POETS OF REALITY

SIX TWENTIETH-CENTURY WRITERS

J. HILLIS MILLER

THE BELKNAP PRESS OF
HARVARD UNIVERSITY PRESS
Cambridge, Massachusetts
1965

FOR ROBIN, MATTHEW, AND SARAH

POETS OF REALITY

Acknowledgments

I wish to express my thanks to the following publishers and individuals who have granted me permission to quote passages from the writings of the six authors who are the subject of this book:

Quotations from the writings of Joseph Conrad are from the Doubleday, Page & Company edition (Garden City, N.Y., 1924–26) and from G. Jean-Aubry, *Joseph Conrad: Life and Letters*, 2 vols. (Garden City, N.Y.: Doubleday, Page & Company, 1927). Permission for these quotations has been granted by Doubleday & Co., Inc., by J. M. Dent & Sons Ltd., and by the Trustees of the Joseph Conrad Estate.

Permission to quote from the writings of W. B. Yeats has been granted by Mrs. W. B. Yeats, Messrs. Macmillan & Co. Ltd., Rupert Hart-Davis Limited, and The Macmillan Company. The following editions of Yeats's writings have been used: *The Autobiography of William Butler Yeats* (New York: The Macmillan Company, 1953), copyright, 1916, 1936, by The Macmillan Company; copyright, 1944, by Bertha Georgie Yeats; *The Collected Poems of W. B Yeats* (New York: The Macmillan Company, 1956), copyright, 1903, 1906, 1907, 1912, 1916, 1918, 1919, 1924, 1928, 1931, 1933, 1934, 1935, 1940, 1944, 1945, 1946, 1950, 1956, by The Macmillan Company; copyright, 1940, by Georgie Yeats; © The Macmillan Company 1956; *The Variorum Edition of the Poems of W. B. Yeats*, ed. Peter Allt and Russell K. Alspach (New York: The Macmillan Company, 1957), copyright, 1903, 1906, 1907, 1912, 1916, 1918, 1919, 1924, 1928, 1931, 1933, 1934, 1935, 1940, 1944, 1945, 1946, 1950, 1956, 1957, by The Macmillan Company; copyright, 1940, by Georgie Yeats; *The Collected Plays of W. B. Yeats* (London: Macmillan & Co. Ltd., 1953), copyright, 1934, 1952, by The Macmillan Company; *Mythologies* (New York: The Macmillan Company, 1959), © Mrs. W. B. Yeats 1959; *Essays and Introductions* (New York: The Macmillan Company, 1961), copyright Mrs. W. B. Yeats, 1961; *A Vision* (New York: The Macmillan Company, 1961), copyright, 1938, by W. B. Yeats; *Explorations* (New York: The Macmillan Company, 1962), copyright © Mrs. W. B. Yeats 1962; *The Letters of W. B. Yeats*, ed. Allan Wade (New York: The Macmillan Company, 1955), copyright, 1953, 1954, by Anne Butler Yeats.

Permission to reprint passages from the following books by T. S. Eliot has been granted. In each case the edition used is identified in parentheses. Permission to quote from *The Use of Poetry and the Use of Criticism* (Cambridge, Mass.: Harvard University Press, 1933), *Notes towards the Definition of Culture* (London: Faber and Faber, 1948), and *Knowledge and Experience in the philosophy of F. H. Bradley* (London: Faber and Faber, 1964) has been granted by Faber and Faber Ltd. Permission to quote from *After Strange Gods: A Primer of Modern Heresy* (New York: Harcourt, Brace, Inc., 1934), *Selected Essays: 1917–1932* (New York: Harcourt, Brace, Inc., 1947), *The Complete Poems and Plays: 1909–1950* (New York: Harcourt, Brace, Inc., 1952), and *Collected Poems: 1909–1962* (New York: Harcourt, Brace & World, 1963) has been granted by Harcourt, Brace & World, Inc., and Faber and Faber Ltd. Passages from *On Poetry and Poets* by T. S. Eliot (New York: Farrar, Straus and Cudahy, 1957), are reprinted by permission of Farrar, Straus and Giroux, Inc., and Faber and Faber Ltd. Copyright © 1943, 1945, 1951, 1954, 1956, 1957 by T. S. Eliot.

Permission to reprint passages from the following books by Dylan Thomas or about him has been granted by their respective publishers. In each case the edition used is identified in parentheses. Permission has been granted by New Directions and J. M. Dent & Sons Ltd. to reprint passages from *The Collected Poems of Dylan Thomas* (New York: New Directions, 1953), copyright 1939, 1942, 1946 by New Directions; copyright 1952, 1953 by Dylan Thomas; *Quite Early One Morning* (New York: New Directions, 1954), copyright 1954 by New Directions; *Portrait of the Artist as a Young Dog* (New York: New Directions, 1955), copyright 1940 by New Directions; *Letters to Vernon Watkins* (New York: New Directions, 1957), The Letters of Dylan Thomas © 1957 by New Directions; editorial contributions and Introduction © 1957 by Vernon Watkins. Permission has been granted by New Directions and the Trustees for the Copyrights of Dylan Thomas to reprint passages from *Adventures in the Skin Trade and other stories* (New York: New Directions, 1955), copyright 1955 by New Directions; copyright 1938, 1939, 1946 by New Directions; copyright 1952, 1953 by Dylan Thomas. Permission to reprint passages from *Dylan Thomas: "Dog Among the Fairies"* by Henry Treece (London: Lindsay Drummond, 1949) has been granted by Ernest Benn Limited and John de Graff, Inc.

Permission has been granted by Alfred A. Knopf Inc. and Faber and Faber Ltd. to reprint passages from the writings of Wallace Stevens. The following editions have been used: *The Necessary Angel: Essays on Reality and the Imagination* (New York: Alfred A. Knopf, 1951), copyright 1951 by Wallace Stevens; *The Collected Poems of Wallace Stevens* (New York: Alfred A. Knopf, 1954), copyright 1954 by Wallace Stevens; *Opus Posthumous* (New York: Alfred A. Knopf, 1957), copyright 1957 by Elsie Stevens and Holly Stevens. A passage from a letter from Wallace Stevens to Henry Church is printed with the kind permission of Mrs. Holly Stevens Stephenson. Part of my chapter on Wallace Stevens appeared in a somewhat different form in my essay "Wallace Stevens' Poetry of Being," in R. H. Pearce and J. H. Miller, eds., *The Act of the Mind: Essays on the Poetry of Wallace Stevens* (Baltimore: The Johns Hopkins Press, 1965). These passages are reprinted with the permission of The Johns Hopkins Press.

Permission to reprint passages from the writings of William Carlos Williams has been granted by Mrs. Florence H. Williams, by New Directions, and by the other publishers of Williams' work, including MacGibbon & Kee Ltd., the British publisher of the various volumes of Williams' poetry. The following editions have been used: *Poems* ([Rutherford, N.J.: privately printed], 1909); *Al Que Quiere!* (Boston: The Four Seas Co., 1917), copyright, 1917, by The Four Seas Company;

Kora in Hell: Improvisations (San Francisco: City Lights, 1957), copyright, 1920, by The Four Seas Company, Boston; © 1957 by William Carlos Williams; *Spring and All* (Dijon: Contact Publishing Co., 1923), copyrighted by the author; *The Great American Novel* (Paris: Contact Editions, 1923), copyright 1923 by William Carlos Williams; copyright © 1960 by Thomas Y. Crowell Co.; *In the American Grain* (New York: New Directions, 1956), copyright 1925 by James Laughlin; copyright 1933 by William Carlos Williams; "An Approach to the Poem," *English Institute Essays: 1947* (New York: Columbia University Press, 1948), pp. 50–75, copyright 1948 Columbia University Press, New York; *The Collected Earlier Poems* (New York: New Directions, 1951), copyright 1938, 1951, by William Carlos Williams; *The Autobiography of William Carlos Williams* (New York: Random House, Inc., 1951), copyright, 1948, 1949, 1951, by William Carlos Williams; *Selected Essays* (New York: Random House, Inc., 1954), copyright, 1931, 1936, 1938, 1939, 1940, 1942, 1946, 1948, 1949, 1951, 1954, by William Carlos Williams; *Selected Letters of William Carlos Williams*, ed. John C. Thirlwall (New York: McDowell, Obolensky, 1957), copyright © 1957 by William Carlos Williams, reprinted here by permission of Ivan Obolensky, Inc.; *I Wanted to Write a Poem: The Autobiography of the Works of a Poet*, reported and edited by Edith Heal (Boston: Beacon Press, 1958), © 1958 by William Carlos Williams; *Yes, Mrs. Williams* (New York: McDowell, Obolensky, 1959), copyright © 1959 by William Carlos Williams, reprinted here by permission of Ivan Obolensky, Inc.; *Many Loves and Other Plays* (New York: New Directions, 1961), copyright 1936, 1942 and 1948 by William Carlos Williams; copyright © 1961 by Florence Williams; *Pictures from Brueghel and Other Poems* (New York: New Directions, 1962), © 1949, 1951, 1952, 1953, 1954, 1955, 1956, 1957, 1959, 1960, 1961 and 1962 by William Carlos Williams; *The Collected Later Poems* (New York: New Directions, 1963), copyright 1944, 1948, 1950 and 1963 by William Carlos Williams; *Paterson* (New York: New Directions, 1963), copyright © 1946, 1948, 1949, 1951, 1958 by W. C. Williams; copyright © 1963 by Florence Williams.

In addition I should like to thank the staffs of the Harvard College Library, the British Museum Library, the Johns Hopkins University Library, and the Yale University Library. I am especially grateful to Mr. Donald Gallup, Curator, Collection of American Literature, Yale University Library, who allowed me to see part of his collection of books by T. S. Eliot and made available to me the Williams holdings in the Beinecke Library at Yale. Finally, I wish to thank the American Philosophical Society for a grant and the John Simon Guggenheim Memorial Foundation for a Fellowship. Without their generous support this book could not have been written.

J. H. M.

CONTENTS

POETS OF REALITY

⌣ I ⌣

The Poetry of Reality

Reality is not that external scene but the life that is lived in it. Reality is things as they are. The general sense of the word proliferates its special senses. It is a jungle in itself.[1]

A change in literature as dramatic as the appearance of romanticism in the late eighteenth century has been taking place during the last fifty years. This book tries to explore the change through a study of six writers who have participated in it. Each of the chapters which follow attempts to show the configuration of themes which permeates one writer's work and unifies it. This chapter describes the historical milieu within which the particular worlds of the six writers may be followed in their planetary trajectories.

My interpretation of these writers questions the assumption that twentieth-century poetry is merely an extension of romanticism. A new kind of poetry has appeared in our day, a poetry which grows out of romanticism, but goes beyond it. Many twentieth-century poets begin with an experience of the nihilism which is one of the possible consequences of romanticism. My chapter on Conrad attempts to identify this nihilism by analysis of a writer who follows it into its darkness and so prepares the way beyond it. Each succeeding chapter describes one version of the journey beyond nihilism toward a poetry of reality. The new art which gradually emerges in the work of Yeats, Eliot, Thomas, and Stevens reaches full development in the poetry of William Carlos Williams.

Much romantic literature presupposes a double bifurcation. Existence is divided into two realms, heaven and earth, supernatural and natural, the "real" world and the derived world. It is also divided into subjective and objective realms. Man as subjective ego opposes himself to everything else. This "everything else" is set

[1] Wallace Stevens, *The Necessary Angel: Essays on Reality and the Imagination* (New York: Alfred A. Knopf, 1951), pp. 25, 26.

against the mind as object of its knowledge. Though some pre-romantic and romantic writers (Smart, Macpherson, Blake) speak from the perspective of a visionary or apocalyptic union of subject and object, earth and heaven, many romantic poets start with both forms of dualism. They must try through the act of poetry to reach the supersensible world by bringing together subject and object. To reach God through the object presupposes the presence of God within the object, and the romantic poets usually believe in one way or another that there is a supernatural power deeply interfused in nature.

Writers of the middle nineteenth century, as I tried to show in *The Disappearance of God*,[2] tend to accept the romantic dichotomy of subject and object, but are no longer able to experience God as both immanent and transcendent. God seems to Tennyson, to Arnold, or to the early Hopkins to have withdrawn beyond the physical world. For such poets God still exists, but he is no longer present in nature. What once was a unity, gathering all together, has exploded into fragments. The isolated ego faces the other dimensions of existence across an empty space. Subject, objects, words, other minds, the supernatural — each of these realms is divorced from the others, and man finds himself one of the "poor fragments of a broken world."[3] Accepting this situation as a necessary beginning, the Victorian poets try to reunite the fragments, to bring God back to earth as a "fusing flame" present in man's heart, in nature, in society, and in language, binding them together in "one common wave of thought and joy."[4]

Another way of thinking grows up side by side with that of the mid-nineteenth-century poets. A God who has disappeared from nature and from the human heart can come to be seen not as invisible but as nonexistent. The unseen God of Arnold or Tennyson becomes the dead God of Nietzsche. If the disappearance of God is presupposed by much Victorian poetry, the death of God is the starting point for many twentieth-century writers.

What does it mean to say that God is dead? Nietzsche's "madman" in *The Joyful Wisdom* announces the death of God, and explains it:

[2] The Belknap Press of Harvard University Press, 1963.
[3] Matthew Arnold's phrase, in "Obermann Once More," *Poetical Works*, ed. C. B. Tinker and H. F. Lowry (London: Oxford University Press, 1950), p. 320.
[4] "Obermann Once More," pp. 320, 323.

"Where is God gone?" he called out. "I mean to tell you! *We have killed him,* —
you and I! We are all his murderers! But how have we done it? How were we
able to drink up the sea? Who gave us the sponge to wipe away the whole horizon?
What did we do when we loosened this earth from its sun? Whither does it now
move? Whither do we move? Away from all suns? Do we not dash on unceasingly?
Backwards, sideways, forewards, in all directions? Is there still an above and
below? Do we not stray, as through infinite nothingness? Does not empty space
breathe upon us? Has it not become colder? Does not night come on continually,
darker and darker? Shall we not have to light lanterns in the morning? Do we not
hear the noise of the grave-diggers who are burying God? Do we not smell the
divine putrefaction? — for even Gods putrefy! God is dead! God remains dead!
And we have killed him!"[5]

Man has killed God by separating his subjectivity from everything but itself. The ego has put everything in doubt, and has defined all outside itself as the object of its thinking power. Cogito ergo
sum: the absolute certainty about the self reached by Descartes'
hyperbolic doubt leads to the assumption that things exist, for me
at least, only because I think them. When everything exists only as
reflected in the ego, then man has drunk up the sea. If man is
defined as subject, everything else turns into object. This includes
God, who now becomes merely the highest object of man's knowledge. God, once the creative sun, the power establishing the
horizon where heaven and earth come together, becomes an object
of thought like any other. When man drinks up the sea he also
drinks up God, the creator of the sea. In this way man is the
murderer of God. Man once was a created being among other
created beings, existing in an objective world sustained by its
creator, and oriented by that creator as to high and low, right and
wrong. Now, to borrow the passage from Bradley which Eliot
quotes in the notes to "The Waste Land," "regarded as an existence which appears in a soul, the whole world for each is peculiar
and private to that soul."

When God and the creation become objects of consciousness,
man becomes a nihilist. Nihilism is the nothingness of consciousness
when consciousness becomes the foundation of everything. Man
the murderer of God and drinker of the sea of creation wanders
through the infinite nothingness of his own ego. Nothing now has
any worth except the arbitrary value he sets on things as he

[5] Book III, Section 125, trans. Thomas Common (New York: Frederick Ungar,
1960), pp. 167, 168.

assimilates them into his consciousness. Nietzsche's transvaluation of values is the expunging of God as the absolute value and source of the valuation of everything else. In the emptiness left after the death of God, man becomes the sovereign valuer, the measure of all things.

Many qualities of modern culture are consonant with the definition of man as a hollow sphere within which everything must appear in order to exist. The devouring nothingness of consciousness is the will to power over things. The will wants to assimilate everything to itself, to make everything a reflection within its mirror. Seen from this perspective, romanticism and technology appear to be similar rather than antithetical.

Romanticism attempts to marry subject and object through the image. The romantic image may be the representation of object within the sphere of the subject, as in Wordsworth, or the carrying of subject into the object, as in Keats, or the wedding of subject and object, as in Coleridge, but in most of its varieties an initial dualism, apparent or real, is assumed. Romanticism develops naturally into the various forms of perspectivism, whether in the poetry of the dramatic monologue or in the novel, which, in its concern for point of view, is perfectly consonant with romanticism. The development of fiction from Jane Austen to Conrad and James is a gradual exploration of the fact that for modern man nothing exists except as it is seen by someone viewing the world from his own perspective. If romantic poetry most often shows the mind assimilating natural objects — urns, nightingales, daffodils, or windhovers — the novel turns its attention to the relations between several minds, but both poetry and fiction usually presuppose the isolation of each mind.

Science and technology, like romanticism, take all things as objects for man's representation. This may appear in a theoretical form, as in the numbers and calculations which transform into mathematical formulas everything from subatomic particles to the farthest and largest galaxies. Or it may appear in a physical form, the humanization of nature, as earths and ores are turned into automobiles, refrigerators, skyscrapers, and rockets, so that no corner of the earth or sky has not been conquered by man and made over in his image.

Romantic literature and modern technology are aspects of a

world-embracing evolution of culture. As this development proceeds, man comes even to forget that he has been the murderer of God. The presence of God within the object, as it existed for the early romantics, is forgotten, and forgotten is the pathos of the Victorians' reaching out for a God disappearing over the horizon of an objectified world. The triumph of technology is the forgetting of the death of God. In the silence of this forgetting the process of universal calculation and reduction to order can go on peacefully extending its dominion. The world no longer offers any resistance to man's limitless hunger for conquest. This process has continued through the first two-thirds of the twentieth century, and is the chief determinant of man's sensibility in many parts of the world today. Many people have forgotten that they have forgotten the death of God, the living God of Abraham and Isaac, Dante and Pascal. Many who believe that they believe in God believe in him only as the highest value, that is, as a creation of man, the inventor of values.

֍

Only if the nihilism latent in our culture would appear as nihilism would it be possible to go beyond it by understanding it. In spite of two world wars, and the shadow of world annihilation, this is a course which our civilization has not yet chosen, or had chosen for it. Nevertheless, a central tradition of modern literature has been a countercurrent moving against the direction of history. In this literature, if not in our culture as a whole, nihilism has gradually been exposed, experienced in its implications, and, in some cases, transcended.

The special place of Joseph Conrad in English literature lies in the fact that in him the nihilism covertly dominant in modern culture is brought to the surface and shown for what it is. Conrad can best be understood as the culmination of a development within the novel, a development particularly well-marked in England, though of course it also exists on the continent and in America. After the attempt to recover an absent God in nineteenth-century poetry, a subsequent stage in man's spiritual history is expressed more fully in fiction than in poetry. The novel shows man attempting to establish a human world based on interpersonal relations.

In the novel man comes more and more to be defined in terms of the strength of his will, and the secret nihilism resulting from his new place as the source of all value is slowly revealed.

Conrad is part of European literature and takes his place with Dostoevsky, Mann, Gide, Proust, and Camus as an explorer of modern perspectivism and nihilism. Within the narrower limits of the English novel, however, he comes at the end of a native tradition. From Dickens and George Eliot through Trollope, Meredith, and Hardy the negative implications of subjectivism become more and more apparent. It remained for Conrad to explore nihilism to its depths, and, in doing so, to point the way toward the transcendence of nihilism by the poets of the twentieth century.

In Conrad's fiction the focus of the novel turns outward from its concentration on relations between man and man within civilized society to a concern for the world-wide expansion of Western man's will to power. Conrad is the novelist not of the city but of imperialism. Several consequences follow from this. He is able to show that society is an arbitrary set of rules and judgments, a house of cards built over an abyss. It was relatively easy for characters in Victorian fiction to be shown taking English society for granted as permanent and right. The fact that Western culture has the fragility of an edifice which might have been constructed differently is brought to light when Conrad sets the "masquerade" of imperialism against the alien jungle. With this revelation, the nature of man's will to power begins to emerge, and at the same time there is a glimpse of an escape from nihilism.

The will to power seemed a subjective thing, a private possession of each separate ego. Though the struggle for dominance of mind against mind might lead to an impasse, nonhuman nature seemed to yield passively to man's sovereign will. Everything, it seemed, could be turned into an object of man's calculation, control, or evaluation. In "Heart of Darkness" (1899) Conrad shows how imperialism becomes the expansion of the will toward unlimited dominion over existence. What begins as greed, the desire for ivory, and as altruism, the desire to carry the torch of civilization to the jungle, becomes the longing to "wring the heart" of the wilderness and "exterminate all the brutes." The benign project of civilizing the dark places of the world becomes the conscious desire to annihilate everything which opposes man's absolute will. Kurtz's megalomania finally becomes limitless. There is "nothing either above or below him." He has "kicked himself loose of the earth," and in doing so has "kicked the very earth to pieces."

It is just here, in the moment of its triumph, that nihilism reverses itself, as, in Mann's *Doktor Faustus*, Leverkühn's last and most diabolical composition leads through the abyss to the sound of children's voices singing. Conrad's work does not yet turn the malign into the benign, but it leads to a reversal which prepares for the daylight of later literature. When Kurtz's will has expanded to boundless dimensions, it reveals itself to be what it has secretly been all along: nothing. Kurtz is "hollow at the core." Into his emptiness comes the darkness. The darkness is in the heart of each man, but it is in the heart of nature too, and transcends both man and nature as their hidden substance and foundation.

ᔓ

When the wilderness finds Kurtz out and takes "a terrible vengeance for the fantastic invasion," [6] then the dawn of an escape from nihilism appears, an escape through the darkness. By following the path of nihilism to the end, man confronts once again a spiritual power external to himself. Though this power appears as an inexpressibly threatening horror, still it is something beyond the self. It offers the possibility of an escape from subjectivism.

The strategy of this escape will appear from the point of view of the tradition it reverses the most dangerous of choices, a leap into the abyss. It will mean giving up the most cherished certainties. The act by which man turns the world inside-out into his mind leads to nihilism. This can be escaped only by a counterrevolution in which man turns himself inside-out and steps, as Wallace Stevens puts it, "barefoot into reality." [7] This leap into the world characterizes the reversal enacted in one way or another by the five poets studied here.

To walk barefoot into reality means abandoning the independence of the ego. Instead of making everything an object for the self,

[6] Quotations from "Heart of Darkness" are cited from *Youth and Two Other Stories* (Garden City, N.Y.: Doubleday, Page, 1925), pp. 118, 131, 144, 148.

[7] "Large Red Man Reading," *The Collected Poems* (New York: Alfred A. Knopf, 1954), p. 423.

the mind must efface itself before reality, or plunge into the density
of an exterior world, dispersing itself in a milieu which exceeds it
and which it has not made. The effacement of the ego before reality means abandoning the will to power over things. This is the most
difficult of acts for a modern man to perform. It goes counter to
all the penchants of our culture. To abandon its project of dominion
the will must will not to will. Only through an abnegation of the
will can objects begin to manifest themselves as they are, in the
integrity of their presence. When man is willing to let things be
then they appear in a space which is no longer that of an objective
world opposed to the mind. In this new space the mind is dispersed
everywhere in things and forms one with them.

This new space is the realm of the twentieth-century poem. It
is a space in which things, the mind, and words coincide in closest
intimacy. In this space flower the chicory and Queen Anne's lace
of William Carlos Williams' poems. In this space his wheelbarrow
and his broken bits of green bottle glass appear. In a similar poetic
space appear "the pans above the stove, the pots on the table, the
tulips among them" of Stevens' "poem of life." The "ghosts" who
"return to earth" in Stevens' poems are those who have been
alienated in the false angelism of subjectivity. They return from the
emptiness of "the wilderness of stars" to step into a tangible reality
of things as they are. There they can "run fingers over leaves/And
against the most coiled thorn." [8]

The return to earth making twentieth-century poetry possible
is accompanied by the abandonment of still another quality of the
old world. This is the dimension of depth. In a number of ways
the world of nineteenth-century poetry is often characterized by
extension and exclusion. The mind is separated from its objects,
and those objects are placed in a predominantly visual space. In
this space each object is detached from the others. To be in one
place is to be excluded from other places, and space stretches out
infinitely in all directions. Beyond those infinite distances is the God
who has absented himself from his creation. The pathos of the
disappearance of God is the pathos of infinite space.

Along with spatial and theological depth go other distances: the
distance of mind from mind, the distance within each self separating
the self from itself. If each subject is separated from all objects, it is

[8] "Large Red Man Reading," pp. 423, 424.

no less divided from other subjects and can encounter them only across a gap generated by its tendency to turn everything into an image. From the assumption of the isolation of the ego develops that conflict of subjectivities which is a central theme of fiction. For Matthew Arnold and other inheritors of romanticism the self is also separated from its own depths, the gulf within the mind which hides the deep buried self. To reach that self is as difficult as to reach God beyond the silence of infinite spaces.

In the new art these depths tend to disappear. The space of separation is turned inside-out, so that elements once dispersed are gathered together in a new region of copresence. This space is often more auditory, tactile, or kinesthetic than visual. To be within it is to possess all of it, and there is no longer a sense of endless distances extending in all directions. The mind, its objects, other minds, and the ground of both mind and things are present in a single realm of proximity.

The disappearance of dimensions of depth in twentieth-century art provides special difficulties for someone trained in the habits of romanticism. An abstract expressionist painting does not "mean" anything in the sense of referring beyond itself in any version of traditional symbolism. It is what it is, paint on canvas, just as Williams' wheelbarrow is what it is. In the space of the new poetry the world is contracted to a point—the wheelbarrow, the chicory flower, the bits of green glass. The poem is "not ideas about the thing but the thing itself," [9] part of the world and not about it. In the same way the characters of Williams' fiction, like those of the French "new novel," have little psychological depth. They exist as their thoughts, their gestures, their speech, and these have the same objective existence as the wheelbarrow or the flower. In such a world "anywhere is everywhere," [10] and the romantic dialectic of movement through stages to attain a goal disappears. In place of advance in steps toward an end there is the continuous present of a poetry which matches in its speed the constant flight of time. Each moment appears out of nothing in the words of the poem and in that instant things emerge anew and move and are dissolved. [11]

If any spiritual power can exist for the new poetry it must be an

[9] Stevens, *The Collected Poems*, p. 534.
[10] William Carlos Williams, *Paterson* (New York: New Directions, 1963), p. 273.
[11] See Wallace Stevens, *Opus Posthumous* (New York: Alfred A. Knopf, 1957), p. 110.

immanent presence. There can be for many writers no return to the traditional conception of God as the highest existence, creator of all other existences, transcending his creation as well as dwelling within it. If there is to be a God in the new world it must be a presence within things and not beyond them. The new poets have at the farthest limit of their experience caught a glimpse of a fugitive presence, something shared by all things in the fact that they are. This presence flows everywhere, like the light which makes things visible, and yet can never be seen as a thing in itself. It is the presence of things present, what Stevens calls "the swarthy water/That flows round the earth and through the skies,/Twisting among the universal spaces." [12] In the same poem he gives this power its simplest name: "It is being." The most familiar object, in coming into the light, reveals being, and poetry brings being into the open by naming things as they are, in their glistening immediacy, the wheelbarrow glazed with rain water, the steeple at Farmington shining and swaying. The new poetry is therefore "the outlines of being and its expressings, the syllables of its law." [13] These outlines are glimpsed as the words of the poem vanish with the moment which brought them into existence. The space of such a poem is the space of the present in its evanescence. This present holds men closely with discovery as, "in the instant of speech,/The breadth of an accelerando moves,/Captives the being, widens — and was there." [14] The instant's motion is a space grown wide, and within that brief space of time all existence is named, captured, and revealed.

These are the characteristics of the domain which twentieth-century literature has come to inhabit. The entry into the new world is not easy to make and has not everywhere been made. Our culture still moves along the track laid out for it by science and dualistic thinking, and many writers remain enclosed within the old world. Moreover, every artist who crosses the frontier does so in his own way, a way to some degree unlike any other. I do not wish to minimize the differences between twentieth-century writers, but to suggest a context in which those differences may be fruitfully explored.

Examples of the new immediacy may be found in widely diver-

[12] "Metaphor as Degeneration," *The Collected Poems*, p. 444.
[13] "Large Red Man Reading," p. 424.
[14] Wallace Stevens, "A Primitive Like an Orb," *The Collected Poems*, p. 440.

gent areas of contemporary thought and art: in the flatness of the
paintings of Mark Rothko and Franz Kline, as opposed to the
romantic depth in the work of Paul Klee; in the "superficiality,"
as of a mystery which is all on the surface, of the novels of Ivy
Compton-Burnett or Alain Robbe-Grillet; in the philosophy of
Martin Heidegger or the German and French phenomenologists;
in the descriptive linguistic analysis of Ludwig Wittgenstein and
the British common language philosophers; in the poetry of Jorge
Guillén, René Char, or Charles Olson; in the literary criticism of
Gaston Bachelard, Jean-Pierre Richard, or Marcel Raymond. All
these writers and artists have in one way or another entered a new
realm, and, for all of them, if there is a fugitive spiritual power
it will be within things and people, not altogether beyond them.

Yeats, Eliot, Thomas, Stevens, and Williams have played important roles in this twentieth-century revolution in man's experience of existence. Each begins with an experience of nihilism or its
concomitants, and each in his own way enters the new reality:
Yeats by his affirmation of the infinite richness of the finite moment;
Eliot by his discovery that the Incarnation is here and now;
Thomas by an acceptance of death which makes the poet an ark
rescuing all things; Stevens by his identification of imagination and
reality in the poetry of being; Williams by his plunge into the
"filthy Passaic." This book traces the itineraries leading these
writers to goals which are different and yet have a family resemblance. The unity of twentieth-century poetry is suggested by the
fact that these authors are in the end poets not of absence but of
proximity. In their work reality comes to be present to the senses,
present to the mind which possesses it through the senses, and
present in the words of the poems which ratify this possession. Such
poetry is often open-ended in form. It follows in its motion the
flowing of time and reveals, through this mobility, the reality of
things as they are. Wallace Stevens speaks for all these poets when
he affirms the union of inner and outer, natural and supernatural,
in the transience and nearness of the real:

> We seek
> Nothing beyond reality. Within it,
>
> Everything, the spirit's alchemicana
> Included, the spirit that goes roundabout
> And through included, not merely the visible,

> The solid, but the movable, the moment,
> The coming on of feasts and the habits of saints,
> The pattern of the heavens and high, night air.[15]

Before following my five poets in their journeys of homecoming toward reality it will be necessary to investigate the spiritual adventure which takes Conrad to the limit of nihilism, and so opens the way beyond it.

[15] "An Ordinary Evening in New Haven," *The Collected Poems*, pp. 471, 472.

II

Joseph Conrad

THE DARKNESS

When near the buildings I met a white man, in such an unexpected elegance of get-up that in the first moment I took him for a sort of vision. I saw a high starched collar, white cuffs, a light alpaca jacket, snowy trousers, a clean necktie, and varnished boots. No hat. Hair parted, brushed, oiled, under a green-lined parasol held in a big white hand. He was amazing, and had a penholder behind his ear. . . . I respected the fellow. . . . His appearance was certainly that of a hairdresser's dummy; but in the great demoralization of the land he kept up his appearance. That's backbone.

Conrad respected those who could keep up appearances in a wilderness. He admired people who could keep their heads clear in any circumstances and remain single-mindedly faithful to a job to be done. The elegantly dressed accountant at a trading station halfway to the heart of darkness is a symbol of this equilibrium in the midst of demoralization. His artificiality of dress and manner is the exact correlative of the artificiality of his accounts. The precision and enumeration of the latter stand against the blur of the surrounding jungle as light stands against darkness in the dominant symbolism of the novel. The accountant represents the triumph of an unceasing act of will, a will to keep the darkness out and to keep what is within the charmed circle of civilization clear, distinct, and inventoried.

The starched and scented accountant is not only an example of one kind of human life. He represents the human enterprise generally as it appeared to Conrad at a certain stage of history. That stage was not the mid-nineteenth century, the time of the triumph, in the Western world, of the middle class, industrialism, and the scientific interpretation of nature. Nor was it our darker time when these forces have reached out to dominate the world, and seem about to reverse themselves and destroy their makers. It was the time of imperialism, when the middle class and the commercial spirit, having conquered the countries of their birth, were spreading outward to conquer the world. In that time "brave young England," in Charles Kingsley's words, was "longing to wing its way out of its island prison, to discover and to traffic, to colonise and to civilise, until no wind can sweep the earth which does not bear the echoes of an English voice." [1] There were still blank places on the map, *terrae incognitae* offering themselves to man's greed for power and knowledge, as the white patch of the Congo fascinated Conrad's Marlow. In the imperialist epoch European countries were still aware of the existence of areas which had not yet submitted to their ideals. Primitive places and primitive peoples still existed, and one would not yet have expected to find a jukebox or a Coca-Cola sign in the midst of every jungle. It was still possible to write a pamphlet on "The Suppression of Savage Customs," because there were still savage customs to suppress.

As a consequence of his vantage point in time, Conrad was able to see, better than we can today, the nature of the historical process unfolding before his eyes. For us the process is more or less complete. There are scarcely any white patches on the map, few dark, savage corners of the world. Enlightenment and progress have triumphed, or seem about to triumph, and one homogeneous civilization has spread almost everywhere. It is difficult for man now to see his civilization clearly because there is nothing to set it against for purposes of comparison, but Conrad could put imperialism against the backdrop of the darkness it was about to conquer.

In Conrad's view civilization is the metamorphosis of darkness into light. It is a process of transforming everything unknown, irrational, or indistinct into clear forms, named and ordered, given a meaning and use by man. Civilization has two sides, curiously in contradiction. To be safe, civilized man must have a blind devotion to immediate practical tasks, a devotion which recalls the Victorian cult of work. For Conrad as for Carlyle work is protection against unwholesome doubt or neurotic paralysis of will. "A man is a worker," says Conrad. "If he is not that he is nothing. . . . For the great mass of mankind the only saving grace that is needed is steady fidelity to what is nearest to hand and heart in the short

[1] *Westward Ho!*, ch. II, quoted in Walter Houghton, *The Victorian Frame of Mind: 1830–1870* (New Haven: Yale University Press, 1957), p. 122.

moment of each human effort." [2] In *The Nigger of the "Narcissus"* he praises the "everlasting children of the mysterious sea" (NN, 25) remaining innocent and inarticulate, faithful to the sailor's code of obedience and devotion to duty, and in *Chance* he speaks of "the peace of the sea," a peace which derives from the fact that the sailors have time only for work and sleep (C, 31, 32). So Marlow in "Heart of Darkness" is protected from the wilderness by the hard work necessary to keep his river steamer going: "I had to watch the steering, and circumvent those snags, and get the tin-pot along by hook or by crook. There was surface-truth enough in these things to save a wiser man" (HD, 97). When Marlow finds in a jungle hut a battered copy of *An Inquiry into Some Points of Seamanship*, the book seems to him an expression of man's power to keep possession of himself through concentrated attention on practical problems: "The simple old sailor, with his talk of chains and purchases, made me forget the jungle and the pilgrims in a delicious sensation of having come upon something unmistakably real" (HD, 99).

Devotion to work is real, with a specifically human reality and sanity, but there is more to the humanizing of the world than "devotion to efficiency" (HD, 50). Behind the efficiency and directing it must be "the idea." Sometimes this idea is the simple one of obedience and fidelity, as when Conrad speaks of his "belief in the solidarity of all mankind in simple ideas and in sincere emotions" (C, xi), or when he affirms his "conviction that the world, the temporal world, rests on a few very simple ideas; so simple that they must be as old as the hills. It rests notably, among others, on the idea of Fidelity" (PR, xxi). Sometimes Conrad means by the idea the grandiose goal of bringing light and civilization to the unillumined peoples of the earth. The idea is civilized man's protection against the anarchic power of atavistic ways of life. It is

---

[2] *Notes on Life and Letters* (Garden City, N.Y.: Doubleday, Page, 1925), pp. 190, 191. The initial quotation in this chapter was from "Heart of Darkness," in *Youth and Two Other Stories*, pp. 67, 68 in the Doubleday, Page edition of 1925. Further passages from Conrad's work will be cited from this edition and from G. Jean-Aubry, *Joseph Conrad: Life and Letters*, 2 vols. (Garden City, N.Y.: Doubleday, Page, 1927). The following abbreviations will be used in citations, accompanied by page numbers in the editions identified above: *An Outcast of the Islands:* OI; *The Nigger of the "Narcissus":* NN; *Lord Jim: A Romance:* LJ; "Heart of Darkness": HD; *Typhoon:* T; "Falk" (in *Typhoon and Other Stories*): F; *Nostromo:* N; *The Secret Agent:* SA; *Under Western Eyes:* UWE; *A Personal Record:* PR; *Chance:* C; *Within the Tides:* WT; *Victory:* V; *The Shadow-Line:* SL; *The Rescue:* R; *Notes on Life and Letters:* NLL; *Joseph Conrad: Life and Letters:* LL.

the guide of devoted work, directing that work as it transforms the world to man's measure. The idea gives meaning to what is wrested from the wilderness, and it builds a barrier making the circle of civilization secure, as the crew of the "Narcissus" triumphs over the formless might of the great storm, or as Kurtz is an "emissary of light" imposing his "ideas," his "plans" on the jungle, or as Marlow's voice, "the speech that cannot be silenced," protects him against the "fiendish row" of the savages (HD, 97). The idea is man's armor against the darkness, and it is the source of the form and the meaning he gives the world.

Civilization is at once a social ideal and an ideal of personal life. The ideal society is imaged in the relation among men on board a well-ordered ship: a hierarchical structure, with those at the bottom owing obedience to those above, and the whole forming a perfect organism. As a personal ideal, submission to civilization may mean being one of the stolid, unimaginative people, like Captain MacWhirr in *Typhoon*. It may also mean setting up for oneself an ideal of glory, the winning of power and fame for the accomplishment of some difficult project. A man who does this accepts as the meaning of his life the value he has in the eyes of other people. "A man's real life," says Conrad, "is that accorded to him in the thoughts of other men by reason of respect or natural love" (UWE, 14).

To live in this way means substituting some goal in the future for gratification in the present. A man who makes glory his aim makes of the present a means to an end, and lives always beyond himself. So Lord Jim hopes for some act of bravery which will make up for his cowardice; Lingard, in *The Rescue*, wants to win renown by reinstating his native friends to power; Razumov, in *Under Western Eyes*, proposes to himself a career as a professor; Nostromo centers all his life on an egotistic dream of personal glory; and Kurtz's goal is the power he will win in Europe for the successful conquering of the jungle. He wants "to have kings meet him at railway-stations on his return from some ghastly Nowhere, where he intend[s] to accomplish great things" (HD, 148). There is more than a nominal form of speech in the way Kurtz refers to his fiancée as his "Intended." That lady, with her "pure brow," "smooth and white, . . . illumined by the unextinguishable light of belief and love" (HD, 157, 158), and her "soul as translucently pure as a cliff of crystal" (HD, 152), is a symbol of the orientation of Kurtz's life. He faces toward an ideal intention which depends on the faith and respect of other people. He lives in terms of an expectation.

Perhaps the intention can never be fulfilled. Perhaps a society based on progress can never reach the far-off divine event when all the darkness will be turned to light. Nevertheless, the project of humanizing the world has in some places been successful, and to dwell in such a place means, as Marlow says, living "with solid pavement under your feet, surrounded by kind neighbours ready to cheer you or to fall on you, stepping delicately between the butcher and the policeman, in the holy terror of scandal and gallows and lunatic asylums" (HD, 116). All the strangeness and danger has been removed or covered up. Everything has been labeled, transformed into a utensil or a significance. The lower regions of human consciousness have been forgotten or buried deep out of sight. The rational mind of man matches the lucid distinctness of forms in a daylight world, and together they form a closed circuit of reciprocal interchanges, each confirming the other. A man's relations to his neighbor are assimilated into the clarity of this world. The strangeness of other people is hidden behind forms, clothes, institutions, and some convention always stands between man and man. Civilization is the triumph of the human, of the all too human. There is nothing, says Conrad in *The Nigger of the "Narcissus,"* which holds people together like the "strong, effective and respectable bond of a sentimental lie" (NN, 155).

∽

The human world is a lie. All human ideals, even the ideal of fidelity, are lies. They are lies in the sense that they are human fabrications. They derive from man himself and are supported by nothing outside him. There is a gap between man and the world, and what remains isolated within the human realm is illusory and insubstantial. Nostromo's goal in life is an egotistic sham, as is Lord Jim's, Lingard's, or Razumov's. Kurtz is not really devoted to a worthy ideal. He is "avid of lying fame, of sham distinction, of all the appearances of success and power" (HD, 147, 148).

Collective social ideals are no less unreal. Each is, like the idea of international fraternity, "un très beau phantome," "les ombres d'une éloquence qui est morte, justement parce qu'elle n'a pas de corps" (LL, I, 269). This dark truth is the source of Conrad's pessimism, of his "désespoir plus sombre que la nuit" (LL, I, 270). A crucial moment in his experience is the time when he must recognize the impossibility of man's hope "for the laying of what is the most obstinate ghost of man's creation, of the uneasy doubt uprising like a mist, secret and gnawing like a worm, and more chilling than the certitude of death — the doubt of the sovereign power enthroned in a fixed standard of conduct" (LJ, 50).

Conrad's pessimism has a double source. It is a recognition that ethical terms have no meaning because they do not refer to something outside man which tells him what he ought to do: "The ethical view of the universe involves us at last in so many cruel and absurd contradictions, where the last vestiges of faith, hope, charity, and even of reason itself, seem ready to perish, that I have come to suspect that the aim of creation cannot be ethical at all" (PR, 92). A fixed standard of conduct is not a sovereign power enthroned above man. It is his own creation. A man obeying an ethical code is trying to lift himself by his own bootstraps, and by bootstraps which have only an imaginary existence. On the other hand, the tragedy of man's existence lies in the fact that he is cut off irrevocably from the truth of the universe. As long as he remains human he will remain exiled in a nightmarish realm of illusion. "A man that is born," says Stein in *Lord Jim*, "falls into a dream like a man who falls into the sea" (LJ, 214). No passage by Conrad expresses more completely this double tragedy of imprisonment within the factitious and exclusion from the truth than a letter of 1898 to R. B. Cunninghame Graham: "Of course reason is hateful, — but why? Because it demonstrates (to those who have the courage) that we, living, are out of life, — utterly out of it. The mysteries of a universe made of drops of fire and clods of mud do not concern us in the least. . . . Life knows us not and we do not know life" (LL, I, 222).

If civilization and each man in it move farther from reality the more completely the humanizing of the world succeeds, is there any chance to escape from the falsity of the human? How can man be liberated from his dream? The aim of all Conrad's fiction is to destroy in the reader his bondage to illusion, and to give him a glimpse of the truth, however dark and disquieting that truth may be. His work might be called an effort of demystification. It attempts to rescue man from his alienation. His problem in reaching this goal is double: to lift the veil of illusion, and to make the truth appear. The second aim is especially difficult, for Conrad's truth is the exact opposite of precise images and events. It is "une ombre sinistre et fuyante dont il est impossible de fixer l'image" (LL, I, 269, 270). Yet fiction must deal in clear and vivid images. How can Conrad use fiction to make the reader see things as they are?

⌇

The first step in his method of demystification consists, strangely enough, in accentuating the lucidity of vision typical of civilized man. The characteristic stance of Conrad's narrators is one of cold, clearheaded, ironic objectivity, what he calls in *A Personal Record* "the detached curiosity of a subtle mind" (PR, 92), or what Henry James in his review of *Chance* calls "a prolonged hovering flight of the subjective over the outstretched ground of the case exposed." [3] James's splendid phrase defines exactly the somber intensity with which Conrad's narrators brood over their stories as they tell and retell them, seeking to reach the elusive truth behind superficial facts. James's image also expresses the distance between Conrad's narrators and the action of the stories. His habit of multiplying narrators and points of view, so that sometimes an event is told filtered through several consciousnesses, his reconstruction of the chronological sequence to make a pattern of progressive revelation, his use of a framing story — all these techniques increase the distance between the reader and the events as they were lived by the characters.

The avowed purpose of this detachment is to permit a clarity of vision which will reach the truth of things, but detachment has, in Conrad's most striking and characteristic passages, another surprising effect. It leads the reader to experience the story with a dreamlike and hallucinatory intensity, to see things as irreducibly strange, separated from their usual meaning. Conrad, more than any other English novelist, is a master of this way of showing things,

[3] "The New Novel," *The Art of Fiction and Other Essays* (New York: Oxford University Press, 1948), p. 204.

and the narrators of all his novels could say what Marlow says in "Heart of Darkness": "It seems to me I am trying to tell you a dream — making a vain attempt, because no relation of a dream can convey the dream-sensation, that commingling of absurdity, surprise, and bewilderment in a tremor of struggling revolt, that notion of being captured by the incredible which is of the very essence of dreams" (HD, 82).

To recognize the dreamlike quality of the waking world does not mean a distortion of civilized man's usual clarity of vision. Tables, chairs, trees, and people are still seen as definite objects, with names, meanings, and forms. The difference lies in a change in the liaison between perceiver and perceived. Ordinarily things are assumed into the process of living and so taken for granted that they are scarcely noticed, only used, as a man does not notice the doorknob he turns a dozen times a day. Conrad shows such things wrested from their context in daily life and put before the spectator as mute, static presences. The interpretations ordinarily connecting man to things are broken, and the world is put in parentheses, seen as pure phenomenon.

Though all men live in a dream, many people are lucky enough to go on with their illusions untouched, in the serene and peaceful state of being deceived. "Of course," says Marlow, "a fool, what with sheer fright and fine sentiments, is always safe" (HD, 97). Some men, like Conrad himself and like most of his heroes, are not so lucky. An experience of solitude, of failure, of adventure, of intense emotion, or simply of unfortunate perspicuity breaks the illusion, and leads such people to see that the dream is a dream.

The most extraordinary aspect of this experience is the deceptive ease with which it occurs. No great catastrophe is necessary. A momentary absence of mind, a new way of looking at a familiar object, a slight change of routine may be enough to shatter the structure of a life. "There are often in men's affairs," says the narrator of "Falk," "unexpectedly — even irrationally — illuminating moments when an otherwise insignificant sound, perhaps only some perfectly commonplace gesture, suffices to reveal to us all the unreason, all the fatuous unreason, of our complacency" (F, 169). Man's fatuous complacency is his assumption that his world is organically unified. The meanings of things, he believes, are identified with the things themselves; all things are bound together in a coherent system; the mind of man forms an integral part of this system. An interpretation of the world of this sort is so fragile that a touch suffices to destroy it. It is as if man were "a tight-rope dancer who, in the midst of his performance, should suddenly discover that he knows nothing about tight-rope dancing." A "broken neck is the result of such untimely wisdom" (LL, I, 247).

This unfortunate fall is often brought about by some insignificant event which detaches the mind ever so slightly from its surroundings. The initial moment of self-consciousness in Conrad is a seemingly benign experience of perplexity or puzzlement, a tiny fissure of separation from the everyday pattern of things. This often takes place when an object is detached from the fabric of its relations to other things. Such an "unexpectedly illuminating" experience causes a double division of the world. The experienced thing is separated from what seemed connected to it by an unbreakable web of relations. When this happens the mind recognizes its isolation from things. The detachment of the object from its surroundings is matched by man's loss of his unthinking engagement in the world. The moment of puzzled detachment rapidly expands to become the recognition that "we, living, are out of life, — utterly out of it." Man discovers that he is an outcast.

Examples of this disastrous moment of self-awareness occur throughout Conrad's work. Wilhelms, in *An Outcast of the Islands*, first understands that his old life has come to an end when he notices the odd look of his house: "He looked at it with a vague surprise to find it there. His past was so utterly gone from him that the dwelling which belonged to it appeared to him incongruous standing there intact, neat, and cheerful in the sunshine of the hot afternoon" (OCI, 23).

The irony of *Typhoon* lies in the fact that the huge storm produces only a gentle ripple on the surface of Captain MacWhirr's stolid complacency: "The hurricane, with its power to madden the seas, to sink ships, to uproot trees, to overturn strong walls and dash the very birds of the air to the ground, had found this taciturn man in its path, and, doing its utmost, had managed to wring out a few words" (T, 90). The climax of the novel comes not at the height of the storm, but during the calm in the middle of it. The Captain returns to his cabin and is irrationally annoyed when he sees how

things there have been slightly disarranged. The right placing of his matchbox is "the symbol of all these little habits that chain us to the weary round of life" (T, 85). Here too the moment of awareness is connected with the sight of objects detached from their usual positions in an orderly world:

> He had not consciously looked at anything by the light of the matches except at the barometer; and yet somehow he had seen that his water-bottle and the two tumblers had been flung out of their stand. It seemed to give him a more intimate knowledge of the tossing the ship had gone through. "I wouldn't have believed it," he thought. And his table had been cleared, too; his rulers, his pencils, the ink-stand — all the things that had their safe appointed places — they were gone, as if a mischievous hand had plucked them out one by one and flung them on the wet floor. The hurricane had broken in upon the orderly arrangements of his privacy. This had never happened before, and the feeling of dismay reached the very seat of his composure. (T, 84, 85)

The detachment of things from one another and from man, so rarely glimpsed by a man like MacWhirr, is expressed throughout Conrad's novels by a precise description of what is there to be seen or heard. A good example of this is Verloc's hat in the murder scene of *The Secret Agent:* "A round hat disclosed in the middle of the floor by the moving of the table rocked slightly on its crown in the wind of her flight" (SA, 265). The hat here has ceased to be Verloc's hat, a useful object in his life. It is simply *a* hat, and its normal motion is in violent contrast to the abnormality of the situation. Such glimpses of the oddity of inanimate things reveal the gap between human passions and the ineluctable "thingness" of external objects. When a man is in a situation of extreme danger or emotional tension, and it seems as if everything should be in an uproar, an everyday object, being itself, impassible and indifferent, often catches the eye. Subjective intensity, by a kind of negative causality, makes the alien quality of the physical world appear.

The same transformation can also affect the way human beings appear. Sometimes people will momentarily seem like sleepwalking actors in an implausible drama, acting out their parts without con-sciousness or volition. These visions are often expressed by Conrad in dehumanizing metaphors which recall those of Dickens. Marlow, in *Lord Jim*, sees the grotesquely fat captain of the "Patna" as "a trained baby elephant walking on hind-legs" (LJ, 37), or as "some-thing round and enormous, resembling a sixteen-hundred-weight sugar-hogshead wrapped in striped flannelette, up-ended in the middle of the . . . floor" (LJ, 38). The captain's entrance into a small gharry is described in a way that makes it seem like a nightmare or hallucination: "The little machine shook and rocked tumultuously, and the crimson nape of that lowered neck, the size of those straining thighs, the immense heaving of that dingy, striped green-and-orange back, the whole burrowing effort of that gaudy and sordid mass troubled one's sense of probability with a droll and fearsome effect, like one of those grotesque and distinct visions that scare and fascinate one in a fever" (LJ, 46, 47). In *Chance*, as Marlow sits with two ordinary people, the Fynes, he suddenly sees the scene as inexplicably strange, like a solemn but senseless masquerade: "We three looked at each other as if on the brink of a disclosure. . . . Nothing more absurd could be conceived. It was delicious. . . . I don't know that I am liable to fits of delirium, but by a sudden and alarming aberration while waiting for her answer I became mentally aware of three trained dogs dancing on their hind legs. I don't know why. Perhaps because of the pervading solemnity. There's nothing more solemn on earth than a dance of trained dogs" (C, 57, 58).

In all his novels Conrad makes images of things and people which cause them to appear mysterious, but perhaps no novel makes a more strategic use of this technique than "Heart of Darkness." That novel is structured as a passing of portals, a traveling through states which leads the reader ever deeper into the darkness. The method of this presentation is to put in question whatever Marlow reaches, to show it as a misleading illusion, something which must be rejected for the sake of the truth behind it. Conrad succeeds in this way in showing civilization as a "fantastic invasion" directed by a "flabby devil," as a "sordid farce acted in front of a sinister back-cloth" (HD, 92, 72, 61). The two silent women knitting in the office of the company in Belgium, "introducing, introducing continuously to the unknown" (HD, 57); the French ship firing shells one after another into the immensity of Africa; the disorder of the first station Marlow reaches, with its dying natives, its aimless dynamiting, its machinery lying broken and useless in ditches; the perfectly dressed accountant keeping up appearances in the jungle; the stout man with mustaches trying to put out a blazing warehouse fire with water carried in a tin pail with a hole in it; the Eldorado expedition with its "absurd air of disorderly flight with the loot of innumerable outfit shops and provision stores" (HD, 87) — each of these is another example of the absurdity of the imperialist invasion.

The first stage in the reader's liberation from his customary dream is a way of presenting human activities and intentions which holds them at arm's length and shows each one as "a mournful and senseless delusion" (HD, 61). What is uncovered when the veil of forms is lifted?

⌐

To see the world without interpretations is to see it reduced to pure quality. Instead of namable things, only patches of dark or light are seen. These can be given no meaning. They are simply there, mute presences. In place of articulate speech, or sounds which can be interpreted, only the duration, timbre, and tone of sounds can be heard. This recognition of the qualitative aspect of sense experience is an ultimate point reached through the vision of the world as dreamlike. A stage of seeing the everyday world as a waking nightmare leads to a moment when the significance is drained out of things, as when a man stares at some familiar object until it suddenly becomes strange, or as when a phrase is repeated over and over until it is emptied of meaning and becomes senseless sound, or as when something is seen too close to the eyes or too highly magnified, and can no longer be identified. What the thing is can no longer be said because the attention is absorbed and fascinated by how it is.[4]

Conrad habitually calls attention to the conflict between the qualitative aspect of things and the interpretation of what is seen into recognizable objects. The world is often perceived simultaneously as colors or incomprehensible sounds and as things which can be identified. The reader is balanced precariously between two ways of being related to the world:

Something like a small white flame in the sky was the carved white coral finial on the gable of the mosque which had caught full the rays of the sun. (R, 251)

[4] The best discussion of this aspect of Conrad's work is in Ramon Fernandez, "L'Art de Conrad," *Messages, première série* (Paris: Gallimard, 1926), pp. 110–119.

. . . a few small islets, black spots in the great blaze, swimming before my troubled eyes. (SL, 96)

I became bothered by curious, irregular sounds of faint tapping on the deck. They could be heard single, in pairs, in groups. While I wondered at this mysterious devilry, I received a slight blow under the left eye and felt an enormous tear run down my cheek. Raindrops. Enormous. Forerunners of something. Tap. Tap. Tap. (SL, 113)

In such passages the work of interpretation is successful, and the spots of color or the inexplicable sounds are translated into recognizable objects. The raindrops are identified, the islets are seen as islets, the white flame is resolved into the finial on the mosque. In other texts the process of interpretation, though successful at first, fails in the end, and the reader is left face to face with a qualitative spectacle. Often this failure is accompanied by the appearance of metaphors. The patches of color are susceptible of alternative explanations. They may be one thing. They may be another:

I beheld him as one sees a fish in an aquarium by the light of an electric bulb, an elusive, phosphorescent shape. (SL, 114)

. . . the sun, all red in a cloudless sky raked the yacht with a parting salvo of crimson rays that shattered themselves into sparks of fire upon the crystal and silver of the dinner-service, put a short flame into the blades of knives, and spread a rosy tint over the white of plates. A trail of purple, like a smear of blood on a blue shield, lay over the sea. (R, 146)

. . . in the still streak of very bright pale orange light I saw the land profiled flatly as if cut out of black paper and seeming to float on the water as light as cork. But the rising sun turned it into mere dark vapour, a doubtful, massive shadow trembling in the hot glare. (SL, 77)

In these texts fish and man, fire and dinner-service, shield and sea, cork, black paper, and land are superimposed. The hovering of the mind between these possibilities leads the spectator to see impressions without interpretation: a phosphorescent shape, a trail of purple, a massive shadow trembling in the glare. Sometimes, however, there is no transition from the perception of things to the sensation of qualities. From the first glimpse nothing is seen but areas of color, light, or dark, and these are never resolved into significant forms. The reader sees nothing but "a belt of orange light" which "faded quickly to gold that melted soon into a blinding and colorless glare" (R, 466), or "a mere stir of black and white in the gathering dusk" (R, 449), or "a black smudge in the darkness" (C, 29).

This sensitivity to the qualitative dimension of experience is conscious as well as instinctive. Conrad articulates it in his theory of impressionism. When he says that the aim of his fiction is above all to make us *see*, he means that he wants the reader to see the true world "buried under the growth of centuries" (R, 153), and behind man's ordinary perception of things. To see things in this way is to see them as they appear to a detached spectator who registers not perceptions but sensations, as the impressionist painters tried to catch the very forms of light. So Conrad defines his aim as a writer as a "scrupulous fidelity to the truth of [his] own sensations" (WT, viii), and in another place asserts that "the unwearied self-forgetful attention to every phase of the living universe reflected in our consciousness may be our appointed task on this earth" (PR, 92).

Such a technique of impressionism is the deliberate method of "Heart of Darkness." "You must remember," says Conrad in a letter about this novel, "that I don't start with an abstract notion. I start with definite images and as their rendering is true some little effect is produced" (LL, I, 268). One aim of the novel is to make it possible for the reader to see the wilderness outside the frail fences guarding the outposts of imperialism, the "silent wilderness surrounding this cleared speck on the earth . . . something great and invincible, like evil or truth, waiting patiently for the passing away of this fantastic invasion" (HD, 76).

The culmination of the vision of the world as pure quality is the recognition that behind "the overwhelming realities of this strange world of plants, and water, and silence" (HD, 93) is something else, something more than human and more than natural, an "implacable force brooding over an inscrutable intention" (HD, 93). This is the darkness. The impressions things make on the senses are no more ultimate reality than their interpretation into meanings and objects. Qualities are a thin layer of scintillating light spread over the formless stuff of things, like the moonlight's silvery glitter on the jungle river or on the primeval mud. The famous sentence in the preface to *The Nigger of the "Narcissus"* about making the reader see is followed by another text not so often quoted: "If I succeed, you shall find there according to your deserts: encouragement, consolation, fear, charm — all you demand — and, perhaps, also that glimpse of truth for which you have forgotten to ask" (NN, xiv). The attempt to render the exact appearances of things is not an end in itself. Its aim is to make the truth of life, something different from any impression or quality, momentarily visible. Not colors or light, but the darkness behind them, is the true reality. What does Conrad mean by the "darkness"?

⤳

The darkness is first of all a sensible experience. Like its opposite, white light, darkness is the vanishing point of visual sensation. It is the blurring of clear forms in an all-engulfing sensation of the fact that there is nothing to sense. A darkness of this sort is experienced by the captain in *The Shadow-Line:* "Such must have been the darkness before creation. It had closed behind me. . . . I was alone, every man was alone where he stood. And every form was gone, too, spar, sail, fittings, rails; everything was blotted out in the dreadful smoothness of that absolute night" (SL, 113).

Again and again in Conrad's novels anything distinct, anything colored or light, shows itself as a scintillating flash against a black background. All things appear as "iridescent gleams on a hard and dark surface" (R, 411). But the darkness is not just a neutral background for intelligible forms or gleams of light. These have come from the darkness, as Ransome appears to the captain in *The Shadow-Line,* "stepping out of the darkness into visibility suddenly, as if just created with his composed face and pleasant voice" (SL, 112), and as the people and scenes of Conrad's stories seem to come out of a darkness within him: "My thought goes wandering through vast spaces filled with shadowy forms. All is yet chaos, but, slowly, the apparitions change into living flesh, the shimmering mists take shape." [5]

If the darkness is the original chaos, it is also, even more frighteningly, the end toward which things hurry to return, "the night that waits for its time to move forward upon the glitter, the splendour, the men, the women" (R, 139). In *The Shadow-Line* the young

[5] *Letters of Joseph Conrad to Marguerite Poradowska, 1890-1920,* trans. and ed. John A. Gee and Paul J. Sturm (New Haven: Yale University Press, 1940), p. 64.

captain has a special experience of darkness as the end of all creation: "When the time came the blackness would overwhelm silently the bit of starlight falling upon the ship, and the end of all things would come without a sigh, stir, or murmur of any kind, and all our hearts would cease to beat like run-down clocks. It was impossible to shake off that sense of finality. The quietness that came over me was like a foretaste of annihilation. It gave me a sort of comfort, as though my soul had become suddenly reconciled to an eternity of blind stillness" (SL, 108).

The universe exists for Conrad, as for Dylan Thomas, as a process of the birth of things out of a genetic darkness and their return to that darkness. Each thing or person has a precarious hold on existence, and is constantly coming out of the darkness and being engulfed by it, as the shore appears and disappears to Lingard in *The Rescue* during a violent thunderstorm: "At every dazzling flash, Hassim's native land seemed to leap nearer at the brig — and disappear instantly as though it had crouched low for the next spring out of an impenetrable darkness" (R, 79). But darkness is more than the origin from which things come, and the end toward which they go. It is a metaphysical entity. The blackness of any night is "the shadow of the outer darkness, the shadow of the uninterrupted, of the everlasting night that fills the universe, the shadow of the night so profound and so vast that the blazing suns lost in it are only like sparks, like pin-points of fire, the restless shadow that like a suspicion of an evil truth darkens everything upon the earth on its passage" (R, 151). The darkness is present at every moment and in every thing and person, underlying them as their secret substance, but also denying them as formlessness denies form, or as impersonality denies personality.

It would be an error to identify Conrad's darkness with Sartrean nothingness, just as it would be an error to identify it with the Freudian unconscious, or with evil, if that implies the existence of some opposing principle of good. The darkness is not nothingness, and it is not limited to the depths of human nature. It is the basic stuff of the universe, the uninterrupted. It is what remains, horrifyingly, when every thing or color has disappeared. In *The Shadow-Line* Conrad describes such an "impenetrable blackness," a darkness which "beset the ship so close that it seemed that by thrusting one's hand over the side one could touch some unearthly substance. There was in it an effect of inconceivable terror and oJ inexpressible mystery" (SL, 108).

The crucial experience for Conrad's characters is the moment when they escape from their enclosures in the sane bounds of everyday life and encounter the heart of darkness which beats at the center of the earth and in the breast of every human being on earth. The darkness is everywhere, like Kurtz's last words, which Marlow hears whispered in the air even when he is back in Europe and safe in a city: "The dusk was repeating them in a persistent whisper all around us, in a whisper that seemed to swell menacingly like the first whisper of a rising wind. 'The horror! the horror!' " (HD, 161). The experience of knowing the darkness takes many forms in Conrad's work, but the darkness remains the same in all its manifestations, as a point reached by diverse radii remains the same center. In any of its forms the darkness causes the collapse of daylight intentions and ideals, the rational forms by which civilized man lives.

The darkness is present in the sheer materiality of things, in the primeval mud of the jungle, but also in the "asphalt and bricks, . . . blind houses and unfeeling stones" (SA, 276) of the city. It is the wild animal clamor of the wilderness or of savagery, which modern man has gone beyond to become civilized. In one way the scrawled note ("Exterminate all the brutes!") at the bottom of Kurtz's pamphlet on "The Suppression of Savage Customs" does not reverse his former eloquence but only states it in another way. The civilizing of the world is the transformation of brute men into restrained human beings. Primitive man and civilized man are related to one another as are, in *The Rescue*, Immada and Edith Travers, who are "the beginning and the end, the flower and the leaf, the phrase and the cry" (R, 148). The human world is made by the extermination of its source, the substitution of Marlow's clarity for the irrational emotion of the native life he sees on the shore.

The darkness is the present nature of man, too, for no man has outgrown his beginning. The heart of darkness exists beneath Apollonian clarity, ready to burst out and change the most civilized man into a savage, as, at the deepest point of his penetration of the darkness, Marlow "confound[s] the beat of the drum with the beating of [his] heart" (HD, 142). The shock to Marlow of his sight of the dancing, howling natives is "the thought of your remote kinship with this wild and passionate uproar," "just the faintest trace of a response to the terrible frankness of that noise, a dim suspicion of there being a meaning in it which you — you so remote from the night of first ages — could comprehend" (HD, 96). At this moment Marlow must recognize that "the mind of man is capable of anything — because everything is in it, all the past as well as all the future" (HD, 96).

Kurtz's return to savagery is striking proof of this terrible law of Conrad's universe. With his plans, his genius, his eloquence, his ideals, he is an example of civilized man at his highest point of development. In spite of this he is swallowed up by the jungle. The fantastic invader is himself invaded and destroyed by the wilderness.

This invasion takes a number of forms, forms which reveal Conrad's sense of what the darkness means as a possible condition of even the most civilized man. Kurtz is driven to substitute the immediate moment of self-forgetful gratification for the satisfaction he has sought in dreams of fame and power. The native woman, apparently Kurtz's mistress, who stands on the shore with her arms upraised, "like the wilderness itself, with an air of brooding over an inscrutable purpose" (HD, 136), is a symbol of the present as Kurtz's Intended with her crystalline brow is a symbol of the future. Sexual abandon, as opposed to spiritualized love, belongs to the darkness. Conrad's misogyny, present in his work from *An Outcast of the Islands* and *Almayer's Folly* onward, derives from his identification of sexual experience with the loss of mental clearness and self-possession. Sex is descent into the darkness of irrational emotion, the blurring of consciousness or its extinction. It is not surprising to find that Conrad identifies sex with the jungle.[6] Both mean the same thing to him: the destruction of lucid consciousness. Kurtz's return to the jungle is "the awakening of forgotten and brutal instincts" (HD, 144). He becomes a god in the wilderness, and is worshiped by his native followers. This means putting absolute sovereignty in place of submission to any law or authority. Religious experience, like sex, is for Conrad a loss of rationality. Kurtz's willingness to think of himself as a god is a special form of

[6] See Thomas Moser, *Joseph Conrad: Achievement and Decline* (Cambridge, Mass.: Harvard University Press, 1957), pp. 53, 54.

that perversion. He replaces reasonable dreams of political or commercial power with a desire for the omnipotence of a god. The riotous dances and unspeakable rites offered to him are forms of the Dionysiac abandon to which he has succumbed.

Kurtz has even unleashed the power of death. Marlow's first understanding of Kurtz's condition comes through his view of the shrunken heads on poles around Kurtz's hut, each "smiling continuously at some endless and jocose dream of that eternal slumber" (HD, 131). If the mind of man is capable of anything this is because it contains all the future as well as the past. The future is death, the return of created things to the night from which they have sprung. To say that the darkness is the end of all things is to identify the darkness with death, and to realize that the truth of the universe can only be recognized by those who have entered the realm of death. In *The Rescue* Jörgenson has come back into the world of action from a deathlike disengagement from life. He understands the triviality of all earthly projects, and is at the beginning of the novel where the hero, Lingard, is going to be at the end. He sees everything as mere appearance because he sees everything from the point of view of death: "Jörgenson, standing by the taffrail, noted the faint reddish glow in the massive blackness of the further shore. Jörgenson noted things quickly, cursorily, perfunctorily, as phenomena unrelated to his own apparitional existence of a visiting ghost. They were but passages in the game of men who were still playing at life. He knew too well how much that game was worth to be concerned about its course. . . . In that world of eternal oblivion, of which he had tasted before Lingard made him step back into the life of men, all things were settled once for all" (R, 382). In "Heart of Darkness," too, death is another form of the darkness. Kurtz's victory comes at the moment of his death and depends on his proximity to death. So Marlow compares his own inconclusive "wrestle with death" to Kurtz's: "True, he had made that last stride, he had stepped over the edge, while I had been permitted to draw back my hesitating foot. And perhaps this is the whole difference; perhaps all the wisdom, and all truth, and all sincerity, are just compressed into that inappreciable moment of time in which we step over the threshold of the invisible" (HD, 151).

The deepest experience of truth is a moment which is neither past, present, nor future, but out of time altogether, like death

itself. Many of Conrad's characters reach this state, but not necessarily by dying. The crucial experience for many of them is a
moment which hovers on the threshold of the invisible. *The Rescue*
offers important examples of this. At different times, but in ways
which have to do with their relation to each other, Lingard and
Mrs. Travers reach a state in which their awareness of themselves
as separate individuals is lost, a state in which the ordinary qualities
of time and space disappear, a state in which they are no one and
nowhere because they are everywhere at once, simultaneously
motionless and moving with infinite velocity. Such a place makes
"this moment of time and . . . this spot on the earth's surface"
a location where the laws of exclusion and succession are no longer
obeyed, and the "moving shadow of the unbroken night [stands]
still to remain . . . forever" (R, 152). Twice Mrs. Travers reaches,
through the combination of physical tension and the perception of
a dark silent night, such a place:

> After a time this absolute silence which she almost could feel pressing upon her
> on all sides induced in Mrs. Travers a state of hallucination. She saw herself
> standing alone, at the end of time, on the brink of days. All was unmoving as if
> the dawn would never come, the stars would never fade, the sun would never rise
> any more . . . (R, 151)

> And all this — the wan burst of light, the faint shock as of something remote
> and immense falling into ruins, was taking place outside the limits of her life which
> remained encircled by an impenetrable darkness and by an impenetrable silence.
> Puffs of wind blew about her head and expired; the sail collapsed, shivered
> audibly, stood full and still in turn; and again the sensation of vertiginous speed
> and of absolute immobility succeeding each other with increasing swiftness merged
> at last into a bizarre state of headlong motion and profound peace. The darkness
> enfolded her like the enervating caress of a sombre universe. It was gentle and
> destructive. Its languor seduced her soul into surrender. Nothing existed and even
> all her memories vanished into space. She was content that nothing should exist.
> (R, 244, 245)

In the same way, Lingard, through his love for Mrs. Travers, is
put in the condition of "a man who, having cast his eyes through
the open gates of Paradise, is rendered insensible by that moment's
vision to all the forms and matters of the earth" (R, 415). He is
driven by his love to abandon his habitual relation to the world.
He has been actively engaged in "the visible surface of life open
in the sun to the conquering tread of an unfettered will" (R, 210).
Now he is taken by his hopeless love into a strange realm of

"wavering gloom" (R, 210). Conrad finds terms to define these two forms of being: "existence" and "life." Existence corresponds to the all-embracing night, to a world of flashes of light, impalpable shapes in the fog. Life corresponds to the vision of things as significant objects projected in broad daylight: "It was as to being alive that he felt not so sure. He had no doubt of his existence; but was this life — this profound indifference, this strange contempt for what his eyes could see, this distaste for words, this unbelief in the importance of things and men? He tried to regain possession of himself, his old self which had things to do, words to speak as well as to hear. But it was too difficult. He was seduced away by the tense feeling of existence far superior to the mere consciousness of life, and which in its immensity of contradictions, delight, dread, exultation and despair could not be faced and yet was not to be evaded. There was no peace in it. But who wanted peace? Surrender was better, the dreadful ease of slack limbs in the sweep of an enormous tide and in a divine emptiness of mind. If this was existence then he knew that he existed" (R, 431, 432).

Life is the voluntary commitment of one's energies to the fulfillment of a noble idea, in Lingard's case his promise to get Hassim and Immada back on their thrones. But life is only an unreal scene performed before a black curtain, and the curtain negates the play acted before it. Black is the color which absorbs all colors, the place where contradictions meet, the force that turns all forms and judgments into nothing, but there is a way of being which is not separate from it: existence. Lingard's love for Mrs. Travers brings him to this state. Existence is passivity, inaction, as opposed to volition and energy. It is an impersonal awareness of an impersonal darkness, rather than the affirmation of personality. Having reached such a condition, Lingard betrays his friends, and abandons his "idea" and all its careful preparation.

People in Conrad's world are in an intolerable situation. The Apollonian realm of reason and intention is a lie. The heart of darkness is the truth, but it is a truth which makes ordinary human life impossible. It is the absorption of all forms in the shapeless night from which they have come. A man who reaches the truth is swallowed up by a force which invades his reason and destroys his awareness of his individuality. To know the darkness is to know the falsity of life, and to understand the leap into emptiness man made when he separated himself from the wild clamor of primitive life.

Throughout his career Conrad recognized that there is no way to relate existence and life, no way to evade the tragic contradictions of the human situation. Captain MacWhirr, after a moment of insight, returns to his imperturable calm, but most of Conrad's heroes are not so fortunate. Their moments of puzzled detachment lead them step by step into the darkness. There is no return from that interior to the fatuous unreason of their complacency. "The habit of profound reflection," says Conrad, ". . . is the most pernicious of all the habits formed by the civilized man" (V, x, xi). Heyst's "fine detachment," in *Victory*, leads him to lose "the habit of asserting himself," and separates him from life. Decoud, in *Nostromo*, is driven to suicide not by some overwhelming experience, but by a few hours alone on the Golfo Placido. His solitude, "from mere outward condition of existence becomes very swiftly a state of soul in which the affectations of irony and skepticism have no place. It takes possession of the mind, and drives forth the thought into the exile of utter unbelief" (N, 497). In novel after novel Conrad presents characters driven to passivity or death by a confrontation with the darkness: Marlow, with his Buddha's pose, Winnie Verloc, driven to suicide by "madness and despair," Lingard, Razumov, Kurtz, and many others.

Is there no way to remain in touch with the darkness without being engulfed by it, no way to be actively engaged in life without becoming part of an empty masquerade?

～

Apparently there is no way. Even those who are not destroyed by their recognition of the darkness seem to have no satisfactory course open to them. Marlow comes back from the darkness. Now he can look down on the citizens of the sepulchral city because, as he says, "I felt so sure they could not possibly know the things I knew" (HD, 152). What good does his wisdom do him? He knows that the lie is a lie, and confirms his allegiance to civilization by the lie he tells Kurtz's Intended. Action which is taken with awareness that the lie is a lie is the only action which is not a mournful and somber delusion, but this authenticity is based on a contradiction.

Action is authentic only insofar as it is recognized that no action is authentic. True action must be based on that which denies it. Its hope is its despair, its meaning its meaninglessness, its reality its proximity to the uninterrupted night, the horror. It is a mistake to define Conrad's solution to the ethical problem by the phrase the "true lie." [7] There is nothing true about any action or judgment except their relation to the darkness, and the darkness makes any positive action impossible. Marlow, in a moment of insight, recognizes the pointlessness of life: "it occurred to me that my speech or my silence, indeed any action of mine, would be a mere futility. What did it matter what any one knew or ignored? What did it matter who was manager? One gets sometimes such a flash of insight. The essentials of this affair lay deep under the surface, beyond my reach, and beyond my power of meddling" (HD, 100). The basis of this somber pessimism is formulated in an early letter to Edward Garnett: "When once the truth is grasped that one's own personality is only a ridiculous and aimless masquerade of something hopelessly unknown, the attainment of serenity is not very far off" (LL, I, 186). It was, no doubt, an understanding of this attitude in Conrad which led the Polish critic Stefan Napierski to ask: "Do they not feel the despair lurking behind these truly nihilistic books?" [8]

Nevertheless, there is someone else present in "Heart of Darkness," someone besides Kurtz, even someone besides Marlow who has come back from the darkness to sit like a dreaming Buddha, contemplating his empty truth and preaching it. There is the narrator, one of those on board the "Nelly," a passive listener whose understanding of the world, it may be, is radically transformed by the story he hears. [9] And there is Conrad himself, the author of the book, the man who after years of active life at sea settled down to decades of solitude, covering thousands upon thousands of blank sheets of paper with words. As he said of himself, remembering Flaubert's *Salammbô:* "Et le misérable écrivait toujours" (LL, II, 64).

[7] See, for example, Robert Penn Warren, "*Nostromo*," *Sewanee Review*, 59:377, 378 (1951).

[8] Quoted in Albert Guerard, Jr., *Joseph Conrad* (New York: New Directions, 1947), p. 77.

[9] See Seymour Gross, "A Further Note on the Function of the Frame in 'Heart of Darkness,' " *Modern Fiction Studies*, 3: 167–170 (1957).

To devote oneself to writing, however, is to engage in the most unreal action of all. Conrad was always tormented by his task, partly by what he called, echoing Baudelaire, "les stérilités des écrivains nerveux" (LL, II, 14), but more painfully still by the sheer unreality of writing: "I have often suffered in connection with my work from a sense of unreality, from an intellectual doubt of the ground I stood upon. This has occurred especially in the periods of difficult production" (LL, II, 14). "It is strange. The unreality of it seems to enter one's real life, penetrate into the bones, and make the very heartbeats pulsate illusions through the arteries. One's will becomes the slave of hallucinations, responds only to shadowy impulses, waits on imagination alone. A strange state, a trying experience, a kind of fiery trial of untruthfulness. And one goes through it with an exaltation as false as all the rest of it. One goes through it, — and there's nothing to show at the end. Nothing! Nothing! Nothing!" (LL, I, 283).

Words, the medium of fiction, are a fabrication of man's intellect. They are part of the human lie. One way to define the darkness is to say that it is incompatible with language. As Marlow gets closer to the heart of darkness he also gets further from it, for he more and more recognizes the gap between words and the darkness they can never express. The expression of Kurtz's genius is his eloquence: "Kurtz discoursed. A voice! a voice! It rang deep to the very last. It survived his strength to hide in the magnificent folds of eloquence the barren darkness of his heart" (HD, 147). The hollowness of Kurtz's eloquence exposes the incompatibility between language and truth, and shows that of all the superficial films putting a glittering surface between man and the darkness, language is the most ephemeral. So Conrad is tormented not only by the unreality of words, but also by a sense of guilt for the mendacity of language. He feels that he is "not half as decent or half as useful" as "the gentlemen in gray who live in Dartmoor" (LL, II, 105).

In spite of this, the separation from the daylight world involved in the act of writing, its forgetting of life in order to penetrate into a realm which does not exist, is the only safe means of reaching truth. Language faces two ways. Words are a sign of man's imprisonment within illusions, but the language of fiction is the substance of a story which has no existence outside words. This detachment of words from their utilitarian function as signs puts language in touch with the unworded darkness. It brings to light the fact that words have always been detached from the everyday world. Language is that which is most intimate to man and therefore flows from the profound dark rather than from the daylight of rationality. The "gift of expression" is double. It is "the bewildering, the illuminating, the most exalted and the most contemptible, the pulsating stream of light, or the deceitful flow from the heart of an impenetrable darkness" (HD, 113, 114).

How, in a novel, can words flow from the darkness and name the nameless? The form of Conrad's fiction gives the answer. Words can name the darkness by describing a double motion of descent into the darkness and return from it. To descend directly into the dark is to be destroyed. The writer must structure the experience of some surrogate in such a way as to reveal its truth. This truth will either destroy that other self, as Kurtz and Decoud are destroyed, or will be hidden from them, as it is hidden from Lord Jim or from Flora de Barral in *Chance*. Conrad's novels are an elaborate manipulation of data in order to make the truth behind the facts appear, and the relation of Marlow to Kurtz may be seen as a dramatization of the writer's relation to his subject. Marlow's real experience, he says, is not his own, but Kurtz's: "It is his extremity that I seem to have lived through" (HD, 151). Each writer must bring the truth back from the darkness, as Marlow carries Kurtz away from the midnight revelry of the natives and bears him toward civilization like a sacred burden.

But Kurtz cannot be rescued. Like Eurydice, he is claimed by the darkness and soon dies, after delivering his terrifying judgment on the universe. Like a new Orpheus, Marlow can only rescue Kurtz indirectly, by transforming his life into words. Writing gives a form to the indefinable. By a return, through language, to the heart of darkness, the writer affirms himself as the power which breaks down the frontier between man and the darkness, and makes the darkness enter for a moment the daylight world. Writing is a dangerous hovering between two realms which are incompatible. Through literature they are brought together and yet kept at a distance. The writer can create a film of words which detaches man from the falsely human by making images of it, and puts him in possession of truth while still protecting him from it. By expressing the experience of someone who has been swallowed up in the darkness, the writer creates a fragile web of narrative between himself and the horror. This web gives the reader a knowledge in no other way available, and at the same time it keeps the devouring darkness at a distance. Writing is the only kind of authentic action. It is in the world and in the darkness at once.

Conrad deliberately uses the precise description of events to reach what is opposed to all visible things. The key to his aesthetic theory is a sentence in *Lord Jim:* "only a meticulous precision of statement would bring out the true horror behind the appalling face of things" (LJ, 30). Through exactly described scenes the horror appears, called by the magical incantation of words, though it is something which cannot be directly defined in words. It is the halo which appears around the reflected light of the moon. In Conrad's fiction an invisible haze is lit up by the glow of bright light, the definite facts, reflected in meticulous words, which make up the action. This, I take it, is the meaning of the famous declaration of the narrator of "Heart of Darkness" when he says that, for Marlow, "the meaning of an episode was not inside like a kernel but outside, enveloping the tale which brought it out only as a glow brings out a haze, in the likeness of one of those misty halos that sometimes are made visible by the spectral illumination of moonshine" (HD, 48). The haze is everywhere, at all times, in the air, everywhere in nature, and at the heart of each human being, like a darkness which is seemingly dissipated by light. The goal of writing is to make darkness visible by means of the light. All words belong to the light, yet for a moment, if the story is successful, they reveal the darkness, for words belong to the darkness too.

But this is not really so. Writing can only oscillate perpetually between truth and falsehood, and endure endlessly its failure to bring what is real, the darkness, permanently into what is human, the light. Every story is necessarily a failure. In the moment that the darkness is caressed into appearing by the words of the story, it disappears. Though writing is the only action which escapes the imposture of the merely human, at the same time all literature is necessarily a sham. It captures in its subtle pages not the reality of the darkness but its verbal image.

Nevertheless, this momentary glimpse of truth is the highest human accomplishment, and it is the aim of all authentic writing. Such is Conrad's claim in the concluding sentences of the preface to *The Nigger of the "Narcissus,"* in a text which recapitulates in brief all the stages of his thought. True art, he says, must shift the gaze of the reader from the unreal dream of the future to the immediate moment of sensation. A meticulous description of the appearances of that moment will lead to a brief glimpse of the truth behind appearance, and that glimpse is the goal of art:

> To arrest, for the space of a breath, the hands busy about the work of the earth, and compel men entranced by the sight of distant goals to glance for a moment at the surrounding vision of form and colour, of sunshine and shadows; to make them pause for a look, for a sigh, for a smile — such is the aim, difficult and evanescent, and reserved only for a very few to achieve. But sometimes, by the deserving and the fortunate, even that task is accomplished. And when it is accomplished — behold! — all the truth of life is there: a moment of vision, a sigh, a smile — and the return to an eternal rest. (NN, xvi)

This return to an eternal rest is the inevitable aftermath of the moment of vision. It is a double return, the return of the darkness to its uninterrupted repose in the flux at the heart of things, and the return of man, after his evanescent glimpse of truth, to the forgetful sleep of everyday life. "Rare moments of awakening when we see, hear, understand ever so much — everything — in a flash" are always followed by a "fall back again into our agreeable somnolence" (LJ, 143). This forgetting of truth after a brief vision of it is the denouement of the Conradian adventure. It is also the most somber moment of all in Conrad's long dialogue with the darkness.

THE SECRET AGENT

> And in those days shall men seek death, and shall not find it; and shall desire to die, and death shall flee from them. (*Revelation* 9: 6)

In *The Secret Agent* Conrad's voice and the voice of the darkness most nearly become one. To explore the meaning of this novel will be to approach as close as possible to the dark heart of Conrad's universe. Its starting place is a certain conception of modern society. Against this background the events of what Conrad, in his dedication to H. G. Wells, calls "This Simple Tale of the XIX Century" (v),[10] enact themselves. Apparently Conrad's notion of modern society is the one implied by the germ idea of the story. That germ was a discussion of anarchist activities, particularly of

[10] Numbers in parentheses in this section refer to pages in the Doubleday, Page edition of *The Secret Agent* (1925).

"the already old story of the attempt to blow up the Greenwich
Observatory; a blood-stained inanity of so fatuous a kind that it was
impossible to fathom its origin by any reasonable or even unreason-
able process of thought" (x). Conrad's attitude is not merely one of
"pity and contempt" for the "criminal futility" of anarchism,
"doctrine, action, mentality," mixed with "indignation" (viii, ix)
deriving from his sense of the threat the anarchists pose to a good
society kept stable by fidelity to duty. Conrad is not a conservative
of this sort at all. Another element had to be added to the story of
the Greenwich explosion before the events and characters of the
novel began to take shape in the indistinction of Conrad's "quieted-
down imagination" (xii). That process he explains by "the analogy
of the addition of the tiniest little drop of the right kind, precipi-
tating the process of crystallization in a test tube containing some
colourless solution" (xi). The metaphor recalls T. S. Eliot's more
famous description of the imagination as the neutral catalyst which,
without itself taking part in the reaction, causes elements otherwise
independent to combine in a chemical fusion. Conrad's metaphor,
however, does not contain Eliot's notion of the detachment and
neutrality of the imagination. The writer's mind, for Conrad, is
both the test tube and its contents. When the right elements were
brought together there, "strange forms, sharp in outline but imperfectly apprehended, appeared and claimed attention as crystals
will do by their bizarre and unexpected shapes" (xii). The tiny drop
that crystallized Conrad's imagination was a passage in a book of
reminiscences by a man who had been Assistant Commissioner of
Police during the dynamite outrages of the eighties.[11] The passage
described the Home Secretary's angry distrust of the police: "your
idea of secrecy over there," he had said, "seems to consist of keep
ing the Home Secretary in the dark" (xi). This anecdote, along
with the Greenwich incident, gave Conrad the combination he
wanted: the vision of an entire society linked in a chain of complicity
with the anarchists, and yet keeping such relations hidden from
one another. Mr. Verloc, secret agent, at once respectable bourgeois
shopkeeper and family man, member of various revolutionary
societies, *agent provocateur* for a reactionary foreign power, and un-

---

[11] For an excellent brief discussion of anarchist activities at this time, see Lionel
Trilling, "*The Princess Casamassima*," *The Liberal Imagination* (New York: The Viking
Press, 1950), pp. 68–74.

official spy for the British police, is a perfect example of the sinister connectedness of all levels of society from bottom to top, from the far left to the far right. The vision of society which informs *The Secret Agent* is not that of a stable civilization threatened by the absurd criminality of a lot of "half-crazy" (ix) anarchists. Conrad sees all society as rotten at the core, as a vast half-deliberate conspiracy of police, thieves, anarchists, tradesmen, aristocratic bluestockings, ministers of state, and ambassadors of foreign powers.

Conrad's symbol for this web of secret connections is London itself, the enormous commercial and industrial city. Within the city everyone is related to everyone else, often in hidden and unlawful ways, and at the same time each person is cut off from his neighbors in a solitude "as lonely and unsafe as though [he] had been situated in the midst of a forest" (201). When the elements which quickened Conrad's imagination combined, there first rose before his mind a picture of London, the greatest city on earth. That image was the dark background from which the characters and events of the story "disengaged" themselves: "Then the vision of an enormous town presented itself, of a monstrous town more populous than some continents and in its man-made might as if indifferent to heaven's frowns and smiles; a cruel devourer of the world's light. There was room enough there to place any story, depth enough there for any passion, variety enough there for any setting, darkness enough to bury five millions of lives" (xii).

The city is the place imposing the mode of human relationship peculiar to modern life. It is also "man-made," a monstrous human construction which surrounds man with his own image, and hides from him the light and truth of nature. The city generates its own darkness, an especially human one, not the transhuman blackness of "Heart of Darkness," but an obscurity made of illusion, fatuity, and blindness, the blindness of five million people who agree, with Winnie Verloc, that "life doesn't stand much looking into" (xiii).

Enclosed within this comfortable darkness, all men — anarchist, policeman, tradesman, and thief — accept certain assumptions. They agree that life is a game with rules everyone must obey, that many of these conventions cannot be talked about openly, and that nothing must be done to upset the delicate balance between thief and policeman, anarchist and reactionary ambassador. All of these classes of men deny their cooperation with the others. All are more or less consciously living a lie. They are alike in their refusal to look for the truth behind the surface of things, and in their determination to maintain the status quo. Like Winnie Verloc, they waste "no portion of this transient life in seeking for fundamental information" (169). Their instinct is not to question themselves or the world, but to be and let be. They remain as little conscious as possible, and as much as possible bound by unthinking habits. Chief Inspector Heat, forced to deal with anarchists, regrets "the world of thieves — sane, without morbid ideals, working by routine, respectful of constituted authorities, free from all taint of hate and despair" (92, 93): "he could understand the mind of a burglar, because, as a matter of fact, the mind and the instincts of a burglar are of the same kind as the mind and the instincts of a police officer. Both recognize the same conventions, and have a working knowledge of each other's methods and of the routine of their respective trades. . . . Products of the same machine, . . . they take the machine for granted in different ways, but with a seriousness essentially the same" (92). Society is a machine, a man-made system of conventions obeyed as much by thief as by policeman. The man-made machine has ended by making men, and by determining their existence within a framework of which many of them are not aware and which they do not wish to question.

What of the revolutionists? Are they not examples of a critical detachment from society? They want to destroy injustice in order to make way for the reign of peace, fraternity, and the triumph of science over nature. Inspector Heat, however, is right about thieves, but wrong about anarchists. With the exception of the Professor, the revolutionists in *The Secret Agent* are as much bound by respectability as any policeman, tradesman, or thief. Conrad is careful to distinguish among them, and to make them form a spectrum of the shades of revolutionary belief in his day, from the dialectical materialism of Michaelis, through Comrade Ossipon's faith in science, to the "terrorism" of Yundt. Nevertheless, all are alike in being completely impotent, and in being parasitically dependent on society. Of each of them Conrad could say what he says of Yundt: "The famous terrorist had never in his life raised personally as much as his little finger against the social edifice" (48). Each is in one way or another fed, clothed, cherished, and comforted by women. Strangely enough, the "mission in life" of Verloc, as of the other revolutionists, is "the protection of the social mechanism, not its perfectionment or even its criticism" (15). The trouble with the anarchists is that they are not anarchistic enough. There is more than simple irony in Conrad's boast that "there had been moments during the writing of the book when I was an extreme revolutionist, I won't say more convinced than they but certainly cherishing a more concentrated purpose than any of them had ever done in the whole course of his life" (xiv).

The Professor is the only true anarchist in *The Secret Agent*, the only one who stands outside society and is free of its infatuations. It is the Professor who most explicitly identifies the attitude of the revolutionists with that of respectable people. "You revolutionists," he says, "are the slaves of the social convention, which is afraid of you; slaves of it as much as the very police that stands up in the defence of that convention. Clearly you are, since you want to revolutionize it. . . . You plan the future, you lose yourselves in reveries of economical systems derived from what is; whereas what's wanted is a clean sweep and a clear start for a new conception of life" (69, 73).

A clean sweep and a clear start — the only hope would be to escape altogether from the darkness of the city, but this would be possible only through the "destruction of what is" (306). All ways of living short of that are the same, whether they seek to maintain things exactly as they are, or whether, like the Marxism of Michaelis, they foresee an inevitable development, governed by the material laws of production, from the present state of things to a better one in the future. Anything derived from what is could only be a rearrangement of elements which suffer from a fatal weakness. They are a human creation, as tools, as money, as laws, as the bricks and stones of the city are shaped by man and therefore without authenticity. Conrad in *The Secret Agent* is not unfaithful to the somber picture of modern civilization which he presents in "Heart of Darkness," in *Nostromo*, and elsewhere. He still sees civilization as an arbitrary creation, resting on no source of value outside humanity. His picture of the sinister cooperation of policemen, anarchists, and ministers of state within the brooding darkness of the enormous town is one of his most impressive dramatizations of this black view of civilized society.

Only if man were in some way liberated from the darkness could he be freed from his fatuous complacency. The purpose of the novel is to bring about such a liberation for the reader by effecting it for the chief characters of the novel, and the objects of Conrad's "inspiring indignation and underlying pity and contempt" are not only the revolutionists of the story, but all men, his readers too, trapped, like the characters of the story, in a blind belief in what is a human fabrication and a lie.

Since *The Secret Agent* is a work of literature, its power to liberate the reader from his infatuation must derive from a certain use of words. Since it is a novel, words must be used in it to describe the appearances of an imagined scene, and to dramatize human actions within that scene. What the scene is we know: the enormous town, generator of its own darkness and devourer of the world's light. To describe this town from the point of view of someone blindly enclosed in it would be no way out of the darkness. The nature of the collective dream is invisible to the dreamers because it determines what is seen and how it is judged. If society is to be exposed there must be a withdrawal to some vantage point outside it. Some dreamers must waken and be able to compare the waking world to the dream.

Conrad chooses two ways of separating his readers from the dark city. The first of these is the point of view of the narrator. His stance is one of ironic detachment. The "purely artistic purpose" of the novel, Conrad says, is "that of applying an ironic method to a subject of that kind" (xiii). The detachment of an ironic perspective is necessary because the clear vision of an uninvolved spectator is the mode of seeing of the waking sleeper, the man who knows all he sees is permeated by the unreality of dreams. Such a man is both inside and outside his dream at once, and can describe it with meticulous precision, while knowing that it is a dream. It is not surprising that Conrad should have said that *The Secret Agent* was written "in the earnest belief that ironic treatment alone would enable me to say all I felt I would have to say in scorn as well as in pity" (xiii).

Conrad wants to do more than show the dream as dream. He

also wants to show what is outside it, to reveal the light which is swallowed up by the city's darkness. In a good novel, the narrator, even if he is omniscient, is limited by the mode of vision possible to the characters in the story. He may present characters as deluded, but it is difficult to show the truth which is hidden from them unless the scales fall from their eyes too. What is not presented as the experience of a character is not properly presented, and "Dramatize! Dramatize!" is the first law of fiction. Conrad must therefore use another method of separating his readers from the urban dream. He must show characters whose enclosure in the dream is destroyed. Only because such people exist in the novel can the narrator describe not only the dream, but what the dream hides.

The plot of *The Secret Agent* is a chain reaction, a sequence of disenchantments started by M. Vladimir's demand that Verloc create a sensational anarchist demonstration. The chain leads from Verloc eventually to Winnie Verloc, and then to the man who survives her and must live on with the terrible knowledge of her death, Comrade Ossipon. One by one these characters are wrested from their complacency and put in a situation which is outside everything they have known, a situation which is, one might say, out of this world. Conrad's ways of describing these cataclysmic experiences are necessarily hyperbolic. Winnie Verloc, after she learns of Stevie's death, is a "free woman." Her freedom is of such a terrifying completeness that she cannot see "what there [is] to keep her in the world at all" (251). Her "moral nature" has been "subjected to a shock of which, in the physical order, the most violent earthquake of history could only be a faint and languid rendering" (255). Similar shocks destroy the unthinking insulation of other characters. Winnie is the central figure only because she goes from the most complete innocence to the most shattering knowledge of what lies beyond the world. Because she moves so far beyond her initial assumptions Conrad can say of her story that it is related reciprocally to its background. It draws its tenebrous gloom from the monstrous town, but it also illuminates the darkness of the city, and shows it as what it is: "Slowly the dawning conviction of Mrs. Verloc's maternal passion grew up to a flame between me and that background, tingeing it with its secret ardour and receiving from it in exchange some of its own sombre colouring.

At last the story of Winnie Verloc stood out complete from the days of her childhood to . . . its anarchistic end of utter desolation, madness and despair" (xii, xv).

A narrator who sees the story with clearheaded pity and contempt, and characters who move toward this detachment — these are the two modes of vision which Conrad uses to "make us *see*" the conditions of life in the city.

∽

When the comfortable dream of a humanized world is rudely shattered, man sees what has been there all along. Reality is always present, but is usually hidden behind the façade of meanings which has been spread over the world. Through the detachment of the ironic narrator and through the experience of the characters the reader is brought to see this dissimulated reality. Such seeing takes several forms, each corresponding to a stage of penetration into reality.

All the levels of this penetration are unobtrusively introduced in an admirable passage at the beginning of the second chapter. This text describes the progress of Mr. Verloc through the streets of London as he walks one spring morning toward the embassy which houses one of his employers:

> The very pavement under Mr. Verloc's feet had an old-gold tinge in that diffused light, in which neither wall, nor tree, nor beast, nor man cast a shadow. Mr. Verloc was going westward through a town without shadows in an atmosphere of powdered old gold. There were red, coppery gleams on the roofs of houses, on the corners of walls, on the panels of carriages, on the very coats of the horses, and on the broad back of Mr. Verloc's overcoat, where they produced a dull effect of rustiness. . . . The polished knockers of the doors gleamed as far as the eye could reach, the clean windows shone with a dark opaque lustre. And all was still. But a milk cart rattled noisily across the distant perspective; a butcher boy, driving with the noble recklessness of a charioteer at Olympic Games, dashed round the corner sitting high above a pair of red wheels. . . . With a turn to the left Mr. Verloc pursued his way along a narrow street by the side of a yellow wall . . . (11, 12, 14)[12]

Conrad has here made use of the fact that weather of a particular sort brings about a startling transformation of the usual look of

[12] My attention was originally called to this passage by Avrom Fleishman. See his essay, "The Symbolic World of *The Secret Agent*," *ELH: A Journal of English Literary History*, 32 (June 1965).

things. The diffused light makes everything look alien. Instead of
seeing houses, walls, carriages, and people as distinct objects, the
spectator also sees the identical gleams which the diffused light
casts on each indiscriminately. It may be, in fact, that nothing
exists except these gleams, since one evidence of the solidity of
objects, the fact that they interrupt the light and cast shadows, is
missing. No thing or person has a shadow, and it is as if they did
not exist as massive forms, but had been dissolved into scintillations
of light. To see things in this way is to understand how little of
what is seen derives from objects themselves, and how much is a
reflection of the pervasive light which makes things visible. The
spectator sees that the world is composed of splotches and blobs
and gleams, gleams which his intelligence distorts by fitting them
into its pre-existent concepts. Such a way of seeing shows that there
is an identity of all red or yellow things which merges them into
cases of a single mode of sensation. What the observer experiences
in this scene, Conrad suggests, is not doors, windows, a wall, the
wheels of a butcher boy's cart, but a "gleam," "a dark opaque
lustre," the color yellow, the color red. He is always sensitive to the
colors of things, and can often persuade the reader of the strangeness of the visible world by insisting on the unlikely colors things
have, as when he describes Winnie's mother during her last cab
ride to the poorhouse: "In the gas-light of the low-fronted shops
her big cheeks glowed with an orange hue under a black and mauve
bonnet" (159).

To see the world as areas of color or flashes of light is no longer
to feel certain of the names man has applied to things. These
identifying labels seem to have detached themselves from things,
and to be wandering around in a sort of limbo halfway between
the spectator and the world, or perhaps to have got attached by
accident to the wrong things. It may be that solid things, obscured
from view by a screen of colors, have, in this unnatural and rarefied
world, begun to stray here and there, defying the law of gravity.
As Mr. Verloc approaches the embassy which is his goal he reaches
a place where all signs are misleading. It is significant that this
approach goes by way of a visible object whose color is its only
identifying characteristic:

Mr. Verloc pursued his way along a narrow street by the side of a yellow wall
which, for some inscrutable reason, had No. 1 Chesham Square written on it in

black letters. Chesham Square was at least sixty yards away, and Mr. Verloc, cosmopolitan enough not to be deceived by London's topographical mysteries, held on steadily, without a sign of surprise or indignation. At last, with business-like persistency, he reached the Square, and made diagonally for the number 10. This belonged to an imposing carriage gate in a high, clean wall between two houses, of which one rationally enough bore the number 9 and the other was numbered 37; but the fact that this last belonged to Porthill Street, a street well known in the neighbourhood, was proclaimed by an inscription placed above the ground-floor windows by whatever highly efficient authority is charged with the duty of keeping track of London's strayed houses. Why powers are not asked of Parliament (a short act would do) for compelling those edifices to return where they belong is one of the mysteries of municipal administration. (14, 15)

In this passage, as elsewhere in *The Secret Agent*, the spectator comes to see how familiar objects exceed the mind's grasp and dwell beyond human meanings. The milk cart and the butcher boy's chariot which appear before Mr. Verloc's eyes have no connection with each other, and no special meaning for Mr. Verloc. They appear one after the other against the drab background of the silent street, and are followed by "a guilty-looking cat issuing from under the stones," and a "thick police constable" who surges "apparently out of a lamp-post" (14). These objects exist with three-dimensional solidity between the spectator and the veil of light which forms the background of the scene. They can be identified, but nothing more can be said of them. Recognitions of the intrinsic absurdity of things most often occur in moments of violence, danger, or surprise, times when man's ordinary engagement in the world is broken. Such moments occur in *The Secret Agent* when Verloc's complacent life is endangered by M. Vladimir, and when the reader first hears of the violent death of Stevie:

He was, in truth, startled and alarmed. . . . And in the silence Mr. Verloc heard against a window-pane the faint buzzing of a fly — his first fly of the year. . . . The useless fussing of that tiny, energetic organism affected unpleasantly this big man threatened in his indolence. (26, 27)

An upright semi-grand piano near the door, flanked by two palms in pots, executed suddenly all by itself a valse tune with aggressive virtuosity. The din it raised was deafening. [Then] it ceased, as abruptly as it had started . . . (61)

⌣

Apparently the shapes and colors of things, their appearance as mute presences, have a quality of firstness before which it is impossible to go. Behind the visible qualities of things, however, is something else: the substance of which they are made. Behind the gleams of colors or light as Mr. Verloc makes his way through the street, behind the houses, walls, carriages, and trees which these gleams reveal and hide, is "the majesty of inorganic nature, of matter that never dies" (14). All things have this in common: they are made of immortal matter.[13] This may be more important, in determining each thing, than the fact that one particular bit of matter has been given just this shape or structure. Repeatedly in *The Secret Agent* Conrad reminds the reader that the forms which man imposes on matter effect only a precarious transformation. At any moment a change in his way of looking at things or a change in the things themselves will force him to see the reality behind surface colors or shapes. This chthonic substance is prior to what had seemed irreducible qualities and is far more alien to man than they. Like the recognition of the strangeness of things, insight into the hostility of matter is brought about by a collapse of man's normal relation to the world. Often this substance, the cold, wet stuff of which London is made, is seen through a window. It seems as though it would be dangerous to face it unprotected: "he pulled up violently the venetian blind, and leaned his forehead against the cold window-pane — a fragile film of glass stretched between him and the enormity of cold, black, wet, muddy, inhospitable accumulation of bricks, slates, and stones, things in themselves unlovely and unfriendly to man. Mr. Verloc felt the latent unfriendliness of all out of doors with a force approaching to positive bodily anguish" (56, and see 100, 269).

Though man's great cities are the expression of his dominion over nature, even there the unfriendliness of the out-of-doors is ready at any moment to appear. This unfriendliness is a stubborn recalcitrance in matter, a passive resistance to man's shapings or valuings. The "majesty of inorganic nature" appears in the solidity, immobility, and inertia of matter. Whatever may be done to it, it remains fundamentally the same. It is outside time, since time cannot change it, and it transcends all attempts to understand or control it. Matter is static and perdurable, and therefore alien to man, that creature of time and change.

[13] Conrad did not know that $E = mc^2$, but energy, after all, is another form of substance. It does not have the insubstantiality of spirit or consciousness.

Man in one way participates in the majesty of matter that never dies. Though his body is organic rather than inorganic, it comes from matter and returns to it. Even while a man is alive his body is as inertly passive as are rocks and bricks. Mr. Verloc marches along the street "steady like a rock — a soft kind of rock" (13), and the thick police constable surges out of a lamppost "as if he, too, were part of inorganic nature" (14). From the point of view of consciousness, the fact that men are in one sense part of nature is the most shocking evidence of the strangeness of matter. If a man exceeds his body by reason of his knowledge, his intentions, memories, and thoughts, in another way he is trapped in his body. He is just this piece of matter here, so many pounds of flesh and blood, like a soft rock, and, like a rock, enclosed within his own bounds. Ordinarily the grossness, or, one might say, the obscenity of a man's enclosure in a thick envelope of flesh is not noticed, so powerful are the evidences of his spirituality, but fat men remind us of the scandal of our incarnation, just as does the sight of a corpse. It is this fact as much as the evidence it gives of gluttony which, it may be, makes obesity seem morally wrong. A fat man seems in danger of ceasing to have a soul and becoming simply a body, and this recalls the grotesque absurdity of our own incarnation. Mr. Verloc can more justly be called "a soft kind of rock" because he is fat than if he were thin. He is "undemonstrative and burly in a fat-pig style" (13), and the police constable who looks as if he had just surged out of a lamppost is "thick."

With something of a shock the reader realizes how many of the characters in *The Secret Agent* are fat. Conrad seems to be insisting on their gross bodies, as if their fatness were connected with the central themes of the novel. Winnie Verloc is "a young woman with a full bust, in a tight bodice, and with broad hips" (5). Her mother is "a stout, wheezy woman, with a large brown face. . . . Her swollen legs rendered her inactive" (6). M. Vladimir has "a large, white, plump hand" (21). Inspector Heat's "determined character" is "marred by too much flesh" (116), a cabman has an "enormous and unwashed countenance" which flames "red in the muddy stretch of the street" (156), and the obesity of the "great personage," a minister of state whom the Assistant Commissioner interviews, is insisted upon at length. He is "vast in bulk and stature," "an expanding man" (136). The most striking example of grotesque fatness in *The Secret Agent* is someone at the other end of the social scale: Michaelis, the ticket-of-leave apostle. This man weighs eighteen stone, has legs like bolsters, and a voice that wheezes "as if deadened and oppressed by the layer of fat on his chest" (41). He has "come out of a highly hygienic prison round like a tub, with an enormous stomach and distended cheeks of a pale, semi-transparent complexion" (41).

A clue to the reason why there are so many fat characters in *The Secret Agent* is given by what happens to Stevie, one of the few characters who is not fat. Stevie is blown to bits when he stumbles with a can of explosives on his way to destroy the Greenwich Observatory. The disappearance of this half-witted boy is the central event of the novel, but it is never directly described. Stevie's end is hinted at, imagined, and approached from various perspectives. It is recounted by various people, but remains hidden, a blank place in the center of the narrative. Stevie's death is proof that human beings are radically different from the majesty of matter that never dies. A man can come to an abrupt end. So a "doctor's brougham arrested in august solitude close to the curbstone" is the "only reminder of mortality" (14) as Mr. Verloc walks to the embassy on the morning which starts the chain of events leading to Stevie's death.

Stevie is dead, but in another sense he is not dead at all. Conrad insists on this other sense. He returns to it, and broods over it, as though it were an important fact in the story. Stevie is not annihilated. He is transformed into "a heap of rags, scorched and bloodstained, half concealing what might have been an accumulation of raw material for a cannibal feast" (86). He is "blown to small bits: limbs, gravel, clothing, bones, splinters — all mixed up together" (210). He becomes "a heap of nameless fragments," like "the by-products of a butcher's shop" (87, 88). Stevie's death is shocking proof of man's incarnation. It proves that a man cannot, even after death, escape from his identification with so many pounds of inorganic nature that never dies. When Stevie dies his consciousness vanishes, but he does not leave a vacuum behind him. He leaves an "enormous hole in the ground under a tree filled with smashed roots and broken branches. All round fragments of a man's body blown to pieces" (70).

Man's identification with his body has another meaning for

Conrad. This meaning is dramatized in the character of the Professor. "Exterminate, exterminate!" he says, echoing the note at the bottom of Kurtz's pamphlet in "Heart of Darkness." "That is the only way of progress. . . . Every taint, every vice, every prejudice, every convention must meet its doom" (303). For this reason he gives explosives to anyone who asks for them. "The condemned social order," as the Professor says, "has not been built up on paper and ink, and I don't fancy that a combination of paper and ink will ever put an end to it" (71). Though the social edifice is made up of a vast system of institutions based on an "idealistic conception of legality" (73), nevertheless these intangible ideals have got themselves embodied in a very tangible form. They exist not only in the bricks and stones of London, but also in the stolid inertia of the citizens of London, shopkeepers, lazy, fat revolutionists, and "thick" policemen alike. Incarnation means more than the imprisonment of spirit in a body. It also means the imprisonment of spirit within the narrow bounds of a set of imperfect assumptions about law and morality. For this reason the Professor's bombs must destroy more than the buildings of modern civilization. They must destroy people too, for in them history is embodied as much as in stones and inscriptions. The Professor's bombs must kill people without killing them. They must "destroy public faith in legality" (81), clear men's minds of the inert residue of traditional beliefs, and yet leave men still alive. The clean sweep and a clear start for a new conception of life must take place in the minds of men. The Professor makes explicit the focus of his destructive aim when, comparing himself to the guardians of law and order, he says that, whereas they depend on life, he depends on death: "Their character is built upon conventional morality. It leans on the social order. Mine stands free from everything artificial. They are bound in all sorts of conventions. They depend on life, which, in this connection, is a historical fact surrounded by all sorts of restraints and considerations, a complex, organized fact open to attack at every point; whereas I depend on death, which knows no restraint and cannot be attacked. My superiority is evident" (68). The Professor wants to employ the power of death in a special way. By using it as the erasure and forgetting of history, he believes he can make the minds of all men pure and empty. Mankind will then be possessors, like himself, of a "sinister freedom." With this freedom will begin a new era in human history, an era of justice and truth.

The Professor fails. He remains poised indefinitely in the moment between the discovery of his sinister freedom and the act which would use that freedom to liberate mankind. The failure of the Professor is as exemplary for our time as was the failure of Chamfort at the time of the French Revolution. Chamfort too sought a spiritual purification, but he died in the frenzies of the Terror. The Professor's failure is strikingly symbolized in his search for a perfect detonator, and in the bomb which he carries on his own person as the expression of his "force of personality" (67). Rather than be captured, he will press the india-rubber ball in his pocket and blow himself and those around him to bits. The only flaw in this "supreme guarantee of his sinister freedom" (81) is the full twenty seconds which must elapse from the moment he presses the detonator until the explosion takes place. The failure of the detonator expresses the contradiction which keeps the Professor hovering interminably in the infinite moment between the decision to bring about the "destruction of what is" and the moment of the explosion. Death is too powerful to be used as an instrument. It is always an end, in more senses than one. The man who tries to bring death into the human world as a means of purification will find that he has committed the world to death. He cannot destroy men's beliefs without actually killing them. To perform such a delicate operation of purification would require infinite time, whereas the Professor's time is finite. One slip, one tiny error, and, instead of bringing death into the world, he will send that world, or part of it, into eternity, and eternity, as Ossipon says, is "a damned hole." "It's time that you need. You — if you met a man who could give you for certain ten years of time, you would call him your master. . . . Wait till you are lying flat on your back at the end of your time. . . . Your scurvy, shabby, mangy little bit of time" (305, 306). Time, in Ossipon's speech, is opposed to eternity, in a juxtaposition which recurs throughout the novel. Time can be measured by man, as it is in the Greenwich Observatory. It can be employed as a dimension within which man fulfills his intentions. Eternity, the realm of death, is a damned hole, of no use to man. The imperfection of the Professor's detonator is a symptom of his inability to reconcile time and eternity.

His failure can be defined in another way. He cannot make a large enough blank place to bring into existence his new conception of life. His bombs are not big enough to make a clean sweep. Mankind is "as numerous as the sands of the seashore, as indestructible, as difficult to handle," and the sound of exploding bombs will be "lost in their immensity of passive grains without an echo" (306). Only if the Professor could destroy mankind at the same moment as he killed himself would he be justified in pressing the india-rubber ball. A vacuum less than total will still leave some men tied to history, believing in the old conventions and laws, and ready to continue the old rather than to initiate the new. The Professor's bombs are too weak, and this weakness alone keeps him from suicide.

The impasse of the Professor explains Conrad's insistence that an explosion does not leave a vacuum but what was there before in a different form. The indestructibility of inorganic nature is identified with the stolid obduracy of human personality. The "constitutional indolence" (169) of so many of the characters in the novel is the exact moral correlative of their obesity. People insist on being themselves in the same way that a grain of sand resists destruction, and the world is dominated by a law of individuality. Each thing or person is just the thing or person it is and no other. This habit of selfhood resists the Professor's attempts to return it to anonymity in order to make a new start. The Professor cannot make a big enough hole. In fact he cannot make any hole at all. Mankind as much resists destruction as do the passive sands of the seashore, which have reached their limit of pulverization, or as do bricks, which are the atomic units of buildings: ". . . after a while he became disagreeably affected by the sight of the roadway thronged with vehicles and of the pavement crowded with men and women. He was in a long, straight street, peopled by a mere fraction of an immense multitude; but all round him, on and on, even to the limits of the horizon hidden by the enormous piles of bricks, he felt the mass of mankind mighty in its numbers. . . . Often while walking abroad, when he happened also to come out of himself, he had such moments of dreadful and sane distrust of mankind. What if nothing could move them?" (81, 82).

"Often while walking abroad" — the Professor's suspicion that nothing can move mankind comes when he himself is moving. To be outside the refuge of his room, that "hermitage of the perfect anarchist" (82), is to be in danger of recognizing "the resisting power of numbers, the unattackable stolidity of a great multitude" (95). It is to be in danger of seeing the heavy weight of history as it is embodied in the present. This happens only occasionally, when the Professor happens to come out of himself as well as out of his room. It is possible for him to go through the streets in complete separation from the surrounding world, as when he walks "with the nerveless gait of a tramp going on, still going on, indifferent to rain or sun in a sinister detachment from the aspects of sky and earth" (96). Verloc walks back from his disastrous interview at the embassy in the same state: "This detachment from the material world was so complete that, though the mortal envelope of Mr. Verloc had not hastened unduly along the streets, that part of him to which it would be unwarrantably rude to refuse immortality, found itself at the shop door all at once, as borne from west to east on the wings of a great wind" (37). Mr. Verloc participates in the majesty of inorganic nature by means of his "mortal envelope," with its paradoxical immortality. He is also able to detach himself from the material world and dwell alone in his mind. If matter is immovable and out of time, consciousness is evanescent and dwells in time. The expression of this insubstantiality is motion. Even a heavy body which is moving is lightened and spiritualized by its motion. It is in one place only for an instant, and the place where it was a moment ago is empty. This emptiness seems to transfer itself to the body and hollow it out. A body in motion slides athwart the solidity of motionless matter like a meteor across the night sky, and seems, like the meteor, to have little in common with its stationary background. Mr. Verloc's detachment from what he sees is expressed in the fact that he is not standing immobile like a lump of matter or a thick police constable, and the stillness of the immobile street, which has the majesty of inorganic nature, is broken, as he walks toward the embassy, by the motion of the milk cart and the butcher.

The effect of motion on an inorganic mass exactly parallels the effect of the presence of mind within a human body. A body inhabited by consciousness is freed from its materiality and seems detached from the surrounding world, just as a man who is walking seems more alive than a motionless one. John Hagan, Jr., has shown the importance of the motif of the interview in *The Secret Agent*.[14] Equally important is the image of walking. It expresses a "sinister freedom" rather than attempts at communication. Verloc, the Professor, the Assistant Commissioner, Inspector Heat, Winnie Verloc, and Comrade Ossipon are at different times shown walking through the streets of London, and an entire chapter is given to an apparently irrelevant description of a journey by cab to the poorhouse. The purpose of this extraordinary chapter is to create a dreamlike atmosphere dramatizing the paradox of man's ability to move himself through the world and thereby escape from it:

> In the narrow streets the progress of the journey was made sensible to those within by the near fronts of the houses gliding past slowly and shakily, with a great rattle and jingling of glass, as if about to collapse behind the cab; and the infirm horse, with the harness hung over his sharp backbone flapping very loose about his thighs, appeared to be dancing mincingly on his toes with infinite patience. . . . And for a time the walls of St. Stephen's, with its towers and pinnacles, contemplated in immobility and silence a cab that jingled. It rolled, too, however. . . . The cab rattled, jingled, jolted; in fact, the last was quite extraordinary. By its disproportionate violence and magnitude it obliterated every sensation of onward movement; and the effect was of being shaken in a stationary apparatus . . . (156, 157, 163)

From inside the cab the buildings seem to be moving, while the cab vibrates up and down without getting anywhere. The horse appears to be executing a stationary dance. The rarefying of matter through its motion appears only to someone who watches the moving object from a stationary point. From the perspective of the moving object, the cab and its passengers remain as solid as ever, and the cab carries its weight as an inescapable burden, however fast and far it goes. Conrad insists on the obesity of Winnie, her mother, and the cabman, and on the immense efforts necessary on the part of the grotesquely feeble horse to transport them through space an inch at a time. People do not escape from themselves by motion. They take their personalities, situations, and bodies with them wherever they go. But they do escape from their immediate surroundings. A fissure is opened between the "immobility and

---

[14] "The Design of Conrad's *The Secret Agent*," *ELH: A Journal of English Literary History*, 22: 148–164 (1955).

silence" of the walls of St. Stephen's and the cab that, after all, does move. The continuity of relations between one part of the world and another is broken when one of those parts is moving. This motion is the only way man has of recognizing the way time undermines what would be, in a stationary world, the changelessness of all things. Man's ability to dwell comfortably in time is one proof of the insubstantiality of his spirit, but when he turns to things it is difficult to find evidence of time and change. A moving object is not altered. It only appears to be changed to someone watching it from the outside. Inside the cab Winnie's mother's legs are as fat and swollen as ever. Nor can the movement of things be detected by the reason. Things are in one place at one time and at another in another, but motion resists logical analysis and leads the mind to contradictions, as in the paradoxes of Zeno. Whenever a man tries to fix the motion of time, it slips away, leaving him face to face with another evidence of motionlessness, so that time seems to stand still. Conrad succeeds in formulating a perfect expression for this presence and absence of time in man's experience of spatially extended things. As in similar passages in Faulkner's novels, the copresence of motion in stillness and stillness in motion is admirably expressed, and this is shown to be the fundamental quality of the ever-created, ever-destroyed now, the present moment or nick of time which, it may be, is the only reality: "Later on, in the wider space of Whitehall, all visual evidences of motion became imperceptible. The rattle and jingle of glass went on indefinitely in front of the long Treasury building — and time itself seemed to stand still" (156, 157).

The theme of *The Secret Agent* seems to be the disjunction between matter and spirit. Matter is solid and resists change. It never dies. Spirit, on the other hand, dwells in time. It moves across matter without being bound by it. Spirit is free. Man lives in both realms. He is incarnated in a body and is therefore part of matter which never dies. He also has a mind. The two dimensions of his existence are incompatible. He can neither incarnate spirit in matter, nor can he immaterialize matter until it takes on the quality of spirit. The gross weight of earth lies untouched behind the façade of the city, and the human mind which created that façade is as fleeting as ever. Man always dies in the end. Conrad's vision seems to culminate in the recognition of an irreconcilable dualism. Man is the meeting place of matter and spirit, and he is riven apart by their contradictions.

Such a notion of the human situation would have at least two consolations. Though man's mind is emptiness and negation, this negation is a power. It is the basis of the changes which have produced civilization. Cities have, after all, been made with stones and bricks. Even though the brute substance of their matter may not have been altered, they have been shaped to man's uses. Society, though it may be based on a lie, still works, as long as everyone agrees to accept the lie as truth. Men have the power to create a vast system based on an "as if." This system is almost as good as if it were real, so effectively has truth been hidden away by the film which man has spread over the world. Though Conrad reveals the factitiousness of human society, he also presents it as a creation which has a pragmatic validity.

There is another comfort in a humanistic world. Though the survivors can see, in Stevie's death, the tragedy of man's participation in deathless matter, Stevie himself, so it seems, is out of this world altogether. He has escaped from what he has correctly called a "bad world for poor people" (171). In the world of atheistic humanism death is a warm blankness surrounding life on all sides. Into that dark womb all men will go at last. There all debts will be paid, and all suffering will be over. So Conrad speaks a requiem over the body of Mr. Verloc, slain by his wife: "Night, the inevitable reward of men's faithful labours on this earth, night had fallen on Mr. Verloc, the tried revolutionist — 'one of the old lot' — the humble guardian of society" (287, 288).

Conrad's view of human life apparently depends on two notions of nothingness, the nothingness of consciousness, and the nothingness of death, and these support his despair and his hope. If society is based on the creative power of man's mind it is based on nothing. If death is nothingness too, it is harmless, and man is free to make of his own nothingness what he will. He can make with impunity an earthly city of man.

ᔕ

Mr. Verloc, getting off the sofa with ponderous reluctance, opened the door leading into the kitchen to get more air, and thus disclosed the innocent Stevie, seated very good and quiet at a deal table, drawing circles, circle, circles; in-numerable circles, concentric, eccentric; a coruscating whirl of circles that by their tangled multitude of repeated curves, uniformity of form, and confusion of intersecting lines suggested a rendering of cosmic chaos, the symbolism of a mad art attempting the inconceivable. (45)

When the half-witted Stevie sits at the kitchen table his mind is not a blank. It is filled with a positive content: circles, innumerable circles, "coruscations of innumerable circles suggesting chaos and eternity" (237). These circles are the objective expression of a state which is far beyond the mind's usual absorption in a single thought. It is, as Conrad says, eternity, but this eternity is not a "damned hole." It has a definite form. It is made of circles. All parts of it have a shape which designates its constant repetiton of itself. Each part goes round and round and round exactly as do all the other parts, for they are all circles. The eternal recurrence of the same perfect figure is the law of this chaos.

Though eternity is not empty, it is filled with something which denies the laws of exclusion and identity. It is the place of a horrible "uniformity of form," the incessant repetition of innumerable ex-amples of the same unique event. In such a place everything is the same as everything else. To be in one place is the same as to be in any other place, just as to be at any one time is the same as to be at any other time. All times are simultaneous in eternity. To say that any one place or time is like any other place or time is to say that in this cosmic chaos there is no center, or, rather, that all places and times are the center. Though eternity is a circle, it is an infinite circle, and though some circles (an infinite number) may be concentric, an equal number are eccentric, and the result is not an orderly geometric diagram, but only a "confusion of intersecting lines," "a tangled multitude of repeated curves."

Stevie's "mad art" is indeed a representation of the "incon-ceivable," for in the realm which his pencil defines the laws of time and space and the laws of logical thought are broken. Stevie's circles represent a place of formless pullulation, a place out of place and a time out of time which is neither nothing nor something but a swarming multiplicity of identical forms which cancel one another out and yet by this mutual destruction leave the same chaos, un-changed and eternal. It is as if one were to destroy everything and were to find that this annihilation did not leave a vacuum behind but a positive presence, a presence which further acts of negation only make more oppressively active, as absolute silence becomes a murmurous sound louder than any noise.

If what lies beyond time and space is not nothingness but this contradictory presence, and if this inconceivable something is the secret ground of every man's consciousness, then the novel will have a different meaning from the one so far identified. This meaning will not so much deny the first as transcend it. Does the notion of a presence beyond ordinary consciousness occur anywhere in the novel but in the descriptions of Stevie's circles?

Of the three deaths in *The Secret Agent*, those of Stevie, Verloc, and Winnie, only one is described directly, Winnie's murder of Verloc, but in the latter case as in the others the emphasis is not on death as escape into nothingness. The focus is rather on the experience of someone who survives the death of another as if it had been his own death and remains behind as a kind of walking corpse. The survivor is transported into a horrible realm where every place is no place, and where time moves without getting anywhere. This metamorphosis is a process of depersonalization. It follows on the breakdown of the ordinary habits linking a person to the sanity of the everyday world. A man ceases to be the person he was, tied by a hundred strands to an enduring role in society, and becomes nobody, an anonymous awareness or wakefulness which cannot be called a self. The horror of this state is the way it suggests that it may be impossible to die. A man who reaches it is still alive, though everything about him is dead. Everything which had defined him as himself is gone, and yet, terrifyingly, he is still there. Only the language of exaggeration will do to describe this condition. After Winnie has killed her husband she becomes "a woman enjoying her complete irresponsibility and endless leisure, almost in the manner of a corpse" (263), and the Assistant Commissioner says of Verloc after the death of Stevie: "It sounds an extravagant way of putting it, . . . but his state of dismay suggested to me an impulsive man who, after committing suicide with the notion that it would end all his troubles, had discovered that it did nothing of the kind" (220).

To be in Verloc's state or Winnie's, is to be unable to die and yet unable to return to life. It is to persist in an interminable moment of freedom, irresponsibility, and leisure. This moment has no content. It is free of everything. Winnie does not "think at all" (263). Yet it is not nothing. It is a positive awareness of nothing. Such a state of mind is, in Conrad's precise words, "madness or despair." It is a living death whose horror is its inability to escape from itself.

The most frightful aspect of this state is the fact that chaos and eternity are not set against man as something he sees from the outside. They are inside, waiting for an opportunity to appear at the surface and engulf him. Mr. Verloc, after M. Vladimir has shattered his enclosure in the routine of his ambiguous existence, is unable to sleep. He is denied that daily oblivion which is a rehearsal of death and an expression of a man's unthinking commitment to his life. Verloc's insomnia anticipates not the forgetfulness of sweet death, but Winnie's terrifying freedom, the freedom of a living corpse. In a similar way, the Assistant Commissioner, when he disguises himself and plunges into the sinister blackness of a wet London night, becomes "unplaced" (149): "It would have been impossible for anybody to guess his occupation" (149, 150). He is absorbed by the anonymous substance of the night: "the Assistant Commissioner, reflecting upon his enterprise, seemed to lose some more of his identity. . . . A pleasurable feeling of independence possessed him when he heard the glass doors swing to behind his back with a sort of imperfect baffled thud. He advanced at once into an immensity of greasy slime and damp plaster interspersed with lamps, and enveloped, oppressed, penetrated, choked, and suffocated by the blackness of a wet London night, which is composed of soot and drops of water" (148, 150). This text suggests that the substance which lies behind the coruscation of colors and the rigidity of intelligible forms is not solid matter, the stuff of which bricks and paving stones are made. It is something even more disquieting, a fluid or pulverized darkness, without form or mass, like the River Thames, which is "a sinister marvel of still shadows and flowing gleams mingling . . . in a black silence" (300). Nothing exists in this darkness except tiny particles, as of soot or drops of water. Everything seems to have come out of this fluidity, and to be in danger of returning to it on any dark, rainy night. So Conrad

several times shows a London which seems to have been over-
whelmed by a great flood or about to be engulfed in a new one.
The fact that Winnie Verloc commits suicide by throwing herself
into the stormy waters of the channel has symbolic as well as
melodramatic value:

> The panes streamed with rain, and the short street . . . lay wet and empty, as
> if swept clear suddenly by a great flood. It was a very trying day, choked in raw
> fog to begin with, and now drowned in cold rain. The flickering, blurred flames
> of gas-lamps seemed to be dissolving in a watery atmosphere. (100)

> His descent into the street was like the descent into a slimy aquarium from
> which the water had been run off. A murky, gloomy dampness enveloped him.
> (147)

> She floundered over the doorstep head forward, arms thrown out, like a person
> falling over the parapet of a bridge. This entrance into the open air had a foretaste
> of drowning; a slimy dampness enveloped her, entered her nostrils, clung to her
> hair. (269)

The "town's colossal forms" are "half lost in the night," in a
darkness "as vast as a sea" (101, 102), and the people too are forced
by a kind of deliquescence to lose their identities and melt into the
fluidity of the darkness. When the Assistant Commissioner goes
out in disguise he is "assimilated" by the "genius of the locality"
and becomes "one more of the queer foreign fish that can be seen
of an evening about there flitting round the dark corners" (147).
In the same way Winnie Verloc is described as "massive and shapeless like a recumbent statue in the rough" (179), or as a "black form
merged in the night, like a figure half chiselled out of a block of
black stone" (280). The shapelessness of Winnie's body is a symbol
of her secret spiritual depths. "She was mysterious," says Conrad,
"with the mysteriousness of living beings" (179, 180); "It was
impossible to say what she knew" (280). These passages reveal the
meaning of the motif of the interview which recurs so often in *The
Secret Agent*. This motif does not express the possibility of a communication between people which might establish a luminous and
honest society. It proves rather the impossibility of communication.
Two people who face one another remain impenetrable mysteries.
Though the clarified upper surface of another personality may be
reached, the real center remains hidden. Each person merges into
an impersonal darkness which is usually hidden even from the
person himself.

To leave the surface levels of the mind and be merged in the night like a statue in the rough is not to lose consciousness or die. Winnie remains very much alive. She survives Stevie's death, which cuts her sole tie to the world, and lives on to drink her "cup of horrors" (298) to the last drop. The emphasis in this section of the novel is not on the death of Verloc, but on Winnie and the extraordinary state of mind she reaches. This state is described in an accumulation of details which shows her progressively approaching a state of anonymity and melting into the blackness of death. Her state is like that of a somnambulist or insomniac. She is awake. She watches with a lucid vigilance, but she does not watch anything. She looks at a blank wall: "[Mr. Verloc] was startled by the inappropriate character of his wife's stare. It was not a wild stare, and it was not inattentive, but its attention was peculiar and not satisfactory, inasmuch that it seemed concentrated upon some point beyond Mr. Verloc's person. The impression was so strong that Mr. Verloc glanced over his shoulder. There was nothing behind him: there was just the whitewashed wall. . . . Mrs. Verloc gazed at the whitewashed wall. A blank wall — perfectly blank. A blankness to run at and dash your head against" (239, 240, 244). Everything Winnie sees has been turned into another expression of death. If what she sees is a symbol of death, she also contains death within herself. This inner death is a bottomless pool which reduces to its own blackness everything she looks at, even the light itself: "[Mr. Verloc] looked straight into his wife's eyes. The enlarged pupils of the woman received his stare into their unfathomable depths" (248); "A tinge of wildness in her aspect was derived . . . from the fixity of her black gaze where the light of the room was absorbed and lost without the trace of a single gleam" (259).

Winnie's depersonalization goes on through the sequence of events leading from her discovery that Verloc has caused Stevie's death to her murder of her husband, her meeting with Comrade Ossipon, their return to the shop, and his abandonment of her on the train going toward the channel boat from which she will leap at last into the dark water. The sea is another expression of the presence which lies behind or within every form and person, and Winnie's suicide is the physical fulfillment of the state she has already reached in her mind. Conrad can say of her that, even while she was alive, when she spoke "it was as if a corpse had spoken"

(247), and that "she was not deadly. She was death itself — the companion of life" (291). Winnie lives on in the endless tossing of the waves and in Ossipon's awareness of how she had died, just as, when she kills Verloc, Stevie is resurrected in her, "as if the homeless soul of Stevie had flown for shelter straight to the breast of his sister, guardian, and protector" (262).

Poor Comrade Ossipon, the unwilling accomplice of Winnie, is the last survivor of the chain reaction which began with M. Vladimir's shattering of Verloc's complacency. He survives to become the inheritor of the terrible knowledge which has destroyed Verloc and Winnie, and to enter a state of living death in which, walking, he does not get anywhere, and in which he finds it impossible to sleep:

> He could walk, He walked. He crossed the bridge. . . . And again Comrade Ossipon walked. His robust form was seen that night in distant parts of the enormous town slumbering monstrously on a carpet of mud under a veil of raw mist. . . . He walked through Squares, Places, Ovals, Commons, through monotonous streets with unknown names where the dust of humanity settles inert and hopeless out of the stream of life. He walked. And suddenly turning into a strip of a front garden with a mangy grass plot, he let himself into a small grimy house with a latchkey he took out of his pocket.
>
> He threw himself down on his bed all dressed, and lay still for a whole quarter of an hour. Then he sat up suddenly, drawing up his knees, and clasping his legs. The first dawn found him open-eyed, in that same posture. This man who could walk so long, so far, so aimlessly, without showing a sign of fatigue, could also remain sitting still for hours without stirring a limb or an eyelid. (300, 301)

The conjunction here of the motifs of walking and insomnia reveals the meaning of each. Walking does not express the freedom of spirit, its ability to skim over the surface of things and break away from the changelessness of matter. It signifies man's inability to escape from himself. Like insomnia, it corresponds to a state of mind which is contradictory or impossible, and yet real. Much earlier in the novel, Verloc's "dreary conviction that there was no sleep for him," his "mute and hopelessly inert . . . fear of darkness" (60), is expressed in the sound of footsteps in the street below his bedroom window: "Down below in the quiet, narrow street measured footsteps approached the house, then died away, unhurried and firm, as if the passer-by had started to pace out all eternity, from gas-lamp to gas-lamp in a night without end" (57). Insomnia is like a walking which begins nowhere and goes nowhere, but moves forever without advancing, always at the same distance from an infinitely distant starting place and an infinitely far-off goal, like the endless ticking of the Verlocs' clock on the staircase. Insomnia puts a man within a time which has not started from any remembered beginning and does not go toward any end. Time passes, but the insomniac can no longer remember when he first lay down to sleep, nor can he anticipate the morning. He seems to have left all that behind him for good. Each moment exactly repeats the others, with the same emptiness, and the same disconnection from anything before or after. The most horrible part of the insomniac's suffering is his sense that his unwinking wakefulness will persist forever in a night without end, an eternal vigilance without object. The clock's steady tick, measure of human time, melts into eternity, just as the dropping of Verloc's blood, which Winnie confounds with the sound of the clock, first accelerates and then becomes a steady flow as he dies. Walking expresses spatially what sleeplessness expresses temporally. Like insomniacs, walkers can move interminably without escaping from themselves. The city is a labyrinth of streets in which a man may go from place to place without getting anywhere, for each place is the same as all the other places. Far from proving the independence of the mind, walking shows how man, living in time and change, possesses death not as the end of his life, but as the substance of his present state.

The social fiction of laws, conventions, ideals, and personalities exists in the past and in the future, never in the present. The present reveals the substance which lies within or behind all things and persons. This secret reality is also expressed by the colors and textures of things, glimpsed evanescently in that wink of the eye between the moment of sensation and its translation into perception. Perceptions always identify an object as like something seen before, or as something which can be manipulated in the future. There is an infinitesimal time-lag which makes the perception that this is a wheel and not just a moving spot of red belong to the past or be projected toward the future. Conrad often links the momentary recognition of qualities to the motion of a thing, as in the case of the red wheels of the butcher boy's cart. The glimpse of the anonymous redness of the wheels reveals an impersonal "thereness" which is another form of the presence apprehended in insomnia and in aimless walking. All examples of the color red repeat one another as do all times in Verloc's insomnia, and as do all places in Ossipon's walking through the interminable straight perspectives of London, and through its Squares, Places, Ovals, Commons, each a monotonous repetition of the others.

Ossipon has by his unintentional complicity in Winnie's crime committed himself to that place out of place and time out of time where nothing exists but the eternal recurrence of the same. After he learns of Winnie's death he re-enacts in terrifying iteration, a repetition like Stevie's innumerable circles, Winnie's end as it was reported in the jargon of the newspaper. In the same way Winnie herself is haunted by the words which describe her anticipated death by hanging ("The drop given was fourteen feet"). Ossipon's brain "pulsates wrongfully to the rhythm of journalistic phrases" (311). He repeats to himself, or some anonymous power within him repeats for him, the banal words which are slowly driving him insane: "An impenetrable mystery seems destined to hang for ever over this act of madness or despair" (307). Death is not the obliteration of everything. It is that which cannot end. The denouement of *The Secret Agent* sets the impasse of the Professor against the disintegration of the robust Comrade Ossipon, his inability to "think, work, sleep, . . . eat," and his absorption by the impersonal wakefulness which has claimed the other characters.

The last paragraphs of the novel juxtapose two walkers, Comrade Ossipon moving toward madness, despair, and the gutter, and the Professor, "terrible in the simplicity of his idea calling madness and despair to the regeneration of the world." This juxtaposition indicates that all the living deaths in the novel are the same death, and that the theme of *The Secret Agent* is the universal death which underlies life. As the characters get closer to death, they approach a condition in which they are equivalents of one another. There all "I's" give way to a collective "we," and communication is possible, communication not between persons, but within that which in each person is the same, the same secret agent at the heart of each.

The Professor can neither make a vacant place where spirit is able to build its own world, nor bring spirit into matter and transform the earth. The madness and despair which he calls on for the regeneration of the world are not pure emptiness of mind. They result from apprehension of the death which lies behind life. Death is a realm of madness because it is a place of contradiction, the copresence of motion and stillness, light and darkness, personality and anonymity, nothingness and substance, speech and silence, meaning and meaninglessness, servitude and freedom, time and eternity, beginning and ending held in a perpetual present. These pairs are all variations of one another, and, though the characters of *The Secret Agent* go toward death in different ways, most of them reach ultimately the same state, a state like that approached by the protagonists of Conrad's other novels, Kurtz, Marlow, Decoud, Flora de Barral, or Mrs. Travers. Conrad's novels all say the same thing, and yet are all different, as all clouds differ and yet are children of the same sky. The Professor faces a double impossibility: the impossibility of escaping from the underlying substance of madness and despair, and the impossibility of using it in any way for the regeneration of the world. He can neither make a secure place where men can create their own culture, nor can he bring the darkness of madness and despair into the world as the foundation of a viable city of man. Between these impossibilities he remains, in the sentences which end the novel, poised forever: "His thoughts caressed the images of ruin and destruction. He walked frail, insignificant, shabby, miserable — and terrible in the simplicity of his idea calling madness and despair to the regeneration of the world. Nobody looked at him. He passed on unsuspected and deadly, like a pest in the street full of men" (311).

III

W. B. Yeats

I was unlike others of my generation in one thing only. I am very religious, and deprived by Huxley and Tyndall, whom I detested, of the simple-minded religion of my childhood, I had made a new religion, almost an infallible church of poetic tradition, of a fardel of stories, and of personages, and of emotions, inseparable from their first expression, passed on from generation to generation by poets and painters with some help from philosophers and theologians. . . . When I listened [those imaginary people] seemed always to speak of one thing only: they, their loves, every incident of their lives, were steeped in the supernatural.

Yeats's starting place is the desire for a transfiguration of the present world and the present self. The everyday world must be transmuted into paradise, and the everyday self must be transformed into an heroic person, steeped in the supernatural. Yeats begins with a certain experience of the death of God: the scientific rationalism of Tyndall and Huxley. For them, as for so many men of the nineteenth century, God is either an exploded myth or is relegated to the realm of Herbert Spencer's "unknowable." In either case the self is defined as a dry collection of faculties, and the environment of the self is equally unliving. Man is left with a dead world of matter in mechanical motion:

> The woods of Arcady are dead,
> And over is their antique joy;
> Of old the world on dreaming fed;
> Grey truth is now her painted toy.

Against this world Yeats passionately rebels. He rebels in the name of a possible immanence of the divine spirit. The whole of human existence, every gesture, every incident, all the most commonplace utensils and acts must be irradiated with spiritual meaning. Only when the world is so transfigured can man be his proper heroic self. The present world is a culture of abstraction, "meaning by abstraction not the distinction but the isolation of occupation, or class or faculty." Each element is separated from the others, and "the world [is] now but a bundle of fragments." Before every corner of life can be steeped in the supernatural, man must, to paraphrase Blake, "build Jerusalem in Ireland's green and pleasant land."

The means of this building will be "dreams," the poetic tradition. "Repelled by what had seemed the sole reality," says Yeats, "we had turned to romantic dreaming, to the nobility of tradition." Ireland was not always fragmented. It was bound together by "a fardel of stories." In its origin each culture had a unity like a "perfectly proportioned human body." This unity is a binding together of man and the supernatural by means of a mythology growing from the mountains and streams of the native land: "Have not all races had their first unity from a mythology, that marries them to rock and hill?" This unity of man, nature, and the supernatural can be recovered by making the poetic tradition current once more. Popular lore is still in touch with the strong earth. If that vital element is made universally active there will be a renewal of the whole culture: "I thought that all art should be a Centaur finding in the popular lore its back and its strong legs. . . . We had in Ireland imaginative stories, which the uneducated classes knew and even sang, and might we not make those stories current among the educated classes . . . ; and at last, it might be, so deepen the political passion of the nation that all, artist and poet, craftsman and day-labourer would accept a common design?" [1]

Folklore has its historical roots in a wider tradition. Beginning with the green shoots of popular legend and song, it may be possible to revivify those roots. Every expression of art, life, philosophy, or

---

[1] Daniel G. Hoffman and others have discussed the problem of the various texts of Yeats's prose. (See Hoffman's review of *Mythologies* in *Journal of American Folklore*, 76: 85, 86 [1963].) Though I have consulted earlier editions I have made citations, whenever possible, from editions currently in print. The following texts have been used. All but the last were published by the Macmillan Company, or, in the case of the volume issued in London, by Macmillan and Co., Limited. Each is followed by the abbreviation which will be hereafter employed in citations. *The Autobiography of William Butler Yeats* (New York, 1953): A; *The Collected Poems of W. B. Yeats* (New York, 1953): CP; *The Variorum Edition of the Poems of W. B. Yeats*, ed. Peter Allt and Russell K. Alspach (New York, 1957): VP; *The Collected Plays of W. B. Yeats* (London, 1953): CPl; *Mythologies* (New York, 1959): M; *Essays and Introductions* (New York, 1961): EI; *A Vision* (New York, 1961): V; *Explorations* (New York, 1962): E; *The Letters of W. B. Yeats*, ed. Allan Wade (New York, 1955): L; *Letters on Poetry from W. B. Yeats to Dorothy Wellesley* (London: Oxford University Press, 1964): LDW. The quotations in the first three paragraphs of this chapter come, respectively, from A, 70, 71; CP, 7; A, 117, 116; E, 372; A, 174, 119, 117, 119.

religion in which human existence is seen as steeped in the supernatural is a valid part of the universal tradition. The unity of this
tradition is one of Yeats's fundamental assumptions and the basis
of his eclecticism. If he believes in the "rooting of mythology in the
earth," [2] he also believes that the Irish tradition, rooted in his own
earth, is only one version of what may be said differently but is
secretly the same in other traditions. He seeks similarities, analogies,
fraternal echoes between his own tradition and the others, as in
the essay called "Swedenborg, Mediums, and the Desolate Places"
(E, 30–70). Spiritism, occultism, theosophy, and ceremonial magic;
romanticism, Platonism, the Cabala, the Cambridge Platonists;
Indian philosophy, the *Bhagavad-Gita*, *The Upanishads*, Noh plays,
and Zen Buddhism; Boehme, Swedenborg, and Blake — all are
authentic, and all are branches of the same tree. The proper attitude toward them is the exact opposite of Cartesian doubt: "one
should believe whatever [has] been believed in all countries and
periods, and only reject any part of it after much evidence, instead
of starting all over afresh and only believing what one [can] prove"
(A, 48).

What power have these learned or ephemeral things, which
seem but foam on the surface of life? What seems so weak is really
the strongest of all. A culture is not made of pragmatic things,
bricks and stones and the doings of active men. Prior to these and
the cause of them are certain disembodied ideas which are cast
over a people by the supernatural: "All civilisation is held together
by the suggestions of an invisible hypnotist — by artificially created
illusions" (A, 293). Yeats's theory of society is magical. Men of
action are puppets of a supernatural showman who pulls the strings
and puts it into their minds to make their institutions in a certain
way.

The instruments of these ghostly influences are emotions and
images. Since these are the special property of solitaries, con-
templatives, philosophers, singers, artists, and poets, these men, who
seem so withdrawn from life, are actually the creators of society.
They are mediators between heaven and earth, the means by which
the supernatural is embodied in the tangible world: "I doubt indeed if the crude circumstance of the world, which seems to create

---

[2] *W. B. Yeats and T. Sturge Moore: Their Correspondence, 1901–1937*, ed. Ursula Bridge
(London: Routledge & Kegan Paul, 1953), p. 114.

all our emotions, does more than reflect, as in multiplying mirrors, the emotions that have come to solitary men in moments of poetical contemplation. . . . [They] receive, as I think, the creative impulse from the lowest of the Nine Hierarchies, and so make and unmake mankind, and even the world itself, for does not 'the eye altering alter all'?" (EI, 158, 159).

The magical power which creates the world is, like all magic, ambiguous. Poets and other contemplative men are "a vessel of the creative power of God" (EI, 202). They "receive" the creative impulse, as womb receives the seed, and so make and unmake mankind. "It is not possible to separate an emotion or a spiritual state from the image that calls it up and gives it expression. Michelangelo's *Moses*, Velasquez' *Philip the Second*, the colour purple, a crucifix, call into life an emotion or state that vanishes with them because they are its only possible expression, and that is why no mind is more valuable than the images it contains" (EI, 286). The earthly representatives of the spiritual world are forms, symbols, images, colors, and the emotions these evoke in mankind. The poet makes images, the painter colored forms. These are in magical harmony with a supernal reality, and they evoke that reality in reader or spectator. "True art is expressive and symbolic, and makes every form, every sound, every colour, every gesture, a signature of some unanalysable imaginative essence" (EI, 140).

In one sense the poet or painter is the passive vessel of revelation. In another sense he might almost be said to create the spiritual reality his work evokes, for it has no earthly existence before he has made his poem or painted his painting. Yeats is careful to respect the doubleness of this process, as in a phrase which recurs throughout *Ideas of Good and Evil:* "create or reveal." The magician, the artist, the poet, for example, "create or reveal a single mind, a single energy" (EI, 28). The words of the poem bring into this world the spiritual reality to which they correspond, but this correspondence is not invented by the poet. Colors and forms are natural symbols of the divine, "for things below are copies, the Great Smaragdine Tablet said" (CP, 283). The artist either knows by intuition these correspondences, or, as in the myth of the sorcerer's apprentice, happens accidentally on a form which has the power to liberate a precise energy from the supernatural. He starts in full control of his art, coldly manipulating familiar materials. At a critical moment the roles of controller and controlled reverse, and an unforeseen power enters the magic circle. The unity of a work of art lies in the organic combination of its parts, and this "musical relation" calls into being a unique emotion, a unique spiritual force. This emotion could not have been known before a certain arrangement of words or colors called it into being, and it has such power that "poets and painters and musicians . . . are continually making and unmaking mankind" (EI, 157).

This "pragmatical, preposterous pig of a world" (CP, 233) is created by the descent of images or emotions from the great sea of moods and symbols. This influx comes only to solitary, contemplative men, and it comes "in a lightning flash" (VP, 825). These instants are followed by darkness and dryness of spirit. The supernatural world makes the natural one, but the two realms do not overlap. At rare intervals a breach of the barrier is made, and through the soul of some man of genius a tiny portion of that all-powerful fire flows into the gross world. Then there is a gradual degeneration, as the glow of the divine lightning cools and fades, for "nature in herself has no power except to die and to forget" (EI, 172). Time and eternity, as Blake said, can only be joined in that instant which is less than the smallest natural measure of time, and therefore brief enough to be an image of eternity.

If the anima mundi enters the world only through isolated men, how can it change a whole society? The man in the street and the man of action do not read the poet and the philosopher. They read the newspaper. Yeats must extend his first sort of magic with a second kind. The influx of power from the soul of the world is "miracle and enthusiasm" (EI, 171) in the literal sense of possession by a God. The transference of this power from solitary contemplative men to society is no less a matter of magic, this time the magical flow of thought from one mind to another. What seems to be chosen or learned may have flowed into the deeps of a man's mind from some more creative mind than his own, some mind which has had a revelation from beyond the world. What at first is thought by a single mind comes eventually to be thought by a whole nation. A nation is therefore to be defined as a group of men and women unconsciously dominated by a single stream of irresistible suggestion. No men are free. All are unwittingly receivers of an impersonal flow of influences. "Is there nation-wide multiform reverie," asks Yeats, "every mind passing through a stream of suggestion, and all streams acting and reacting upon one another no matter how distant the minds, how dumb the lips?" (A, 158).

The process by which society is made and unmade cannot be distinguished from the process of self-realization in the makers. At the center of Yeats's idea of selfhood is the notion of "unyielding personality, manner at once cold and passionate" (A, 125), a self full of "unpremeditated joyous energy" (A, 92). Only such a self is worthy to be an avenue by which the supernatural enters society. So *Per Amica Silentia Lunae* is divided into two sections, one about the soul of man and one about the soul of the world. Binding these together is the poet, singing songs which are simultaneously expressions of a personal emotion and the dramatization of a universal mythology. Only in the self-expression of the whole man can an impersonal mythology be incarnated, for only "the actual thoughts of a man at a passionate moment of life" (A, 62) are real.

Yeats started out in life with the project of transfiguring Ireland. He also "set out on life with the thought of putting [his] very self into poetry" (EI, 271). Since abstraction is impersonal he feared it so much that he deliberately kept all generalizations out of his early poetry (A, 115, 116). Gradually he came to see that the most obscure mathematical abstraction can be given life if it is presented as the speech of some violent man in a moment of emotion, but a conviction that only dramatic utterance is valid remains his fundamental principle of style. His subject matter is "intellectual essences" (EI, 271), but these must be embodied. This explains his constant habit, in his prose, of coming suddenly from an abstraction to a cryptic restatement of the same notion in a concrete image, an anecdote, or a reminiscence. For example, he ends a dry discussion of the way a visionary man must avoid politics with a sentence which parallels one of his more difficult poems: "Is it not certain that the Creator yawns in earthquake and thunder and other popular displays, but toils in rounding the delicate spiral of a shell?" (A, 151). Or he begins an abstract discourse, like *Per Amica Silentia Lunae*, with a little story or drama. This alternation between theory and image gives Yeats's style its characteristic flavor. The richness of his language, but also its vagueness are partly a result of this alternation. As Yeats well knows, there is more inexplicable depth in an image than in a clear abstraction, and often, just when a poem or an essay seems crystallizing into a lucid formulation, he turns back, as at the very end of *A Vision*, to an image brilliant in its opacity, trembling with the multiplicity of its associations and meanings: "Shall we follow the image of Heracles that walks through the darkness bow in hand, or mount to that other Heracles, man, not image, he that has for his bride Hebe, 'The daughter of Zeus, the mighty, and Hera, shod with gold'?" (V, 302).

The human body is Yeats's favorite image of the concrete and real. His habitual expression of Unity of Being is a phrase from Dante about "a perfectly proportioned human body," and, when he speaks of the importance of form in art, his ideal of unity is again the human body: "you cannot give a body to something that moves beyond the senses, unless your words are as subtle, as complex, as full of mysterious life, as the body of a flower or of a woman" (EI, 164). Incarnate man or woman holds the center of the stage because ultimate reality is not something vague and impalpable, the "One," or the "Idea of Ideas." It is a person or a congeries of persons. Yeats chooses for Plotinus, as he understands him, against Plato, and believes that behind all phenomena are not archetypal ideas but archetypal persons. The cosmos is made of the transformations of these eternal figures, "nothing exists but a stream of souls," and therefore "all knowledge is biography" (E, 397). If personality is the ground of existence, then "the whole man — blood, imagination, intellect, running together" (EI, 266), is the only incarnation of reality in space and time, and the process by which the poet receives impulses from the lowest of the Nine Hierarchies is no different from the process by which he actualizes his true self. "The wholeness of the supernatural world can only express itself in personal form, because it has no epitome but man" (A, 150).

～

When Yeats tries to carry his project into practice, instead of a poetry "as cold/And passionate as the dawn" (CP, 146), he can achieve only vagueness and wavering. An ominous vacillation is present in the essays from *Ideas of Good and Evil*. The notion that the poet can bring down intellectual essences from heaven is countered by an opposing goal: the transformation of the pragmatical pig of a world into the intangibility of spirit. "True art is the flame of the Last Day, which begins for every man when he is first moved by beauty, and which seeks to burn all things until they become 'infinite and holy' " (EI, 140). Civilization has been moving toward the idea that only matter exists. Yeats wants to ascend the stair man has been descending, and to believe that only a world of blurred soft outlines, of dreams and ideals, exists. He wants everything to be "consumed and become a vision" (EI, 184). It must melt into an "invisible life" (EI, 195) and become "an almost disembodied ecstasy" (EI, 194). In this transmutation "familiar woods and rivers should fade into symbol with so gradual a change that [a man] may never discover, no, not even in ecstasy itself, that he is beyond space, and that time alone keeps him from Primum Mobile, Supernal Eden, Yellow Rose over all" (EI, 297). In tension with the goal of an incarnation of the supernatural, there is the desire for a disembodiment of the world. Yeats dreams of an "autumn of the body" in which everything material will fade away and leave nothing tangible behind. He believes our scientific, critical age is about to pass and give way to "an age of imagination, of emotion, of moods, of revelation" (EI, 197).

If there is a contradiction in Yeats's early essays between praise for disembodiment and an urge to descend toward earth, the early plays and poems are unambiguously concerned with "the essences of things, and not with things" (EI, 193). Everywhere there are half-lights, faint outlines, velleities, "wavering, meditative, organic rhythms" (EI, 163). This poetry describes "a world where anything might flow and change, and become any other thing" (EI, 178). Nothing has sharp boundaries, but is always partly one thing, partly another, or about to melt into something else. It is the moment of transition: autumn, or twilight, the "Celtic Twilight." "Cultic twalette," James Joyce called it, and cruelly defined Yeats's early poetry by calling it onanistic. In these dreamy, melancholy poems the speaker, like Narcissus admiring his image in the pool, hovers over his emotions, luxuriating in them, brooding over them, and refining them until they reach, in a hothouse isolation, a decadent purity.

Certain words or phrases occur again and again: "dove-grey," "pearl-pale," "numberless dreams," "shimmering," "whirling," "wandering," "trembling," "flickering." These words, like the times of autumn and twilight, are appropriate to a transition state. "Dove-grey" and "pearl-pale" are iridescent colors, "faint mixed tints" (A, 210). Like "murmuring silk" (CP, 353), they change liquidly from one intermediate shade to another as the light changes on them. Such colors form an opalescent surface, filling the eye with a subdued brilliance, but forbidding it to go beyond the superficial glistening. Ladies, clothes, landscapes, ships — all things are elements in a multicolored shimmering:

> [Oisin] found on the dove-grey edge of the sea
> A pearl-pale, high-born lady, who rode
> On a horse with a bridle of findrinny;
> And like a sunset were her lips,
> A stormy sunset on doomed ships;
> A citron colour gloomed in her hair,
> But down to her feet white vesture flowed,
> And with the glimmering crimson glowed
> Of many a figured embroidery;
> And it was bound with a pearl-pale shell
> That wavered like the summer streams,
> As her soft bosom rose and fell. (CP, 351)

Image after image has the same quality, and describes, for example, "a gleam of light/Upon a sword" (CP, 33), or "glimmering white" eyes (CP, 59), or the "flicker and glow" of fire (CP, 58), or mother-of-pearl adorning:

> . . . many a trumpet-twisted shell
> That in immortal silence sleeps
> Dreaming of her own melting hues,
> Her golds, her ambers, and her blues. (CP, 355)

When Yeats yields himself to these kaleidoscopic images he is "astray upon the Path of the Chameleon, upon *Hodos Chameliontos*." "But now," he says, "image called up image in an endless procession, and I could not always choose among them with any confidence; and when I did choose, the image lost its intensity, or changed into some other image" (A, 163).

The recurring present participles, so characteristic of these early poems, are usually verbs of motion transformed into terms for a constant movement which repeats itself in an ever-renewed present, like the vibration of aspen leaves. The spectator sees a wavering surface, shimmering, whirling, trembling, or flickering. Though everything is in motion, this movement is constantly reversing itself, and all remains the same, as in the refrain of one of the earliest poems: "They will not hush, the leaves a-flutter round me, the beech leaves old" (CP, 16). The world seems caught permanently in the moment when something is about to happen, and announces itself by premonitory flutterings, as of a wing in stone, or a child in the womb. But, instead of the birth of the new, there is only a hesitation, and then a further repetition of the signs which announce it.

These motifs are a precise representation of the present epoch of history. The world is now about to dissolve and become an essence, but so far this transition has not occurred, and Yeats's poems must describe, not the accomplished fact, but the crisis when the change is just going to take place. The phrase "almost disembodied ecstasy" wavers with characteristic hesitation. The ecstasy will be almost disembodied, but not quite, as "dove-grey" is not quite grey, and as the fluttering of leaves is a motion which is also stasis. Yeats often imagines himself as an old, old man, worn out by life, about to die, living in an autumn world which is on the point of being transfigured, and the characteristic situation of the early poems and plays involves someone who has had a bewitching glimpse of the land of heart's desire and is about to be absorbed into it, as are the lovers in *The Shadowy Waters*.

Each personage in Yeats's early poems becomes aware of himself as "a whirling and a wandering fire" (CP, 16), a sequence of many moods. Exhausted by this inner oscillation, he longs for fixity in the midst of whirling, but he finds only more moods, each replaced in a moment by another. The endless autumn of the mind will not give way to the immobility of winter. Since all inside is unstable, he turns to what is outside and beyond him. He goes to nature as the abiding place of an immanent spiritual force. Because he has had a glimpse of this beauty, he can find no peace in the everyday world. At the center of the "Rose of all Roses" (CP, 37), though not at the petals' edge, it may be that there is peace.

When such a man seeks to reach peace at the center of the rose, his real adventure begins. He finds that he cannot reach eternal beauty in any of its earthly manifestations. The "glimmering girl" with apple blossom in her hair, formed magically from the little silver fish, runs over hill and valley, and cannot be caught (CP, 57,

58), and Oisin seeks everywhere for an undiscoverable repose. These men are doomed to an eternity of dissatisfaction, the endless pursuit of a phantom which always eludes the outstretched hand. The word "wandering" expresses exactly the dominant motif of Yeats's early work. Everyone wanders vainly, seeking a goal which exists but which can never be reached.

The situation of Yeats's personages is even worse than that of most men who seek eternal beauty. His early poems are based on a certain apprehension of the supernatural which he never betrays, even in his latest work. Instead of feeling that the divine world is a Platonic place of permanence and peace, Yeats experiences it as instability and turbulence. It is "eternal beauty wandering on her way" (CP, 31). At the center of the rose may be "the whirlpool's motionless centre" (V, 195), but all outside this, though it belongs to God, is in motion. It is "the wind among the reeds" (CP, 53), a lonely wandering of spirit, now here, now there, without direction or purpose. Even in the country of the blessed Yeats's characters find no escape from restless movement, but only, like Oisin, or like Baile and Aillinn, more wandering. Oisin's adventures are a perpetually renewed quest for a goal which can never be reached. In this eternity of wandering the same phantoms, "emblematical of eternal pursuit," are seen again and again (E, 392). Even in death Oisin does not find peace, but only another version of his eternally repeated adventure. Immortal peace itself has a "wild heart" (CP, 398), and is a "wandering quiet" (CP, 11).

There is no resting place in heaven because Yeats sees the supernatural as involved in space and time. As Blake said in the "Proverbs of Hell," "eternity is in love with the productions of time," and the divine world is locked in a close embrace with earth. The supernatural is not something which man may pursue in his wanderings as a place of escape from all motion. It permeates the earthly world, as the wind blows everywhere across the landscape. It is a tumultuous force, not a unitary stillness, and this energy causes nature to ebb and flow, shimmer and tremble. The supernatural manifests itself in the "great Powers of falling wave and wind and windy fire" (CP, 69), or in the hosting of the Sidhe, those spirits dwelling in the wind among the reeds. Yeats recognizes that his vision of the supernatural, though based on Irish myth, is different from the usual European tradition. In a note of 1925 on his early work he says: "I notice upon reading these poems for the first time for several years that the quality symbolized as The Rose differs from the Intellectual Beauty of Shelley and of Spenser in that I have imagined it as suffering with man and not as something pursued and seen from afar" (CP, 447). The source of the interior fluctuation of the soul is the wavering of a spiritual force, dwelling in nature, which fascinates man, makes it impossible for him to commit himself to any daily task, and imbues him with its own eternal unrest.

The only hope is to turn away from "the sweet everlasting Voices" which "call in birds, in wind on the hill,/In shaken boughs, in tide on the shore" (CP, 53). Man must seek in mortal love or in withdrawal to some secluded spot escape from the fluttering of the beech leaves and the turbulent spiritual energy they reveal. So Yeats imagines a woman who says: "The shadowy blossom of my hair/Will hide us from the bitter storm" (CP, 58), or he plans, in a reverie which haunted his young manhood, to go to the Lake Isle of Innisfree, and there live in a peaceful world at last. An island in a lake is an admirable image of the still point in the midst of motion, peace at the center of the rose. At the periphery is the noisy outside world, but it is hidden by the lapping waves, symbols of the oscillation of spirit. The island is the heart of the rose, an image of fixity and peace. There Yeats can live in his hut, alone or with his beloved, protected from the fluctuation of the supernatural and also from the loud materialism of the world.

He finds, however, that neither love nor isolation offer an escape from wavering. In poem after poem the only rest he can find is an attenuated wandering. The most stable situation he can imagine still has a slight trembling, and even in the arms of his beloved or alone on an island he cannot escape from fluctuation. In "The Indian to His Love," the speaker promises tranquillity to his beloved on a tropical island, but it is an island where "peahens dance on a smooth lawn," and "a parrot sways upon a tree." There the lovers will participate not in fixity, but become "one with the tide that gleams, the wings that gleam and dart" (CP, 14). The peace of Innisfree, with its "lake water lapping with low sounds by the shore," is only the slowing down of motion, not its cessation. It is "some peace," not complete peace (CP, 39).

Movement is everywhere, as the host of the air is everywhere.

Once a man has had a vision of eternal beauty wandering on her way, he can never cease to be haunted by it. He is doomed to be unquiet forever, for "The winds that awakened the stars/Are blowing through [his] blood" (CP, 68). This world and the supernatural are realms of eternal unsatisfied yearning, the yearning of the lover whose "breast will not lie by the breast/Of [his] beloved in sleep" "Until the axle break/That keeps the stars in their round" (CP, 65). Everyone in Yeats's early poetry is in the condition of those in "The Rose of Battle," "the sad, the lonely, the insatiable," who have been claimed by God, and as a consequence have "hearts, that may not live nor die" (CP, 37, 38). Their destiny is to wander perpetually, neither living nor able to die. Rather than finding an ideal identity, they have discovered that they are fated to live constantly outside themselves.

One last possibility may provide escape: the destruction of everything that is, including the frustrate self, the explosive demolition of the multitudinous round, leaving only the fecund darkness out of which all things came. Yeats was fascinated by the Irish myth of the great battle of the forces of good and evil, light and darkness, warmth and cold, the Tuath De Danaan and the Fomoroh (VP, 796). Only at the end of the world, when "God burn[s] time" (CP, 64), will his breast lie by the breast of his beloved in sleep, and only then will his wandering end. So the drunken sleeper in "The Hour before Dawn" tells the beggar that all his unhappiness is really a yearning for the obliteration of self and world at the Last Day, when there will be "nothing but God left" (CP, 116, 117).

If peace lies only in oblivion, then the fundamental project of Yeats's early work is doomed to failure. His poetry and his practical work as politician and organizer of the Irish Theater come to nothing, and he must recognize that "the dream of [his] early manhood, that a modern nation can return to Unity of Culture, is false" (A, 176). The matching aim for the individual has also turned out to be impossible. The self can never poise its two halves and is condemned to chase itself perpetually. Far from "putting his very self into poetry," Yeats has discovered that the self always hovers before him, just out of reach, however hard he tries to attain it. Instead of finding himself through his attempt to steep self and world in the supernatural, he has got further and further into the impalpable inane of "intellectual essences" and poems about ab-

stractions like "Sleep, Hope, Dream, endless Desire" (CP, 60),
poems full of unrealities like "thought-woven sails" above a sea
made not of salt water but of "hours" (CP, 37).

Nevertheless, this experience of failure is a positive gain. Only
by the collapse of his attempt to bring together culture and the
supernatural, man and his buried self, can Yeats discover the
ecstatic liberation of defeat. This secret exultation is "of all things
known" "most difficult" (CP, 107). Such difficult knowledge accompanies the discovery that Unity of Being is possible only at rare
moments of history. At all other times earth and heaven are incompatible, and to try to fuse them leads only to emptiness and
unreality. This discovery leads Yeats to a crossroads, the "choice of
choices."

ᔦ

The choice confronted when natural and supernatural are seen
to be incompatible is both literary and personal. Yeats has sought
in his writing to marry rock and hill to mythology. Now he finds
that there are two forms of art. A writer may commit himself to
one or the other, but not to both simultaneously. One kind of art
takes delight "in essences, in states of mind, in pure imagination,
in all that comes to us most easily in elaborate music" (EI, 266).
The other delights in the whole man — blood, imagination, intellect, running together. One art leads upward to mystic ecstasy. The
other leads to an art of "force," "personality," "the tumult of the
blood" (EI, 267). Even the greatest artists of intellectual essences
cannot carry the body to the summit of ecstasy, and even the
greatest artists of personality cannot bring soul all the way to earth.
A poet must choose either for personality or for the essences. "There
are two ways before literature — upward into ever-growing subtlety, with Verhaeren, with Mallarmé, with Maeterlinck, until at
last, it may be, a new agreement among refined and studious men
gives birth to a new passion, and what seems literature becomes
religion; or downward, taking the soul with us until all is simplified
and solidified again. That is the choice of choices — the way of the
bird until common eyes have lost us, or to the market carts" (EI,
266, 267).

The choice of a way of art is contingent on the choice of a way of life. Only the artist who is committed to mysticism can create an art of intellectual essences, and only an artist who delights in the tumult of the blood will go to the carts. In life as in art the choice is between the way up and the way down, the center of the circle or the periphery. To choose for the center is to choose for the supernatural. To choose for the periphery is to choose the sufferings of the whole man, engaged in life's circling alternations between desire and weariness, illuminated only at rare moments by that sun which the saint desires to possess always, for "if it be true that God is a circle whose centre is everywhere, the saint goes to the centre, the poet and artist to the ring where everything comes round again" (EI, 287). It is the same either/or, but with a difference. There is an incompatibility between the aim of the poet and the aim of the saint. The artist wants to make perfect works of art, while the saint seeks his own perfection, and "works in his own flesh and blood and not in paper or parchment" (M, 333). Only the saint can go to the center of the circle. The poet "may not stand within the sacred house but lives amid the whirlwinds that beset its threshold" (M, 333). A man must choose for "perfection of the life, or of the work" (CP, 242). If the choice is for the second, he must renounce all thoughts of salvation, turn his back on heaven, and commit himself to the suffering of fallen life.

Now Yeats can see why his early art has led to vagueness and unreality, and why his search for self-fulfillment has turned into a chase after will-o'-the-wisps. His personal mistake has been to assume that he is destined to be a saint, just as his political mistake has been to assume that the Ireland of his day can achieve Unity of Being. He has believed that the life of the saint and the life of the poet can be reconciled and, through his attempt to combine them, has discovered their incompatibility. This discovery is a revelation about both art and selfhood. It shows him that there is no art of the way up. Art is permitted to ascend only so far toward the ideal as it can carry "the normal, passionate, reasoning self, the personality as a whole" (EI, 272). As soon as body is left behind art becomes shadowy, the poet's style "cold and monotonous," his sense of beauty "faint and sickly" (EI, 287), his images "broken, fleeting, uncertain," and "all grows unsubstantial and fantastic" (EI, 293). Moreover, the man who tries to combine saint and poet will botch both roles. Yeats has sought to put himself into poetry, and at the same time to make that self-expression the embodiment of an ideal beauty. Can he not become a saintly personage, steeped in the supernatural, and is not the aim of art a disembodied beauty? He has thought of himself as simultaneously inside and outside himself. His true identity is inside his mind and body, like a grain of sand, and he need only put its visions into words. At the same time the self is outside, within his exterior visions, and the attempt at self-expression is mirrored in dramas of the pursuit of an ideal which always eludes the outstretched hand.

Yeats is in these assumptions triply wrong, and this multiple wrongness leads to the wavering mistiness of his early poetry. Art is not the pursuit of a disembodied beauty, and the self is neither already there like a grain of sand, nor is it, except for the saint, an ideal being, fit to dwell in heaven. All but the saint must seek selfhood in the peripheral world of serpent circling from desire to weariness and back to desire again. The poet especially must accept earthly existence. Only when he seeks self-fulfillment in the adventures of the personality as a whole can self-expression and the making of true art coincide:

> I thought of myself as something unmoving and silent living in the middle of my own mind and body, a grain of sand in Bloomsbury or in Connacht that Satan's watch-fiends cannot find. Then one day I understood quite suddenly, as the way is, that I was seeking something unchanging and unmixed and always outside myself, a Stone or an Elixir that was always out of reach, and that I myself was the fleeting thing that held out its hand. The more I tried to make my art deliberately beautiful, the more did I follow the opposite of myself, for deliberate beauty is like a woman always desiring man's desire. Presently I found that I entered into myself and pictured myself and not some essence when I was not seeking beauty at all, but merely to lighten the mind of some burden of love or bitterness thrown upon it by the events of life. We are only permitted to desire life . . . (EI, 271, 272)

This passage testifies to a crucial reversal in Yeats's theory of life and art, a pivoting which is the basis of his mature work. Now that the situation is clear to him, he makes his choice resolutely. He rejects the "desire to get out of form, to get some kind of disembodied beauty," and chooses "to create form, to carry the realization of beauty as far as possible" (L, 402). He makes his choice because he must. Reality, for him at least, lies only in the serpent's mouth. Though he remains true to this decision, the fact that two ways of life exist becomes an axis of his thought. He is troubled by recurrent longings for the straight way to heaven, and writes "A Dialogue of Self and Soul" in which the self, with its commitment to love and war, wins out over his soul, but with difficulty. When, near the end of his life, he sums up his life in a phrase, he puts it in terms of the old dichotomy: "The swordsman throughout repudiates the saint, but not without vacillation" (L, 798). The poem called "Vacillation" is the best statement of the alternatives, and of the reasons for Yeats's choice. Ultimately Yeats would rather be poet than saint. The poet must sing of this world, and would, as saint, be "struck dumb" by the fire of mystic experience. The subject of all literature since poetry began is the tragic imperfection of this world: "What theme had Homer but original sin?" (CP, 247).[3]

Yeats has come a long way from his early belief that the supernatural can permeate the solid earth. Now he knows that the universe is divided against itself, riven and fractured. The world is split into irreconcilable antinomies, and therefore "we begin to live when we have conceived life as tragedy" (A, 116). The tragedy of life is the incompatibility of time and eternity. This is manifested in an unappeasable conflict of contraries. Yeats did not expect this revelation. It is an insight born of his own hard experience, an experience which puts him forever beyond his naive beginnings. On this foundation he builds the complex structure of his poetic thought.

∾

I have a Chinese painting of three old sages sitting together, one with a deer at his side, one with a scroll open at the symbol of *yen* and *yin*, those two forms that whirl perpetually, creating and re-creating all things. (E, 396)

The universe is a multitude of battles, and, since "no battle has been finally won or lost" (E, 396), all battles must be fought over again forever. This notion is Yeats's "centric myth" (L, 829). As he knows, it is a return to the thought of the presocratics. Like Empedocles and Heraclitus, Yeats sees πόλεμος as the underlying principle of things. "Discord or War," as Heraclitus said, is "God

---

[3] Yeats comments on this poem in a letter: "I feel that this is the choice of the saint (St Theresa's ecstasy, Gandhi's smiling face): comedy; and the heroic choice: Tragedy (Dante, Don Quixote). Live Tragically but be not deceived (not the fool's Tragedy)" (L, 790).

of all and Father of all, some it has made gods and some men, some bond and some free" (V, 67). If the source of things is a clash of incompatibles, rather than a perfect One which has split into multiplicity, then each thing born of this generative war will mirror the discord in its father. Yeats's early apprehension of the supernatural as restless motion is fulfilled in his later vision of life as "a whirling and a bitterness" "which turns, now here, now there" (V, 52). He remains true to his early image of the divine as wavering instability when he rejects, in *A Vision*, the Platonic or Cabalistic theory of emanations from a still center in favor of his own intuition of life as "no orderly descent from level to level, no waterfall but a whirlpool, a gyre" (V, 40).

The center is discord, as the middle of the maelstrom is the most violent place of all, the very womb of war. In another sense the center of the whirlpool is the stillness of that which is moving so fast that its speed is infinite and therefore beyond motion, and the oneness of that which has absorbed multiplicity into an all-inclusive point, as all radii of a circle meet in its center. Was not Heraclitus' symbol for Discord, which fathers all, the "simplicity of fire," and did he not say: "All things are one," and "All things are an equal exchange for fire and fire for all things"? Heraclitus' fire is at once many and one, storm and calm. It is the lightninglike energy which gathers the greatest multiplicity, for "thunderbolt steers all things." [4] Yeats has a similar notion of the contradictions of the divine. It brings multitudinous motion into motionless unity, and, destroying neither motion nor multiplicity, holds them together in the transport of extreme tension. This strange unity cannot be apprehended or expressed directly, but only referred to as "there" (CP, 284).

The divine, though one, can only appear to man as motion and the divergence of opposites. Yeats cites the Aeslepius dialogue from the *Hermetic Books* for this idea: "Eternity also, . . . though motionless itself, appears to be in motion" (V, 211). Ultimate reality is beyond the antinomies. Yeats's symbol for this is again presocratic: the perfect sphere of Parmenides, everywhere one with itself. This reality is not exempt from the universal law limiting

[4] Fragments 50, 90, 64. I have used the translations in G. S. Kirk and J. E. Raven, *The Presocratic Philosophers* (Cambridge, England: Cambridge University Press, 1957), pp. 188, 199.

human experience, and as soon as it manifests itself it becomes split into contraries, chance and choice, death and life, gods and men. "The ultimate reality because neither one nor many, concord nor discord, is symbolised as a phaseless sphere, but . . . all things fall into a series of antinomies in human experience" (V, 193).

One of the chief contradictions of the ground of being is the way it is single and multiple at once. There is both one God and a multitude of gods. The divine appears to one people in terms of monotheism, to another as polytheism, and both peoples are right. Christianity has seen God as one, but the new age will know ultimate reality as multitudinousness. Yeats remembers Joachim of Floris' cyclical theory of history in *The Eternal Gospel*, and believes that man is about to have a new revelation governed by the Third Person of the Trinity, as early epochs have been dominated successively by Father and Son: "Our civilisation was about to reverse itself, or some new civilisation about to be born from all that our age had rejected, from all that my stories ["Rosa Alchemica" and "The Adoration of the Magi"] symbolised as a harlot, and take after its mother; because we had worshipped a single god it would worship many or receive from Joachim de Flora's Holy Spirit a multitudinous influx" (E, 393). The alternation between polytheism and monotheism is one of the most important antinomies. Either apprehension of God is authentic, and reality is both "a congeries of beings and a single being" (V, 52).

Ultimate reality is a multitude of patterns, each the model for a certain set of existences in space and time. God "contains archetypes of all possible existences" (E, 368), every bird, beast, man, or flower, and the birth of things is not the creation of novelty, but the actualization in matter of what has already existed eternally in the bosom of divinity. Nothing is created from something other than itself and given a derived life. All things are self-begotten, like God, for each thing is a "portion of Divinity," as Blake said. It is fantastically wrong to think of things as constructed of elements other than themselves, or to imagine "Building-yard and stormy shore,/Winding-sheet and swaddling-clothes" (CP, 264).

It is as mistaken to believe in winding sheets as in swaddling clothes. All things which have ever existed still exist in God, and one of the articles of Yeats's faith is the idea that events of the past may be re-enacted in time and space. This is the basis of two of his plays, *The Words Upon the Window-Pane* and *Purgatory*, and is expressed again and again in his prose and verse from the *The Celtic Twilight* to the end. The presupposition which makes plausible the idea that things can come back and occur again on earth is the notion that God is the assembly of things real or possible, existing forever in their vitality: "All things remain in God" (CP, 254).

If God is "a congeries of beings" he is also "a single being." Each created being incarnates one archetype, and each archetype is a version of the great archetype which contains all without ceasing to be individual. God is all-inclusive and yet has the uniqueness of a person. Each part of ultimate reality, though unlike the others, mirrors it all, as every cell in a living body contains the genetic pattern of the whole, or as every poem by a great poet is a unique expression of his single vision, or as the sun is the same and yet different in everybody's eyes. The universe is a complex organism of interlocking units, lying "one inside another, each complete in itself, like those perforated Chinese ivory balls" (E, 434). It is like certain Dutch paintings which contain in one corner a miniature painting of the larger painting, in one corner of that a miniature of the miniature, and so on. At whatever level the world is divided a whole remains which is a complete mirroring of the totality. This whole, however small, can always be cut into smaller pieces which will themselves mirror all in a unique way: "a fragment may be an image of the whole, the moon's still scarce crumbled image, as it were, in a glass of wine" (A, 177), and every unit, however large, up to the divine ground itself, can be assimilated into larger units, each an irreplaceable reflection of the totality. At the heart of reality is the "unintelligible" fact of unity in multiplicity, and for Yeats it is Plotinus who presides over the apprehension of this mystery. This is not inappropriate, since the notions of plenitude and *concordia discors* are both present in the Third *Ennead*, and are transmitted to later generations by that text. "We may come to think . . . with Plotinus," says Yeats, "that every soul is unique; that these souls, these eternal archetypes, combine into greater units as days and nights into months, months into years, and at last into the final unit that differs in nothing from that which they were at the beginning: everywhere that antinomy of the One and the Many that Plato thought in his *Parmenides* insoluble, though

Blake thought it soluble 'at the bottom of the graves' " (E, 397).

Though this mystery is insoluble, it can, like other mysteries, be expressed in poetry. Yeats achieves this with a symbolism derived from Blake: the description of the unity of the infinitely large in terms of the unity of the infinitesimally small. Infinitely large and infinitesimally small are also an antinomy, but they meet in God, for did not Blake see a world in a grain of sand? Yeats too finds the universe enclosed in the smallest natural units, and speaks now of the way "All things hang like a drop of dew/Upon a blade of grass" (CP, 249), now of the way "All the stream that's roaring by/Came out of a needle's eye" (CP, 287). The stream of time is driven by that which takes up no room in time or space. Within a needle's eye all things past and to come lie enfolded in a point and a moment: "Things unborn, things that are gone,/From needle's eye still goad it on" (CP, 287).

Yeat's best expression of this is certain magnificent verses in "Words for Music Perhaps." Here he uses neither the image of the needle's eye nor the image of a drop of dew, but speaks of the eye of God himself. Speaking through Tom the lunatic, he declares his faith that the living things of time, in the full intensity of their vitality, remain eternally in the circuit of God's eye, as all that a man sees is brought to a focus and enclosed in his vision:

> Whatever stands in field or flood,
> Bird, beast, fish or man,
> Mare or stallion, cock or hen,
> Stands in God's unchanging eye
> In all the vigour of its blood;
> In that faith I live or die. (CP, 264)

If all things stand in God's unchanging eye, what need is there for them to sail out of perfection? Why was the world not complete as soon as the archetypes existed in the divine ground, that is, from the beginning?

Yeats believes that the descent into material existence adds something to the eternal archetypes. Spatial and temporal existence is in one sense a fall. In another sense it makes the perfect more perfect. Material existence adds the violence of physical existence, and without these the archetypes are incomplete. If wisdom is "incompatible with life," "power" is "a property of the living" (CP, 234). Yeats remembers the ancient belief that spirits are hungry for blood, and will materialize if blood is poured for them (M, 350; E, 366). He believes with Blake that the divine needs the human in order to act or be (M, 352), declares in *Per Amica Silentia Lunae* that each man's Daimon has as much need of his earthly counterpart as the man has need of his Daimon, and, in *The Celtic Twilight*, affirms that spirits cannot even play without man's help (M, 9). The archetypes need material existence in order to fulfill themselves, just as the things of this world would be unreal without the archetypes as models. Yeats repeatedly refers to a voice he once heard in the night. The voice affirmed the boundless love of God for every soul. Each makes real in flesh and blood one potentiality of deity, and "no other can satisfy the same need in God" (M, 348). Things are made neither of time nor of eternity, but of both in their relation. Yeats characteristically expresses this conjunction as sexual union. Eternity wants to incarnate in matter all its forms, and, quoting Tom again, Yeats sees this as a pro-creative drive:

> The stallion Eternity
> Mounted the mare of Time,
> 'Gat the foal of the world. (CP, 264)

So, in "Leda and the Swan" the divine power cannot come to Leda without borrowing the power of blood from that which is less than man. The divine knowledge of the god can only be transmitted through his carnal knowledge of Leda. He cannot, by himself, engender "The broken wall, the burning roof and tower/And Agamemnon dead" (CP, 212). He must use Leda as an avenue through which to enter time. History is made of the conjunction of divine and human, eternal and temporal, but this union can only be momentary. After begetting the Trojan war and all its effects, Zeus must withdraw, the "indifferent beak" must "let her drop," and he must leave Leda and her progeny to bear history — in both senses of bear.

The eternal archetypes, though already perfect, need the descent into matter in order to complete themselves, even though that descent is a tearing apart of the whole. The fall into matter is an entry into violence and conflict which deflowers what in eternity is virginally pure. Through this desecration the things of eternity attain a new perfection. At the end of *A Full Moon in March* one attendant asks why the divine beings, who carry pitchers wherein "tight . . . all time's completed treasure is," must descend into time: "Why must those holy, haughty feet descend/From emblematic niches . . . ? What do they seek for? Why must they descend? . . . What do they lack?" And the other attendant gives the answer: "Their desecration and the lover's night" (CPl, 629, 630). Crazy Jane too knows that the purity of heavenly love can only be fulfilled in the violence of copulation. Fair love needs foul love, which man has "in common/With every noble beast" (CP, 297). She knows that this is only one mode of the general law by which heaven must be torn apart in time in order to be made complete at last, "For nothing can be sole or whole/That has not been rent" (CP, 255).

What wholeness is there in desecration? In the ground of being all the antinomies are copresent without incompatibility. There body and soul are not opposites, nor do beauty and wisdom each entail its own appropriate suffering. There things do not have to develop slowly through time, as the flower grows from seed to blossom, nor are things divided into spatially separate parts. A thing is not separated from its function, nor from that in which it participates. There all is the harmony of reconciled opposites, as dancer, dance, and music are one, or as leaf, blossom, and bole make up the tree. Eternity is a *concordia discors*, and can be described only as the negation of the terrestrial condition, or by the supreme images of poetry, as in Yeats's famous symbols of the chestnut tree and the dancer.

As soon as they enter time and space the antinomies become violently incompatible. Yeats, like his compatriot Joyce, returns to the ideas of Bruno and Nicholas of Cusa. In heaven things are perfect and at one, but on earth "all things are from antithesis" (V, 268). Each thing can manifest itself only in terms of its opposite, as a color cannot be seen unless it is set against another color, or as heat exists only in terms of cold, light in terms of darkness. The human soul "would not be conscious were it not suspended between contraries, the greater the contrast the more intense the consciousness" (VP, 824), and the system of *A Vision* "is founded upon the belief that the ultimate reality, symbolised as the Sphere, falls in human consciousness, as Nicholas of Cusa was the first to demonstrate, into a series of antinomies" (V, 187).

The opposition between eternity and time might be called the vertical antinomy, for it is a conflict between time and timelessness rather than among the things of time. It is a true antinomy, made of both love and war, discord and concord. Time and eternity are mutually negating, and whatever can be said of one must be denied of the other: "There are two realities, the terrestrial and the condition of fire. All power is from the terrestrial condition, for there all opposites meet and there only is the extreme of choice possible, full freedom. And there the heterogeneous is, and evil, for evil is the strain one upon another of opposites; but in the condition of fire is all music and all rest" (M, 356, 357). Like two halves of an hourglass, or like two intersecting cones whirling within one another, point to base and base to point, time and eternity are opposed and yet related, face to face in the intimacy of opposition. Love is founded upon hate and concord upon discord. As the sand flows into one half of the hourglass it flows out of the other, and as the thread winds on one gyre it unwinds from the other. When it is one season here it is the opposite season in the country of heaven, as Yeats affirms in that sentence which, so he says, was written by a beggar upon the walls of Babylon: "There are two living countries, one visible and one invisible, and when it is summer there, it is winter here, and when it is November with us, it is lambing-time there" (CPl, 301).

The parallel on the human scale to this relation of the two countries is the warfare of man and his Daimon. Man and Daimon are not only mirror images of one another. They are opposites too, like the two countries, and seek one another as a man seeks a woman. There is an analogy between Daimon and sweetheart "that evades the intellect" (M, 336). To reach eternity would be to escape from the clash of antinomies, for in the condition of fire all is music and rest. In another sense man cannot escape by death from the war of opposites, for eternity is but one side of the greatest antinomy, and as in Heraclitus' philosophy there is a constant transfer of energy between man and Daimon, time and eternity, earth and fire. Earth and heaven are contraries whirling perpetually. "Death cannot solve the antinomy: death and life are its expression" (V, 52), and Yeats affirms as an important special case of the Heraclitean law that "opposites are everywhere face to face, dying each other's life, living each other's death" (E, 430) the way the divine and human worlds live in a relation of support and destruction, hatred and love: "Your words are clear at last, O Heraclitus. God and man die each other's life, live each other's death" (CPl, 594). God and man form a unity of opposites in tension, like "the yolk and white of the one shell," to alter Plato's parable (CP, 213), for the universe is "a great egg that turns inside-out perpetually without breaking its shell" (V, 33).

The vertical antinomy is an opposition between that which is beyond antinomies and that which is dominated by them. This vertical hourglass is accompanied by horizontal gyres. Time and eternity, though opposites, are each in a way complete, reflections of one another in different modes. Each side of a temporal opposition is incomplete and unhappy because of this imperfection. What is in eternity spherically complete is refracted in time, as white light is divided by a prism. Each ray is only a portion of eternity, the fragment of a whole: "The acts and nature of a Spirit during any one life are a section or abstraction of reality and are unhappy because incomplete. They are a gyre or part of a gyre, whereas reality is a sphere." [5]

The incompleteness of the things of time drives them to seek completion, as the divided halves of Aristophanes' spherical man sought one another through the world. This urge to wholeness is the impetus of time and keeps the wheel of life turning. For Yeats, as for Blake, "without contraries is no progression." If the antinomies of time are "those combatants who turn the wheel of life" (E, 393), they are also in love. Each contrary seeks to join its fellow and become perfect, but in time and space things are either one thing or its contrary, never both. The flow of time is the desire of each point on the wheel to be everywhere at once. This yearning for totality can only be satisfied beyond time, where all the planets drop in the sun. In every season we call on the others, "Nor know

---

[5] Quoted from an unpublished manuscript in Hazard Adams, *Blake and Yeats: The Contrary Vision* (Ithaca: Cornell University Press, 1955), p. 288.

that what disturbs our blood/Is but its longing for the tomb" (CP, 208).

The wheel of the seasons is only one example of the circling of frustrated contraries. The image of whirling antinomies dominates Yeats's vision of human life. Youth and age, bodily pleasure and wisdom, subjective and objective attitudes — man can have only one side of each of these pairs at once, but whichever he has dissatisfies him. If he is on one side of the wheel he longs for the other, but when he reaches the other side he has lost what he had before and longs to be back where he was. Young he longs for wisdom, but in old age he wants youth again and its tumult of the blood:

> . . . O that I were young again
> And held her in my arms! (CP, 337)

The elaborate discussion of human existence in "The Phases of the Moon" and *A Vision* is a codification of this insight. Each man's nature may be characterized by one of the twenty-eight phases of the moon, for each man is a certain combination of the moon's dark and full, objectivity and subjectivity, "primary" and "antithetical." At any moment each man is a certain balance of four faculties, "Will," "Mask," "Creative Mind," and "Body of Fate." These stand, as it were, in opposite quarters of the circle, since "every phase is in itself a wheel" (V, 89). Every man is tormented by the limitations of his phase, and longs to possess simultaneously the modes of existence appropriate to all twenty-eight phases. Life is an impossible attempt to be what one must be and what one would be at the same time. It is "an endeavour, made vain by the four sails of its mill, to come to a double contemplation, that of the chosen Image, that of the fated Image" (V, 94).

This desire for completeness turns the mill of life. Though each man may be defined by a single phase of the moon, he also moves in his lifetime through all twenty-eight phases, from the subjectivity of passionate youth to the objective wisdom of old age, or, it may be, from the cold objectivity of youth, seeking to know what is outside itself, to the wisdom of blinded Oedipus, who has absorbed the world into himself, and though he speaks but his own mind, knows and controls all things. Oedipus in old age "knew nothing but his mind, and yet because he spoke that mind fate possessed it

and kingdoms changed according to his blessing and his cursing"
(V, 28). Two series of poems, "A Man Young and Old" and "A
Woman Young and Old," demonstrate how a man and a woman,
in the temporal circuit of their lives, pass one by one through all the
phases of the moon. What they would wish to have in a moment
they are fated to have only as a succession:

> Between extremities
> Man runs his course . . . (CP, 245)

However an individual human life is divided, from each thought
or action up to the whole course of it, it remains a wheel around
which the man whirls in a vain attempt to reconcile contraries.
The relations of man to his fellows also express the antinomies of life.
"Sometimes individuals are *primary* and *antithetical* to one another
and joined by a bond so powerful that they form a common gyre
or series of gyres" (V, 237). The relation which most interests
Yeats is the sexual one. His treatment of sex is dominated by the
idea that a man and a woman are contraries and in their relation
make an impossible attempt to unify opposites. Love is "a kiss/In
the mid-battle . . ./A brief forgiveness between opposites" (CPl,
259). The sexual relation is a mixture of love and hate, like its
vertical analogy, the relation of a man and his Daimon. Lovers,
though they need one another as the moon needs the sun, torment
one another with "cruelties of Choice and Chance." "Love is like
the lion's tooth," and "has a spider's eye/To find out some appropriate pain . . ./For every nerve" (CP, 255, 175). All lovers
seek in their amorous combat a perfect union joining the antinomies
of male and female, body and soul, the brief ecstasy of physical
pleasure and the permanence of spiritual love. When this union is
attained the lovers will escape from the circling bitterness of life,
all that winding of the gyres, and, as the "Zodiac is changed into a
sphere" (CP, 268), find completeness in one another's arms.

A perfect sexual act, Yeats affirms in "Solomon and the Witch,"
would do more than liberate the lovers from the wheel of life. If
Choice and Chance were ever reconciled in the love embrace, the
whole world would return to eternity (CP, 175), but of course this
can never happen. No sexual act can be perfect, or change, for
more than a moment, the Zodiac into a sphere. Never can soul's
love and body's love be unified. Never can "Love cram love's two

divisions/Yet keep his substance whole" (CP, 297). Only the sexual relation of supernatural beings can be complete. According to a sentence from Swedenborg which Yeats often quoted, "the sexual intercourse of the angels is a conflagration of the whole being" (L, 805, and see CP, 282).

Since the lovers of heaven possess one another completely, they also possess all time in an eternal moment, and "lad and lass,/Nerve touching nerve upon that happy ground,/Are bobbins where all time is bound and wound" (CPl, 633). No human lovers can reach such unity, and, as a result, sex is not a means of liberation from the whirling of time. At most it is a momentary expression of the place where contraries meet, and therefore all the more a sign of the limitation of earthly life. Lovers catch a glimpse in their ecstasy of the bliss of heaven, but in their attempt to make this joy eternal they exhaust it, and fall back into "the common round of day" (CP, 284). This failure of love is a constant refrain of Yeats's thought: "The marriage bed is the symbol of the solved antinomy, and were more than symbol could a man there lose and keep his identity, but he falls asleep" (V, 52); "Exhausted by the cry that it can never end, my love ends" (V, 40); "The tragedy of sexual intercourse is the perpetual virginity of the soul" (LDW, 174).

All love is doomed to imperfection and evanescence. Yeats's symbol for this circling frustration is the dance. Like dancing, love is a mixture of harmony and opposition. Both are a constant motion in an ever-renewed, ever-unsuccessful attempt to reach a poise which is beyond movement. The dancers whirl round, each trying to merge with the other, but, when the other side of the circle is reached, the partners have merely reversed sides. They attain only for an instant in the height of their spinning the moment when they are moving so fast that they seem to be everywhere on the circle at once, each melted into the other. These dancing lovers are like the sun and the moon, or like constellations of the "whirling Zodiac" (CP, 268). As one rises the other sets, and never can they satisfy their longing for completion (CP, 135). Or, it may be, the woman trying to hold the man is like the earth trying to keep the sun from rising out of its embracing darkness (CP, 268).

The temporal existence of larger groups is no less a matter of opposites, each living the other's death, dying the other's life. The whirling of the golden king and silver lady is an expression of

the gyres of history as well as of the gyres of sex, and is cited in
A Vision to describe that larger "horizontal dance" (V, 270). The
figure of the whirling gyres "is true also of history, for the end of an
age, which always receives the revelation of the character of the
next age, is represented by the coming of one gyre to its place of
greatest expansion and of the other to that of its greatest con-
traction" (VP, 824, 825). Yeats's vision of history is an application
of his fundamental intuition on a larger scale. Every age, civilization, or nation, like every human life, can be characterized by
one of the phases of the moon. It is a combination of subjectivity
and objectivity. Each civilization, like each man, is driven by a
tragic desire to be the whole without ceasing to be itself. This
attempt only more quickly brings decadence, "the artificial unity"
of "dead sticks . . . tied into convenient bundles" (L, 869) which
marks the approaching end of every civilization. "Things fall
apart; the centre cannot hold" (CP, 184), and at last the desiccated
shell collapses. Then the cry of revelation heralds the birth of the
new age which has been gradually preparing in secret as the old
culture has died. "An age is the reversal of an age" (CP, 275);
"Each age unwinds the thread another age had wound" (V, 270);
and opposing cultures follow one another as the dark of the moon
follows the full.

～

The brevity of each individual or cultural accomplishment is not
a matter of choice, nor is it time alone which brings love "nearer
death" with "every touch" the lovers give (CP, 257). God himself
decrees that "all things pass away" (CP, 247). Ultimate reality
wants all things to be actualized in time, and this fulfillment,
though complete in an eternal moment in heaven, takes time in
time. A man's selfhood requires a lifetime to complete, and a
civilization takes a measurable number of centuries to go from
vital youth to tired decadence. God does not want things to remain
in static perfection, a hollow image of eternity. Once they have
fulfilled the allotted circle of their existence, they have satisfied the
need of the archetypes for material existence, and God then destroys
them. He drives them to go beyond themselves into emptiness.
There is only so much room in space at any one time, and the stage

must be cleared for the next act of history. The plenitude of possible forms lives in the needle's eye of God, forcing the stream of time to flow forward into extinction in order to make room for new incarnations. To put it another way, all men are dancers, but they are not free to call the tune. They are "constrained, arraigned, baffled, bent and unbent," "obedient to some hidden magical breath" (CP, 167, 168). A great supernatural choreographer or puppetmaster, like a strong wind bending the trees, or like a magnetic field constraining iron filings, forces the dancers to his will, whirling them round until they have completed themselves in their own destruction:

> When Loie Fuller's Chinese dancers enwound
> A shining web, a floating ribbon of cloth,
> It seemed that a dragon of air
> Had fallen among the dancers, had whirled them round
> Or hurried them off on its own furious path;
> So the Platonic Year
> Whirls out new right and wrong,
> Whirls in the old instead:
> All men are dancers and their tread
> Goes to the barbarous clangour of a gong. (CP, 205, 206)

Yeats's vision of history leads him, as this passage shows, to reaffirm the doctrine of "the Great Year of the ancients." There is an elaborate discussion of this tradition in *A Vision* (V, 243–263), and it is the basis of his cyclical theory of history. It means first the Indian or Platonic notion that after a certain long span of time, thirty-six thousand years or some multiple of that, all the archetypes will have incarnated themselves in time. There will have been one version of each possible form, and time will be fulfilled. The slow precession of the equinoxes will have completed a cycle, the movement of the zodiacal constellations will bring them back to their original position, and Aries will once more preside over the coming of spring. The creation will be returned to the beginning, and the impulse of eternity to actualize itself in time will be exhausted at last (E, 395, 396; V, 251–254).

Yeats escapes from the terror of history by affirming that everything is inevitable. All happenings occur according to a pre-established plan. Neither in a man's life, nor in the life of nations is there gratuitous novelty, and no man need feel responsible for the tragedies and sufferings of his own life or of history. Each man and each culture will begin at a certain time and will last exactly so long and no longer. "I do not doubt," writes Yeats, "those heaving circles, those winding arcs, whether in one man's life or in that of an age, are mathematical, and that some in the world, or beyond the world, have foreknown the event and pricked upon the calendar the life-span of a Christ, a Buddha, a Napoleon" (M, 340).

Even though Yeats modifies this, in *A Vision*, with the notion that the future is to some degree unpredictable, nevertheless the past can be seen as perfectly orderly, a sequence of cycles which has happened in a regular way — so many years for the Roman Empire, so many for the Byzantine, and so on, according to the divine measure. All men past and present are understandable in terms of the twenty-eight phases of the moon. What a pleasure to be able to place Christ, Buddha, Napoleon, and all one's friends in the same paradigm, to control them by making them explicable! One of Yeats's strongest motivations is the desire for a systematic comprehension of the universe. He praises energy, intensity, the irrational, and says, "Passion is to me the essential" (L, 791), but he also has a great need to include particulars under ever larger and more abstract rubrics, and at last to have the whole universe, time, space, eternity, and all, reduced to one pattern, like "the diagrams in Law's *Boehme*, where one lifts a flap of paper to discover both the human entrails and the starry heavens" (V, 23, 24).

Yeats is referring to the discrepancy between the uniqueness of the particular and the mathematical abstractions of the system, when, in a famous passage in *A Vision*, he says that his "circuits of sun and moon," which "divide actual history into periods of equal length," are "stylistic arrangements of experience comparable to the cubes in the drawing of Wyndham Lewis and to the ovoids in the sculpture of Brancusi" (V, 24, 25). This does not mean that he considers his circuits arbitrary inventions, "metaphors for poetry," taking poetry to mean human fiction. Yeats never believes that poetry is made of baseless fantasy. In the next sentence, not so often quoted, he says of his stylistic arrangements of experience: "They have helped me to hold in a single thought reality and justice" (V, 25). Reality is the irrational intensity of actual experience, and justice is the hidden law behind it. Yeats always seeks to hold these in a single thought. Respect for the tumult of the blood and a rage for order — these are the contraries in Yeats's own nature, dying each other's life, living each other's death. At times there is a wild oscillation from one extreme to the other, but his best work draws its strength from a tense copresence of these contraries. This is truest, perhaps, when it is least obviously the case. Yeats's most magically simple, sensuous, and passionate lyrics often hide his most esoteric thought. As the poet himself said: "We can (those hard symbolic bones under the skin) substitute for a treatise on logic the *Divine Comedy*, or some little song about a rose, or be content to live our thought" (V, 24).

The pattern of Yeats's thought involves a horizontal counterpart of the ascent of the universe from minute particulars up to God. Time as a whole is a great year, one incarnation of the plenitude of God. This is divided into lesser units, each an image of the whole, each with its own circular perfection. Every lesser unit is in turn divided into smaller circuits, and so on down to the smallest creature, whose life repeats the great year in miniature. Time is made of wheels within wheels within wheels. The great year is divided into innumerable smaller wheels, each of which is itself a year and contains the whole, eternity in an hour. Like Proclus, Yeats gives "to the smallest living creature its individual year" (V, 202). Elsewhere the same thought is put more vividly: "a Greatest Year for whale and gudgeon alike must exhaust the multiplication table" (E, 396). Whale or gudgeon, every portion of the whole is destined to proceed through a circuit traversing in its own way the permutations of existence, subjective and objective, chance and choice, and the rest. When the great year is complete, it will be as if all the little wheels within the biggest wheel had simultaneously come round again to zero: "It is as though innumerable dials, some that recorded minutes alone, some seconds alone, some hours alone, some months alone, some years alone, were all to complete their circles when Big Ben struck twelve upon the last night of the century" (V, 248).

In whatever way spatial and temporal existence is divided, the same universal law governs all. The smallest piece of the world is not spherically complete. A tiny set of the gyres whirls incessantly within it, in obedience to the law by which all things are divided into irreconcilable contraries. Within every portion of the universe "a being racing into the future passes a being racing into the past, two footprints perpetually obliterating one another, toe to heel, heel to toe" (V, 210). The Greatest Year is also divided against itself, and wears itself out in an unsuccessful attempt to merge its opposing impulses. It divides "into waxing and waning, day and night, or summer and winter. There [is] everywhere a conflict . . . between two principles or 'elemental forms of the mind' " (E, 396).

The gyres govern everything, and "all creation is from conflict" (A, 342).

⌐

Yeats has come a long way from the structureless, wavering universe of his early poetry, but, though he now has a comprehensive vision of things, his world is still tragically divided against itself. Moreover, all is laid out in advance. "When had I my own will?" he asks. "O not since life began" (CP, 167). Man plays a fated role, like an actor in some great tragic drama. He is destined to enact one part and no other in a play written before time began:

> All perform their tragic play,
> There struts Hamlet, there is Lear,
> That's Ophelia, that Cordelia . . . (CP, 292)

When a man recognizes that he plays a predetermined role his life seems arbitrary and factitious, the rigid following of a mathematical pattern. It is not his own life, but some other life which is making use of his body and soul to incarnate itself. He cannot escape this coercion, but at best can hasten the performance of the play, and this is his only liberty, for "the more rapid the development of the figure the greater the freedom of the soul" (VP, 824). Such an existence is worse than determined. My own life and all the lives that have ever been lived have one outcome: "Everything that man esteems/Endures a moment or a day" (CP, 211); "Man is in love and loves what vanishes" (CP, 205). Ephemerality is the first law of life. No work of art or intellect lasts for long. Each life ends in death, and every civilization comes at last to the desert. Again and again Yeats sings in a kind of shocked amazement of the obliterating power of the "levelling wind" (CP, 207). His imagination is most stirred by the wanton destruction of great works of art, "handiwork of Callimachus" (CP, 292), or "Phidias' famous ivories" (CP, 204). No effort of preservation can be successful. "Day brings round the night," and "before dawn" man's "glory and his monuments are gone" (CP, 287). This panorama of savage destruction is made all the more horrifying by its inevitability. The intensity with which man plunges into a creative act causes him to go beyond construction to the obliteration of what he has made, and "every movement, in feeling or in thought, prepares in the dark by its own increasing clarity and confidence its own executioner" (M, 340). This is the tragedy of man's involvement in time. It is as if he were on a circular track and forced to strain every nerve and muscle to reach his heart's goal, but the momentum of his intensity carries him past the goal and back to deprivation again. "Things thought too long can be no longer thought" (CP, 291). There is an uncontrollable energy in every individual and civilization which forces them to bring their forms to perfection and then destroy them:

> Whatever flames upon the night
> Man's own resinous heart has fed. (CP, 211)

Man seeks an absolute consummation of his life. Enraged by the limitation or factitiousness of what he has made, he is driven to demolish it, to go beyond it, "Ravening, raging, and uprooting that he may come/Into the desolation of reality" (CP, 287). The feeling that reality is desolation is a special possession of the twentieth century. Yeats, as much as any other writer in English, is the spokesman for our apocalyptic sense of doom, our terror of destruction, rage for destruction. Western civilization, Yeats with passionate horror believes, is nearing its end. As early as "The Adoration of the Magi" he foresees a great flood of irrationalism, of wars, hatred, and violence. The First World War and the Irish rebellion and civil war then seem the first wave of terror. He begins "to imagine, as always at [his] left side just out of the range of the sight, a brazen winged beast" which he associates with "laughing, ecstatic destruction" (E, 393). Romanticism, symbolism, and the decadence, his tradition in art, are the trembling of the veil, the presage of the end. "After Stephane Mallarmé, after Paul Verlaine, after Gustave Moreau, after Puvis de Chavannes, after our own verse, after all our subtle colour and nervous rhythm, after the faint mixed tints of Conder, what more is possible? After us the Savage God" (A, 210).

The pale wavering of Yeats's early work is the dying gasp of the old dispensation wandering feebly out to the extreme edge of the expiring gyre. The lightning flash of revelation comes always as a divine act of violence, the rape of Leda, the terror of Christ's resurrection. Yeats believes that the revelation about to occur will be especially destructive. The age which Christ initiated was objective, an age of peace, love, and reason. The new age will reverse all that. It will be violent in itself, as well as initiated by violence. Its symbol is not the virgin but the harlot, not Christ "who, crucified standing up, went into the abstract sky soul and body," but a new Oedipus, who, like his prototype, will sink down "soul and body into the earth" (V, 27). "After an age of necessity, truth, goodness, mechanism, science, democracy, abstraction, peace, comes an age of freedom, fiction, evil, kindred, art, aristocracy, particularity, war. Has our age burned to the socket?" (V, 52).

The new age will be a return to values lost since the coming of Christ, or, it may be, since the Unity of Being of Byzantium or the Renaissance. The second coming will "disinter/The workman, noble and saint," and all things will "run/On that unfashionable gyre again" (CP, 291), but before the construction of the new there must be a destruction of the old. The sense of a loosening of control, the staining of earth with "irrational streams of blood" (CP, 291), is expressed in Yeats's most powerful poems about contemporary history. Everything that he most admires in civilization, tradition, wit, "the ceremony of innocence" (CP, 185), a life directed by elaborate codes and yet heroically intense, all that he associates with the Renaissance and with the life of his own Irish ancestors, or with Lady Gregory and Coole Park — all this is coming to an end, and he must be the terrified witness of the descent of an irrational force which seizes men and makes them act like beasts. Worse yet, he cannot remain a passive spectator, but comes to take pleasure in the destruction of all that has been dearest to him. Horror turns to sensual delight, and this is more horrifying yet:

> We, who seven years ago
> Talked of honour and of truth,
> Shriek with pleasure if we show
> The weasel's twist, the weasel's tooth. (CP, 207)

The final consequence of Yeats's sense of history is the worst of all. Not only is history determined and everywhere the same tale of violence, terror, and defeat, but each man is doomed, like each civilization, to suffer the same failure again and again. Yeats's vision of history culminates in a belief in the eternal return, for "a system symbolising the phenomenal world as irrational because a series of unresolved antinomies, must find its representation in a perpetual return to the starting-point" (V, 194, 195).

Everything in Yeats's thought leads him to reaffirm this doctrine. On the ring of history "everything comes round again." What is to prevent it from beginning again, and going round the same circle once more? The Platonic year which drives history, like a dragon of air among the dancers, brings in its whirling not new right and wrong but the "old instead," that is, it brings a new enactment of events which have already taken place an infinite number of times before. No event is novel, but all are re-enactments of the old, like performances of a tragic drama which must be ritually played over and over for the satisfaction of some audience hungry for pity and terror. The text is the celestial archetypes, and these must be endlessly repeated on the stage of history. The rape of Leda, the Trojan War, Jason's search for the golden fleece, the crucifixion, all the violent events of history have happened innumerable times (CP, 210).

The audience for this cosmic play, insatiable for suffering and blood, is God. God wishes to see repeatedly his own death, his descent to earth to suffer material existence to the end. The play he witnesses is the perpetual reincarnation of the congeries of beings which is himself. It is as if God were some rich king who must see himself mirrored in what he creates. The world is the overflow of the joyous plenitude of God, for "the Universal Self is a fountain, not a cistern, the Supreme Good must perpetually give itself. The world is necessary to the Self, must receive 'the excess of its delights' " (EI, 483).

What is joyous self-expression to God is a whirling and a bitterness here. Man longs to return to his origin, to "perish into the One," but God is not satisfied with one performance of each drama of history. He wants to behold each one over and over, for none is a perfect image of his fullness. Each man in each incarnation strives to satisfy God with a perfect living of his assigned role. He swings around his circle to its fated end, and, longing for the center, asks: "Now, O Lord, is that enough?" But God flings him once more out to the periphery, driving him around the serpent's path again and yet again. Yeats makes the Magi a symbol of the multitudinous divinity in its need for the re-enactment of the tragic shows of history. One performance of the birth and death of Christ was not enough. The Magi, the "pale unsatisfied ones," hover over the earth, "their eyes still fixed, hoping to find once more,/Being by Calvary's turbulence unsatisfied,/The uncontrollable mystery on the bestial floor" (CP, 124).

An awareness of the eternal return adds its particular flavor of horror to the knowledge that all is determined and that "all men live in suffering" (CP, 308). To know that I play a role which has been acted countless times before seems to empty my life of meaning. My existence appears an alien costume which I am forced to wear, and my role is altogether arbitrary. I am Hamlet, but might just as well have been Lear or the fool. The role has been played so often before that it has lost all significance. I am a puppet reliving someone else's life. My existence is as pointless and ephemeral as if I should "have been always an insect in the roots of the grass" (E, 398).

This feeling slips into the eerie anguish of the sense of _déjà vu_. The life which I am living at this moment, with all its sensations and details, down to the most trivial and absurd, I have lived in exactly the same way a thousand times before, and shall live again in the future. The sensation of _déjà vu_ combines horror and futility: the horror of being possessed by a life not my own, as if I should, like Shelley's Zoroaster, meet my own image walking in the garden; the futility of utter meaninglessness, of being like a phrase which has been repeated so often that it has become mere noise: "I murmured, as I have countless times, 'I have been part of it always and there is maybe no escape, forgetting and returning life after life like an insect in the roots of the grass.' "[6]

[6] _A Vision_, first edition (London: privately printed . . . by T. Werner Laurie, 1925), p. xiii. Compare the following passage from Nietzsche's _Joyful Wisdom_, trans. Thomas Common (New York: Frederick Ungar, 1960), pp. 270, 271: "What if a demon crept after thee into thy loneliest loneliness some day or night, and said to thee: 'This life, as thou livest it at present, and hast lived it, thou must live it once more, and also innumerable times; and there will be nothing new in it, but every pain and every joy and every thought and every sigh, and all the unspeakably small and great in thy life must come to thee again, and all in the same series and sequence — and similarly this

One final form of suffering will complete the description of the wheel of existence. The Universal Self wishes each soul to endure innumerable versions of the same life, but, seeking to give each soul a spherical perfection like its own, it also dooms every man to traverse the whole round of incarnations and suffer all possible lives. To the horror of reincarnation is added the horror of metempsychosis, and to one infinity of rebirths is added another, as Yeats learned from Mohini Chatterjee (CP, 242).

Yeats has reduced everything to a comprehensive system, but it is a system which deprives human life of freedom and significance. No man's life is fortuitous. Each is patterned on eternal models. In spite of this, and even because of it, each life is meaningless suffering. Every man is condemned to a quadruple limitation. His life is determined. All lives destroy themselves through their search for permanence, as the painter's brush consumes his dream, and as "all true love must die" (CP, 257). Each life repeats itself eternally, "turning its revolving wheel again and again" (V, 237). Man must suffer not only the eternal return of the same life but also the eternal return of all possible lives. It seems that he will be racked on the wheel of time forever.

Only the saint can shoot the arrow which goes straight to the sun. The poet cannot escape the path of the serpent. If he tries to leap off the wheel and go directly to God, he is rebuffed by Paradise and cast out to go around the wheel again. Even death is no escape, for the sharp spades and strong muscles of the gravediggers but "thrust their buried men/Back in the human mind again" (CP, 341). Man must not come to God by negation. To seek such a liberation is to imagine the plunge into God as the return of nothing to nothing. God is not a purity beyond positive qualities, but the plenitude of them all, and therefore it is futile to try to reach God by emptying out all the particulars of life. There is only one valid

---

spider and this moonlight among the trees, and similarly this moment, and I myself. The eternal sand-glass of existence will ever be turned once more, and thou with it, thou speck of dust!' — Wouldst thou not throw thyself down and gnash thy teeth, and curse the demon that so spake?" Though Nietzsche is by no means the only source for the idea of the eternal return in Yeats, he was reading Nietzsche with great enthusiasm in 1903, when the fully developed notion of repetition began to appear in his work.

strategy. Man must turn his back on God and willingly choose, with all his heart, to live the life he has been fated to live, and even to live it over and over again. A halfhearted playing of his role will have to be re-enacted. Only a full commitment to the destined life, however painful or trivial that life may be, will have any hope of exhausting it. "To seek God too soon is not less sinful than to seek God too late; we must love, man, woman, or child, we must exhaust ambition, intellect, desire, dedicating all things as they pass, or we come to God with empty hands" (EI, 483).

Yeats discovers that the longest way round is the shortest way home. As in *Through the Looking-Glass*, to go directly toward the garden on the hill is to get even farther from it. Only by moving in the opposite direction does a man find himself miraculously at his goal. As Yeats puts it in a sentence which is the key to all his later thought: "Hatred of God may bring the soul to God" (CP, 284). It is not a question now of the attempt to take the world to heaven set against the attempt to bring heaven to earth. Now the way up, in the new sense of leaving earth for heaven, is opposed to what might be called the way around: the attempt to live a fated life so intensely as to be liberated from it. "Neither between death and birth nor between birth and death can the soul find more than momentary happiness; its object is to pass rapidly round its circle and find freedom from that circle" (V, 236). The idea of rapidity is important here. A man's eternal archetype has in an eternal instant what the man must laboriously experience in succession. The only approach of time to eternity would be a movement around the periphery so rapid that one would be at all points of the circle at once and thereby reach spherical completeness. The perfection out of which man sailed would be regained at last, and he could return to heaven: "Escape may be for individuals alone who know how to exhaust their possible lives, to set, as it were, the hands of the clock racing" (E, 398). This might be called a theory of liberation by addition. When the soul has added one to another enough diverse experiences it will be an image of the plenitude of God and worthy to be gathered into the artifice of eternity. The passage of the soul through its vicissitudes will repeat in miniature the whole course of time: "Human life is . . . a transformation of the character defined in the horoscope into timeless and spaceless existence. The whole passage from birth to birth should be an epitome of the whole passage of the universe through time and back to its timeless and spaceless condition." [7]

Yeats's earliest expression of the reaching of totality by addition is the doctrine of the Mask. This doctrine receives its first full statement in the diary of 1909, is elaborately developed in *Per Amica Silentia Lunae*, and is the basis of the analysis of Dowson, Johnson, Beardsley, and Wilde in the *Autobiographies*. Each man is limited in character. He is one phase of the moon, one point on the periphery, one mixture of subjectivity and objectivity. By an heroic discipline he can take the role of that person who is most unlike himself, and by being both himself and the opposite of himself achieve spherical wholeness. My anti-self is not really foreign to me. He is my mirror image and has been all along secretly part of my being: "We could not find him if he were not in some sense of our being, and yet of our being but as water with fire, a noise with silence" (M, 332). The anti-self is both adored and loathed, loathed because he is that which is least natural to me, adored because he is that which I need to escape the torment of my limitation. "Then after some years," says Yeats of the genesis of the idea, "came the thought that a man always tried to become his opposite, to become what he would abhor if he did not desire it" (E, 394). To wear the mask of the anti-self takes an enormous effort of will. It means the abnegation of all easy self-expression. A man of this sort lives in extreme tension, continually destroying the natural self and replacing it with an artificial self which has the stylized formality of the masks and costumes of Japanese Noh actors. To do this is "of all things not impossible the most difficult" (M, 332). Only what requires such extraordinary discipline can be an authentic accomplishment of the soul and become "a portion of our being" (M, 332). All great writers and artists have expressed not the natural self but its opposite. Dante the lecher found in his poetry "the most exalted lady loved by a man" (M, 322); Landor, a man of savage violence in his daily life, wrote poetry and prose of a marmoreal calm, and so on. From the wearing of the mask of the anti-self all creativity comes, and "active virtue as distinguished from the passive acceptance of a current code is therefore theatrical, consciously dramatic, the wearing of a mask. It is the condition of arduous full life" (A, 285).

[7] Adams, *Blake and Yeats*, p. 288.

Yeats assimilates his idea of the polarity of the sexes into the more inclusive doctrine of the Mask. Anti-self may be sought as much in the loved one as in the notion of what is unlike oneself, and in the sexual embrace a man may achieve escape from limitation. "When a man loves a girl it should be because her face and character offer what he lacks; the more profound his nature the more he should realise his lack and the greater be the difference. It is as though he wanted to take his own death into his arms and beget a stronger life upon that death" (E, 430).

In its full implications the doctrine of the Mask is more than the idea that a man reaches completion through love or by playing the role of the self least like his spontaneous nature. The idea of the Mask began with a strange visionary experience: "I woke one night to find myself lying upon my back with all my limbs rigid, and to hear a ceremonial measured voice, which did not seem to be mine, speaking through my lips, 'We make an image of him who sleeps,' it said, 'and it is not him who sleeps, and we call it Emmanuel' " (A, 227). Yeats interpreted this vision by means of his theory of the Daimon, the idea that the anti-self needs me as I need him, and in order to merge with me drives me to play the role of that self I least resemble (M, 335, 336). My Daimon is the representative of my archetypal self in a realm a little lower than ultimate reality. My archetype is myself as I shall be when I have entered into the eternal possession of myself in a single moment. The Daimon drives me to stretch to the utmost my possibilities of being so that I may melt into that archetype. My Daimon wants me to become Emmanuel, the universal man, what Blake called "Albion." Yeats remembers the theological idea that Christ is the model for all created things and the tradition "which declares . . . that Christ alone was exactly six feet high, perfect physical man" (V, 273, and see V, 232, 233). All things "proclaim" Christ by being themselves, for Christ is the prototype for all. He is the "one that is perfect or at peace" (CP, 263), and the whole creation dances around him:

> All that could run or leap or swim
> Whether in wood, water or cloud,
> Acclaiming, proclaiming, declaiming Him. (CP, 263)

Man can attain only through great effort his likeness to the Universal Man. One life on earth, though a man is driven by his Daimon to expand it far beyond its instinctive limitation, cannot be an epitome of the universe. Life from "birth to birth" is necessary to epitomize the universe, not merely life from birth to death. The period after death must also be used for the completion of the soul. Yeats's theories of Mask, love, and Daimon are therefore extended by his notions of the "dreaming back" and the other adventures of the soul beyond the grave.

His account of the soul's experiences after death in "The Soul in Judgment" (V, 219–240) and elsewhere in his work is complex enough. It is part of that "arbitrary, harsh, difficult symbolism" (V, 23), "all those gyres and cubes and midnight things" (CP, 444) which the poet found necessary to hold justice and reality in a single thought. Nevertheless, one idea determines this aspect of his thinking: the notion that the soul after death can gradually perfect its life. It can be slowly freed from the heterogeneity of its earthly life and, having achieved a simplicity like God's, "sink into its own delight at last" (CP, 225). "All that keeps the *Spirit* from its freedom," says Yeats, "may be compared to a knot that has to be untied or to an oscillation or a violence that must end in a return to equilibrium" (V, 226); "the individual soul is awakened by a violent oscillation (one thinks of Verlaine oscillating between the church and the brothel) until it sinks in on that Whole where the contraries are united, the antinomies resolved" (V, 89).

Man cannot come to God with empty hands, but neither can he come with the obscurity of material existence. The soul must transform all that mishmash into its own nature, draw "backward into itself, into its own changeless purity, all it has felt or known" (V, 220, 221). Dominant in Yeats's idea of the soul's adventures after death is the image of a slow patterning of the multiple and confused. What was the blind tumult of the blood must become transparent, reasonable, spiritualized. Man must bring God an incarnation of one archetype made worthy to be reabsorbed into the simplicity of fire:

> . . . body gone he sleeps no more,
> And till his intellect grows sure
> That all's arranged in one clear view,
> Pursues the thoughts that I pursue

> Then stands in judgment on his soul,
> And, all work done, dismisses all
> Out of intellect and sight
> And sinks at last into the night. (CP, 338)

How does a man accomplish this cleaning of his "dirty slate" (CP, 338)? Yeats distinguishes three stages in the spiritualization of the opaque and confused. First, man must exhaust his emotional entanglement in the events of his earthly life. The ghost must live over and over, in the limbo between earth and heaven, the experiences of his life, especially those of great passion, until finally that passion is worn out and so completed. "In the *Dreaming Back* the *Spirit* is compelled to live over and over again the events that had most moved it; there can be nothing new, but the old events stand forth in a light which is dim or bright according to the intensity of the passion that accompanied them. They occur in the order of their intensity or luminosity, the more intense first, and the painful are commonly the more intense, and repeat themselves again and again" (V, 226). This explains those ghosts in *Purgatory* who reappear at fated intervals, lighting up a ruined house, and re-enact there a scene of love and violence from their past lives.

Even such a re-enactment is not enough. Each event in life must also be followed to its source, and all its consequences explored. In this way a man can be freed from the eternal return, for "only that which is completed can be known and dismissed" (V, 230). Man must "trace every passionate event to its cause until all are related and understood, turned into knowledge, made a part of [the soul]" (V, 226). This is the meaning of the theme of remorse in Yeats's poetry. By turning back on what he has done and brooding on its effects, taking the blame "out of all sense and reason" (CP, 123), a man may exhaust his life and reach the ecstasy of liberation. On the one hand the torment of remorse; on the other hand the sudden liberation from it which comes from acceptance of the irrevocable:

> When such as I cast out remorse
> So great a sweetness flows into the breast
> We must laugh and we must sing,
> We are blest by everything,
> Everything we look upon is blest. (CP, 232)

Man must go further yet. He must experience in the limbo between death and birth all that was most foreign to him while he lived: "In so far as the man did good without knowing evil, or evil without knowing good, his nature is reversed until that knowledge is obtained" (V, 231). The experiences of the soul after death combine two incompatibles, gradual purification and the addition of more and more elements until the soul becomes an image of the universe. By proceeding in these contrary directions at once the soul can become, like God, both one and many.

One last idea will complete the description of what happens to man after death. The stages of liberation are reversals of the process by which the soul descended into matter. The string which was wound up on the bobbin of life must be unwound in order for a man to return to his original state. "Hades' bobbin bound in mummy-cloth/May unwind the winding path" (CP, 243), and after death each man must "live backward through time" (E, 366), proceeding slowly from the heterogeneous complexity of old age back through youth to childhood, and finally to the divine simplicity of prenatal existence. Like Blake ("The Mental Traveller"), Shelley ("Epipsychidion"), Wyndham Lewis (*Childermass*), or Plato ("The Statesman")[8] Yeats comes to believe that time can be redeemed by being reversed, until the beginning is reached, the point where time and the things of time can be reintegrated into eternity. The skein of love or war will be unwound, and, like Robert Gregory (CP, 142, 143), or like Crazy Jane, each man will "leap into the light lost/In [his] mother's womb" (CP, 253).

Through this long purgatorial process the soul can return to God. This return is reached by turning one's back on the center and choosing to spin on the circle as rapidly as possible, until gradually the "blood-dimmed tide" of the world is transformed into rhythmic motion and then into the fire at the center. It is

[8] Though these may have been Yeats's primary sources, the idea of a reversal of time is traditional and may be found widely among archaic peoples. See Mircea Éliade, *Le Yoga: immortalité et liberté* (Paris: Payot, 1954), pp. 186–191, and "Le Mythe du bon sauvage ou les prestiges de l'origine," *La Nouvelle Nouvelle Revue Française* (August 1955), pp. 241–243. "Or l'un des moyens de 'brûler' les résidus karmiques," says Éliade in the latter text, "est constitué par la technique du 'retour en arrière,' afin de connaître ses existences antérieures. C'est une technique pan-indienne. . . . [E]n partant d'un moment quelconque de la durée temporelle, on peut arriver à *épuiser* cette durée en la parcourant à rebours et déboucher finalement dans le Non-Temps, dans l'éternité. Mais c'est là transcender la condition humaine et récupérer l'état non conditionné qui a précédé la chute dans le Temps et la roue des existences."

"always to the Condition of Fire . . . that we would rise"
(M, 364). The aim of all souls "is to enter at last into their own
archetype, or into all being: into that which is there always"
(E, 366). The discontinuous, fragmentary, and confused must be
changed into the perfection and harmony of the cosmic dance, just
as in "Nineteen Hundred and Nineteen" the particulars of history
are thrown into the crucible of the poem and assimilated into a
unity which harmonizes diversity. The poet imitates the purification of history, and, it may be, helps it to take place, until all is
"changed, changed utterly:/A terrible beauty is born" (CP, 178).
Yeats's poems about the history of his time are part of that history
and have helped to give it whatever heroic stature it may have.
This transfiguration of history in art is only possible because the
poet believes that the change takes place in reality as well as in
imagination.

In certain eloquent passages in his work he uses the traditional
symbolism of the four elements to describe a soul or group of souls
moving from earth through water and air to the simplicity of
God's holy fire. In *Per Amica Silentia Lunae*, for example, he speaks
of a "running together and running of all to a center" (M, 356),
the slow patterning of relived memories in the afterlife until the
souls achieve perfection: "When all sequence comes to an end,
time comes to an end, and the soul puts on the rhythmic or spiritual
body or luminous body and contemplates all the events of its
memory and every possible impulse in an eternal possession of
itself in one single moment" (M, 357). The best expressions of this
movement of Yeats's thought, however, are the descriptions, in
"News for the Delphic Oracle" and "Byzantium," of souls dancing
"through their ancestral patterns" (CP, 324), coming from "the
fury and the mire of human veins" through "that dolphin-torn,
that gong-tormented sea," the realm of purification, to the condition of fire, where "Marbles of the dancing floor/Break bitter
furies of complexity" and, as in the Noh play which was one of
Yeat's sources for "Byzantium," purgatorial flames reduce everything to the ecstatic rhythm of a dance (CP, 244).

⌣

Is not this dying into a trancelike dance perilously close to the
saint's way? To be like a planet that drops into the sun is to be

"struck dumb in the simplicity of fire," and this way Yeats emphatically repudiates in "Vacillation" and "A Dialogue of Self and Soul." It is not quite true to say that "Byzantium" affirms the soul's need to lose all distinction in order to reach a God without qualities, but the poem comes close to saying this. The multitudinous experiences of the self are gradually patterned in the dance and ascend into heaven, but the emphasis is more on the unity than on the harmonized multiplicity of the result. It is rather a process of losing idiosyncrasy through fiery purification than one of adding elements to reach totality.

Yeats describes this yielding to God as the phase of total objectivity. It is characterized by "complete passivity, complete plasticity," "liquefaction," "pounding up" (V, 183). The recalcitrant particularity of person or event is smoothed out until all souls begin to flow together, and at last everything is absorbed in the undifferentiated flames. The energy needed is all on the part of God. The "golden smithies of the Emperor" "break the flood" (CP, 244), and man needs only to yield himself to the refining fire. The heroic choice of the periphery is given up for the pleasure of a fall into the center, and the self-sufficient vitality which Yeats associates with the life of swordsman is repudiated. Knowledge is now sought not for its own sake, but so that it may be dedicated to God and dismissed, for what the soul seeks is the "trance/Of sweeter ignorance" (CP, 143). Though a man may in this way find himself in God, he finds himself by losing himself and by losing what Yeats values more than salvation. Yeats is never for long willing to give up the pleasure of being this unique person here, in all the vigor of his blood. The lure of the condition of fire must be described as a recurrent vacillation away from the hard path of the swordsman toward the path of the saint. Though beginning with an apparent choice of the periphery, it is surreptitiously a choice of the center. It goes to the circle only to escape it. This way, the way around and up, will not satisfy him for long.

There is no guarantee, moreover, that a man will rise permanently to the condition of fire, however willingly he yields to its purgatorial simplifications. Some men may, but the rest almost reach the center only to be cast out to the periphery again. The account of the soul in judgment in *Per Amica Silentia Lunae* and *A Vision* is completed by the idea of rebirth. To be born again is the fate of most souls. In *Per Amica* Yeats finds a powerful image to describe man's continually frustrated attempt to reach liberation from the wheel. Like Sisyphus, each man pushes the burden of his selfhood toward liberation, and like Sisyphus he can never reach the summit, but falls back into time and is born again: "A friend once dreamed that she saw many dragons climbing upon the steep side of a cliff and continually falling. Henry More thought that those who, after centuries of life, failed to find the rhythmic body and to pass into the Condition of Fire, were born again" (M, 363).

There is, however, another means of liberation, liberation by assimilation. With this new way it is no longer a question of exhausting experience in order to dismiss it and sink into God. The soul must resume all possibilities in itself and oppose itself to God, gathering all things to itself in an attempt to rival his fullness, until ultimately there is nothing left but the single soul. The soul must not seek the dark of the moon, when it is closest to God and has no light of its own. It must attain the full of the moon, total subjectivity, and try to mirror God in its round completeness by going as far as possible from him. Such a soul:

> . . . sings as the moon sings:
> "I am I, am I;
> The greater grows my light
> The further that I fly."
> All creation shivers
> With that sweet cry. (CP, 285)

All creation shivers because it seems as if the soul is about to substitute itself for God, become "self-born, self-begotten," and absorb creation into itself. Only a being which is in no sense contingent can say, in echo of God himself, "I am I, am I."

In the state of complete subjectivity "all thought has become image . . . . All that the being has experienced as thought is visible to its eyes as a whole, and in this way it perceives, not as they are to others, but according to its own perception, all orders of existence" (V, 136). *On the Boiler* describes a reverie in which, as the poet sinks deeper and deeper into his own mind, it seems to him, first, that it contains the minds of all his ancestors, and, finally, that it contains everybody's mind. His soul recapitulates all souls. He wonders if he can balance these perfectly enough so that they will find, in him, a harmony like that of the divine dance.

If this were to happen the world would end, having been perfectly assimilated in a single soul, just as the cock of Hades would crow the world away if Solomon and Sheba were to make love perfectly and annul the antinomies. Vico presides over this intuition, for he "was the first modern philosopher to discover in his own mind, and in the European past, all human destiny. 'We can know nothing,' he said, 'that we have not made' " (E, 429).

When a man reaches the point where it seems to him that he has made everything, then he has gone as far as possible from the passive humility in which the soul returns all to God. Now the soul claims to have created all, even heaven itself. It is the opposite extreme, but accomplishes the same end. Tormented by the antinomy which sets the soul against God in eternal warfare, a man may seek to unwind all from his gyre onto the gyre of God, or he may seek to wind all things on his own bobbin. In either case he would escape from the struggle of contraries. The first way involves the abnegation of the soul's individuality and volition. The new way is an act requiring the defiant virtues of the swordsman. It seems as if in this way a man might satisfy both his needs: to be himself and at the same time to be everything.

Some admirable lines in "The Tower" express the joy which a man feels when he affirms himself as the unique creator. There is no longer any distinction between what the soul wants and what God wants. "Its own sweet will is Heaven's will" (CP, 187), and the soul is its own God. Such is the poet's sense of power that he feels even death to be his own creation: "He knows death to the bone —/Man has created death" (CP, 230). Yeats associates this attitude with the rejection of Platonism, which he calls, sarcastically, "all that talk of the Good and the One," "all that cabinet of perfection" (V, 28). In its most powerful expression he makes it explicitly a defiance of Plato and Plotinus, a defiance as scornful as Crazy Jane's rejection of the Bishop. Whereas Platonism wants to free the soul from itself and melt it into God, Yeats asserts, with "an old man's frenzy" (CP, 299), the soul's desire to make itself the origin of everything:

> And I declare my faith:
> I mock Plotinus' thought
> And cry in Plato's teeth,
> Death and life were not

Till man made up the whole,
Made lock, stock and barrel
Out of his bitter soul . . . (CP, 196)

This vision of the soul's power to assimilate all into itself is related to Yeats's theories of history and especially to his sense of the uniqueness of his own time. The revelation made through Christ was objective and led man to self-abnegation. The revelation about to come will be subjective, like the one which initiated Greek culture, and therefore it will be from within us, rather than coming from a virgin's womb. It will affirm self-sufficient beauty, not the ascetic's emaciated form, the full moon, not the dark. The new revelation will require man to take existence into his own hands rather than to yield all to God.

Yeats's play about the beginning of the Christian dispensation, *The Resurrection*, describes Christ's rising from the grave as the victory of God and the death of man. Now, two thousand years later, it is man's turn to live the death of God. He must destroy the old objective civilization, take all into himself, and out of some "rich, dark nothing" create a new civilization, a culture which will derive from man himself. It may be that man can this time go beyond previous subjective cultures and achieve total freedom. If this were to happen, the next age would be more than another turn of the gyres. It would be the fulfillment of time, the end of history, the establishment on earth of that Unity of Being which Greece, Byzantium, and the Renaissance almost attained.

The idea that the new age will be a time of violence, of wars, of Nietzschean supermen asserting their sovereign will over the herd-like masses brings Yeats momentarily to sympathize with Fascism. Fascism seems the first dawning of an age which will reconcile the freedom and form of the Renaissance with the autonomous power of all-organizing mind, and thereby bring the millennium. "Dear predatory birds," cries his spokesman, Michael Robartes. "prepare for war, prepare your children and all that you can reach . . . . Love war because of its horror, that belief may be changed, civilisation renewed" (V, 52, 53).

Sometimes Yeats speaks as if the next age would be a repetition of the last subjective age, the germination of "mummy wheat" which has been lying dormant for two thousand years (CP, 287, and V, 302), but he has a strong sense of the unpredictability of the future. History involves forces which cannot be put neatly in a pattern, and the coming revelation may be not the return of an old gyre, but the destruction of all gyres, the coming of what Yeats calls the "thirteenth cone," the time of total freedom and therefore of totally destructive violence. Such a revelation would necessarily be created by the human mind itself. That mind would be the embodiment of the brazen winged beast of laughing, ecstatic destruction and would absorb the whole world into itself. It is called the thirteenth cone because the great year is made up of twelve gyres of two thousand years apiece. The thirteenth cone will appear when all time is complete. It is in fact a sphere, the sphere of freedom from the antinomies. It is the antithesis of the human state, hence appears as the opposing gyre to man's gyre, but in itself it is a sphere (V, 193, 202, 210).

Just here Yeats's thought turns back curiously on itself and extremes meet. Complete subjectivity and complete objectivity are, it may be, exactly the same. Both are the spherical reconciliation of antinomies. Both are symbolized as phaseless spheres. The absorption of all things by the autonomous soul turns out to be exactly the same thing as the engulfing of the soul by God. In both cases the soul becomes God, God becomes the soul. To carry to its extreme either subjectivity or objectivity results in the same merger, and Yeats uses the same language to describe the objective soul liberated into God as he uses to describe the autonomy of the subjective soul which has become God can say, "I am I, am I." In the dark of the moon the soul plunges into the sun. In the full of the moon the soul shines in spherical fullness, but this light, after all, is reflected from the sun. The soul has, in affirming its independence from God, rediscovered its dependence on him. It is doomed to eternal warfare with God, a warfare which is also love, and will end only in the unimaginable midnight when the soul and its maker, like wife and husband, become one without ceasing to be distinct:

> Now his wars on God begin,
> At stroke of midnight God shall win. (CP, 286)

The soul can only know what it makes and creates the whole world, sun, moon, stars, and all, from moment to moment. On the other hand it is just as true to say that the soul needs God, as bride needs bridegroom, and cannot see or know anything unless God makes it possible:

> What can she take until her Master give!
> Where can she look until He make the show!
> What can she know until He bid her know!
> How can she live till in her blood He live! (CP, 285)

To say that the soul makes all, or that God makes the soul is to say the same thing in different ways. Yeats recognizes this when, in a footnote to the lines in which he mocks Plato and Plotinus, he makes his amends to the two philosophers and confesses his awareness that Plotinus teaches as much the divine independence of the soul as its reliance on God. The soul too is part of God, and shares the creativity of the deity (CP, 454).

Yeats's attempt to reach a Godlike completion by the addition of experiences has brought him again to affirm the whirling of the vertical gyres, God and man dying each other's life, living each other's death. He has come to see the universe as a great dance or sexual embrace. Energy flows outward from God until the physical world is almost made divine, and then flows back again toward God, only to ebb once more toward the world. The relation between the earthly and divine realms is that of inter-penetration and withdrawal, the momentary ecstasy of revelation, the irrational cry, Leda's submission to the swan, followed by the creation of a culture which slowly decays as "confusion falls upon our thought," until a new revelation comes at last. The cosmic dance, like the Indian dance of Siva, is a rhythmic fluctuation, a systole and diastole in which unity is almost lost in multiplicity, and then multiplicity almost absorbed in divine unity, and so on forever. From the point of view of the single soul this appears as an endless alternation between a melting toward God and an attempt to dissolve everything in the self. There is an eternal "conflict between Moon and Sun, or . . . between a Moon that has taken the Sun's light into itself, 'I am yourself,' and the Moon lost in the Sun's light, between Sun in Moon and Moon in Sun" (EI, 470).

Neither extreme can be reached. The soul can neither be wholly itself nor wholly God. Having almost merged with God, man is born again. Even the perfection and exhaustion of a life is no guarantee against reincarnation. Moreover, Yeats is not satisfied with the simplicity of fire. He must also have a vital personal life. Neither of these goals is attainable or desirable by itself, and the soul remains at war with God, going eternally from one opposite to the other. At the end of all Yeats's attempts to imagine escape from the wheel by an intensity of addition he must admit failure and reaffirm the circling of the eternal return: "Perhaps some early Christian . . . thought as I do, saw in the changes of the moon all the cycles: the soul realising its separate being in the full moon, then, as the moon seems to approach the sun and dwindle away, all but realising its absorption in God, only to whirl away once more" (E, 403).

⌐

. . . in a breath
A mouthful held the extreme of life and death. (CP, 329)

One movement of the soul remains to be tried. The way up and the way around have failed. Each leads back to the eternal return, and all ways to the center seem closed. The soul can but turn its back on God, and in rage, hatred, and defiance choose the circle, choose the brevity and incompleteness of earthly life, choose even its repetition for ever and ever. Now the circle is chosen not for the sake of eventual liberation but for its own sake. Man cannot will his liberation from the wheel, however intensely he tries, for, the more violent his energy, the more rapidly the present is exhausted, the wheel whirled round, and the same point on the periphery brought back once more. Freedom lies in the abnegation of any hope of reaching heaven and in the resolute choice of the opposite course. God forbids all access to his central fire, so man must, like Crazy Jane, spit in the face of the Bishop, and choose demoniacally to go as far as possible from God. The morality of obedience and purification is only a trap which makes it possible for God all the more effectively to frustrate man. Rebuffed in every attempt to approach God, man must take the only course open to him and reject God utterly. It is the choice of the way down: to will, with all one's passion and strength, the eternal repetition of earthly existence with all its tragic suffering.

Man must not secretly face God while pretending to turn away from him. The repudiation of God must be real hatred and not love in disguise. One must reject unambiguously the simplicity of fire, "learn to accept even innumerable lives with happy humility . . . and, putting aside calculating scruples, be ever ready to wager all upon the dice" (E, 398). The proud humility of this choice of "the second-best" (CP, 309) is one of the most difficult of spiritual acts. It requires the utmost of abnegation, in one direction, and the utmost of will in the other. It is an act of will which is physical in its violent affirmation of the earth and its suffering. Yeats's reversal of his instinctive orientation gives rise to some of his most powerful lines, lines which express the supreme energy necessary to transform the fated into the freely chosen. The eternal return is transformed, as in Nietzsche's thought, from "terror" to "exultation":[9]

> I am content to live it all again
> And yet again, if it be life to pitch
> Into the frog-spawn of a blind man's ditch,
> A blind man battering blind men . . . (CP, 232)

Man can free himself neither from his personal role nor from the determined course of history. Living in the twentieth century, he cannot choose to live in the Renaissance. Being old, he cannot choose to be young. Must he relax in passive despair, or must he live in the panic of the hysterical women in "Lapis Lazuli," those who are full of resentment and self-pity, and would "break up their lines to weep" (CP, 292)? There is one other possibility. With passionate intensity and with full awareness that his life is doomed to end tragically man may affirm what is fated. The fact that "things pass away" must become: "Let all things pass away" (CP, 247). To will what is fated changes man from a passive tool of history into the creator of his own destiny. In "Lapis Lazuli" the heroic men and women act their fated parts with a gaiety "transfiguring all that dread" (CP, 292). They are gay because they know that though all things end, they return again, and the same insouciance which endures their passing away will be able to build them anew.

Such men "laugh in tragic joy" (CP, 291) as they witness the coming of anarchy. They can laugh because they know that what is destroyed will be built again, to be destroyed again, and so on

---

[9] *A Vision* (1925), p. xiii.

forever. Though all things end in darkness, they return again, and if a man wills his life intensely enough it has infinite value, even though that intensity speeds the coming of death. Tragic joy sees life from the point of view of all that negates its value, sees it from the perspective of death and the eternal return, and yet affirms the infinite value of "what is past, or passing, or to come" (CP, 192). Such joy accepts a limited role, in full knowledge of its evanescence, and this intensity of will brings a momentary ecstasy which is freedom from the wheel of time.

Tragic joy is "tragic" because it means the acceptance of perhaps innumerable lives, as when Léon Bloy somewhere says: "There is but one sadness and that is for us not to be saints." It is "joy" because the willing acceptance of interminable suffering brings about a sudden liberation from the chains of determinism. Man will be free of the bondage of time only when he puts aside all calculating scruples and no longer looks upon the present moment as a means to the end of liberation. The present must be its own end, and a man must be willing to sacrifice even his chance of salvation for the sovereign pleasure of the moment. Only an instant of "zig-zag wantonness" (CP, 139) can be cut off from past and future, and therefore an image of eternity. "An aimless joy is a pure joy" (CP, 139), and "only the wasteful virtues earn the sun" (CP, 99).

Yeats experiences a number of such moments. He associates them with the joy of creativity as well as with spiritual insight, but he emphasizes more than anything else their undetermined quality and the triviality of the circumstances which surround them. These circumstances seem wholly incommensurate with the joy which leaps out of them. As he sits drinking tea in a crowded London shop his body suddenly "blazes," and it seems that he is blessèd and can bless (CP, 246, and see M, 364, 365). Such ecstasy comes from nowhere, is altogether unpredictable, and cannot be deliberately brought about. "We seek reality with the slow toil of our weakness and are smitten from the boundless and the unforeseen" (M, 340). During such lightning flashes a man seems to be "self-born, born anew" (CP, 250). This experience has no explicable meaning and no use. It cannot be made part of any utilitarian scheme of things, nor can it be absorbed into the systems of the "logic-choppers" (CP, 139). It is an end in itself. Only the man who has escaped from hatred and desire, which bind him to time, can experience such moments. The attitude which brings them about is foreign to the rational morality of those who have "marked a distant object down" (CP, 139), and make of each moment a step toward a future goal. Yeats associates tragic joy with a savage rage for destruction, as if the whole world should be burned in a moment to feed the pleasure of the present. To experience such joy a man must make a wanton sacrifice, even of his own good. He must be "like a country drunkard who has thrown a wisp into his own thatch," and so "burn up time" (M, 365). Tragic joy is creative, for it brings the delight which is worth more than everything else, but it is also destructive, for it obliterates all else for the sake of the present:

> The swan has leaped into the desolate heaven:
> That image can bring wildness, bring a rage
> To end all things, to end
> What my laborious life imagined, even
> The half-imagined, the half-written page . . .
>
> (CP, 206, and see CP, 133, 229, 457)

Such creative-destructive moments are most possible when a man is face to face with death, for all sovereign joy is secretly related to death. As long as I know that I shall survive the present moment some element of impurity remains, but if my joy comes in the teeth of death, then no element of calculation mars it. As death is that which is most to be feared, so the man who can be joyful in the face of it will triumph over the greatest obstacle, and in this way there is a "concordance of achievement and death" (L, 917). Yeats reserves his most enthusiastic praise for those who "come/ Proud, open-eyed and laughing to the tomb" (CP, 246), those who willingly meet "Black out; Heaven blazing into the head" (CP, 292). Tragic joy is the supreme experience because it is joy in the face of impossible barriers and brings the soul to its greatest intensity. This intensity gathers the antinomies of life closer and closer until finally they fuse in a moment which is beyond time or limitation. "The arts are all the bridal chambers of joy. No tragedy is legitimate unless it leads some great character to his final joy. . . . Some Frenchman has said that farce is the struggle against a ridiculous object, comedy against a movable object, tragedy against an immovable; and because the will, or energy, is greatest in tragedy, tragedy is the more noble; but I add that 'will or energy is eternal delight,' and when its limit is reached it may become a pure, aimless joy. . . . It has, as it were, thrust up its arms towards those angels who have, as Villiers de L'Isle-Adam quotes from St. Thomas Aquinas, returned into themselves in an eternal moment" (E, 448, 449).

It is not necessary to wait for the end of time or for the slow purgation of perhaps innumerable incarnations to reach liberation. After seeking it in vain through the world, Yeats has at last found what he wants at his own doorstep. He has discovered that every moment of life, in all its lowliness, can be the divine center itself. All direct approaches to God lead to further exile on the periphery. By renouncing them and choosing the circle in its poverty, Yeats finds himself miraculously at the center. This unexpected reversal is like the tangent curve in mathematics which disappears at infinity only to reappear again from the other direction. "Transdescendence," to borrow Jean Wahl's terms, turns out to be a better means of reaching God than "transascendence." Having gone far enough away from God, man finds himself in the midst of paradise. As Yeats learned from Blake, contraries meet if carried far enough. "Excess of sorrow laughs. Excess of joy weeps," and "the roaring of lions, the howling of wolves, the raging of the stormy sea, and the destructive sword" (quoted in EI, 103) are as much aspects of God as the bleating of lambs. This is the true meaning of Ribh's claim that hatred of God may bring the soul to God. Such a God is more akin to the divinity of Heraclitus, Boehme, or Nicholas of Cusa (all writers known to Yeats) than to the God of Plato or of Abraham. It is a God beyond good and evil rather than a God who establishes right and wrong. Only a God who is the coincidence of opposites allows man to reach one extreme by exhausting its contrary.

Yeats's way of expressing the paradoxical nature of such a God revives an old definition of the deity. It is a definition which first appears in a twelfth-century pseudo-Hermetic treatise, the "Liber XXIV philosophorum": "God is an infinite circle, a circle whose center is everywhere and circumference nowhere." If this is the case, then God is not the stillness and distance of transcendence, off somewhere beyond or above his creation. He is everywhere, in all his plenitude. Eternity is here and now, in each man's heart, in each grain of sand and field mouse squeaking in the corn. Every finite life or event can constitute itself as the center of the universe, the point where contraries are reconciled, the vortex where things gather as around their origin, principle, and end. "The resolved antinomy appears not in a lofty source but in the whirlpool's motionless centre, or beyond its edge" (V, 195). In the center or outside the periphery — both places come in the end to the same thing, for the center is everywhere, and either extreme has escaped the whirling. God is no lofty source. He permeates the universe, from highest to lowest, equally present in all, and Crazy Jane's unholy body, possessed by all, is the place where all things remain in God.

ᔐ

The smallest units of space and time — drop of dew, needle's eye, or gleam on water — are more than images of heaven. The indivisible concrete event actually contains eternity, and in that indissoluble unit all contraries are present in tense reconciliation. The concrete moment *is* the infinite. There and only there is God's plenitude freely available to those dwelling in time and space. "Every action of man," says Michael Robartes, "declares the soul's ultimate, particular freedom, and the soul's disappearance in God" (V, 52).

Every action — not all of them added together through a long life or lives, but each one in its particularity. The momentary event which evades the contraries must be "concrete, sensuous, bodily" (V, 214) because only the physical resists mental analysis. As soon as a thing is thought it divides into abstract opposites, for consciousness is to be identified with conflict (V, 214). Only the thing as it is lived escapes the antinomies, and if man can keep his experience on this side of the mind's diffracting power the most insignificant gesture or sensation will take on a mysterious depth and reveal itself as an irreplaceable version of totality. The least event is inexhaustible, and we can find "all the world there, as we find the sun in the bright spot under the burning glass" (VP, 836). So Yeats prays that his thought may be married to his body: "He that sings a lasting song/Thinks in a marrow-bone" (CP, 281).

Consciousness is the great enemy. It hides the infinite riches lying close at hand in every moment of life. Mental knowledge changes everything into language, number, or measure, and these are known, not the thing itself: "We know the world through abstractions, statistics, time tables, through images that refuse to compose themselves into a clear design. Such knowledge thins the blood. To know it in the concrete we must know it near at hand" (VP, 836). There are two kinds of knowledge: abstract, mediated, systematic knowledge, which reduces everything to common measure, making each man the exact copy of his neighbor, and immediate, irrational knowledge, the thought in a marrowbone. The latter is the kind of knowledge which Leda had of Zeus through the rape, and this sustains an affirmative answer to the question posed at the end of the poem: "Did she put on his knowledge with his power/Before the indifferent beak could let her drop?" (CP, 212). Against the skeletonlike dryness of abstract thought must be set the living reality of bird, beast, fish, or man. These express ultimate truth, without knowing it, in every action. "My imagination was for a time haunted by figures that, muttering 'The great systems,' held out to me the sun-dried skeletons of birds, and it seemed to me that this image was meant to turn my thoughts to the living bird. That bird signifies truth when it eats, evacuates, builds its nest, engenders, feeds its young; do not all intelligible truths lie in its passage from egg to dust?" (V, 214).

Ultimate truth cannot be known; it can only be incarnated in the action of some vital being. As soon as a man tries to know truth he cuts himself off from it, and falls into the realm of contradiction and abstraction. Only if he becomes as spontaneous as a nursery rhyme or as the bird eating, evacuating, engendering can he embody truth. When a man knows least he is closest to truth. This notion, Yeats came to feel, was his fundamental insight, and it is expressed, with serene confidence, in his last letter, written only three weeks before his death. "I am happy and I think full of an energy, of an energy I had despaired of. It seems to me that I have found what I wanted. When I try to put all into a phrase I say, 'Man can embody truth but he cannot know it.' I must embody it in the completion of my life. The abstract is not life and everywhere draws out its contradictions. You can refute Hegel but not the Saint or the Song of Sixpence" (L, 922).

Through his understanding of the richness of bodily life Yeats frees himself at last from the horror of the eternal return. His notion of repetition is significantly different from Nietzsche's. In Nietzsche it has a quasi-materialistic cause. Time is infinitely long; there is an infinite reservoir of energy; the amount of matter in the universe is finite; matter undergoes transformations according to unalterable laws; therefore in the course of time exactly the same arrangement of atoms will inevitably recur. The universe is a machine for repeating itself. In Yeats's thought, on the other hand, the eternal return is caused by the hunger of God for a perfect incarnation of the archetypes. God is an infinite potentiality, and therefore the supply of forms can never be exhausted. The Argo, the Trojan War, Leda, Helen, Hamlet, Ophelia, Lear's rage under the lightning — all these will return an infinite number of times, but each repetition will be slightly different from the others, as every performance of a play differs from all previous enactments, for "no man can do the same thing twice if he has to put much mind into it" (E, 430). Every person, object, or event, though modeled on an archetypal pattern, is unique, and the cycles of history bring back the same, but never exactly the same. Nature is a place of "unique irreplaceable individuals," not "something that can be chopped and measured like a piece of cheese" (E, 436). Every man, wave, or leaf differs from all the others, "for these things return, but not wholly, for no two faces are alike, and, it may be, had we more learned eyes, no two flowers" (EI, 288). The poet, like all men who are passionately engaged in life, may commit himself safely to the circle, for, though the things of time return, they return differently each time: "Nature or reality as known to poets and tramps has no moment, no impression, no perception like another, everything is unique, and nothing unique is measurable" (E, 435).

This affirmation of the Leibnizian principle of indiscernibles is a way of preserving the infinite fecundity of the divine source, as against the poverty of God implied in any notion of exact repetition. Infinity, for Nietzsche, lies in the temporal dimension, in the way the motion of things continues forever, bringing the same objects and events back in innumerable repetitions. For Yeats, as for Blake, there is an infinite plenitude in every object, since each is unique. Each "bird, beast, fish or man" is a special representation of the totality and therefore of God himself. For a man to assert his limited situation with enough "heroic passion," forgetting all else, is to assert at the same time every other possibility and therefore to escape from limitation. Through narrowness he attains his ultimate particular freedom and his soul's disappearance in God.

‿

Yeats has finally found what he sought in his youth, when he was deprived of his religion by Tyndall and Huxley. He has recovered an inherence of the supernatural in every corner of life. His long battle against the nineteenth-century experience of the death of God has been won, and his work as a whole is an un-expectedly successful recovery of immanence. Yeats in the end is far from Platonism, with its splitting apart of the universe and its distrust of bodily existence. If any parallel is needed for his funda-mental thought it can be found in Zen Buddhism, and the poet turns to some passages from "Zazuki's *Zen Buddhism*, an admirable and exciting book" (V, 215), when on a crucial page of *A Vision* he tries to express his sense of the divine richness of the concrete and momentary:

Passages written by Japanese monks on attaining Nirvana, and one by an Indian, run in my head. "I sit upon the side of the mountain and look at a little farm. I say to the old farmer, 'How many times have you mortgaged your farm and paid off the mortgage?' I take pleasure in the sound of the rushes." "No more does the young man come from behind the embroidered curtain amid the sweet clouds of incense; he goes among his friends, he goes among the flute-players; something very nice has happened to the young man, but he can only tell it to his sweetheart." "You ask me what is my religion and I hit you upon the mouth." "Ah! Ah! The lightning crosses the heavens, it passes from end to end of the heavens. Ah! Ah!" (V, 214, 215)

The incoherent ejaculation; the violent sense experience, filling the moment like a bolt of lightning; the calm description of a commonplace action — these self-enclosed atoms can, like a drop of dew, contain more than the widest-sweeping intellectual system, more than the soul which has multiplied experiences through many incarnations. But "man's life is thought," and, though every bird and beast may live in the immediacy of truth, man dwells most of the time in his mind. Only with difficulty can he find his way out of this realm of discontinuity, where each person is separate from other things and people. Violent experiences lift a man out of himself into union with God. God himself is irrational fury, the "there" where all opposites fuse. He can be most closely approached by man in experiences which carry the contraries to the point where they merge. So Yeats praises battle, drunkenness, rage, brutality, laughter, madness, revelry, wanton destruction or waste, the experience of great loss or failure, the moment of death. In these a man is most outside himself and can best receive the lightning bolt of revelation. They carry a man away from the rational world of distinctions and utility into the place where everything is present at once:

> . . . when all words are said
> And a man is fighting mad,
> Something drops from eyes long blind,
> He completes his partial mind,
> For an instant stands at ease,
> Laughs aloud, his heart at peace. (CP, 342)

The fool, the beggar, the warrior, and the drunken reveler are Yeats's heroes, but most of all he praises sexual experience as a means of reaching divine fusion. He is obsessed by the notion of a kinship between the erotic and the divine. Sex, which seems least like the holiness of heaven, is actually the human experience which most intensely combines the opposites and therefore is nearest to God. Yeats uses an image of shocking intensity to describe Ribh's vision of the "cause or ground" of himself and all things. The divine is a paroxysm of sexual energy where "Godhead on Godhead in sexual spasm [begets]/Godhead" (CP, 284). If God is unrestrained sexuality, the experience on earth which is most like heaven is erotic frenzy. Sensual abandon will take man to God, and sexual ecstasy is identical with spiritual ecstasy. Man most copies God in that action which Puritanism has called most distant from God, for "natural and supernatural with the self-same ring are wed" (CP, 283), and if man or beast could prolong sexual pleasure they could, like God, "beget or bear themselves" (CP, 283) instead of producing a separate offspring, and engendering another link in the serpent-circle of time. While the sexual moment lasts a man and a woman are out of time and identical with God. Hence the attempt, in the Tantric practice of *sahaja*, to prolong the erotic embrace indefinitely: "An Indian devotee may recognise that he approaches the Self through a transfiguration of sexual desire; he repeats thousands of times a day words of adoration, calls before his eyes a thousand times the divine image. He is not always solitary, there is another method, that of the Tantric philosophy, where a man and woman, when in sexual union, transfigure each other's images into the masculine and feminine characters of God, but the man must not finish, vitality must not pass beyond his body, beyond his being" (EI, 484).

Battle, drunkenness, rage, and sex are among the best means of liberation, but one other way remains, and perhaps the most important: art. Like drunkenness and sex, dancing is a means of losing oneself to find oneself, and poetry is also a way of liberation. The culmination of Yeats's experience is a mode of poetry as well as a mode of life. His best poems begin with elements which are opposed or apparently unrelated, and bring them closer and closer in the dancelike rhythm of the poem until at the climax the opposites fuse in an explosion of intensity.

This explosion is the image. Yeats's use of an image, violent in its irrational particularity, as the resolution of a poem accords exactly with his praise of the intense moment of sense experience. Both are escape from the wheel of time. Both are a reconciliation of contraries. In Yeats's best poems the effect of the climactic image exactly parallels the experience it names. In the exclamatory image, wholly concrete, wholly resisting logical analysis, all the world and all the power of poetry are present at once, just as they are present in lightning flashing across the sky and obliterating past and future. In these final images Yeats reaches the summit of his art and at the same time the summit of his apprehension of life.

In "Nineteen Hundred and Nineteen" he absorbs into the poem European and Irish history of the year after the First World War. The poem says that man can change history from determined suffering to tragic freedom only by willing its destructive violence. The verses are themselves that violence which sweeps among the dancers and offers them to the savage God. The poem ends with an image expressing an acquiescence in destructive evil which is both sexual submission and the sacrifice of artistic beauty. As beauty is given up to the brazen beast of laughing, ecstatic destruction, it is won again in the perfection of the image which expresses this sacrifice:

> . . . thereupon
> There lurches past, his great eyes without thought
> Under the shadow of stupid straw-pale locks,
> That insolent fiend Robert Artisson
> To whom the love-lorn Lady Kyteler brought
> Bronzed peacock feathers, red combs of her cocks. (CP, 208)

In "High Talk," a poem about poetry, Yeats abandons the explicable imagery of metaphor and allegory in order to break through to the absolute poetry of the irrational image, the image which means only itself. The final lines are a defiant assertion of the power of the self-sufficient image in poetry. Such an image is identical with the revelation it describes:

> . . . A barnacle goose
> Far up in the stretches of night; night splits and the dawn breaks loose;
> I, through the terrible novelty of light, stalk on, stalk on;
> Those great sea-horses bare their teeth and laugh at the dawn. (CP, 331)

In "News for the Delphic Oracle," to give a final example, Yeats rejects the pale heaven of Porphyry, a paradise of discontinuity, where Oisin, Pythagoras, Plotinus, and the other "golden codgers" "sigh for love," each in frustrated separation. He reverses the oracle's account of Plotinus' liberation and affirms that the sage was closest to divine continuity when he was wallowing in the mire and blood of the sea of generation. When he tried to free himself from the body he moved away from his goal, not toward it. In this poem, as elsewhere, Yeats defiantly rejects the way up and celebrates the way down. Here three fundamental Yeatsian themes are joined: art, sex, and the supernatural.[10] Art and sex are the best means of reaching the supernatural, and Pan's "intolerable music" is identified with Dionysiac revelry. The two together, in the last image, bring that ecstatic release which Platonic abstraction can never attain:

> . . . nymphs and satyrs
> Copulate in the foam. (CP, 324)

[10] Dorothy Wellesley said of Yeats in old age: "Sex, Philosophy, and the Occult preoccupy him. He strangely intermingles the three" (LDW, 174).

IV

T. S. Eliot

Immediate experience, at either the beginning or end of our journey, is annihilation and utter night.

Every differentiated entity has developed out of an all-inclusive whole, as the embryo grows by division of a single primitive cell. Eliot, following F. H. Bradley, calls this original unity "immediate experience."

Immediate experience is an "undistinguished unity," a "sort of confusion." Another name for it is "feeling." It is, in another phrase Eliot borrows from Bradley, "the general condition before distinctions and relations have been developed." Though every term and relation emerges from immediate experience, that unity does not vanish in the entities which derive from it. It "remains at the bottom throughout as fundamental," a "felt background" for every modification of experience.

Eliot means the word "immediate" in a spatial as well as temporal sense. Immediate experience is present in the present, with no stretching out toward a distant past or future, no separation into "there" and "here." There are no mediating bridges between one part of it and another. To say that it is "immediate" is to say that it is without parts or distinctions.

In one sense immediate experience is the only thing which is irreducibly given and not a construction. In another sense it does not exist at all. Immediate experience is nonrelational, but, since every experience of which we can be aware must be differentiated into terms and relations, it follows that "non-relational experience does not exist." Immediate experience is incompatible with consciousness, and, paradoxically, is not experience at all. Eliot returns again and again to formulations of this paradox: "no actual experience could be merely immediate, for if it were, we should certainly know nothing about it"; "in order that it should be feeling at all, it must be conscious, but so far as it is conscious it ceases to be merely feeling"; "Experience, we may assert, both begins and ends in something which is not conscious."

Our "journey" starts and finishes in the absurdity of an experience which cannot be experienced. This initial datum is neither the consciousness of an ego, nor any other form of the Cogito. Eliot's starting place is just the reverse of the Cartesian or Lockean derivation of everything from the experience of the self. Immediate experience is prior to any thinking or sensing. This means that selfhood, far from being the foundation of everything else, is an appearance, a construction, an illusion. If there is an "I" to think at all, that "I" may be sure that its existence proves its alienation from fundamental reality. "I think and feel, therefore I am only an appearance" — this is Eliot's negative version of the Cogito. "We must be on guard," he says, ". . . against identifying experience with consciousness, or against considering experience as the adjective of a subject. We must not confuse immediate experience with sensation, we must not think of it as a sort of panorama passing before a reviewer, and we must avoid thinking of it as the content or substance of a mind." In immediate experience there may be distinguished neither mind, nor selfhood, nor sensation, nor perception, nor objects to perceive, nor language to name them by, nor time, nor space, nor positions in space as "points of view" on the whole. Immediate experience is "outside of time altogether, inasmuch as there is no further point of view from which it can be inspected." Outside of time, it is also outside of space, for space too depends on the existence of points of view. Where there are no distances and distinctions there can be neither time nor space. Immediate experience, therefore, "is a timeless unity which is not as such present either any*where* or to any*one*." [1]

---

[1] The following texts of Eliot's work have been used in this chapter. Each is accompanied by the abbreviation which will hereafter be employed in citations. *The Sacred Wood: Essays on Poetry and Criticism* (London: Methuen, 1928): SW; *For Lancelot Andrewes: Essays on Style and Order* (London: Faber & Gwyer, 1928): FLA; *The Use of Poetry and the Use of Criticism: Studies in the Relation of Criticism to Poetry in England* (Cambridge, Mass.: Harvard University Press, 1933): UPUC; *Elizabethan Essays* (London: Faber & Faber, 1934): EE; *After Strange Gods: A Primer of Modern Heresy* (New York: Harcourt, Brace, 1934): ASG; *Selected Essays: 1917–1932* (New York: Harcourt, Brace, 1947): SE; *Notes towards the Definition of Culture* (London: Faber and Faber, 1948): NTDC; *The Complete Poems and Plays: 1909–1950* (New York: Harcourt, Brace, 1952): CPP; *On Poetry and Poets* (New York: Farrar, Straus and Cudahy, 1957): OPP; *The Elder Statesman* (London: Faber and Faber, 1959): ES; *Collected Poems: 1909–1962* (New

Though neither subject nor object nor any of their usual qualities can be distinguished in the dark night of immediate experience, they are all there, in an inextricable confusion of "many in one" (KE, 21). Both idealism and realism may be refuted by showing that subject and object are appearances which presuppose one another because they have been detached from their original unity in immediate experience. Any attempt to make subject the source of object or object the source of subject will fail, for both equally find their source in the unity from which they have come. Both arise spontaneously as reflexes of one another. If there is subject, there is object; if object, subject; but neither is the origin of the other. Idealism and realism are equally false and equally true. Each is a plausible appearance which develops by looking at things from a certain point of view. "That objects are dependent upon consciousness, or consciousness upon objects, we most resolutely deny. Consciousness, we shall find, is reducible to relations between objects, and objects we shall find to be reducible to relations between different states of consciousness; and neither point of view is more nearly ultimate than the other" (KE, 29, 30).

The central chapters of *Knowledge and Experience*, those on "The Psychologist's Treatment of Knowledge" and "The Epistemologist's Theory of Knowledge," show the absurdities to which thinkers are led who try to make the physical world from the mental one or the mental from the physical. "[N]o definition can anywhere be found to throw the mental on one side and the physical on the other," and "we can never construct the external world from the mental, for the external is already implied in the mental" (KE, 84); "If you will find the mechanical anywhere, you will find it in the workings of mind; and to inspect living mind, you must look nowhere but in the world outside" (KE, 154).

Eliot's philosophy is therefore a "monistic metaphysic," but the division of unity into duality which accompanies the appearance of consciousness means that reality "contains irreducible contradictions and irreconcilable points of view" (KE, 112). All these points of view — idealism, materialism, solipsism, or realism — are

York: Harcourt, Brace & World, 1963): CP; *Knowledge and Experience in the philosophy of F. H. Bradley* (London: Faber and Faber, 1964): KE. The quotations in the initial paragraphs of this chapter come, respectively, from KE, 31, 20, 19, 16, 16, 28, 27, 18, 20, 28, 15, 22, and 31.

both true and false, true relatively, false absolutely, for "the ideal and the real, the mental and the non-mental, the active and the passive . . . are terms which apply only to *appearance*" (KE, 157).

Because subject and object have their source in the same undistinguished unity, the analysis of one will always lead to a recognition that the other has been surreptitiously assumed from the beginning. By arguing that immediate experience is "the reality out of which subject and object are sorted, and upon which as background they have their meaning" (KE, 157), Eliot shows that all dualistic positions are untenable, and that *some* dualistic position is inevitable. "By the failure of any experience to be merely immediate, by its lack of harmony and cohesion, we find ourselves as conscious souls in a world of objects" (KE, 31).

A situation in which subject and object have "emerged" (KE, 20) out of the confusion of feeling is the only situation man can know, and so destined is it to be contradictory and inconsistent that any point of view is both proper and improper. All points of view are relative, but all points of view may be sustained. "Everything, from one point of view, is subjective; and everything, from another point of view, is objective; and there is no *absolute* point of view from which a decision may be pronounced" (KE, 21, 22). Only an absolute point of view could be true, but there is no absolute point of view, so all positions are relative, and therefore relatively true. As a result, "metaphysical systems are condemned to go up like a rocket and come down like a stick," and though the world "exists only as it is found in the experiences of finite centres" (KE, 168), each of these experiences "is a paradox in that it means to be absolute, and yet is relative" (KE, 166).

This is the view of reality which Eliot expounds with great subtlety and penetration in his dissertation. The essay was completed in April 1916, and so is more or less contemporary with his early poems. It may be taken as the starting point from which all his later development emerges.

The dualism of subject and object, I am arguing in this book, is a fundamental presupposition of much nineteenth-century literature, and in many important twentieth-century writers there is a return to some form of monism. Eliot's thought is striking confirmation of this idea. The return to monism is not enacted gradually through his career, but in the reasoning of *Knowledge and Experience*, his first book. Eliot's position, however, allows him to recognize the inevitability of dualism, and the way it is an alienation from reality. The monism of immediate experience is the truth, but men are condemned to the contradictions and eccentricities of dualism, or, in the sentence from Heraclitus which Eliot cites many years later as an epigraph to "Burnt Norton": "Although the Logos is common the many live as though they had a private understanding."[2] Grover Smith, Jr.'s witty paraphrase of this in terminology closer to Eliot's own is appropriate even for the initial stage of the poet's thought: "Although there is but one Center, most men live in centers of their own."[3] Though the definition of immediate experience as the still center is absent from *Knowledge and Experience*, the notion of man's imprisonment in the eccentric location of his own "finite center" is as pervasive and fundamental in the dissertation as in the early poetry.

Eliot in his preface of 1964 repudiates the dissertation and says that he is "unable to think in the terminology of this essay" or even to understand it (KE, 10). Even so, the appositeness of the epigraph from Heraclitus both to the dissertation and to the pattern of *Four Quartets* is good evidence of the continuity of Eliot's thought through all its transformations. The opposition between reality and appearance, authentic and alienated existence, may be traced throughout, from *Knowledge and Experience* to *The Elder Statesman*.

In spite of Eliot's later use of Heraclitus, Parmenides, among the Presocratics, is closer than Heraclitus to the metaphysics of *Knowledge and Experience*. For Eliot as for Parmenides the "Way of Truth" is one, an inextricable confusion of subject and object, inner and outer, which might not inappropriately be symbolized by Parmenides' sphere, "equal to itself on every side."[4] Though reality is unity, all men, by the fact that they exist as conscious selves, are alienated from it, and must travel the path of appearance, the "Way of Seeming." The truth of immediate experience cannot be experienced, nor can it be described except negatively.

[2] Fragment 2. I have cited the translation in G. S. Kirk and J. E. Raven, *The Presocratic Philosophers* (Cambridge, England: Cambridge University Press, 1960), p. 188.

[3] *T. S. Eliot's Poetry and Plays: A Study in Sources and Meaning* (Chicago: University of Chicago Press, 1956), p. 251.

[4] Kirk and Raven, *The Presocratic Philosophers*, p. 276.

The pathos of the human condition is man's inescapable exclusion from absolute experience.

⤳

This pathos, in all its complexity, is the chief subject matter of Eliot's early poetry. This poetry is a dramatization of the fact that though my private experience, just because it is my private experience, is an illusory appearance, nevertheless "what is subjective is the whole world — the whole world as it is for me — which, because it is (for me) the whole world, cannot be contrasted with anything else 'objective' " (KE, 24). Whatever exists for the self, exists as already part of the self, and the self can never encounter anything other than itself. I am because I am everything. If I should cease to exist, everything would cease with me, go out like a snuffed candle. At least this is the way it appears from the perspective of my consciousness, and what other perspective could I have? Just this notion of the validity of subjectivism is expressed in the passage from Bradley's *Appearance and Reality* which is cited in the notes to "The Waste Land" and in one of the essays on Leibniz published in *The Monist:* "My external sensations are no less private to myself than are my thoughts or my feelings. In either case my experience falls within my own circle, a circle closed on the outside; and, with all its elements alike, every sphere is opaque to the others which surround it" (CP, 75).

Like Leibniz's monad and Bradley's finite center, each mind in Eliot's early poetry is isolated from all the others. "Each expanded to completion, to the full latent reality within it, would be identical with the whole universe" (KE, 202). Each is " 'while it lasts,' the whole world" (KE, 204), and "everything, the whole world, is private to myself" (KE, 204). This assumption is a constant refrain in *Knowledge and Experience.* Even though subjectivism is only an "appearance," a prison which has appeared magically with the development of consciousness out of confused feeling, still, from the point of view of the single mind, everything is an aspect of the ego, and has no independent existence. "And outside of the objectivity of objects appearing to finite centres, there is no objectivity at all" (KE, 141); "reality exists only through its appearances"

(KE, 40). "I can know no point of view but my own" (KE, 141), and, therefore, "so far as experiences go, we may be said in a sense to live each in a different world" (KE, 149).

Eliot's early poetry is a dramatization of the situation in which there is a "circle described about each point of view" (KE, 141). The comedy of these poems derives from the fact that their protagonists are imprisoned behind barriers which are only a mirage and yet appear to be impenetrable. In "The Love Song of J. Alfred Prufrock" the reader is plunged with the first words into the spherical enclosure of Prufrock's mind. Everything exists because Prufrock thinks of it, and the bubble of his thought is never broken. The objectivity of nineteenth-century fiction, on the other hand, is guaranteed not so much by the presence of independent material objects as by the presence of more than one consciousness. The realism of fiction is a realism of intersubjectivity. Eliot recognizes this in his early essays on fiction. The "real hero" of James's novels, he says, is "a collectivity," and he describes Hawthorne's method as the ability to "grasp character through the relation of two or more persons to each other." [5] The poetry of the dramatic monologue collapses this realism into the isolation of a single mind. Henry James can find a novel in "The Ring and the Book" because it presents the same events through many points of view, but Pompilia's monologue alone, or Guido's alone, like Andrea del Sarto's, would tend to be an opaque sphere closed in on itself. This tradition of the dramatic monologue is inherited by Eliot, and explored to its limit in his early poems.

Browning's monologuists are usually speaking to someone, and the reader is conscious of the other mind throughout the poem. The presence of another person generates a sense of the substantiality of the external world. If both speaker and auditor can see the portrait of the last duchess or the statue of Neptune taming a sea horse, then these objects have an existence which would continue even if the duke were not there. Browning's monologues are further unified by being modes of the poet's own experience, and, beyond that, by being ways in which God actualizes himself in time, space, and matter. All these escapes from subjectivism disappear in Eliot:

[5] "In Memory of Henry James," *The Egoist*, 5: 2 (1918); "The Hawthorne Aspect," *The Little Review*, 5: 50 (1918).

> Let us go then, you and I,
> When the evening is spread out against the sky
> Like a patient etherised upon a table . . . (CP, 3)

No other mind is present to violate the integrity of Prufrock's isolation. He has split himself into two persons, and speaks to himself alone. Since there is no other mind to limit the expansive tendency of his finite center, his consciousness has "spread out" to engulf in its spherical bounds the sky which is the limit of his vision. Prufrock *is* the evening, and includes in his mind all the scene. In the same way, in the fourth "Prelude," the soul of the protagonist is "stretched tight across the skies/That fade behind a city block" (CP, 14), and the ring of lamplight on the stair in "Rhapsody on a Windy Night" symbolizes the closed circle of the speaker's consciousness. In another poem "the damp souls of housemaids/[Sprout] despondently at area gates" (CP, 19), and in "Burnt Norton" there is an "Eructation of unhealthy souls/Into the faded air" (CP, 179). This coincidence of subject and object is the justification for the celebrated image of the etherized patient in "Prufrock." The evening sky is like a man under anesthesia because it is enclosed within Prufrock's numbed mind and expresses the quality of that mind.

In Eliot's poems the reader never witnesses the process whereby an independent object is teased by the mind, turned this way and that until it can be assimilated and become a symbol of the mind's emotional tone. The external world is always already humanized, and for Eliot as for Bradley, "nothing is real, except experience present in finite centres" (KE, 203). There can never be for him that effacement of the mind before the solidity of objects which is so important in the poetry of Hopkins or William Carlos Williams. Eliot's difficulty is the same as that of Leibniz or Bradley: "to maintain that there is any world at all, to find any objects for these mirrors to mirror" (KE, 202). The mirroring ego has swallowed up the world, and everything exists inside the looking glass.

It follows that "objective correlatives" are not invented by the poet. They are encountered in an all-inclusive subjective realm. It is appropriate that the first image in "Prufrock" should be a personification. All the images of Eliot's early poetry are overtly or covertly expressions of the coincidence of subject and object presupposed in this figure of speech. The streets in "Prufrock" "follow like a tedious argument/Of insidious intent" (CP, 3), and the feline behavior of the fog picks up the image of the etherized patient to express Prufrock's wish that he too could curl once about the house, and fall asleep (CP, 3). Everything in the poem expresses the texture of Prufrock's mind. It has already been made over to conform to that texture.

Prufrock's paralysis follows naturally from this subjectivizing of everything. If each consciousness is an opaque sphere, then Prufrock has no hope of being understood by others. "No experience," says Bradley in a phrase Eliot quotes, "can lie open to inspection from outside" (KE, 203). Prufrock's vision is incommunicable, and whatever he says to the lady will be answered by, "That is not what I meant at all./That is not it, at all" (CP, 6). The lady is also imprisoned in her own sphere, and the two spheres can never, like soap bubbles, become one. Each is impenetrable to the other.

If other consciousnesses exist only as opaque objects for Prufrock, he has an equally unhappy relation to time and space. One of the puzzles of the poem is the question as to whether Prufrock ever leaves his room. It appears that he does not, so infirm is his will, so ready "for a hundred indecisions,/And for a hundred visions and revisions,/Before the taking of a toast and tea" (CP, 4). In another sense Prufrock would be unable to go anywhere, however hard he tried. If all space has been assimilated into his mind, then spatial movement would really be movement in the same place, like a man running in a dream. There is no way to distinguish between actual movement and imaginary movement. However far Prufrock goes, he remains imprisoned in his own subjective space, and all his experience is imaginary. It seems to be some perception of this which keeps him in his room, content to imagine himself going through the streets, ascending the lady's stair, and telling her "all," like Lazarus back from the dead. There is no resurrection from the death which has undone him, and this is one meaning of the epigraph from Dante.

Time disappears in the same way. Space must be exterior to the self if movement through it is to be more than the following of a tedious argument in the mind. In the same way only an objective time can be other than the self, so that the flow of time can mean change for that self. But time, like space, has only a subjective existence for Prufrock. As a result, past, present, and future are equally immediate, and Prufrock is paralyzed. Like one of Bradley's finite centers, he "is not in time," and "contains [his] own past and future" (KE, 205). Memories, ironic echoes of earlier poetry, present sensations, anticipations of what he might do in the future ("I grow old . . . I grow old . . . /I shall wear the bottoms of my trousers rolled" [CP, 7]) — these are equally present. There is a systematic confusion of tenses and times in the poem, so that it is difficult to tell whether certain images exist in past, present, or future. Prufrock begins by talking of his visit to the lady as something yet to be done, and later talks of his failure to make the visit as something long past ("And would it have been worth it, after all,/Would it have been worth while" [CP, 6]). Like the women talking of Michelangelo, he exists in an eternal present, a frozen time in which everything that might possibly happen to him is as if it had already happened: "For I have known them all already, known them all" (CP, 4). In this time of endless repetition Prufrock cannot disturb the universe even if he should presume to try to do so. Everything that might happen is foreknown, and in a world where only one mind exists the foreknown has in effect already happened and no action is possible. Prufrock's infirmity of will is not so much a moral deficiency as a consequence of his subjectivism. He lives in that perpetual present described in the opening lines of "Burnt Norton":

> Time present and time past
> Are both perhaps present in time future,
> And time future contained in time past.
> If all time is eternally present
> All time is unredeemable. (CP, 175)

One final avenue of escape is closed for Prufrock. The presence of the one God in Browning's characters unifies his monologues. His men and women are rays from the infinite center rather than exclusive finite centers, but the people in Eliot's early poems are bereft of God. In his essay on Leibniz and Bradley, Eliot firmly rejects the latter's idea of an "Absolute" which unifies all finite centers. The Absolute can only be imagined as the expansion of one such center to include all things and all points of view at once. "But in doing so it would lose the actuality, the here and now, which is essential to the small reality which it actually achieves" (KE, 202). Reality exists only in limitation, in the here and now.

The Absolute would be everywhere at all times, and such a vaporous blandness could not exist. "The Absolute responds only to an imaginary demand of thought, and satisfies only an imaginary demand of feeling. Pretending to be something which makes finite centres cohere, it turns out to be merely the assertion that they do" (KE, 202). If Bradley's Absolute is an unreal wish, then his universe "falls away into the isolated finite experiences out of which it is put together" (KE, 202).

The same thing can be said of the universe of Eliot's early poems. God exists in these poems, but he is unavailable, "more distant than stars" (CP, 105). He is the center of an infinite circle, and each man is his own finite center on the periphery, an unimaginable distance from the true center. Men in this situation are tormented by "hints and guesses" (CP, 199) of an ideal which they can neither reach nor bring into the "twittering world" (CP, 179) of peripheral motion. They are caught between the "sordid, dreary daily world" (OPP, 87) and the "deeper, unnamed feelings which form the substratum of our being, to which we rarely penetrate" (UPUC, 149). A metaphor of depth is as essential to Eliot's picture of human personality as it is to Matthew Arnold's. In both cases the depths are emotive, and in both cases man has intermittent contact with them through "airs, and floating echoes," "as from an infinitely distant land." [6] These glimpses come only at rare moments, moments "in and out of time" (CP, 199). To possess the depths, even in this indirect and evanescent way, is, for Eliot as for Arnold, to possess not only the true self, but also the divine source of the self, the infinitely distant center.

This insight may be mysteriously generated by man's reaction to things. Nature is not an avenue to God for Eliot any more than it is for Arnold, but internalized by the self, as things are as soon as they are known at all, objects become images, memories. These remembered images seem inexplicably in resonance with man's emotive depths, and have the power to release them. "Why," asks Eliot, "for all of us, out of all that we have heard, seen, felt, in a lifetime, do certain images recur, charged with emotion, rather than others? The song of one bird, the leap of one fish, at a particular place and time, the scent of one flower, an old woman on

---

[6] "The Buried Life," ll. 75, 74, *The Poetical Works of Matthew Arnold*, ed. C. B. Tinker and H. F. Lowry (London: Oxford University Press, 1950), p. 247.

a German mountain path, six ruffians seen through an open window playing cards at night at a small French railway junction where there was a water-mill: such memories may have symbolic value, but of what we cannot tell, for they come to represent the depth of feeling into which we cannot peer" (UPUC, 141). The emotively charged image gives us knowledge which is not knowledge, and of depths which remain unfathomably deep.

Relations to other people, once more in a way reminiscent of Arnold, can also give momentary insight into the divine center. In "The Buried Life" the "lost pulse of feeling stirs again" only when "our eyes can in another's eyes read clear" (ll. 85, 81). Eliot's poetry from "Prufrock" to "Marina" makes use of the same idea. A woman, in the tradition which, for Eliot, probably derives from *La Vita Nuova*, can be a mediator of religious illumination. The girl on the stairs in "La Figlia che Piange" is a momentary revelation; in "Marina" the father's approach toward the shore where his daughter waits is also his approach to that place "under sleep, where all the waters meet" (CP, 105); and an image in Shakespeare, "saturated while it lay in the depths of [his] memory," is commended for rising "like Anadyomene from the sea" (UPUC, 140). The image of the woman, like other images, comes from the depths and can open those depths in the beholder.

Even so, love releases only a fleeting insight into something which remains distant and unpossessed. The theme of love appears in Eliot's early poetry either as the revelation of an unattainable ideal, as in "La Figlia che Piange," or in the debased form of relations merely sexual, as in "Dans le Restaurant," "The Waste Land," or "Fragment of an Agon." Eliot's early protagonists remain unable to advance beyond their knowledge that God, though infinitely distant, does exist. The divine center is never immediately present to dissolve the isolation of the ego, nor does God's immanence guarantee the communion of one self with others. Though God exists, the self is unable to reach him except as a haunting presence-absence, no more than a "feeling which we can only detect, so to speak, out of the corner of the eye and can never completely focus" (OPP, 93). Such a self, like Prufrock, has "heard the mermaids singing, each to each" (CP, 7), but knows they will not sing to him.

ى

This is the situation to which romanticism in poetry and idealism in philosophy have brought Eliot. Each man seems destined to remain enclosed in his separate sphere, unable to break out to external things, to other people, to an objective time and space, or to God. All these exist, but as qualifications of the inner world which is peculiar and private to the self.

Perhaps it will be possible to accept this situation and make a tolerable life out of it. Instead of beating futilely against the walls of its prison, the self should turn within, inspect the contents of inner space, and try to reduce them to harmony. Though all things are only modes of the self they do have at least that form of existence. If they can be put in patterned order the self, though still isolated, will be like a little world made cunningly. A world of this sort, the universe squeezed into a ball, may not possess God as the immanent principle of its order, but it may have that secondary form of possession which is called resonance.

The notion of attunement is of great importance for Eliot. It is one reason why he gives so much value to formal design. Pattern is not so much a good in itself as it is a means of reaching the otherwise unattainable stillness at the center. The finite self is hopelessly peripheral, but if its elements can be brought into order they may vibrate, though at an infinite distance, in harmony with the divine pattern. This bringing into order is Eliot's fundamental definition of art. Though art and religion are always to be distinguished, art is not an end in itself. It can take man only part of the way toward salvation, but its reason for being is precisely to take him that part of the way. This it does through an ordering of reality which leads to an artistic stillness oriented toward the divine stillness and echoing it.

This is the meaning of Eliot's most explicit definition of the use of art: "For it is ultimately the function of art, in imposing a credible order upon ordinary reality, and thereby eliciting some perception of an order *in* reality, to bring us to a condition of serenity, stillness, and reconciliation; and then leave us, as Virgil left Dante, to proceed toward a region where that guide can avail us no farther" (OPP, 94). The passage is another version of an ambiguity basic in romanticism from Keats and Shelley to Yeats. Just as Yeats, in *Ideas of Good and Evil*, cannot decide whether the poet "creates" or "reveals" his symbols, so art for Eliot imposes pattern in order to reveal one which has been there invisibly all along. This pre-existent order is shy to reveal itself and can be brought to light only by a created order, the "musical design" (OPP, 80) of art. The pattern in reality may be there already, but it is brought into being for human beings only through art. Art is the Virgil who leads us to the borders of that realm where only Beatrice can lead us farther. Such a notion of art as design vibrating in resonance with the divine stillness is, in "Burnt Norton," admirably expressed in the image of the Chinese jar:

> Words, after speech, reach
> Into the silence. Only by the form, the pattern,
> Can words or music reach
> The stillness, as a Chinese jar still
> Moves perpetually in its stillness. (CP, 180)

Abandoning his impotent yearning to escape from himself, the poet turns inward to search within his own sphere for the patterns which may grant him an indirect possession of the divine harmony. It may be that the inner world of the isolated ego falls naturally into orderly design.

No such design can be discovered. Two qualities define existence inside the self: mobility and fragmentation. Here again Eliot recalls Matthew Arnold, for in Eliot as in Arnold a dizzy mobility and an incoherent fragmentation pervade both time and space. Eliot's early poems are full of things broken, twisted, or incomplete. Prufrock's mind is occupied by images which express his passivity and the incoherence of his revery. His visions are not of finished scenes but of bits and pieces of people: faces, hands, eyes, arms, and legs. He never faces a situation directly, but avoids it by focusing on seemingly irrelevant details. These details betray his infantile concentration on oral and tactile images. Like a baby he wants to be fed and then caressed into sleep. The fog licks its tongue; a question is dropped on Prufrock's plate; he has measured out his life with coffee spoons, and thinks of spitting out the butt-ends of his days and ways, or of biting off the matter with a smile. There is talk of tea and cakes and ices, of marmalade, of teacups, and Prufrock envies the afternoon which "sleeps so peacefully!/ Smoothed by long fingers" (CP, 5).

The inner space of "Preludes" is like that of "Prufrock." Each thing there is broken in itself, or incomplete, and the whole collec-

tion of things forms no coherent order. It is a heterogeneous
assembly of fragmentary objects thrown together in pell-mell confusion, smell of steaks, scraps of leaves and newspapers, broken
blinds and chimney pots, feet, hands, "short square fingers stuffing
pipes," and "eyes/Assured of certain certainties" (CP, 14). These
dissociated pieces of bodies express the half-conscious, half-human
existences of the city-dwellers. These feet, these fingers, these eyes
seem detached from any normally conscious mind, and to be living
a horribly detached life of their own.

"The Waste Land" is also a structure of fragments. In place of
the bric-a-brac of a single city there are bits of scenes from all times
and places, broken quotations, parodies, "fragments" shored
against ruins in the manner of a cubist collage. Like so much
other twentieth-century art "The Waste Land" works by the
abrupt juxtaposition, without connectives, of jagged pieces from
diverse contexts. The meaning emerges from the clash of adjacent
images or from a line of action which the reader creates for himself.
The poem works like those children's puzzles in which a lion or a
rabbit emerges from nowhere when the numbered dots are connected in sequence. Who is to say that the animal is really there?
It may be an illegitimate patterning of what is in fact without
pattern.

These poems are filled with broken things packed side by side,
close but not touching, each detached from the context which
would normally complete it. One assumption justifying this incoherence is a psychological one. "The natural wakeful life of our
Ego is a perceiving" (CP, 125), and what the ego perceives is
"The thousand sordid images/Of which [the] soul [is] constituted"
(CP, 14). Whether the world in itself is orderly cannot be known,
for the ego can only know itself. By the time things have been
perceived, they have been broken to pieces and disconnected from
one another, perhaps by some anarchic power in the soul itself.

Human time in Eliot's early poetry has the same qualities as
subjective space. There is often a spontaneous spatializing of time,
so that a poem exists in a perpetual present. The simultaneity of
its parts is guaranteed by the fact that past, present, and future
exist at once for the imprisoned ego. The reader must hold all the
images of a poem in his mind at once, and set each against the
others in order to apprehend the full meaning. These parts come

from many different times. They are, like Prufrock's mind, a whole constituted by memories and anticipations as well as by present sensations.

This possession of the past through memory is often said to be derived from Bergson, whose lectures Eliot heard in Paris, but it would be difficult to find two intuitions of time more different in quality. In place of the fluid continuity of Bergsonian memory, the presence of all the past in a musical harmony, Eliot dramatizes a memory which has the same disconnected quality as the present. If "Preludes" is a poem about the "thousand sordid images" of the present, "Rhapsody on a Windy Night" (CP, 16–18) is a poem about the relation of the present to the past. The speaker walks through the streets in a movement which is matched by the passage of time. (Bergson would have found distasteful this spatializing of time into linear motion.) The midnight walk by moonlight releases the speaker's memory, and things he sees on his walk recall, by a simple process of association, things from the past. Two qualities characterize the past which is released: its incoherence and the fragmentary quality of its parts. The structure of memory is exactly the same as the structure of the present, and broken images of the present call forth broken images of the past. The midnight is a "madman" who "shakes the memory" as if it were "a dead geranium," and "lunar incantations/Dissolve the floors of memory." The sight of a twist in the corner of the eye of a woman in a doorway causes the memory to throw up high and dry "a crowd of twisted things," a twisted branch, a broken spring in a factory yard. The space of memory is imposed on the space of the present, and the two are found to be perfectly congruent in their shape and content. The poem ends with "the last twist of the knife," a recognition that the future will exactly repeat the present and past.

The anarchic swarm of images which fill the ego is in constant, aimless motion. Even though the spatializing of time has in a sense stilled its movement, since "all time is eternally present," everything within the space-time of simultaneity is still moving at random, like fish in a fishbowl or snowflakes in a storm. Eliot is horrified as much as Arnold was by this violent motion and the instability it generates. The "simple soul" is born "To a flat world of changing lights and noise,/To light, dark, dry or damp, chilly or warm" (CP, 103), and the succession of sensations passing aimlessly one after the other ceases only with death.

Images of a desert, a labyrinth, the subway, and, most pervasively, of circular motion, express Eliot's sense of the swirling mobility of human existence. Prufrock's thoughts follow one another like labyrinthine streets; history, in "Gerontion," is also a labyrinth; Madame Sosostris sees "crowds of people, walking round in a ring" (CP, 54); De Bailhache, Fresca, and Mrs. Cammel, in "Gerontion," are "whirled/Beyond the circuit of the shuddering Bear/In fractured atoms" (CP, 31); earthly existence, in "Burnt Norton," is like the Circle Line of the London underground, in which people ride around in a circle, "Distracted from distraction by distraction . . . , whirled by the cold wind/That blows before and after time" (CP, 178, 179); Harry, in *The Family Reunion*, sees human life as "an endless drift/Of shrieking forms in a circular desert" (CPP, 277), or as:

> The sudden solitude in a crowded desert
> In a thick smoke, many creatures moving
> Without direction, for no direction
> Leads anywhere but round and round in that vapour — (CPP, 235)

Fragmentation, disorder, vertiginous motion — these qualities are bad enough, but there is a final characteristic which completes the disorder of the isolated ego. Though each consciousness is cut off from all other finite centers, it is aware of their existence. It includes them within itself as impenetrable nodes in the general transparency of its inner space. This is implied in the passage from the *Monadology* which Eliot cites in the refutation of solipsism in *Knowledge and Experience:* "it is as if there were so many different universes, which, nevertheless, are nothing but aspects (*perspectives*) of a single universe, according to the special point of view of each monad" (KE, 146). Awareness of the existence of other points of view gives man a further sense of his instability and insecurity, for the world, even the private world of the ego, seems to be made of the copresence of an indefinite number of points of view, "masquerades/That time resumes" (CP, 13), all crisscrossing, contradicting, jostling, canceling one another out, never able to be reconciled, "experiences so mad and strange that they will be boiled away before you boil them down to one homogeneous mass" (KE, 168). Though one mind can never have direct communication with others, it knows they are there, and this knowledge generates a sense of the disorderly assembly of all the isolated minds. The universe is not harmonized by any encompassing Absolute, but is a collection of contradictory worlds, each isolated from the others, and each rotating with its own aimless motion:

> The worlds revolve like ancient women
> Gathering fuel in vacant lots. (CP, 15)

When the ego abandons its attempt to break out of itself and turns within, it finds no harmony of any kind. Human existence is a nightmare of incoherence and eccentricity. The famous "dissociation of sensibility" is one version of this. The separation of thought and feeling which "set in" after the metaphysical poets, and "from which we have never recovered" (SE, 247), is a literary example of that fragmentation which is characteristic of human experience generally. If Tennyson and Browning, like other modern poets, "thought and felt by fits, unbalanced" (SE, 248), they were in this no different from the "ordinary man," whose experience is "chaotic, irregular, fragmentary" (SE, 247).

～

To see this is to see why Eliot so admires the good poets, and perhaps also to see the reason for his choice of poetry as a vocation. The true poet is a man who can cause the dissociated elements swarming within the ego to flow together into harmonious order. This definition of poetry is a recurrent theme in Eliot's criticism. "When a poet's mind is perfectly equipped for its work," he says, "it is constantly amalgamating disparate experience . . . . [The ordinary man] falls in love, or reads Spinoza, and these two experiences have nothing to do with each other, or with the noise of the typewriter or the smell of cooking; in the mind of the poet these experiences are always forming new wholes" (SE, 247). In another place the poet's mind is defined as "a receptacle for seizing and storing up numberless feelings, phrases, images, which remain there until all the particles which can unite to form a new compound are present together" (SE, 8). This new unity is "a fusion of elements" (SE, 9). As late as 1956 Eliot still describes poetic originality as "largely an original way of assembling the most disparate and unlikely material to make a new whole" (OPP, 119).

Fusion, synthesis, amalgamation — these are the accomplishments of the poet. Order is not a given quality of subjectivity. It must be made. The poet can put together the elements of experience and achieve a willed wholeness. There is in Eliot's criticism a fully developed individualistic theory of poetry which follows from this idea. In spite of his distaste for romanticism in all its varieties, this theory is the heir of romantic definitions of art. In his version of romanticism the origin of poetry is emotion, and the meaning of the finished product is emotive too. Though he may sometimes speak of "the pernicious effect of emotion" (SW, 13), and though he may sometimes try to distinguish between feelings and emotions, or between inartistic emotions, which are personal, and impersonal emotions, which are the substance of art, nevertheless he has a strong conviction that emotions are the origin and end of poetry. Poetry, he says in a late essay, "has primarily to do with the expression of feeling and emotion" (OPP, 8).

If Eliot's theory of art is emotive, he stresses in addition the way authentic art is the expression of the artist's personality. He often affirms the uniqueness of the good work of art and the way this derives from the uniqueness of the self. The arts "require that a man be not a member of a family or of a caste or of a party or of a coterie, but simply and solely himself" (SW, 32); "The creation of a work of art, we will say the creation of a character in a drama, consists in the process of transfusion of the personality, or, in a deeper sense, the life, of the author into the character" (SE, 137); "a dramatic poet cannot create characters of the greatest intensity of life unless his personages, in their reciprocal actions and behaviour in their story, are somehow dramatizing, but in no obvious form, an action or struggle for harmony in the soul of the poet" (SE, 172, 173).

It is easy to see why Eliot should be attracted by an affective and individualistic theory of poetry. Emotions are fluid and permeating. They can diffuse themselves throughout jagged, heterogeneous elements and reduce them to unity. A poetic drama has a "structural emotion," and its "whole effect" "is due to the fact that a number of floating feelings, having an affinity to this emotion by no means superficially evident, have combined with it to give us a new art emotion" (SE, 10). As Hugh Kenner and H. Marshall McLuhan have seen, Eliot inherited from romantic and symbolist poetry the idea of indefinite, suggestive, emotive images. Images of this sort will fuse into a phrase the substance of a poet's self, for the only constant among the elements of the self is a pervasive emotive note. The overtones of an image of the right blurred sort will proliferate indefinitely and synthesize a private world in a breath.

The emotive image will also solve the problem of communication between persons. The poet may use rational language to describe as exactly as he can his thoughts and feelings, but other people, like Prufrock's lady, will not understand him. The emotive image has a magical power to generate in the reader a feeling exactly like that which bred the image in the poet. This idea of the miraculous power of verbal images is codified in the concept of the objective correlative: "The only way of expressing emotion in the form of art is by finding an 'objective correlative'; in other words, a set of objects, a situation, a chain of events which shall be the formula of that *particular* emotion; such that when the external facts, which must terminate in sensory experience, are given, the emotion is immediately evoked" (SE, 124, 125).

This sentence has certain assumptions and implications which make it relevant only to Eliot's own theory of poetry. Like Joyce's epiphany, Eliot's objective correlative becomes a term so vague as to be useless when it is applied to all poetry or even to all modern poetry. Only in the context of one area of his thought does the concept have full meaning. It presupposes the isolation of each ego from the others. It assumes that the business of art is to express unique emotions, emotions particular and private to the artist. Though art may in the end be impersonal, it begins with feelings which are special to the artist and therefore incommunicable in the abstractions of ordinary language. Shakespeare "was occupied with the struggle — which alone constitutes life for a poet — to transmute his personal and private agonies into something rich and strange, something universal and impersonal" (SE, 117). The image in the background here is one of descent into the emotive depths of the self and return with the image. Images are pearls that were eyes. If eyes are private, pearls are public, impersonal.

They can be valued and possessed by everyone. The song from *The Tempest* is used in another text, and more explicitly, to describe the genesis of the image. Speaking of "Kubla Khan," Eliot says: "The imagery of that fragment, certainly, whatever its origins in Coleridge's reading, sank to the depths of Coleridge's feeling, was saturated, transformed there — 'those are pearls that were his eyes' — and brought up into daylight again" (UPUC, 139).

There is an apparent contradiction in this metaphor and in the idea which lies behind it. If the sea is the depths of the self, the pearl is secreted from the hidden resources of that self and can scarcely be public or impersonal. On the other hand, the objective correlative is, precisely, *objective*. It is a set of objects, a situation, a chain of events which magically corresponds to a particular emotion. The contradiction is resolved by Eliot's instinctive commitment to the notion that things only exist or have value for man when they have been made subjective. The objective correlative is not the external facts themselves, but these facts after they have "terminated in sensory experience," that is, after they have been taken within the inner space of poet or reader and transformed into mind-stuff. The pearls are not public objects in the sense that a materialist would mean this, but are things which can be experienced alternately by poet and by reader. They are bridges carrying the particular emotion to the reader and evoking it there. The verbalizing of objects might be said to represent their rich and strange transmutation, since poetry never gives the external facts but only those facts turned into words.

The way in which the objective correlative is not really objective is shown by the context of Eliot's description of it. Hamlet the man and *Hamlet* the play are failures for parallel reasons. Hamlet the man is "dominated by an emotion which is inexpressible, because it is in *excess* of the facts as they appear" (SE, 125), and the play fails because Shakespeare could not express the emotions he wanted to put into it. He was in the grip of "intense feeling, ecstatic or terrible, without an object or exceeding its object" (SE, 126), but it is the business of the artist to express emotions objectively, and so he must "intensify the world to his emotions" (SE, 126). This phrase implies that the world in itself is not as intense as those emotions, ecstatic or terrible, which art must communicate. The world must be intensified, and it is just this process which turns

external facts into the precious pearls of imagery, objective correlatives which will evoke the otherwise incommunicable emotion
in the reader.

Two apparently insoluble problems have been solved by the
theory of the emotive image. Emotive images can unify the swarm
of fragmentary elements in the ego, and they can break through
the opaque walls of the self to communicate the incommunicable.
If Prufrock were a poet the lady might understand, as the reader
does understand, Prufrock's state of mind, just as "the state of
mind of Lady Macbeth walking in her sleep has been communi-
cated . . . by a skilful accumulation of imagined sensory impressions" (SE, 125).

Two additional limitations of Eliot's initial situation are avoided
by his emotive theory of poetry. If the wakeful ego is separated
from other people it is also separated from itself. Like Matthew
Arnold once again, Eliot believes that the bewildering series of
distractions and fancies which makes up the conscious life of an
ordinary man is an exclusion from the true self. Like Arnold he
places that self deep beneath the surface of everyday consciousness.
The only true deep-buried self is emotive in substance, and the
core of selfhood is those deeper, unnamed feelings which form the
substratum of our being. It is the business of poetry to name these
unnamable feelings, to drag them out of the dark abyss of selfhood
into the light of day. In doing so poetry goes beyond integration
of the superficial contents of consciousness, and beyond the communication of that unity to others. It brings surface and depths
together and gives a man possession of his true self.

The emotive center of selfhood is the "unknown, dark *psychic
material* — we might say, the octopus or angel with which the poet
struggles" (OPP, 110). The intolerable wrestle with words and
meanings is the effort necessary to bring this psychic material to
the surface and embody it in words. In itself the emotive center
can scarcely be glimpsed by the conscious mind, much less possessed. Only when it is embodied in a poem does it belong to the
daylight world. Matching the notion of the objective correlative
as a means of communication between minds, there is the notion
that the poetic image is a means of self-possession. In authentic
poetry the deep-buried self, octopus or angel, is given an objective
existence which replaces with the precision of words and rhythms

the inarticulate sense that there is something lurking in the darkness. The poet, in a metaphor borrowed from Gottfried Benn, is said to have "something germinating in him for which he must find words; but he cannot know what words he wants until he has found the words; he cannot identify this embryo until it has been transformed into an arrangement of the right words in the right order. When you have the words for it, the 'thing' for which the words had to be found has disappeared, replaced by a poem" (OPP, 106).

In bringing the hidden self from the deeps, poetry reveals the divine power which underlies the self. To do this is to go beyond the haunting sense of an unattainable God which torments Prufrock. The "unknown, dark psychic material" is divine as well as human, and to bring it to light is to bring God within the sphere of the self as an irradiating presence, emotive like the deep-buried self and, in conjunction with that self, fusing the disparate elements of consciousness into a harmonious whole. Here again Eliot's language is curiously like Arnold's, in spite of his attack on Arnold in *The Use of Poetry and the Use of Criticism* for confounding poetry and religion. For Arnold, possession of the buried life gives a man knowledge of "The hills where his life rose,/And the sea where it goes" ("The Buried Life," ll. 97, 98). To reach before the beginning and after the ending is to reach the eternity which surrounds time. Eternity may also be reached in subterranean depths. Horizontal and vertical dimensions coincide if followed far enough, and to reach one limit is simultaneously to reach the other. Like Arnold's momentary possession of the buried life, Eliot's instant in and out of time, the moment of "sudden illumination" (CP, 194), coincides with the revelation achieved by "The backward look behind the assurance/Of recorded history, the backward half-look/Over the shoulder, towards the primitive terror" (CP, 195). Angel and octopus may be the same, and the beginning and end of time are the same too: "And the way up is the way down, the way forward is the way back" (CP, 196). On all sides the opaque sphere of the self is surrounded by God, and a poet has the unique power to go down or up, forward or back, to reach the place where God is present. He can then return to embody his illumination in rhythmic language. "What I call the 'auditory imagination' is the feeling for syllable and rhythm, penetrating far below the conscious levels of thought and feeling, invigorating every word; sinking to the most primitive and forgotten, returning to the origin and bringing something back, seeking the beginning and the end" (UPUC, 111).

This is Eliot's ambitious program for a poetry which will express the unique emotions of a unique individual. Though emotions seem as irrevocably imprisoned within the self as the other elements of the private world, they turn out to provide an escape from the enclosures and disabilities of the solitary ego. Emotive language will unify the chaos within the self, and put it in communication with other people, with the buried self, and with God.

᠊ᢏ

The attempted accomplishment of this program for poetry is less impressive than the project itself. Only the poetry written prior to "Gerontion" and "The Waste Land" remains limited to the assumptions of subjective idealism, and themes of fragmentation, of isolation, and of the inability to reach other people or God are dominant there. In the early poetry irony is the only mode of fusion which is successful, and irony becomes even more pervasive in the volume of 1920, the volume which contains the Sweeney poems, "Burbank with a Baedeker: Bleistein with a Cigar," and the poems in French.

Irony, whether imitated from Jules Laforgue or not, is a synthesis which, bringing things together, recognizes their separateness. The disparates remain disparate, the fragments fragmented, and unity emerges from a clash of these which affirms the ideal and at the same time admits the unattainability of the ideal. The images in such poems have that powerful suggestiveness which Eliot wants, but the pervading emotions are distaste for a sordid reality and poignant longing for the lost ideal. "Lune de Miel," to give one example, sets the reality of the bedbug-bitten honeymooners at Ravenna against Saint Apollinaire in Classe which "tient encore/Dans ses pierres écroulantes la forme précise de Byzance" (CP, 40). This method of affirming unity in disunity through irony persists throughout Eliot's early poetry, from Prufrock's mermaids juxtaposed against the tea and cakes and ices to Apeneck Sweeney set against Agamemnon and the Convent of the Sacred Heart. Irony harmonizes only to admit disharmony.

The same admission of disharmony is present in Eliot's picture of the poet making "new wholes" of the experiences of falling in love, reading Spinoza, hearing the typewriter, and smelling the cooking. These *are* a miscellaneous lot, and it is hard to imagine a fusion of them which would be other than wry or incongruous. Eliot's choice of such random examples betrays his feeling that experience is in fact chaotic, and that its elements are only harmonized through being yoked by violence together. The metaphysical poets are admired by Eliot because of their power to bring the actually disparate into ironic conjunction. They "possessed a mechanism of sensibility which could devour any kind of experience" (SE, 247).

Eliot's individualistic theory of poetry does not in practice achieve the goals he sets for it. The inner world remains a "heterogeneity of material compelled into unity by the operation of the poet's mind" (SE, 243), and the communication with other people, with the central self, and with God remains only communication at a distance, not true possession. In Eliot's poetry and criticism there is scarcely a trace of belief in the elaborate system of analogical participation which unified the hierarchical universe of the Middle Ages and the Renaissance. The structure of correspondences, as used by Donne, Herbert, or Vaughan, presupposes an interpenetration of heaven and earth, but Eliot tends to see the metaphysical poets as artists like Baudelaire, Laforgue, and himself, writers who ironically unify the disparate through private harmonies of feeling. Through the utmost efforts of his rhythmical skill the poet, in Eliot's view, can at best create an emotive image which vibrates in rapport with the hidden emotions of other people, with the hidden self, and with the hidden God. Possession through resonance is no real possession. What is desired remains distant and unobtainable. Within its opaque walls the soul is as fragmented and as isolated as ever. Only if it could in some way expand those walls to include within itself what now appears inalterably exterior could it find a way out of its solitude.

⤸

Just such an escape is already implicit in certain tendencies of Eliot's early poetry and criticism as well as in his dissertation. By extending these directions of his thought he transforms the idealism of the solitary self into what might be called a "collective idealism." The basic presupposition of this change is the assumption that everything which exists at all for man has a mental existence. How could he otherwise know of it? This slips over into the idea that what exists outside the sphere of the individual ego is not an objective world of time, space, and matter, but an impersonal subjective realm, a realm in which everything already has a mental existence. If the separate ego could bring itself to sacrifice its centrality it might dissolve the walls of its prison and find itself in possession of a universal kingdom of subjectivity, a kingdom as wide as all time and space. The self by abnegating itself might achieve that all-inclusiveness it seeks. Through self-effacement, infinite expansion, but only if a collective consciousness is already there waiting to be entered.

The strategy of this dissolution into the whole is already implied in the refutation of solipsism in *Knowledge and Experience*. Just as idealism and materialism are both equally true and false, according to one's point of view, so each mind is a private world and at the same time a perspective on a social world which it interpenetrates. Other minds are both hidden and available, depending on how one looks at them, and this is another version of the paradoxical relativism which runs through Eliot's thesis. The way in which one side of the paradox can be exploited is explored in "Tradition and the Individual Talent." All Eliot's later prose and verse attempts to define this approach further and to carry it out in practice.

"Tradition and the Individual Talent" is in two sections. The place of individual talent in the writing of poetry depends on the definition of "tradition" given in the first part of the essay. Tradition is the presence in an all-inclusive subjective space of the whole history of a culture. There is a "mind of Europe," a mind much more important than the poet's private mind, and this collective mind "abandons nothing *en route*." It "does not superannuate either Shakespeare, or Homer, or the rock drawing of the Magdalenian draughtsmen" (SE, 6). If such a mind exists, then a man can write authentic poems only by obliterating his separate ego and participating in the personality of his culture. The poet can "procure the consciousness of the past" (SE, 6) only by self-effacement, and must make "a continual surrender of himself as he is at the moment to something which is more valuable." For this reason, "the progress of an artist is a continual self-sacrifice, a continual extinction of personality" (SE, 6, 7).

The sense of history attained through this self-sacrifice apprehends the past of Europe as a spatial panorama containing in ordered interdependence all expressions of that culture from the beginning to the present. "[T]he historical sense involves a perception, not only of the pastness of the past, but of its presence; the historical sense compels a man to write not merely with his own generation in his bones, but with a feeling that the whole of the literature of Europe from Homer and within it the whole of the literature of his own country has a simultaneous existence and composes a simultaneous order" (SE, 4). Just as the private ego possesses its past and future in a perpetual present, so the mind of Europe is a timeless whole, the "present moment of the past" (SE, 11).

Two complementary facts may be deduced from the nature of this collective mind. No individual poet has his complete meaning alone. "His significance, his appreciation is the appreciation of his relation to the dead poets and artists. You cannot value him alone; you must set him, for contrast and comparison, among the dead" (SE, 4). On the other hand, if the individual work has value only as it fits into the timeless pattern of a culture, that pattern is altered in all its parts by the introduction of an authentic work. The collective mind is a living whole. Each part shares the vitality of the other parts and is changed by any change in them. Eliot's statement of this idea is elegant and precise. It leaves no corner of validity for the poet who affirms the independence and idiosyncrasy of his ego: "what happens when a new work of art is created is something that happens simultaneously to all the works of art which preceded it. The existing monuments form an ideal order among themselves, which is modified by the introduction of the new (the really new) work of art among them. The existing order is complete before the new work arrives; for order to persist after the supervention of novelty, the *whole* existing order must be, if ever so slightly, altered; and so the relations, proportions, values of each work of art toward the whole are readjusted; and this is conformity between the old and the new" (SE, 5).

The ideal order made of all the works of art is not a fiction or a convention, not an "ideal" existing only in the mind of someone who unifies the works in his imagination. It is independent of the mind of any individual, and the private ego can reach it only by self-surrender. It existed before each man was born and will continue to exist after his death. A man can only isolate himself from it, or melt into it. Eliot's language strongly affirms the independence of the collective mind. The new work of art does not have to be recognized by critics and readers in order to join the previous body of works. As soon as it is written it "spontaneously" adds itself to them, and the order and proportions of the old order are instantaneously altered by the new work. This readjustment does not depend on the evaluations of any individual or group. It just happens, magically, in a moment. It occurs because the ideal order has its own life, a life independent of any private ego, though it is in its qualities much like a private ego enormously expanded.

If the notion of the objective correlative makes sense only in the context of an individualistic and emotive theory of poetry, another celebrated description of the poetic process in Eliot's prose is valid only as a corollary of the idea that a true poem takes its place in an impersonal subjective order. This other theory of art, the notion of the poet as catalyst, seems to follow naturally from the failure of the first theory to provide a way out of the prison of the isolated ego. According to this alternative conception, "poetry is not a turning loose of emotion, but an escape from emotion; it is not the expression of personality, but an escape from personality" (SE, 10). If poetry is still to be seen as expressing emotions, these now must inhere in the words of the poem and be embodied there. They have nothing to do with the private emotions of the poet, for there should be a complete separation between "the man who suffers and the mind which creates" (SE, 8), and "the emotion of art is impersonal" (SE, 11). This impersonality is achieved by a turning inside-out of the enclosed sphere of the self so that its private emotive core disappears and the poet's consciousness enters the surrounding medium of the collective mind. Only in this way can the poet succeed in "surrendering himself wholly to the work to be done" (SE, 11).

The work to be done is a new fusion of elements already existing in the collective mind. In this sense the poet's mind is a catalyst. Though nothing happens in the writing of a poem to the poet's private mind, and though poetry is not self-expression or self-validation, the mind of a poet is a neutral element whose presence is necessary to the fusion of cultural elements which makes a new poem. This gives a fresh meaning to the description of the poet as "a receptacle for seizing and storing up numberless feelings, phrases, images, which remain there until all the particles which can unite to form a new compound are present together." The numberless feelings, phrases, images are not, in this new theory, private to the in-turned ego. They are floating in a universal subjectivity, waiting for the poet's mind to synthesize them into the new unity of the poem. "[T]he mind of the mature poet differs from that of the immature one . . . by being a more finely perfected medium in which special, or very varied, feelings are at liberty to enter into new combinations" (SE, 7). In this way the poet is like a shred of platinum, the catalyst in whose presence gases unite to form sulphuric acid, while the platinum remains "inert, neutral, and unchanged" (SE, 7). The idea of the independence of elements in an impersonal realm is once more affirmed in the phrase "are at liberty to enter into new combinations." If the effect of the platinum is quasi-magical, the fusion of elements is no less so. They seem hungry to flow together to form a harmony embodying the impersonal emotion of art. When the mind of the poet is turned inside-out into the mind of Europe he becomes a "medium," with a power of combination almost like that of a man in a trance who speaks in many tongues. In another sense of the word, the mind of Europe, with all its heritage of ideas, images, and feelings, is the medium which the poet assembles in a new order. "[T]he poet has, not a 'personality' to express, but a particular medium, which is only a medium and not a personality, in which impressions and experiences combine in peculiar and unexpected ways" (SE, 9).

The derivation of this theory of poetry from one fundamental assumption appears clearly here. This assumption is the idea that it is impossible to reach an independent objective world from any human starting point. This notion leads to the disappearance of that intercourse of subject and object which generates the action of so much romantic poetry. Everything is already subjective for Eliot, and the mind can never bump into anything other than itself, anything stubbornly recalcitrant to its devouring power to assimilate everything. The mind cannot watch itself turning things into feelings or images. By the time it encounters them they already exist in this form. Eliot's impersonal theory of poetry merely substitutes a universal mind for a private one. In neither case can there be an encounter with anything other than mental.

Several aspects of this reduction of all to mind may be noted. One is the absence in Eliot of that process, so important in Keats or Stevens, whereby the imagination works on an independent object and finally raises it to the status of a symbol by taking it into the mind. All the symbols exist from the beginning for Eliot. Novelty is only a new arrangement of them, and one of the sources of Eliot's distaste for romanticism is his rejection of the idea that novel images might be introduced into literature by an original poet. The romantic idea of progress in poetry puts the Rimbaudian *voyeur* out at the frontiers of experience. Artists are the antennae of the race. Against this Eliot sets his notion of a stasis at best, for the mind of Europe abandons nothing en route, and "this development, refinement perhaps, complication certainly, is not, from the point of view of the artist, any improvement" (SE, 6).

The progress of poetry may even be seen as an odd kind of deterioration, for "when a great poet has lived, certain things have been done once for all, and cannot be achieved again" (NTDC, 114). "Not only every great poet, but every genuine, though lesser poet, fulfills once for all some possibility of the language, and so leaves one possibility less for his successors" (OPP, 66). This notion is also central in Ezra Pound's theory of poetry. Even though the possibilities of poetry may be inexhaustible, and even though "every great poet adds something to the complex material out of which future poetry will be written" (NTDC, 114), still every new poet reduces by that much the opportunities for the future. Now that the *Divine Comedy* and *King Lear* have been written, no new poet can write them again, and all forms, genres, or conventions ultimately exhaust themselves, leaving the mind richer in one sense, but, from the point of view of a young poet, impoverished. The feeling that we live in a late age of literature, when there is relatively little left to be done, runs through all Eliot's criticism. A poet like William Carlos Williams would bid Eliot turn his senses to the inexhaustible richness and novelty of nature, but this is just what Eliot cannot do, and for good reasons of his own.

Another quality of Eliot's descriptions of the poetic process is the relative absence of any recognition that poetry is written with words. Poetry is made of "feelings, phrases, images." Eliot makes no distinction here between words and emotions. The process whereby a feeling is turned into a phrase need never be shown because the naming of things has already happened. The mode of existence of the mind of Europe is chiefly verbal, and it is language which the poet inherits when he surrenders himself to that mind. Another way to say that everything is subjective is to say that everything has already been named. Language may therefore be taken completely for granted. Within the collective subjectivity names are married to feelings and images, and the relation of language to the mind, in one direction, and to things, in the other, need never be questioned. Eliot suffers none of that anguished doubt of the validity of language which accompanies dualistic thought and is central in so much modern poetry and philosophy. Sometimes he may speak of the decay of language, but that decay is part of the general disintegration of modern culture. The ancient whole is fragmenting. Each man thinks his own eccentric thoughts and makes his own eccentric use of words. This is not Eliot's problem with words, since he belongs, or wants to belong, to the old order. When he tells how "words strain,/Crack and sometimes break, under the burden,/Under the tension, slip, slide, perish,/Decay with imprecision, will not stay in place,/Will not stay still" (CP, 180), he is describing, not the difficulty of naming things, but the difficulty of putting named things in such a pattern that they will reach beyond time and space. Within the collective mind of Europe the coincidence of consciousness, word, and feeling can be assumed without question, and all the names, in Greek, Latin, Sanscrit, French, Italian, or German, are part of the poet who has the indispensable "historical sense."

⌇

The theory of poetry worked out in "Tradition and the Individual Talent" is the basis of most of Eliot's literary criticism. Those essays which have done so much to form the taste of twentieth-century readers covertly assume that literature exists in a universal mental space. Everywhere latent is the idea of a unified whole made up of a complex network of relations. The individual part has meaning only in the way it fits into the parts around it. This idea is present in *Knowledge and Experience*, as when Eliot says that "the world, so far as it is a world at all, tends to organize itself into an articulate whole" (KE, 82), or in the statement that "the reality of the object does not lie in the object itself, but in the extent of the relations which the object possesses without significant falsification of itself" (KE, 91), or in the definition of the goal of science as "a system of terms in relation, of terms the nature of each of which would be constituted by its place in the system; which would be completely definable by their position, and which would have no characteristics which could be isolated from the system" (KE, 73). This is Eliot's version of the concept of organic unity, so influential today, and it may be seen operating as a basis of judgment in all the contexts of his criticism. It is important to remember the idealist associations of this notion in Eliot. Such attachments give the idea a meaning very different from the positivistic or psychologistic versions more current in America. It is possible to believe that poetry should be an organic unity without believing that the mind of a culture is a "collective personality" (OPP, 58) with an independent existence of its own.

One mode of organic wholeness is the individual poem. The music of a poem arises from the fact that its words work rhythmically together like figures in a dance. A single word in a good poem is a node concentrating in itself all the relations it has to the words around it. It is like a point in the middle of a spider web toward which the filaments converge. "The music of a word is, so to speak, at a point of intersection: it arises from its relation first to the words immediately preceding and following it, and indefinitely to the rest of its context; and from another relation, that of its immediate meaning in that context to all the other meanings which it has had in other contexts, to its greater or less wealth of association" (OPP, 25).

A poem is good or bad depending on whether it has this kind of unity. "Kubla Khan" is rejected on the grounds that the material, however "inspired," has not been composed into a whole. "The poem has not been written. A single verse is not poetry unless it is a one verse poem; and even the finest line draws its life from its context. Organisation is necessary as well as 'inspiration' " (UPUC,

139). A poetic drama, like a lyric poem, must have "a unity of inspiration," "an emotional unity," "a dominant tone" (SE, 134, 190). Romantic comedy is rejected because it is "a skilful concoction of inconsistent emotion, a *revue* of emotion," "a concatenation of emotions which signifies nothing" (SE, 190). The *Divine Comedy*, on the other hand, "is a whole; . . . you must in the end come to understand every part in order to understand any part" (SE, 219).

The next larger context is that of all the work of a single writer. Eliot's essays on the Elizabethan and Jacobean dramatists presuppose the idea that all the works of a dramatist form a whole, an *œuvre*. Shakespeare is a supreme writer partly because his plays form an elaborate pattern. His work is "*one* poem" (SE, 179). The reader must know all the plays in order to understand any one of them, and taken together they are the gradual exploration of the themes which most concerned their author. "What is 'the whole man' is not simply his greatest or maturest achievement, but the whole pattern formed by the sequence of plays; so that we may say confidently that the full meaning of any one of his plays is not in itself alone, but in that play in the order in which it was written, in its relation to all of Shakespeare's other plays, earlier and later: we must know all of Shakespeare's work in order to know any of it" (SE, 170).

The idea that a poet expresses himself in his poems must be understood in the context of these larger and smaller wholes, organic unities within organic unities, spheres within spheres. Genuine poets create in their works "small worlds," "drawn to scale in every part" (SE, 137). Marlowe and Jonson, like Shakespeare, were such poets. Their plays "were a view of life; they were, as great literature is, the transformation of a personality into a personal work of art, their lifetime's work, long or short" (SE, 192). Beaumont and Fletcher, on the other hand, are meretricious because they lack this irradiating unity. The blossoms of their imagination are "cut and slightly withered flowers stuck into sand" (SE, 135), and the "evocative quality" of their verse "depends upon a clever appeal to emotions and associations which they have not themselves grasped; it is hollow. It is superficial, with a vacuum behind it" (SE, 135). In the same way Massinger's personality "hardly exists." "He did not, out of his own personality, build a world of art, as Shakespeare and Marlowe and Jonson built" (SE, 192).

Outside the *œuvre* of the single poet is a medium surrounding it on every side and penetrating it through and through: the literary tradition. The notion of literary history as the growth of a living organism is everywhere assumed in Eliot's criticism. This organism is independent of the individuals who make it up and uses them to bring about developments which are suprapersonal necessities of its own.

The fullest working out of these assumptions is in the essays on English drama. The playwrights from Marlowe to Shirley were engaged, without being aware of it, in the exploration and gradual exhaustion of a particular form of drama. The work of each authentic dramatist forms a little world complete in itself, but the little worlds are planets within a larger system. This is perhaps most succinctly expressed in a curious metaphor about versification. "The development of blank verse may be likened to the analysis of that astonishing industrial product coal-tar. Marlowe's verse is one of the earlier derivatives, but it possesses properties which are not repeated in any of the analytic or synthetic blank verses discovered somewhat later" (SE, 101). The metaphor implies that blank verse was a pre-existing entity, one potentiality of the mind of Europe. The Elizabethan and Jacobean dramatists did not invent blank verse and its variations. They were servants of the development of something outside themselves, something transindividual, just as a system of geometry may be thought of as having always had a potential existence which is rendered actual by the mathematician who "invents" it. What this metaphor implies for blank verse is equally assumed for every other aspect of literature. A "mature literature" has "a history behind it: a history, that is not merely a chronicle, an accumulation of manuscripts and writings of this kind and that, but an ordered though unconscious progress of a language to realize its own potentialities within its own limitations" (OPP, 55). Like blank verse a language has a life of its own and makes particular poets the unconscious servants of its urge to realize itself.

The notion that European literature forms a living whole is applied in detail in Eliot's judgments of individual poets or movements. The basic tools of criticism are "comparison and analysis" (SW, 37). Comparison in fact predominates in Eliot's criticism.

His constant habit is to set one writer against another, or to place a writer in his cultural context. The unstated presupposition is that the works of all the writers are, or ought to be, present together in the same medium, for "European literature is a whole, the several members of which cannot flourish, if the same blood-stream does not circulate throughout the whole body" (OPP, 72, 73). Virgil is a classic because he has a complete literature behind him. "[H]e was, in a sense, re-writing Latin poetry — as when he borrows a phrase or a device from a predecessor and improves upon it" (OPP, 64). The dissociation of sensibility was a catastrophe which happened within the mind of Europe, and individual poets were the victims of an impersonal process. Eliot's ancient animus against Milton, softened in the later essays, is not just a distaste for Milton's poetry. Milton represents the moment in history when certain disasters happened to the mind of Europe, and Eliot most dislikes him for the effect he had on later poetry. He stands as a "Chinese Wall" (SE, 100), forbidding return to the unified sensibility of Donne and his contemporaries, who felt their thought "as immediately as the odour of a rose" (SE, 247).

Milton, however, at least existed within the mind of Europe, even though he did that mind irreparable damage. Eliot's deepest abhorrence is reserved for those eccentric poets, heretics all, who detached themselves from the collective mind and presumed to think and feel for themselves. The great poet is "one who in his poetry re-twines as many straying strands of tradition as possible" (UPUC, 77). Wordsworth is superior to Landor because Wordsworth has a significant "place in the pattern of history," while Landor is "only a magnificent by-product" (UPUC, 79). The good poets live at a time when culture is unified; so Dante "thought in a way in which every man of his culture in the whole of Europe then thought" (SE, 203). Ideas in poetry are not valuable in themselves, but are of use only if they are shared with a culture, and can guarantee a community of outlook. Blake, though a poet of genius, illustrates the deplorable "crankiness, the eccentricity, which frequently affects writers outside of the Latin traditions" (SE, 279). "What his genius required, and what it sadly lacked, was a framework of accepted and traditional ideas which would have prevented him from indulging in a philosophy of his own, and concentrated his attention upon the problems of the poet" (SE, 279, 280). As for writers like Hardy and Lawrence, Eliot reserves for them the un-measured condescension and disdain which makes *After Strange Gods* his most intransigent polemic. Such writers represent the "tendency of a nimble but myopic minority to progenerate hetero-doxies" (UPUC, 101). Joyce is "the most ethically orthodox of the more eminent writers of [Eliot's] time," but Lawrence is "an almost perfect example of the heretic" (ASG, 41). Yeats's verse "is stimu-lated by folklore, occultism, mythology and symbolism, crystal-gazing and hermetic writings" (ASG, 48), and Hardy is "an interesting example of a powerful personality uncurbed by any institutional attachment or by submission to any objective beliefs" (ASG, 59).

In Eliot's estimations of Virgil, Dante, Hardy, or Lawrence his idealist assumptions are particularly evident. There is no notion that a poet might make new discoveries by turning his senses toward an objective world. Poetry for Eliot is almost entirely incorporeal. The reader of his criticism is rarely reminded that poets have bodies and are impinged upon by the tangibility of external things. This perhaps explains his claim that clear visual imagery is essential in good poetry. Dante is a supreme poet in part because of his "peculiar lucidity" (SE, 201), a lucidity associated with his use of "clear visual images" (SE 204). This "visual imagination" is one reason for his universality, since "speech varies, but our eyes are all the same" (SE, 205). On the other hand, Eliot deplores the "opacity, or inspissation of poetic style" which set in "throughout Europe after the Renaissance" (SE, 202). This obscurity in litera-ture shows that the unity of the European mind was dissolving. Eliot's discussions of poetry jump all the way from visual imagery to the emotions it expresses, and suggest that poetry should be made exclusively of these two elements. Dante's poetry is "the one uni-versal school of style for the writing of poetry in any language" (SE, 228, 229), not only because his poetry is composed of sharp visual images, but because these images are used to express "a complete scale of the *depths* and *heights* of human emotion" (SE, 229).

There is little recognition in Eliot's poetry or criticism that men have other senses beside eyesight, and that words may express the experiences of these senses. There is little of that tactile or kines-thetic imagery so pervasive in the work of Browning or William

Carlos Williams. Such imagery constantly reminds the reader that the poet has a muscular body engaged in the world, at grips with something other than itself, but Eliot's muscles are slack. He regards passively, with his mind's eye, a swarm of ideal images which have sharp outlines but are disembodied, detached from the spectator's consciousness, like two-dimensional figures on a screen. Eliot's criticism is the expression of a judicious mind locked in his study, surrounded by books, making discriminations, comparisons, and abstractions in a region of pure subjectivity.

This criticism is least impressive when the process of abstraction reaches a point where judgments and comparisons seem to be fencing in a void. The reader gasps for air, as with Arnold's criticism, and longs for a breath of tangible reality. Eliot discusses at length, for example, the way poetry must be "the precise expression of finer shades of feeling and thought" (OPP, 59), without specifying in the least the objects of these feelings and thoughts. In another essay he affirms that great poetry must have "Universality," "Abundance, Amplitude and Unity" (OPP, 251, 250), leaving the perplexed and exasperated reader to ask: "Universality, Abundance, Amplitude, and Unity of *what?*" Or he gets trapped in the sequence of his definitions and is led farther and farther into a realm where verbal distinctions multiply themselves and could proliferate indefinitely: "The important thing is that if fiction can be divided into creative fiction and critical fiction, Jonson's is creative. That he was a great critic, our first great critic, does not affect this assertion. Every creator is also a critic; Jonson was a conscious critic, but he was also conscious in his creations. Certainly, one sense in which the term 'critical' may be applied to fiction is a sense in which the term might be used of a method antithetical to Jonson's" (SE, 131). "Creative," "critical," "conscious," "unconscious" — the terms multiply in a vacuum and have no more precision than Arnold's use of "creative" and "critical" in "The Function of Criticism at the Present Time," or than do his "reason," "will of God," "current of true and fresh ideas," and "the best that is known and thought in the world."

Once more there is an unexpected similarity between Arnold and Eliot, a similarity which derives from the similarity of their metaphysical positions. For both poets the divine center exists, but is seemingly at an infinite distance. In Eliot this leads to an inability to believe in the significance of any isolated person or thing. Only as a nexus of relations importing meaning from without can any man or object be of value. The concrete particular disappears in the network of its relations. The disembodied quality of much of Eliot's criticism follows from his feeling that a genuine individual must be almost entirely defined by his context and brings little of his own to the whole. At the limit this tendency dissolves the pattern too, for the whole is, after all, made of particulars. The system of relations becomes more and more impalpable. Finally it dissipates in Universality, Abundance, Amplitude, and Unity. Virgil can be a great poet only if he rewrites Latin poetry, retwines as many strands of tradition as possible. Nothing in his poetry may come freshly from outside the already existing mind of Europe. His work must rearrange and synthesize images, motifs, phrases which are inherited from the past. Lawrence, on the other hand, is a great heretic because he thinks and feels for himself. Whether Eliot praises or deplores a poet the assumptions of his literary criticism remain the same. Unless a writer dwells centrally within the collective personality, cherishes and extends it, he cannot be authentic and must be banished for whoring after strange gods.

～

   The whole made up of all true literature, enclosing within itself the smaller spheres of single poems and collected works, is not the most inclusive cultural organism. Outside literature, supporting it and drawing life from it in reciprocal interchange, is the entire culture.

   Eliot's assumptions here are exactly the same as those for the less inclusive spheres. His theory of social order in *Notes towards the Definition of Culture* and *The Idea of a Christian Society* presupposes the idea of a society which is as organically unified as a good poem. The proper culture is one "of order and stability, of equilibrium and harmony" (OPP, 57). There should be "a way of feeling and acting which characterises a group throughout generations" and is "largely . . . unconscious" (ASG, 31). Eliot often emphasizes the spontaneous quality of a living culture. Collective attitudes should permeate each individual so completely that he is not even aware of the habits which determine his life. Just as a mature literature is the product of the unconscious striving of a language to realize its potentialities, and just as the chief effect of style and rhythm in dramatic speech "should be unconscious" (OPP, 77), so a civilization functions largely below the level of awareness. "Culture cannot altogether be brought to consciousness; and the culture of which we are wholly conscious is never the whole of culture: the effective culture is that which is directing the activities of those who are manipulating that which they *call* culture" (NTDC, 107). Eliot's praise of unconsciousness seems to be partly a fear of the annihilating effects of a relativistic historical sense. To be aware of the history of one's own culture is admirable, but to see it from the outside as a culture among others is to be so detached from it as to be unable to participate in it. Only by being unconscious can a man be penetrated through and through by a culture. Consciousness means separation. Eliot's list of the elements included in English culture recalls Henry James's famous description in his book on Hawthorne of the things America lacks. English culture embraces "all the characteristic activities and interests of a people: Derby Day, Henley Regatta, Cowes, the twelfth of August, a cup final, the dog races, the pin table, the dart board, Wensleydale cheese, boiled cabbage cut into sections, beetroot in vinegar, nineteenth-century Gothic churches and the music of Elgar" (NTDC, 31). A thin parsonical smile may be glimpsed here on the Old Possum's face as he specifies the riches of English civilization. Nevertheless, this is the living reality of England, and a man cannot be an Englishman without the boiled cabbage.

In a proper culture the individual is never idiosyncratic or unique. He is only a node within a series of concentric circles which associate him in close intimacy with ever larger groups of people. The nation is "only one fluctuating circle of loyalties between the centre of the family and the local community, and the periphery of humanity entire" (ASG, 21). The conservatism and anti-egalitarianism of Eliot's social thought follows naturally from his idealist presuppositions. It is not surprising that he should have declared himself to be "classicist in literature, royalist in politics, and anglo-catholic in religion" (FLA, ix). If society is to be an organic whole, the individual must be willing to sacrifice himself for the sake of the whole, and an established religion of dogmatic orthodoxy is an important requirement of a valid culture. In one sense the truth of the religion is not in question, only its power to hold a people together. "I do not believe," he says, "that the culture of Europe could survive the complete disappearance of the Christian Faith. And I am convinced of that, not merely because I am a Christian myself, but as a student of social biology. If Christianity goes, the whole of our culture goes" (NTDC, 122).

Literature must grow naturally from the surrounding cultural milieu, for "in a healthy society there is a continuous reciprocal influence and interaction of each part upon the others" (OPP, 12). Poetry is a living body within a larger body, and "a classic can only occur when a civilization is mature" (OPP, 54). If authentic literature derives from the life of a people and is determined by it, it also reacts on the culture. Poetry "makes a difference to the speech, to the sensibility, to the lives of all the members of a society, to all the members of the community, to the whole people, whether they read and enjoy poetry or not" (OPP, 12). The poet's duty is first to language, to "preserve," "extend and improve" (OPP, 9) that language, to develop "a music latent in the common speech of [his] time" (OPP, 24), but language is the indispensable vehicle of culture. Unless a people goes on producing great poets, "their language will deteriorate, their culture will deteriorate and perhaps become absorbed in a stronger one" (OPP, 10). The disappearance of a language means the disappearance of a culture, and poetry has the same relation to society that individual words have to the organic unity of a poem. Eliot's highest praise for a writer is to say, as he says of Yeats, that he "was one of those few [poets] whose history is the history of their own time, who are a part of the consciousness of an age which cannot be understood without them" (OPP, 308).

From the single poem, to the *œuvre* of a writer, to the literature of Europe, to the whole culture of which that literature is a part Eliot's model is the same. Everywhere operative is the notion that human beings dwell within a universal subjective realm dissolving the particular in the fabric of its relations. One example of the importance of this idea is the frequency with which he confesses to the impossibility of being too precise in his definitions. For a writer so eloquent and exact this admission seems odd, but it follows naturally from the nature of the system he is describing. Any image, poem, writer, or epoch exists within a shifting, overlapping milieu of evasive entities, evasive because they are so inextricably inter-related. The impossibility of achieving complete precision is a consequence of the complex context of any particular. The milieu contains such a multiplicity of elements that an individual item is impinged upon by a web of relations too large to hold clearly in the mind at once. This is another version of that dissolution of the particular in its environment so characteristic of Eliot's thought.

The impossibility of distinguishing any element from the integument of its relations is a basic motif in *Knowledge and Experience*. The only reality is immediate experience. All else is appearance. One proof of this is man's failure to be able to draw a firm boundary line around any entity, whether it is subjective or objective. "[T]he line between the experienced, or the given, and the constructed can nowhere be clearly drawn" (KE, 18), just as the "objectivity" of minds "is continuous with their subjectivity, the mental continuous with the merely mechanistic" (KE, 145). The "*ignis fatuus* of epistemology" is "the search for terms, which persist in dissolving into relations" (KE, 98), and "in knowing as we experience it the aspect which is knowing is continuous with the other aspects and can never be definitely separated from them at any point" (KE, 86).

The paradoxes of relationship are stated and restated in Eliot's later prose. Of the liaison between religion and culture he says: "From one point of view we may identify: from another, we must separate" (NTDC, 31). The distinction between prose and verse is one which cannot be made rigidly, for language will not do justice to the complexity of the relation between them: "Where terminology is loose, where we have not the vocabulary for distinctions which we feel, our only precision is found in being aware of the imperfection of our tools, and of the different senses in which we are using the same words" (OPP, 293, 294). There is a distinction to be made between poets who use ideas as the primary material of a poem and poets who subordinate ideas to rhythm and imagery, but this is a distinction which must be made "without precision" and is "incapable of exact calculation" (UPUC, 87, 88). A similarly indefinite relation between two cultures is expressed in the *Aeneid*, for, "behind the story of Aeneas is the consciousness of a more radical distinction, a distinction which is at the same time a statement of *relatedness*, between two great cultures" (OPP, 63).

In all these cases, a single entity cannot be pinned down exactly in itself because it does not exist in itself. It exists only in terms of its overlapping relatedness to other objects.

⤸

The image of structural unity pervades Eliot's social and literary criticism. What of his own poetry? Is he able to reach his goal of organic unity and write poems which live because they share the life of the European mind?

Most of Eliot's poems depend on the assumption that the poet can enlarge his private consciousness to coincide with a collective consciousness. This assumption is so easily and persuasively sustained that it is easy to forget what an extraordinary arrogation of power it is. Only a few early poems, such as "Prufrock" or "Portrait of a Lady," are limited to the perspective of a single ego. In most poems the reader is placed within everybody's mind at once. An act of self-surrender has expanded the private mind of the poet into the universal sphere of the mind of Europe. It may take long years of hard work to assimilate the riches of that mind, but this is now the exploration of an inner space, not the effort to comprehend something other than the self. This claim of universality is not a matter of saying that the individual ego has the power to know other egos from the outside. The knowledge of others affirmed by the speaker in Eliot's poems is internal and intimate. Other people are known as inwardly as Prufrock knows himself, and the poet has the power to identify himself with a pervasive mind which possesses all minds at once. The transparency of other subjectivities to the poet is an extraordinary gift which is denied to most people in this twittering, whirling world. Even in poems which, like "The Waste Land," assert the inescapable privacy of each ego ("I have heard the key/Turn in the door once and turn once only" [CP, 69]), the reader shares with the protagonist the privilege of being in all minds at once.

This privilege is enjoyed as early as "Preludes." That poem places the reader within the minds of all the people who live in the city at a certain time. The enclosed sphere of the poem is made up of the interaction of their incompatible consciousness, each a revolving world. The first prelude is in the present tense and consists of a list of the images which are present in the mind of the speaker. Only in the word "your" is any individuality ascribed to him, and in the context of the other words this seems rather the momentary identification of an impersonal mind with one center of consciousness than an assertion that the speaker's mind is limited. The first line of the poem places the reader within a mind as wide as the whole winter evening, just as the second prelude tells, not of the waking of one person, but of how "the morning comes to consciousness" (CP, 13). The images of the poem are appearances within a ubiquitous mind which includes awareness of "all the hands/That are raising dingy shades/In a thousand furnished rooms" (CP, 13). In the third prelude the all-embracing personality focuses on the contents of a single mind within it, the "thousand sordid images" which make up the ego of the girl with dirty hands, yellow soles of feet, and curlpapers in her hair. She has "such a vision of the street/As the street hardly understands" (CP, 14), but the "hardly" makes the necessary qualification. The consciousness of the speaker includes the mind of the girl and the mind of the street, and understands both at once. The fourth prelude returns to "the conscience of a blackened street." It sums up the mind of the city, reservoir of all the individual minds, as "some infinitely gentle/Infinitely suffering thing" (CP, 15). Though it is possible to draw from this poem evidence about Eliot's notion of the isolated ego, the individual minds in it are embraced by a general consciousness. Just as the poem shifts from present tense to past, to present, to an imperative facing the future, and thereby exists in a perpetual present, so it moves from "your" to "one" to "you" to "his" to "I" to "your" again. The systematic confusion of times and pronouns confirms the fact that the mind of the protagonist is a collective personality containing all times and persons at once.

The assumptions latent in the structure and grammar of "Preludes" are given their fullest development in "Gerontion" and "The Waste Land." The old man in "Gerontion" is far more universal than the city-mind of "Preludes." The "thoughts of a dry brain in a dry season" (CP, 31) are the images making up the poem, and they include all history from the Fall to the present. The entire circuit of the peripheral world, from Thermopylae to Belle Isle and the Horn, even out to the sphere of the stars, is enclosed in the old man's "dull head among windy spaces" (CP,

29). Gerontion has "nor youth nor age," and knows all times and places as his "after dinner sleep" (CP, 29).

Eliot was dissuaded by Ezra Pound from publishing "Gerontion" as a prelude to "The Waste Land." Like Gerontion, Tiresias resumes all human history in himself. The blind prophet who has been both man and woman seems an appropriate specification of such inclusiveness, especially if it is remembered that a prophet is not so much a man who can foresee the future as one who sees things from God's point of view, that central point to which every time, place, and person is equally present. The personages of "The Waste Land" are aspects of Tiresias' all-knowing mind, just as the conscience of the street in "Preludes" includes images which are private to the girl with curlpapers in her hair. "Preludes" involves only one city, but "The Waste Land" recapitulates the experience of all mankind, as Eliot says in his notes to the poem: "Tiresias, although a mere spectator and not indeed a 'character,' is yet the most important personage in the poem, uniting all the rest. Just as the one-eyed merchant, seller of currants, melts into the Phoenician Sailor, and the latter is not wholly distant from Ferdinand Prince of Naples, so all the women are one woman, and the two sexes meet in Tiresias. What Tiresias *sees*, in fact, is the substance of the poem" (CP, 72).

This power of expansion is also assumed, though less theatrically, in Eliot's later poetry. The speaker in "Ash-Wednesday" is spokesman for all Christians at the beginning of Lent, and "Four Quartets," though in some ways the most intimate of Eliot's poems, still has his characteristic impersonality. The speaker can move anywhere in space and time, and includes items from the widest variety of contexts. Eliot's plays are perfectly continuous with the assumptions of his mature lyric poetry. As the real hero of a James novel is a "collectivity," so the unity of Eliot's plays is made by the interpenetration of the characters. Since a dramatist has no way to make a personage live "except to have a profound sympathy with that character" (OPP, 101), and since in a play "character is created and made real only in an action, a communication between imaginary people" (OPP, 104), the dramatist should be as it were the Tiresias of his play, present in all the characters and living their life.

Eliot's aim of identification in drama goes even further. It extends to the idea that the audience seeing the play is assimilated into the consciousness expressed in the play. The reader of "The Waste Land" sits in isolation in his room, but, if he goes to see *The Cocktail Party* or *The Confidential Clerk*, he will, Eliot hopes, be joined not only to the impersonal mind pervading the play but also to the minds of the other members of the audience. Eliot turns from lyric poetry to the writing of plays at least partly because drama seems to him the form of verse most working for social cohesion. "The ideal medium for poetry, to my mind," he says, "and the most direct means of social 'usefulness' for poetry, is the theatre. In a play of Shakespeare you get several levels of significance. For the simplest auditors there is the plot, for the more thoughtful the character and conflict of character, for the more literary the words and phrasing, for the more musically sensitive the rhythm, and for auditors of greater sensitiveness and understanding a meaning which reveals itself gradually" (UPUC, 146). A play brings together the minds of the audience by appealing to each according to his ability to respond to the words. But "the classification is [not] so clear-cut as this" (UPUC, 146). Each auditor "is acted upon by all these elements at once" (UPUC, 146), and therefore is in himself a unique version of the structure of the audience. Guiding Eliot's decision to write plays is the same ideal of organic unity which is the basis of his literary and social criticism, and from "Gerontion" to *The Elder Statesman* his verse is an attempt to affirm his participation in the mind of Europe.

The notion of a collective personality is also the rationale for the bits and pieces of quotation and allusion which have so exercised students of Eliot's poetry. A positivistic critic may be justified in picturing the poet busily at work reading Jacobean plays, the Loeb Classical Library, and all the rest of his "sources," marking passages, remembering them, and later weaving them into the pastiche of his verse. To take the poetry on its own terms, however, is to assume that the echoes were not assimilated from the outside but were encountered by the poet on his voyage of exploration through inner space. To put it another way, the reader must believe that Gerontion and Tiresias need only bring to the surface of their minds phrases and images from many languages and contexts. These are there waiting to be recalled to the center of attention. The quotations, echoes, and parodies which make up

"The Waste Land" are a poetic device of great power. Each phrase concentrates in itself a whole context, and the poem is made of the contours and clashes of these condensations as they are juxtaposed, but the reader is not to think of the poet as assembling fragments from outside himself and putting them together like a cubist collage. Critics have complained that "The Waste Land" does not develop, but, since it is a selection from the perpetual present of the European mind, it cannot develop. All its images, experiences, and feelings hover side by side in a "simultaneous order." The poem has in a sense already been written by European culture in its development, and the poet need only copy it down, or make a selection from a pre-existing pattern.

This selection is made according to the resonance which elements from the mind of Europe have for the unique feelings of a particular poet. Though the poem is made of images from the past, it also expresses personal feelings of the poet who assembles those images. This notion allows Eliot to reconcile his impersonal theory of art with the idea that art is self-expressive. The image of the snowy bear in "Gerontion" is borrowed from Chapman, who borrowed it from Seneca. The three poets' use of the same image affirms the unity of European culture and Eliot's participation in it. But for each poet the image had a different "personal saturation value." "What gives it such intensity as it has in each case is its saturation . . . with feelings too obscure for the authors even to know quite what they were" (UPUC, 140, 141). The notion that deep, obscure feelings are the poet's way of being related to the divine center will justify saying that the meaning of the image, though special to each poet, is nevertheless the same each time. The image of "fractured atoms" "whirled/Beyond the circuit of the shuddering Bear" is in fact one version of the motif of "the unstilled world still whirled/About the centre of the silent Word" (CP, 92).

Eliot's use of myth shares the same subjectivistic justification. In "Ulysses, Order, and Myth" [7] he hails Joyce's method as a discovery which makes the contemporary world possible for art. The immense panorama of futility, anarchy, and decay which is modern life is given an aesthetic pattern by being ordered according to the ideal form of a myth. In "The Waste Land" not modern life but all history is organized by the myth of the Grail quest. The implied

[7] *The Dial*, 75: 480–483 (1923).

assumption is that human life falls into certain ideal patterns, patterns which are constantly re-enacting themselves in new forms and new contexts. People are always unwittingly reliving dramas which exist outside history and structure it in recurring shapes. The Grail legend is one such shape, and Eliot's use of it in "The Waste Land" must not be thought of as the imposition of pattern on what is without order. The poet is "*older* than other human beings" (UPUC, 148). One sign of this age is his ability to sink beneath or before history or rise above it to the place where universal myths abide. The words of the greatest poets "have often a network of tentacular roots reaching down to the deepest terrors and desires" (SE, 135). Having reached such depths, the poet can re-enter time and see apparently miscellaneous events and persons organizing themselves according to an ideal design. "The Waste Land" takes elements from the most diverse times and places, Philomel and Cleopatra, Mrs. Porter and Lil, St. Augustine and Mr. Eugenides, and reveals their secret conformity to the universal story he found in *From Ritual to Romance*.

The recurrence of mythical patterns in all times and places of history is no accident. It is evidence of the hand of God in time, the still center radiating out to organize the whirling world. Eliot's use of stories from Greek drama in his plays is also based on this assumption. The rather ordinary twentieth-century people in *The Cocktail Party* or *The Elder Statesman* are repeating, in ways obscure to themselves, eternal forms of human experience. Of Yeats's later plays Eliot says: "the myth is not presented for its own sake, but as a vehicle for a situation of universal meaning" (OPP, 305). The same thing could be said of Eliot's covert use of myth in his own plays. The myths are not used to recall *The Eumenides*, *Alcestis*, or *Oedipus at Colonus*, but as an assertion that the Greek and modern dramas are versions of pervasive patterns of the collective consciousness of mankind.

In his theory and in his practice Eliot seems to have freed himself triumphantly from the prison of his ego. Without abandoning his subjectivist assumptions, he has expanded the tiny sphere of the self to encompass the whole history of mankind. His development of a poetry of allusion and quotation and his use of ordering myths has given him techniques for concentrating this all-but-infinite sphere in the finite space of a poem. He has made of his solitude everything, and has won for the poet the role of expressing the organic unity of that everything.

⤻

This triumph is really defeat. The quality of the life of the mind of Europe is exactly the same as the experience of the solitary ego. Though Eliot has expanded his mind to include all history he is within the same prison, the prison of the absence of God, errancy from God: "The cycles of Heaven in twenty centuries/Bring us farther from GOD and nearer to the Dust" (CP, 147). Like the little world of the self-enclosed ego, the larger world of history is characterized by fragmentation, aimless motion, lovelessness, frustrated longing. The quest in "The Waste Land" is a failure. The life-giving rain has not yet fallen at the end, though distant thunder can be heard. All men and women together are on the Circle Line, like the disaffected riders on the underground in "Burnt Norton," and the movement of time is the sign of man's eccentricity, of his tragic distance from the still center.

All men are guilty of original sin. This keeps them separated from God, locked within a consciousness which may contract to a private ego or expand to universality but will forever be peripheral, spun on the wheel of suffering that is man's distance from God. History is a labyrinth in which each individual is lost. In one of the most poignant passages in his poetry Eliot shows man lost in the maze of history, never able to find satisfaction, led by his very strengths and virtues to wander farther and farther from God. It is a terrifying description of history as a long tale of frustration and error, the same story, repeated in millions of lives, of man's failure to reach God, or to possess anything which satisfies his cravings. History is an endless movement away from salvation, all deriving from man's first sin in the Garden:

> After such knowledge, what forgiveness? Think now
> History has many cunning passages, contrived corridors
> And issues, deceives with whispering ambitions,
> Guides us by vanities. Think now
>
> . . .
>
> Neither fear nor courage saves us. Unnatural vices
> Are fathered by our heroism. Virtues

Are forced upon us by our impudent crimes.
These tears are shaken from the wrath-bearing tree. (CP, 30)

The knowledge which seems unforgivable is not only the knowledge of good and evil, fruit of the wrath-bearing tree, but also man's knowledge of history. The self-surrender which turned the ego inside-out into the European mind seemed a means of salvation, but it leads instead to recognition of each man's participation in the collective guilt of mankind. This guilt perhaps consists as much as anything in the autonomy of the impersonal mind which makes up culture. Eliot's social and literary criticism has depended on idealist assumptions which put everything within a universal subjectivity. Time, space, nature, man and his works — all are inside the same sphere. The divine presence is inside it too, if that presence is to exist for man, and if God exists only as an aspect of the human mind he cannot be defined as an omnipotent creator. Whether Eliot as a student of social biology is thinking of Christianity as the indispensable cohesive force in European culture, or whether he thinks of the emotions of the individual poet as in resonance with a divine emotion in the depths of his mind, his assumptions are still idealistic. God is merely one part of the all-embracing system of relations which makes up the collective mind. Eliot can only become a Christian when he ceases to be an idealist.

╰

The reversal which makes him a Christian takes place in his poetry in the transition from "The Waste Land" to "Ash-Wednesday." Traces of idealist thinking still remain in his later prose and testify to the almost irresistible tendency for Christian thought in our time to contaminate itself with idealism. But "Ash-Wednesday," the "Four Quartets," and Eliot's plays show that his later experience is genuinely Christian. His career as a whole may be seen as an heroic effort to free himself from the limitations of nineteenth-century idealism and romanticism. If the reversal from individualism to collectivism involves painful self-surrender, the reversal which transforms idealism into Christianity is even more painful, for it requires not only that Eliot should resist the natural direction of modern history, but that he should resist the most powerful penchants of his own nature, penchants which involve a strong distaste for the body and a longing for the purely spiritual.

If Eliot seems at times to represent a twentieth-century continuation of Matthew Arnold's line of thought, this is perhaps most
true in his rejection of the body and in the insubstantiality of some
of his thinking. But Arnold remained trapped within his own spirit,
hovering between two worlds, able only to see at a distance the
return of God which would assuage his longing. Eliot, on the other
hand, is able to transcend the assumptions which kept Arnold
paralyzed, and this makes his work one more example of that recovery of immanence which has been the inner drama of twentieth-
century literature. Eliot's reversal is all the more impressive because
it seems so unlikely that such a goal could be reached from the
uncompromising narrowness of his initial position. Unlike Yeats,
Stevens, or Williams, Eliot represents a specifically Christian
version of the recovery of immanence, a version which may be
defined as a reaffirmation of the Incarnation. It is loss of belief
in Incarnation which turns Christianity into idealism, and Eliot
can only become a Christian when the Incarnation is a reality for
him.

Two steps are necessary to complete this recovery. The first is
a recognition of the sterility of idealist thought. The second is
another turning inside-out of the mind, a reversal which recognizes
that time, nature, other people, and God are external to the self
rather than elements in "some spectral woof of impalpable abstractions, or unearthly ballet of bloodless categories," to borrow phrases
from Bradley's eloquent rejection of "the notion that existence
could be the same as understanding" (SE, 361). The first of these
steps is taken in "The Hollow Men," the second in "Ash-Wednesday." Only when he sees the emptiness of collective subjectivism
can he find the humility to see that existence is outside himself and
not the same as his understanding of it. Eliot's poetry reflects, in its
sequence from "Prufrock" to the plays, a journey as personal and
dramatic as that of the pilgrim in the *Divine Comedy*. This journey
takes him, like Lord Claverton in *The Elder Statesman*, from a
"spectral existence into something like reality" (ES, 85).

In "The Hollow Men" all the richness and complexity of culture
which gives "The Waste Land" such thickness of texture disappears. The poem takes place in a twilight realm of disembodied
men and forces. The complexity of relations making up the sub-

jective realm in Eliot's ideal descriptions of it is replaced by the vagueness and impalpability of "Shape without form, shade without colour,/Paralysed force, gesture without motion" (CP, 79). The hollow men are walking corpses ("Mistah Kurtz — he dead"), and their emptiness is the vacuity of pure mind detached from any reality. They are cut off from one another. Their voices are whispers, "quiet and meaningless" (CP, 79). Groping together, they "avoid speech" (CP, 81). They are detached from nature, and live in a place which is devoid of any spiritual presence, a "dead land," a "cactus land," a "valley of dying stars," hollow like the men themselves (CP, 80, 81). The eyes of the hollow men are not only averted from one another, but from those other eyes, the returning look from the divine place which those who cross "with direct eyes" to "death's other Kingdom" will encounter. There are no eyes in the hollow valley, and the empty men are bereft of God. Even within their own hollowness detachment is the law. The "Shadow" which falls between idea and reality, conception and creation, emotion and response, desire and spasm, potency and existence (CP, 81, 82), is the paralysis which seizes men who live in a completely subjective world. Mind had seemed the medium which binds all things together in the unity of an organic culture. Now it is revealed to be the Shadow which isolates things from one another, reduces them to abstraction, and makes movement, feeling, and creativity impossible. "The Hollow Men" is an eloquent analysis of the vacuity of subjective idealism, and the state of the hollow men appears in Eliot's later work as the "distraction, delusion, escape into dream, pretence" (CPP, 210) of the unenlightened people in his plays, each one of whom is a "fugitive from reality" (ES, 70), or as that horrid form of hell described in *Murder in the Cathedral*, the hell of "the Void," of "emptiness, absence, separation from God" in "the empty land/Which is no land," where "there are no objects, no tones,/No colours, no forms to distract, to divert the soul/From seeing itself, foully united forever, nothing with nothing" (CPP, 210).

If "The Hollow Men" shows where idealism leads, it offers a fleeting glimpse of a way out of emptiness. Though nature, other people, and God have an almost entirely negative existence in the poem, they do exist as something outside the hollow men. The poem places the "stuffed men" in the context of an external world,

God's world. Their state is defined as that of the trimmers in the third canto of the *Inferno*, those wretched souls, "gathered on this beach of the tumid river," who lived without blame or praise, and, like the neutral angels, were neither rebellious nor faithful to God, but lived for themselves. Far better to be one of the "lost/Violent souls" (CP, 79), for they were at least capable of damnation, as Baudelaire, in Eliot's essay, "walked secure in this high vocation, that he was capable of a damnation denied to the politicians and newspaper editors of Paris" (SE, 344). To recognize the possibility of damnation is in a way to become capable of it, and therefore capable of the salvation which is denied to the trimmers. The trimmers in Dante have no hope of another death, but Eliot's hollow men understand dimly that if they endure the death which is prelude to rebirth they have some hope of salvation. Though Eliot's language is deliberately ambiguous, it implies that the sightless eyes of the hollow men may see again, and confront the divine eyes which are "The hope only/Of empty men" and will reappear as "the perpetual star/Multifoliate rose" of heaven itself (CP, 81). The idealists of "The Hollow Men" have stepped out of themselves into the barrenness of an external world, and the fragments of the Lord's prayer ("For Thine is/. . . For Thine is the" [CP, 82]) which they mutter at the end of the poem are moving appeals to a God who may be infinitely distant, but who is independent of their minds and therefore may have power to save them.

If "The Hollow Men" is Eliot's rejection of idealism, "Ash-Wednesday" (CP, 85–95) is the act of humility whereby he accepts the conditions of the real world. The poem, as is appropriate for the first day of Lent, is an intricate pattern of acts of resignation. Eliot gives up one by one all the hopes offered by collective idealism, and prays, in abject humility and deprivation, for the descent of God's grace. The first line of the poem ("Because I do not hope to turn again") establishes the controlling metaphor of ascent up the staircase of spiritual perfection. To climb that stair means to turn away from the realm which had seemed to offer a way of salvation. Eliot must give up his hunger for "this man's gift and that man's scope," the desire for universal power which it seemed possible to satisfy by participation in the mind of Europe. To turn away from idealism means giving up those moments of sudden illumination which have validated poetic imagery through their release of emotions from the obscure depths of the self. These moments were a response not to an objective world, but to the memory of details fixed in the mind and transformed into images, the leap of a fish, the scent of a flower, a phrase from Chapman. The illumination took place through an interchange among parts of the isolated self, and now Eliot sees that such a "glory of the positive hour" is "infirm." This glory is not the "one veritable transitory power," but only "nothing again," the nothing of self-enclosed spirit. The poet knows that he "cannot drink/There, where trees flower, and springs flow." He has separated himself from the plenitude of external nature, and must turn away from the mirrored existence it has within himself.

If the illumination of the moment must be sacrificed so must the power to expand that moment through its relations until it possesses all time and space in a subjectivized whole. To remember the value Eliot places on the idea of history as an inclusive system of simultaneous relations is to see the poignancy of his recognition in "Ash-Wednesday" that "time is always time/And place is always and only place/And what is actual is actual only for one time/And only for one place." The parts of the all-embracing unity Eliot has constructed are dispersed, like the bones of the speaker in the second part of the poem, and he sees that "neither division nor unity/Matters." The expansive energy of the will which has yearned to fly outward to encompass everything must be renounced ("Why should the agèd eagle stretch its wings?"). Those wings by which he once dominated space "are no longer wings to fly."

Having abandoned the powers which accompanied his identification with the mind of Europe, Eliot must abandon even the hope of a temporal immortality which is its last temptation. As long as European culture lasts, Homer, Virgil, Dante, and Shakespeare will continue to live, and Eliot will have the same permanence if he can write poems worthy to join the simultaneous order of the literature of Europe. But this immortality is an idealist sham, and the poet must "proffer [his] deeds to oblivion," and pray to be forgotten utterly, like scattered bones in the desert. Only when he has shorn himself of all the hopes of subjectivism can he walk naked into reality, and in complete self-abnegation pray that, through the intercession of the Virgin, the grace of God may descend upon him. Having died to the old self, he must have the courage to "sit still" even though he finds himself in a desert. The only movement now must come from God, and only God can hear his cry and "suffer [him] not to be separated."

Time can be annihilated neither by the spatializing of it involved in the claim that all the elements of a culture have a simultaneous existence, nor by dreamlike moments of sudden illumination which seem to belong to eternity. Only when the poet has yielded himself to a time ordered by God rather than by man is it possible to "redeem the time," and, in doing so, to "redeem/The unread vision in the higher dream," the dream that is "the token of the word unheard, unspoken" (CP, 90, 91). The movement of reversal and self-sacrifice begun in "The Hollow Men" culminates with the humility of "Ash-Wednesday," and is completed in the affirmations of the "Four Quartets" and the plays. These affirmations are both a new means of personal salvation and a new definition of the role of poetry.

ᔋ

In all their aspects these affirmations depend on the idea of the Incarnation. Eliot's early poetry is dominated by disgust for the body. The protagonists of his first poems scarcely seem to have bodies at all. They recall James's heroes in their fastidious distaste for "Arms that are braceleted and white and bare/(But in the lamplight, downed with light brown hair!)" (CP, 5). The men and women in Eliot's early poems are unable to reconcile sexual love and spiritual love. Spiritual love is represented by Prufrock's glimpse of the mermaids, or by the girl with "her hair over her arms and her arms full of flowers" (CP, 26) in "La Figlia che Piange," or by the hyacinth girl in "The Waste Land," who comes from "the heart of light, the silence" (CP, 54). Sexual love is always sordid, a fall into unredeemed matter, like the unholy loves of Sweeney, or like the tales of rape or betrayal or of sex as "the ecstasy of the animals" (CP, 105) in "The Waste Land." Though at first there seems no way to bring the two loves together, Eliot's later work recognizes that body and spirit must work together for a proper human life. "For Man is joined spirit and body," says one of the choruses from "The Rock," and "you must not deny the body" (CP, 168). Acceptance of the body appears in Eliot's later work primarily in the theme of marriage. The fertility dancers in "East Coker" dance around the bonfire "two and two," in a "necessarye coniunction," "signifying matrimonie" (CP, 183), and marriage as the acceptance of a God-given earthly role is an important motif in the plays.

If Eliot comes to accept the fact that men and women have bodies, he also comes to recover a physical world, external to himself and with a life of its own. Hints of this may already be seen in "Ash-Wednesday." The first section rejects the spiritualized, emotionalized nature which makes natural images in Eliot's early poetry merely aspects of the solitary self. The sixth section gives the reader a glimpse through the staircase window of the objective nature which has rarely appeared before in Eliot's poetry. Even though he may present this only to reject it, after the hermetic enclosure of the early poems it is like a breath of fresh air to find again "the lost lilac and the lost sea voices," "the bent golden-rod and the lost sea smell," "the cry of quail and the whirling plover," "the salt savour of the sandy earth" (CP, 94). These images appeal to all the senses, not just to eyesight, and they show Eliot beginning to know a real world by means of a real body engaged in that world. This return from idealist isolation to a physical world is one dimension, and not the least moving, of "Marina." The old man sailing toward a shore where he will recover his daughter, and, through her, the divine vision, approaches also toward "scent of pine and the woodthrush singing through the fog" (CP, 105). The "Four Quartets" everywhere presuppose this possession, through the senses and the body, of a nature external to the self, as in the lines in "Burnt Norton," affirming that "the dance along the artery" and "the circulation of the lymph" are "figured in the drift of stars" (CP, 177), or as in the exquisitely beautiful lines at the beginning of "The Dry Salvages" about the river and the sea.

The human body and the world's body — these are two forms of incarnation. Another is that social form of embodiment which is a man's acceptance of a limited role in his community. This theme is central in Eliot's plays. *Murder in the Cathedral* associates it explicitly with the Incarnation. Becket's last temptation, the one most difficult for him to resist, is the lure of a pure spirituality, the version of subjective idealism appropriate to tempt a saint. The Fourth Tempter shows Thomas a vision of himself high above the earth, "dwelling forever in presence of God," looking down on the poor human race and the damned in hell with ineffable condescension:

> Seek the way of martyrdom, make yourself the lowest
> On earth, to be high in heaven.
> And see far off below you, where the gulf is fixed,
> Your persecutors, in timeless torment . . . (CPP, 192, 193)

Thomas must reject this motive for martyrdom. It is the sin of angelism and would lead to "damnation in pride" (CPP, 193). To accept martyrdom means going beyond the tempters' vision of human life as "a cheat and a disappointment" in which "All things are unreal,/Unreal or disappointing" (CPP, 194). Martyrdom is the imitation of Christ, and the center of Christ's life is the acceptance of the Passion, that is, the acceptance of his Incarnation even to the death of the body. This is the lesson of the Archbishop's Christmas morning sermon, and it is fulfilled in Thomas' humble sacrifice of his life for the local good of the Church: "The martyr no longer desires anything for himself, not even the glory of martyrdom" (CPP, 199, 200).

Though the theme of martyrdom as an imitation of Christ returns in the death of Celia Coplestone in *The Cocktail Party*, perhaps an even more important mode of incarnation is the life of those who are not saints or martyrs. How easy, and how glorious, it would seem to discover that one has been chosen for the role of martyr, but suppose a man discovers that God has chosen for him not to be a saint? He must work out his salvation in humble acceptance of an unheroic role in the community, struggling unsuccessfully against the temptation to sin, able to love others only imperfectly and occasionally. The form of incarnation involved in becoming an obscure member of the body of believers is in a way more difficult to accept than martyrdom, and it is just this unheroic life which most of the people in *The Cocktail Party*, *The Confidential Clerk*, and *The Elder Statesman* must choose for themselves as the role God would have them play.

Another form of incarnation in Eliot's later work is a transformation of the idea of pattern and therefore a transformation of his earlier idea of poetry. The poet had been defined as the man who can unify heterogeneous elements into a dancelike form. Now that notion must be abandoned, along with the idea of the infinite value of those subjective images which accompany moments of sudden illumination. Man's attempt to transcend temporality either by experiencing eternal moments or by making a spatialized pattern of all the times of history leads only to a parody of the real pattern. The true pattern is God's order of history, an objective rather than subjective design organized around the central event of the Incarnation.

This abnegation of any humanly imposed pattern in order to recover the divine pattern is the central theme of the "Four Quartets." It is announced in the epigraph to "Burnt Norton" cited earlier: "Although the Logos is common the many live as though they had a private understanding." Only when a man ceases to trust in his own understanding and its power to make order can he see the order which has been there all along and has its source in the Word. This theme appears within the poems in the idea that a man must give up the precious moments of consciousness which take him out of time. Only when these instants find their place in a pattern of memory can their significance be perceived. Time can only be redeemed through submission to time, for "We had the experience but missed the meaning,/And approach to the meaning restores the experience/In a different form" (CP, 194). The approach to the meaning can only be made by allowing present moments to fall into the past and become part of the objective pattern of God's presence in history:

> . . . only in time can the moment in the rose-garden,
> The moment in the arbour where the rain beat,
> The moment in the draughty church at smokefall
> Be remembered; involved with past and future.
> Only through time time is conquered. (CP, 178)

History is not a fixed spatialization of time, but constant movement and a constant introduction of novelty which changes all that preceded. This means that man can never fully understand history:

> The knowledge imposes a pattern, and falsifies,
> For the pattern is new in every moment
> And every moment is a new and shocking
> Valuation of all we have been. (CP, 185)

The word "pattern" recurs throughout the "Four Quartets," and always in contexts where Eliot is trying to express his idea that order has a divine rather than human source and can be glimpsed only through patience and submission. This submission means first letting things become part of the past, and then coming to see that "history is a pattern/Of timeless moments" (CP, 208), moments of the presence of the timeless God within time:

> See, now they vanish,
> The faces and places, with the self which, as it could, loved them,
> To become renewed, transfigured, in another pattern. (CP, 205)

The new pattern is the form God gives to history. The presence of God in history, of the timeless in time, is the Incarnation. The Incarnation occurred at a particular moment in time, and yet is constantly recurring at every moment as that which creates time by creating the design of time. The Incarnation was "a moment not out of time, but in time, in what we call history." It was "a moment in time but not like a moment of time,/A moment in time but time was made through that moment: for without the meaning there is no time, and the moment of time gave the meaning" (CP, 163).

The still point is present at every point on the periphery, but this can only be perceived when the place of each point in God's pattern of the whole is seen. It is for this reason that "a people without history/Is not redeemed from time" (CP, 208). The possession of the historical past is not for the sake of belonging to the eternal fixity of an idealized culture. The historical sense is necessary to release the recognition that God is present in each moment as it passes. In the same way, the patterning of the words of a poem so that they move like a Chinese jar still moving in its stillness or like a "complete consort dancing together" (CP, 208) is not for the sake of the perfection of the poem. It leads to the perception that the apparently anarchic world is really a pattern, a pattern imposed by God.

This is the use of poetic drama. In a successful play the spectators come to "perceive a pattern behind the pattern into which the characters deliberately involve themselves; the kind of pattern which we perceive in our own lives only at rare moments of inattention and detachment, drowsing in the sunlight" (EE, 194). This is also the use of lyric poetry: to lead to a recognition of the presence of God in every moment and every event of time. It is possible to give now its full meaning to Eliot's statement in "Poetry and Drama": "For it is ultimately the function of art, in imposing a credible order upon ordinary reality, and thereby eliciting some perception of an order *in* reality, to bring us to a condition of serenity, stillness, and reconciliation." Eliot is more than a continuator of nineteenth-century idealism. He belongs to the twentieth century, and the course of his poetry, like the course of twentieth-century poetry generally, is a recovery of immanence, in his case a recovery of the God immanent in reality and revealed by the musical patterns of poetry. Eliot too goes beyond the vanishing of God.

The pattern's revelation of the meaning of each moment returns the poet to the moment itself, and now its infinite depth is available. Incarnation is not in the total design only, but in each moment of it, and Eliot's poetry, like so much recent poetry, must in the end be defined as poetry of the moment. "The hint half guessed, the gift half understood, is Incarnation" (CP, 199). The moment of Incarnation reconciles time and eternity, past and future, in an "impossible union/Of spheres of existence" (CP, 199).

The course of Eliot's development is in some ways curiously parallel to that of Yeats. Like Yeats, Eliot begins in exclusion and deprivation, then expands outward to include all time and space, and finally narrows again to the concrete moment which concentrates everything in the radiant presence of the present. The Yeatsian moment of violent sensation is of course very different from Eliot's moment of the "point of intersection of the timeless/With time" (CP, 198). The latter retains the dimensions of depth, mystery, and transcendence which are characteristic of Christian thought. Nevertheless, the culminating passages of Eliot's poetry, as of Yeats's, are certain images which affirm the infinite plenitude of the instant of intense experience. The "voice of the hidden waterfall" (CP, 208), the "hidden laughter/Of children in the foliage" (CP, 181), bird song, the "wild thyme unseen, or the winter lightning" (CP, 199) are proof that the still point of the turning world is not unattainably distant, but here and now and always:

> Quick now, here, now, always —
> Ridiculous the waste sad time
> Stretching before and after. (CP, 181)

V

Dylan Thomas

On my haunches, eager and alone, casting an ebony shadow, with the Gorsehill jungle swarming, the violent, impossible birds and fishes leaping, hidden under four-stemmed flowers the height of horses, in the early evening in a dingle near Carmarthen, . . . I felt all my young body like an excited animal surrounding me, the torn knees bent, the bumping heart, the long heat and depth between the legs, the sweat prickling in the hands, the tunnels down to the eardrums, the little balls of dirt between the toes, the eyes in the sockets, the tucked-up voice, the blood racing . . . . There, playing Indians in the evening, I was aware of me myself in the exact middle of a living story, and my body was my adventure and my name.

From the very first moment of its existence, even in the womb, even when the "seed [is] at-zero," the self, for Dylan Thomas, includes all the cosmos, lives its life and is lived by its life. There is no need to achieve by expansive stratagems of sensation or imagination an identification with all things. That identification is given with existence itself and can never be withdrawn. There is no initial separation between subject and object. The self is not set apart from things or people which are other than itself. Thomas' early poetry, according to the poet himself, with all its "very many lives and deaths," describes events which took place "in the tumultuous world of [his] own being." Echoing Rimbaud's "Je est un Autre," Thomas once said, "I *am* lots of people." Even when his poems are dialogues they are not the confrontation of two separate existences, but of two opposing parts of a single existence. It is not a question, as for Rimbaud, of a first-person-singular self which becomes "another" and enters a new state of existence. Thomas from the beginning contains in himself the farthest star. He is the center of an adventure which is the total cosmic adventure, and, after the first experience of a birth which is a coming into existence of everything, there is no possibility of adding more to the self. What exists for Thomas as soon as anything exists at all is a single continuous realm which is at once consciousness, body, cosmos, and the words which express all three at once.

At the center is "me myself," the consciousness and self-identity by which he is "aware." He knows himself not as an interior emptiness, not as a pure lucidity of consciousness, but as being "in the exact middle of a living story." The self is of the story; the story is of the self. The milieu of their interpenetration is his body, "the excited animal surrounding me." "My body," says Thomas, "was my adventure." The body is identified with consciousness, in one direction, and, in the other, with the adventure, the cosmic process in which it participates. The plenitude of existence is within the self. In a letter to Vernon Watkins the poet describes himself as feeling as if he has tightly packed everything he has and knows "into a mad-doctor's bag." "[A]ll you can see is the bag, all you can know is that it's full to the clasp, all you have to trust is that the invisible and intangible things packed away are . . . worth quite a lot." [1]

The poet's body is, finally, "my name." It is identified with the primary word, the name of the self, and, by implication, with all language, the "churning bulk of the words" (LVW, 25) which name the multiplicity that self becomes in its all-embracing adventure:

> And from the first declension of the flesh
> I learnt man's tongue, to twist the shapes of thoughts
> Into the stony idiom of the brain,
> To shade and knit anew the patch of words
> Left by the dead . . .
> What had been one was many sounding minded. (CP, 25)

The realm of existence, soon after it is entered, becomes diversified into an immense number of sensations, some proper to the body itself, some happening within the body through its possession of the world. These sensations do not blend with one another to form a

---

[1] The following texts of Thomas' work have been used in this chapter. Each is accompanied by the abbreviation which will hereafter be employed in citations. *The Collected Poems of Dylan Thomas* (New York: New Directions, 1953): CP; *Quite Early One Morning* (New York: New Directions, 1954): QE; *Adventures in the Skin Trade and other stories* (New York: New Directions, 1955): A; *Portrait of the Artist as a Young Dog* (New York: New Directions, 1955): P; *Letters to Vernon Watkins* (New York: New Directions, 1957): LVW; *Explorations*, No. 4 (Toronto, 1955): E; "Poetic Manifesto," *The Texas Quarterly*, 4: 45–53 (1961): PM; Henry Treece, *Dylan Thomas: "Dog Among the Fairies"* (London: Lindsay Drummond, 1949): T. Quotations in the initial paragraphs of this chapter come, respectively, from P, 22, 23; CP, 49; QE, 174, 175; E, 37; LVW, 25.

totality. Each event, however many are apprehended at once, remains separate and distinct, with its own sharpness of individuality,
as in the striking description of an apprehension of the earth in the
story called "A Prospect of the Sea": "He walked to the last rail
before pitch space; though the earth bowled round quickly, he saw
every plough crease and beast's print, man track and water drop,
comb, crest, and plume mark, dust and death groove and signature
and time-cast shade, from ice field to ice field, sea rims to sea
centres, all over the apple-shaped ball" (A, 188, 189).

More than the present moment is possessed by consciousness,
identical with its being. The past too is available, and waits to
come when called, or even to come spontaneously out of the realm
of memory. The boy crouching in the thicket, playing Indians, is
aware not only of each singular sensation of his body and of each
event in the surrounding jungle, but also of "the memory around
and within flying, jumping, swimming, and waiting to pounce"
(P, 23). Memory has the same swarming, importunate existence
as the environing world and the body of the present moment. In
"A Prospect of the Sea" the protagonist performs an extraordinary
act of retrospective perception, seeing down through all the layers
of civilization superimposed on the outstretched earth, seeing down
even to the beginning of history, still green and undrowned Eden.
It is an act of perception and not really of memory, for all past
history is as vividly present to the senses as every mark on the
earth: "He saw through the black thumbprint of a man's city to
the fossil thumb of a once-lively man of meadows; through the
grass and clover fossil of the country print to the whole hand of a
forgotten city drowned under Europe; through the handprint to
the arm of an empire broken like Venus; through the arm to the
breast, from history to the thigh, through the thigh in the dark to
the first and West print between the dark and the green Eden; and
the garden was undrowned, to this next minute and for ever, under
Asia in the earth that rolled on to its music in the beginning evening" (A, 189).

It is no accident that Thomas speaks of this descent into the
still-existing past as the exploration of ever more secret parts of a
human body. The entire expanse of the cosmos, both spatial and
temporal, is as close to him and as intimately known as his own
body, or as the body of a woman he loves. He is always "in the safe

centre of his own identity, the familiar world about him like another flesh" (P, 143). Thomas' use of the traditional relation of microcosm and macrocosm is more than the manipulation of a metaphor. It is a way of expressing a literal fact in the universe of his poems. To understand and accept this literalness is the key by which his most difficult poems may be unlocked. The contradictory images of his poems are not metaphors or symbols. They describe something as exactly as the poet knows how. "It is impossible to be too clear" (E, 35), he once said, and on another occasion he reproved Edith Sitwell for not reading his poetry literally: "Miss Edith Sitwell's analysis . . . of the lines: 'The atlas-eater with a jaw for news/Bit out the mandrake with tomorrow's scream' seems to me very vague. She says the lines refer to 'the violent speed and the sensation-loving, horror-loving craze of modern life.' She doesn't take the literal meaning: that a world-devouring ghost-creature bit out the horror of to-morrow from a gentleman's loins. . . . This poem is a particular incident in a particular adventure, not a general, elliptical deprecation of this 'horrible, crazy, speed-life' " (T, 149, 150). As Elder Olson has pointed out,[2] "atlas-eater" does not literally mean "world-devouring." Just here, however, in Thomas' assertion that they are identical in meaning, the fundamental principle justifying all the complexities of his style can be detected. For Thomas an atlas, the world transformed into a human representation of it, *is* the world, the only world there is. Throughout his poetry what might in another poet be asserted as a metaphor or simile is affirmed as literally true. He does not say: "It seemed as if the water-birds and the birds of the winged trees were speaking my name." He says:

> My birthday began with the water-
> Birds and the birds of the winged trees flying my name
> Above the farms and the white horses
> And I rose
> In rainy autumn
> And walked abroad in a shower of all my days. (CP, 113)

The autumn shower is not like the poet's memory of his life; they are the same thing. An occurrence in the outside world is not the symbol of an occurrence in the mind or in the private world of the

---

[2] Elder Olson, *The Poetry of Dylan Thomas* (Chicago: University of Chicago Press, 1954), p. 4.

body. They are identical. "Light breaks where no sun shines" is a poem about the secret processes within the poet's body and mind. Its method is to describe interior events as if they coincided with cosmic events, as if they *were* cosmic events. The language of the poem mingles inextricably words which refer to bodily, mental, and natural events. The poem ends with an apparent reversal of what had gone before: the assertion that sensations make things happen in the interior world. The implication is that neither is prior. To say it in terms of exterior space or in terms of interior space is to say the same thing in different ways. "Especially when the October wind" again asserts the coincidence of thought and world. The locus of their crossing is the blood, which is at once "chemic" and "syllabic" (CP, 19, 20). "In the beginning," to give another example, describes as identical events the creation of the universe by God, the creation of Adam, the formation of the poet's body in the womb, and his attainment of consciousness. If anything is prior here it is God's all-creating Word, but this is identical with the coming to consciousness of the poet. Godlike, he makes the world anew, and makes it again whenever he wakes in the morning. "Every morning I make,/God in bed, . . . The death-staged scatter-breath/Mammoth and sparrow fall/Everybody's earth" (CP, 150). The poet's mind and body, and God's creating Word are also identical with the "mounting fire" of the primary physical cause which "set alight the weathers from a spark," the life force which "Burst in the roots, pumped from the earth and rock/The secret oils that drive the grass" (CP, 27).

This overlapping of mind, body, and world means that language which in conventional speech would apply to only one of these realms can be used by Thomas to describe all three simultaneously. The difficulty of so many of his poems derives from this assertion as literally true of what would usually be thought of as metaphorical relations. The result is statements which apparently do not make sense, which are contradictory, paradoxical, or absurd:

> The photograph is married to the eye . . . (CP, 17)
>
> [T]he owls were bearing the farm away . . . (CP, 179)
>
> A hill touches an angel! (CP, 182)
>
> My world is pyramid. (CP, 36)

Thomas tries to create structures of words which cannot be understood piece by piece, but only by a single leap which carries the reader into the meaning. Sometimes this meaning grows slowly, not as something which is directly accessible in the words, present as logic, but as something which enters through the powerful impression of sound and feeling which the poem makes even when it is not understood. Of his early poetry Thomas said: "I thought it enough to leave an impression of sound and feeling and let the meaning seep in later" (E, 35, 36). This does not mean that there is no meaning, but that the poet refuses to give the reader easy access to it.

Thomas' language calls attention to itself as language. It is not an instrument which dissolves in its own use, but is its own world. It is not a transparent medium through which the reader sees undistorted an object which remains detached from consciousness. In an admirable passage in praise of words written two years before his death Thomas asserts that a fascination with language was the genesis of his vocation as a poet. What fascinated him was not the meanings of words, but "the *sound* of them," "the shape and shade and size and noise of the words as they hummed, strummed, jigged and galloped along" (PM, 45, 46). Words were not signs of something external to themselves, but the "substance" of poetry, in the same way that marble is the substance of sculpture. "What I like to do," says Thomas, "is to treat words as a craftsman does his wood or stone or what-have-you, to hew, carve, mould, coil, polish & plane them into patterns, sequences, sculptures, fugues of sound" (PM, 46). Though words, taken as things in themselves and not as names or meanings, are the stuff of poetry, nevertheless these entities, "seemingly lifeless, made only of black and white" (PM, 45), contain all the sensible richness of the physical world. "Out of them came the gusts and grunts and hiccups and heehaws of the common fun of the earth" (PM, 46). Without words, mind and world would be split apart. Language is the place of their interpenetration. When he was a child, words were "as the notes of bells, the sounds of musical instruments, the noises of wind, sea, and rain, the rattle of milkcarts, the clopping of hooves on cobbles, the fingering of branches on a window pane, might be to someone, deaf from birth, who has miraculously found his hearing" (PM, 45).

Language is the transposition of world into consciousness, and Thomas' images therefore name not an external object, but the thing already classified, thought, assumed into the human mind and body. The world is atlas as soon as it is known at all. The poet's blood flows through the words of the poem, but that blood is also, through the agency of the poem, "the blood of leaves, wells, weirs, fonts, shells, echoes, rainbows, olives, bells, oracles, sorrows" (LVW, 38).

This does not mean that the existence of things in Thomas' poems is, as for Mallarmé, merely conceptual, "the notion of an object, escaping, that fails to be," an essence which is "absent from all bouquets." Thomas' things, things in a world which is atlas, are objects of immediate sensation. They *are* immediate sensation. Even though he is "shut . . . in a tower of words" (CP, 19), that tower is identical with his spiritual-physical being. "[Y]ou secluded in your Tower know and learn more of the world outside than the outside-man who is mixed up so personally and inextricably with the mud and the unlovely people . . . and the four bloody muddy winds" (LVW, 23, 24). The poet, because of his possession of the world through the "five and country senses," contains all the universe:

> My images stalk the trees and the slant sap's tunnel . . . (CP, 41)

> Am I not all of you by the directed sea
> Where bird and shell are babbling in my tower? (CP, 54)

This possession of the world through its spontaneous transformation into images is not dry, cerebral, or abstract. It coincides with the passionate apprehension of things through the senses. The poet penetrates the world, identifies himself with its processes, lives its secret life. "I breathe" the world, "now that my symbols have outelbowed space" (CP, 47). If the transformation of world into words is the way the poet interiorizes the world, it is also the way he is invaded and possessed by the world in all its sensuous immediacy. The sensible world is the substance of the poet's words. The birds by the sea's side are "dark-vowelled" (CP, 20); the shade of the trees is "a word of many shades" (CP, 98); the stones speak "with tongues that talk all tongues" (CP, 52); and the world may be read like a book:

I open the leaves of the water at a passage
Of psalms and shadows among the pincered sandcrabs prancing

And read . . . (CP, 188)

⌒

What does the book of sensations tell the poet about the all-inclusive realm made up of the participation of words, consciousness, body, and world? Thomas learns when he reads the book of sensations that the world is, first of all, a totality. This must be called simply "it":

> All the sun long it was running, it was lovely, the hay
> Fields high as the house, the tunes from the chimneys, it was air
>   And playing, lovely and watery
>   And fire green as grass. (CP, 178)

The "it" is the anonymous subject of all possible activities or things. "It" is connected with each by a form of the verb to be: "All the sun long it was running, it was lovely, . . . it was air and playing." To put it another way, the word "it" is the name for the undifferentiated substance which underlies all activities and entities. "It" is the fact that something is, the unnamable, unthinkable fact of existence itself, a property which may be attributed equally to anything that is. *It is.* All things which are, share a single property: they exist, they are. Participles, nouns, adjectives, and adverbs, rather than defining distinct modes of existence, share a single mode of it. The phrase "it was" may have as its object "running," "playing," "watery," "lovely," "air," "the hay fields," "the tunes from the chimneys," and "fire green as grass." All are, like subject and object, inextricably mixed, aspects of the single unitary "it."

The "it" exists not as a substance, static, solid, and enduring, but as a perpetual motion and activity. It is a world which is primarily verbal, not substantial, a world in which nothing can maintain longer than an instant a motionless identity. In such a universe things are what they do. They exist as a process of becoming, in which "the green blooms ride upward, to the drive of time" (CP, 58). For Thomas a noun does not come into existence until it has been linked to a verb expressing a vital activity, and then

modified by an adjective which is a transposed verb, or is another
noun which has been given a verbal aspect. The effect is an
explosion of activity in which all these linguistic forms cooperate:

> . . . the sun blooms
> And the tusked, ramshackling sea exults . . . (CP, 193)

> In the mustardseed sun,
> By full tilt river and switchback sea . . . (CP, 190)

> . . . I, a spinning man,
> Glory also this star, bird
> Roared, sea born, man torn, blood blest. (CP, xvi)

As the last quotation suggests, it is not a world of isolated activities, but one in which the unity of simultaneous activities is affirmed
by the participation of each activity in others. From the point of
view of any center chosen as focus, every other activity is a modification or adjective of the central activity. Thomas' way of expressing this is to add "-ed" to a noun, thereby turning it into a verbal
adjective. He does not say "a tree full of robins." He says "robin
breasted tree" (CP, 182). The tree and its robins do not exist in
isolation from one another, but share each other's life. The robins
are attributes of the tree. The tree is robin breasted. Just as consciousness has no separate existence, but exists in interpenetration
with all things, so each entity is inextricably entangled with all the
others:

> And yellow was the multiplying sand,
> Each golden grain spat life into its fellow . . . (CP, 24)

Again and again Thomas invents phrases which assert the reciprocal participation in one another, as activities, of what would
ordinarily be thought of as isolated objects: "the mountain ravened
eaves," "the starred well" (CP, 182), "the mussel pooled and the
heron/Priested shore" (CP, 113), "scummed, starfish sands,"
"men/Tackled with clouds" (CP, xv), "the frozen hold/Flocked
with the sheep white smoke of the farm house cowl/In the river
wended vales" (CP, 131).

Certain culminating passages in his late poetry are magnificent
expressions of a world which is a single activity in the present
moment of a thousand separate forms of life, each asserting its
distinct violence of existence to make a total "sermon of blood"

(CP, 184). It is a world neither of vegetable nor of human existence, but full of "animals thick as thieves/On God's rough tumbling grounds" (CP, xvii). It is the realm of a feral life whose blood penetrates even the trees of the forest and extends from deep under the sea to heaven itself:

> Among the cocks like fire the red fox
>
> Burning! Night and the vein of birds in the winged, sloe wrist
> Of the wood! Pastoral beat of blood through the laced leaves!
> The stream from the priest black wristed spinney and sleeves
> Of thistling frost
> Of the nightingale's din and tale! (CP, 184)
>
> . . . the vaulting does roister, the horned bucks climb
> Quick in the wood at love, where a torch of foxes foams,
> All birds and beasts of the linked night uproar and chime . . . (CP, 198)

The fact that the act of love is the best symbol of the inter-penetration of all things in the "linked night" shows the transiency of any instant of the cosmic life. If things can only continue to exist as a process, this means that they can only continue to exist by changing. To live is to burn like a fiery torch through time, but it is possible that the torch may burn out, and it is certainly necessary that new fuel continually be added to the fire. In Thomas' world nothing remains itself for long. Forms are continuously changing into other forms. It is a world of metamorphosis, of perpetual move-ment and alteration, in which nothing can long remain its solid self.

In some cases this appears as a continuous modulation of forms, evolutionary changes in size, appearance, and color, like those in a delirious dream, or like those in Rimbaud's *Illuminations*, a possible source for Thomas' prose poems:

> Real things kept changing place with unreal . . . . But she returned ten times, in ten different shapes. (A, 164)
>
> . . . a waterfall turning to fishdust and ash . . . (A, 230)
>
> The salmon of the still sail turned to the blue of the birds' eggs in the tips of the fringing forest of each wave. The feathers crackled from the birds and drifted down and fell upon bare rods and stalks that fenced the island entrance, the rods and stalks grew into trees with musical leaves still burning. (A, 229)

"Kept changing place," "turning to," "drifted down," "grew into" — such expressions suggest that for Thomas change takes place in a leisurely fashion modeled on organic growth. In one poem he describes the temporal motion of the heavens as "the night's eternal, curving act" (CP, 197), and in "A Prospect of the Sea" the hero watches a landscape go through a bewildering metamorphosis. The present participles suggest the smooth continuity of even vertiginous changes: "the boy stared down at the river disappearing, the corn blowing back into the soil, the hundred house trees dwindling to a stalk, and the four corners of the yellow field meeting in a square that he could cover with his hand. He saw the many-coloured county shrink like a coat in the wash. Then a new wind sprang from the pennyworth of water at the river-drop's end, blowing the hill field to its full size, and the corn stood up as before, and the one stalk that hid the house was split into a hundred trees. It happened in half a second" (A, 184). The last sentence, however, shows that the transformations in Thomas' world do not happen by degrees, or even in a continuous evolutionary curve of change. They happen instantaneously. In a moment, like a flash of lightning, one form is destroyed and a new creation appears. Temporal duration is made up of discontinuous moments between which there is a gap. Nothing can endure as itself for more than an instant, and what replaces it is not a modulated form of what filled the previous moment. It is something entirely different, depending not on continuity with what preceded but on its complete annihilation. In order for one instant to come into being there must be a destruction of what existed the moment before, and out of this void the solidity of the new moment comes. Thomas often insists on the suddenness of these changes, and on the dissimilarity of what is changed and what it is changed into:

A woman turns into a hill. (A, 158)

Late evening turned to night . . . suddenly . . . (A, 156)

The dream had changed. Where the women were was an avenue of trees. And the trees leant forward and interlaced their hands, turning into a black forest. . . . Stepping on a dead twig, he was bitten. (A, 152)

In another passage Thomas shows how a mountain cannot go on enduring, but must proceed through time in a series of full stops and leaps made of alternate appearances and disappearances. The mountain continually comes into being out of nothing: "Through the mist . . . came a mountain in a moment. . . . [T]he mountain vanished leaving a hole in space to keep the shape of his horror as he sank . . . . [T]he hollow shape of his horror was filled with crags and turrets, rock webs and dens, spinning black balconies, the loud packed smashing of separate seas, and the abominable substances of a new colour. The world happened at once. There was the furnished mountain built in a flash and thunderclap colliding" (A, 231, 232). The universe is a place of perpetual novelty, in which there is a constant appearance of the abominable substances of a new color. These new colors are abominable because they have nothing in common with any color which has ever existed before. They are the scandal of absolute novelty.

There is no intermediary stage between the sermon of blood, the affirmation of existence in the mode of present participles, and the complete change of that moment into something different. Within the confines of a single moment there is nothing, a hole in space, then crags and turrets, rock webs and dens, spinning black balconies, the loud packed smashing of separate seas, a space full of crowded substantiality and violent activity. Then, still within the same instant, there is the hollow shape of horror again, making way for the next surging forth of a world as new-made as the Garden of Eden. There is no transition but vacancy between the exultant assertion of vitality in the moment of its being and a change to something else. Even if this is another version of what existed before, it has no temporal link with its previous double.

In the end this discontinuity becomes a law of continuity. It is certain that the next instant will have nothing to do with the present one. This fact comes to be experienced as something constant, as a succession of moments which, whatever their content, express the same weariness and suffering, the same failure of any instant to generate something like itself: "There had been seven women, in a mad play by a Greek, each with the same face, crowned by the same hoop of mad, black hair. One by one they trod the ruler of turf, then vanished. They turned the same face to him, intolerably weary with the same suffering" (A, 151, 152).

The experience of time is expressed by Thomas in two contradictory ways, both of which are simultaneously present in any instant of life. Since endurance through time is a continual destruction of what one has just become, it is like nothing so much as a perpetual falling, a descent which is the continual annihilation of what miraculously continues to exist, though as a constant destruction and falling away, a flowing like the hemorrhage from some great wound. Nowhere in Thomas has this been more magnificently expressed than in the poem called "In country sleep":

> This night and each night since the falling star you were born,
> Ever and ever he finds a way, as the snow falls,
>
> As the rain falls, hail on the fleece, as the vale mist rides
> Through the haygold stalls, as the dew falls on the wind-
> Milled dust of the apple tree and the pounded islands
> Of the morning leaves, as the star falls, as the winged
>   Apple seed glides,
> And falls, and flowers in the yawning wound at our sides,
> As the world falls, silent as the cyclone of silence. (CP, 183)

At the same time, as temporal existence is a perpetual dying and falling away, it is, since the motion of simultaneous birth and death persists throughout, something stationary, like a photograph which freezes rapid motion in mid-air:

> The ball I threw while playing in the park
> Has not yet reached the ground. (CP, 72)

Time in Thomas' world is an ever-experienced discontinuity. Of all earthly things it is true to say: "time has set its maggot on their track" (CP, 59). Every instant is "beginning with doom in the bulb" (CP, 40), and "murder of Eden and green genesis" (CP, 47). Time is a perpetually repeated moment of beginning and immediate destruction. Even "a timeless insect/Says the world wears away" (CP, 53), and the unborn child in the womb, in the instant of its conception, is, in spite of God's promise to the contrary, murdered by Time:

> "Time shall not murder you," He said,
> "Nor the green nought be hurt;
> Who could hack out your unsucked heart,
> O green and unborn and undead?"
> I saw time murder me. (CP, 79)

The child in the womb weaves, not the tissue of his living body, but his shroud; and the sun, symbol of the driving force of time, is "meat-eating" (CP, 110). It lives on the destruction of man's body.

To come into life is to be "dressed to die," and the "sensual strut" (CP, 110) is for that reason undermined by death. Wherever Thomas opens the book of earth he reads a single fact, the fact of death. Death is spoken in all things by the presence in them of the inexorable passage of time. This is like the song of wind over rocks or through snowflakes, or like the endless sound of the sea in a shell, or like the eternal motion of the stars:

> The carved mouths in the rock are wind swept strings.
> Time sings through the intricately dead snow drop. Listen. (CP, 134)

To live is to foreknow one's death, and therefore to forelive it. Even the "Young/Green chickens of the bay and bushes cluck, 'dilly dilly,/Come let us die' " (CP, 188). Since any moment of life contains beginning and ending, birth and death, all moments of life are the same, and their succession is experienced not as a progression, but as a moving stasis which persists interminably: "In the final direction of the elementary town/I advance for as long as forever is" (CP, 110).

⤵

This elementary town is God. God is an anonymous totality of being. He is "the god of beginning in the intricate seawhirl" (CP, 44). He is the source and end of all things, a dark fluid background against which they surge into being, and which they negate by being specific objects rather than the inclusive *I am*. Man always remains "this side of the truth" (CP, 116), this side of a deity who combines contradictions and to whom moral terms do not apply. To God distinctions of good and bad, innocent and guilty, are nothing, since he sees all created things in terms of their inevitable return into "the winding dark" where "each truth, each lie" will "die in unjudging love" (CP, 116, 117).

It would be possible to believe that the world was liberated for good from the ground of being when it was created. If this were so, the world would have substantiality and continuity even if all things were forced to submit to constant metamorphosis. But objects in Thomas' world do not have power to continue on their own. As soon as they come into existence, they die altogether and fall back into the source from which they sprang. When they enter the world of time they immediately crumble away, like bodies long preserved in an Egyptian tomb and then exposed to light and air.

Things are unable to support themselves in existence. Their only support is the creative ground which is their source, and that ground is no support. It yields under them, gives way, and they sink back and vanish. Anything which continues from moment to moment must be brought back into being again and again. Time and all the things of time must constantly recommence. In describing a world of "endless beginning" (CP, 109), Thomas, like Descartes or Malebranche, affirms the old doctrine of continuous creation. The death that obsesses him and undermines his world is not the change of one form of existence into another. It is the perpetual return of all things into the neutrality of God. As soon as the first thing came into being, it died, and in dying revealed the true horror of time. The creation is given over to death, death not as the end point of a long course of existence, but death permanent, incessant, the continual evaporation into God of all things, and the continual resurgence of things which are immediately stricken with death. "After the first death, there is no other" (CP, 112). After the first disappearance of the first thing revealed the fact that the world is possessed by death, there was no other death. Each new death is another example and proof of the same death. "Death is all metaphors" (CP, 80), and God is "the mankind making/Bird beast and flower/Fathering and all humbling darkness" (CP, 112). Into this night, a darkness made of anonymous particles which humble all because they deny all, the dead child goes in "A Refusal to Mourn the Death, by Fire, of a Child in London":

> Deep with the first dead lies London's daughter,
> Robed in the long friends,
> The grains beyond age, the dark veins of her mother . . . (CP, 112)

The temporal existence of things is a perpetual genesis out of the fathomless darkness of things which continually fall back into their source, like water in a fountain. It is two simultaneous motions of beginning and ending: "darkness kindled back into beginning" (CP, 143), and "beginning crumbled back to darkness" (CP, 145). This ever-new genesis rises, in "Ceremony After a Fire Raid," like a life-giving fountain out of the destructive fire burning the cathedral where a dead child lies as a sacrifice on the altar:

The masses of the sea
The masses of the sea under
The masses of the infant-bearing sea
Erupt, fountain, and enter to utter for ever
Glory glory glory
The sundering ultimate kingdom of genesis' thunder. (CP, 146)

∽

Human beings can reach the darkness of the genetic sea in a way which is possible to no other creatures. A man may reach God through the intermediary of another human being. This possibility is explored in all Thomas' poems about love. It is the key to the meaning he gives to sexual experience. Love is never an end in itself. Other people interest Thomas because they offer the opportunity of a special access to the divine darkness. This is so, paradoxically, because of man's inveterate betrayal of love. "All over the world love is being betrayed as always, and a million years have not calmed the uncalculated ferocity of each betrayal or the terrible loneliness afterwards" (LVW, 92). A man's sexual partner is inevitably and necessarily unfaithful, but not merely because, as in the poem called "Into her Lying Down Head," "his runaway beloved" is sexually possessed in her sleep by "his enemies," "Juan aflame" and savage "young King Lear," "Samson drowned in his hair" and even by "once seen strangers or shades on a stair." This "libidinous betrayal," in which the woman "whores with the whole night" (LVW, 92), is only a symbol of the woman's contact with "fountains of origin," "the deep/Forgotten dark," the indeterminate ground of being itself, appearing here as "the always anonymous beast" (CP, 125–127).

Sexual intercourse is a way of attaining the fountains of origin through the woman as mediator. In the last story in Thomas' autobiography the protagonist imagines his possession of a young woman as death by endless falling: "He and Lou could go down together, one cool body weighted with a boiling stone, on to the falling, blank white, entirely empty sea, and never rise. . . . He wished that the light would fail. In the darkness he and Lou could creep beneath the clothes and imitate the dead" (P, 154, 155). When the hero leaves the room for a moment he is unable to find Lou again. He finds himself on "a silent patch of stairway at the top of the house." In place of the vanished girl and the vanished room, there is a long fall in the darkness: "he put out his hand, but the rail was broken and nothing there prevented a long drop to the ground down a twisted shaft that would echo and double his cry" (P, 158). The genetic sea can be experienced only as a bottomless gulf, even when it is reached through sexual experience.

Attainment of the all fathering and all humbling darkness through a deathlike sexual fall is necessary to the continuation of the world. The woman's submission to "the naked shadow," "the incestuous secret brother" (CP, 127), has a cosmic significance. It is able to "perpetuate the stars" (CP, 127). Without her constant immersion in the dark sea of origin, the creation could not endure, and would blink back into darkness. For a man too sexual intercourse can be a renewing experience of the flowing forth of things from the sea of being. The Virgin, mother of Christ and, through him, of the world, is the type of all women:

> And taken by light in her arms at long and dear last
> I may without fail
> Suffer the first vision that set fire to the stars. (CP, 119)

> O my true love, hold me.
> In your every inch and glance is the globe of genesis spun,
> And the living earth your sons. (CP, 122)

After the fall, the resurrection, after death the "resuffered pain" (CP, 34) of a new birth. Sexual experience is, like the copresence of "beginning crumbled back to darkness" and "darkness kindled back into beginning," the immobile motion of a perpetually flowing fountain, a fountain which, in the climax of "A Winter's Tale," is at once fire, water and a flower: "And she rose with him flowering in her melting snow" (CP, 137).

╰╮

Only a certain kind of poetry will be possible in such a world, so detached is each moment from all the others. The best clue to Thomas' conception of his poetry is a letter to Henry Treece. This letter is an excellent description of the form of his poems and an exact picture of the metaphysical nature of the world these poems represent. It is, necessarily, both at the same time. "[I]t consciously is not my method," writes Thomas, "to move concentrically round a central image. . . . A poem by myself *needs* a host of images, because its centre is a host of images. I make one image — though 'make' is not the word; I let, perhaps, an image be 'made' emotionally in me and then apply to it what intellectual and critical forces I possess — let it breed another, let that image contradict the first, make, of the third image bred out of the other two together, a fourth contradictory image, and let them all, within my imposed formal limits, conflict" (T, 47).

The center here is the poet's consciousness, but it is also the anonymous darkness, the "god of beginning" out of which all images come. The poet "lets" an image be made in him. It is not a matter of volition or reasoning. These operate only in the construction of the finished poem out of its raw material, or, rather, the poet's will operates in a negative way in the genesis of a poem. He permits the images to come into being within his consciousness. The center is "a host of images," that is, at once the possibility of a vast number of images and the negation of each one, since none is commensurate with its source. The host of images is beyond contradiction. It both contains and denies all the images which may come from it. Each image is as isolated and evanescent as an instant of time, as fragile as the appearing and disappearing mountain in the passage cited earlier. An image does not derive from the one which preceded it, nor does it lead to the next image. "[A]ny sequence of my images must be a sequence of creations, recreations, destructions, contradictions" (T, 48). Each image derives from the center and returns to that center after a momentary and fading existence: "the life must come out of the centre; an image must be born and die in another" (T, 48). The only possible relation between successive images is that of contradiction, or that of a parodoxical breeding in which what is bred utterly denies the breeder. The real father is the "central seed," which not only gives each image its life but is the source of its death: "Each image holds within it the seed of its own destruction, and my dialectal [dialectical?] method, as I understand it, is a constant building up and breaking down of the images that come out of the central seed, which is itself destructive and constructive at the same time" (T, 47, 48). The central seed both validates all images and makes a poetry of continuity impossible. No image which does not come from the central seed will be the stuff of real poetry, and yet the central seed demands that any poem must be what Picasso once called his paintings: "a horde of destructions."

Can the name of poetry be given to a group of contradictory images, each born of the destruction of the preceding one, and forming not a true progression but a chaos of unrelated images? Such poetry, like much important contemporary art, has as its reason for being to be the living proof that art is impossible. Thomas' poetry testifies to the impossibility of bringing alive into the light of day the central seed which is the source of all true poetry. The origin of poetry is the negation of poetry, "destructive and constructive at the same time," and it is this negation to which poetry must testify at the same time that it testifies to the inexhaustible fecundity of the source. Poetry, like its origin, must be "creative destruction, destructive creation" (LVW, 38). When asked if he found increasing satisfaction in his own poetry, Thomas answered: "There is never any satisfaction — that's why I write another poem" (E, 36). Literature is the search for a definitive expression of what can never be expressed, a seeking to say the unsayable, to contain in language what transcends all language. "Poetry is the rhythmic . . . movement from an overclothed blindness to a naked vision . . . . My poetry . . . is the record of my individual struggle from darkness towards some measure of light . . . . Whatever is hidden should be made naked. To be stripped of darkness is to be clean, to strip of darkness is to make clean. . . . Benefiting by the sight of the light and the knowledge of the hidden nakedness, poetry must drag further into the clean nakedness of light more even of the hidden causes than Freud could realize" (QE, 188, 190). And, in one of his last poems, a poem about the relation of the process of living to the place which is death, the poet says: "Dark is a way and light is a place" (CP, 191). The endless advance in the direction of the "elementary town" is darkness, but to be there would be to reach the immobile perception of a dazzling brightness.

Poetry in the sense of an organic structure of words cannot, it would seem, be created out of "naked vision," out of the perception of a light so bright that it can only be experienced as darkness. One answer to this dilemma is the notion that a poem, even if it is made up of a group of conflicting images, can be held together by a narrative line. Thomas' poems are not a conglomeration of disconnected images, but a group of conflicting images centering on a

single event or sequence of events. He will have nothing to do with
the surrealists' random placing of images dredged from the subconscious. One aim of poetry "is to make comprehensible and
articulate what might emerge from subconscious sources; one of the
great main uses of the intellect is to *select* from the amorphous mass
of subconscious images, those that will best further his imaginative
purpose, which is to write the best poem he can" (PM, 52). To
subordinate all to a dramatic action is a good means of shaping and
selection. "Narrative is essential" (QE, 189); "I believe in the
simple thread of action through a poem, but that is an intellectual
thing aimed at lucidity through narrative" (T, 48). Yes, it is an
intellectual thing, merely an intellectual thing, and not the essence
of the poem, not its hidden cause. The poet, it seems, can do nothing
to make this essence available to the reader.

In another passage in the letter to Treece, however, Thomas
describes a transmutation the poem can make of the destructive
and constructive seed which is the origin and denial of poetry.
It is a text which goes to the heart of his conception of the function
of poetry: "Out of the inevitable conflict of images — inevitable,
because of the creative, recreative, destructive and contradictory
nature of the motivating centre, the womb of war — I try to make
that momentary peace which is a poem" (T, 48). How can a poem
both contain and free itself from the central seed? How can it make
of a poem which is "a series of conflicting images" (QE, 169) a
stasis in which "all warring images . . . [are] reconciled for that
small stop of time" (T, 48)? To do so would be to transcend a
situation which seems to make poetry impossible, and to make
human experience a succession of broken and isolated moments
whose single meaning is the affirmation of death.

⌁

Assuming a certain measure of freedom, the freedom at least to
choose an attitude, the poet can relate himself in several ways to
such a world.

He may attempt to yield to the motion of time, to follow that
motion so closely that it will no longer be distinguished as motion:
"Hold hard, these ancient minutes in the cuckoo's month" (CP,
58). This is the tension of an exact following of the curve of time.

It escapes the pain of time, not by denying it or by entering an eternal realm, but by holding it so hard that all sense of movement ceases in a poised moment which is a hyperbolic intensification of time rather than freedom from it.

But does this change anything? Man is already completely identified with the process of nature. "The force that through the green fuse drives the flower/Drives my green age" (CP, 10). However hard I may hold to this force, such holding is nothing more than the acceptance of what is already an accomplished fact. The seasons "must be challenged or they totter/Into a chiming quarter/Where, punctual as death, we ring the stars" (CP, 2). How can the seasons be challenged?

One way is to withdraw from the world and live shut in one's body, or, even more narrowly, in one's consciousness. Thomas considers this possibility in "Ears in the turrets hear." The self is imaged as an enclosed tower with the living world outside knocking for entrance at the door of the senses. "Shall I unbolt," asks Thomas, "or stay/Alone till the day I die/Unseen by stranger-eyes/In this white house?" (CP, 67). This movement of withdrawal is rarely considered by the poet, both because it is in fact impossible, and because he never really wants isolation. The world, with all its horror, is too sweet, too full of light and pleasure:

> I cannot murder, like a fool,
> Season and sunshine, grace and girl,
> Nor can I smother the sweet waking. (CP, 75)

One final possibility remains. Man may deny the seasons, negate them. Negation is the sole power which only human beings have, the power which sets them apart from animals and plants, and even, it may be, from God. Can negation be for Thomas, as for Hegel and Mallarmé, a magical power which makes life of death, and by negating negation produces something positive?

Negation appears first in Thomas simply as defiance, as the refusal of the "dark deniers" (CP, 2) to accept things as they are. It appears as an absolute saying no:

> Now
> Say nay . . . (CP, 60)

> And death shall have no dominion. (CP, 77)

Dry as a tomb, your coloured lids
Shall not be latched while magic glides
Sage on the earth and sky . . . (CP, 12)

Such an attitude of rebellion pretends that, by the assertion of
the contrary of what actually exists, its opposite can be created by
the magical power of words. The imagination of the poet has power
to put rivers in dry riverbeds, to transform death into immortality,
to replace the shrunken corpse of poor Ann Jones, "her wits drilled
hollow," with a "sculptured Ann" who is "seventy years of stone."
The poet, by transmuting dead Ann into the monumental statue
which is the poem, is able to change the entire world and make of
its death, life:

These cloud-sopped, marble hands, this monumental
Argument of the hewn voice, gesture and psalm,
Storm me forever over her grave until
The stuffed lung of the fox twitch and cry Love
And the strutting fern lay seeds on the black sill. (CP, 97)

In the end this defiance accomplishes nothing. It is the hopeless
rage of the man who cannot alter what is happening, but only
refuse to submit to it. Such rage has a shrillness which betrays the
impotence of the defier:

Rebel against the binding moon
And the parliament of sky . . . .
Rebel against the flesh and bone,
The word of the blood, the wily skin,
And the maggot no man can slay. (CP, 74)

Do not go gentle into that good night.
Rage, rage against the dying of the light. (CP, 128)

Death is the maggot no man can slay, not even by such denial of
its power. To refuse with rage to go into that good night does not
change the fact. One goes all the same. Even God cannot keep time
from murdering the green child in the womb. Defiance is negative
in a bad sense, sterile, subsisting in the tension of rejection of whatever happens, but without power to keep it from happening. Its
only grandeur is the grandeur of passive resistance. So Thomas
described his own father, "who, he said, had been a militant
atheist, whose atheism had nothing to do with whether there was a
God or not, but was a violent and personal dislike for God. He

would glance out of the window and growl: 'It's raining, blast Him!' or 'The sun is shining — Lord, what foolishness!' " (E, 38). This defiance, far from producing the momentary peace which is a poem, is an endless impotent anger whose only pleasure is the pleasure of asserting the opposite of what is really the case.

There is no help for it. Man must accept the world and his identification with it.

To accept the world means to embrace even those parts of it which are not immediately present. Human beings can remember in one season the other seasons. They can live winter in terms of summer and summer in terms of winter. So the "boys of summer," the "dark deniers," "Setting no store by harvest, freeze the soils;/There in their heat the winter floods/Of frozen loves they fetch their girls,/And drown the cargoed apples in their tides" (CP, 1, 2). If they "summon/Death from a summer woman," and "from the planted womb the man of straw," they are also able to bring the fecund ocean to the dry desert, to "Pick the world's ball of wave and froth/To choke the deserts with her tides" (CP, 2). The poet, like the boys of summer, must live all the seasons at once, "graft these four-fruited ridings on [his] country" (CP, 69). He must accept his overlapping with the world, the fact that neither he nor his poetry can escape from the stream that is flowing all ways. When he does this, he finds that he can qualitatively affect the world, that he can make a watertight section of the stream, and stop the flowing all ways for an infinitesimal moment of time. He can stop it for the moment when things are poised in a tension of polar opposites: "O see the poles are kissing as they cross" (CP, 3). It is impossible to return the world to the "one windy nothing" (CP, 24) of its primal unity. All that can be attained is a poised equilibrium of opposites. The boy in "A Prospect of the Sea," for example, recovers not the one original Garden of Eden but a balance of "the dark and the green Eden" (A, 189). In the letter to Treece, Thomas says: "I do not want a poem of mine to be, nor can it be, a circular piece of experience placed nearly outside the living stream of time from which it came; a poem of mine is, or should be, a watertight section of the stream that is flowing all ways" (T, 48). The poem is within experience, within the contradictory stream of time. It does not deny it or withdraw from it, and yet it makes a momentary stasis for that small stop of time. Within the watertight compartment of the poem all things are rescued, and Thomas can "rail with [his] wizard's ribs the heart-shaped planet" (CP, 69).

The poet, says the "Author's Prologue" to Thomas' collected poems, is Noah, and the poem is an ark in which the world is received and saved from the flood of time:

> Hark: I trumpet the place,
> From fish to jumping hill! Look:
> I build my bellowing ark
> To the best of my love
> As the flood begins . . . (CP, xvi)

This notion of the poet as Noah must not be misunderstood. To accept all the world means accepting death too, since death is everywhere present in life. To accept death is to anticipate it, but this transfigures the small deaths of all living things. It changes them by putting them in touch with the prospective death of the world. Then each brief event in the world is seen as the image of itself, the ghost of itself. The power to imagine the future makes the present also an image. The poet's "images" roar and rise "on heaven's hill" (CP, 44) in the phoenixlike apotheosis of the poem. It is not the world itself which is reborn, but the world transformed into image through what Thomas calls "the lovely gift of the gab" (CP, 104). Everything is put into the interior of the poem, into a space where only the images of things exist. Thomas' later poetry sees all earthly things as if their deaths had already happened. In the ark of the poem they are rescued and reaffirmed in their disappearance, in their death, as the long-dead girls of "In the white giant's thigh" are resurrected by the poet's celebration of them: "And the daughters of darkness flame like Fawkes fires still" (CP, 199).

This extravagant feat of imagination is the essential poetic act. It underlies the magnificent poems of Thomas' last period: "In country sleep," "Over Sir John's hill," "Poem on his birthday," and "In the white giant's thigh." These poems were to be part of a long series of poems to be called "In Country Heaven," which the poet left unfinished when he died. The series was to be written as if from the perspective of the dead in heaven after the self-destruction of the world: "The Earth has killed itself. It is black, petrified, wizened, poisoned, burst; insanity has blown it rotten; and no creatures at all, joyful, despairing, cruel, kind, dumb, afire, loving, dull, shortly and brutishly hunt their days down like enemies on that corrupted face" (QE, 179). In the darkness of heaven, as God weeps for the death of the earth and "Light and His tears glide down together, hand in hand" (QE, 179), the dead give the shriveled and blackened earth an eternal existence in their memory of it. This is not a matter, as it is for Mallarmé, of the hyperbolic destruction, in imagination, of the world, and then the creation, within the emptiness remaining after this annihilation, of "an ideal which exists by means of its own dream." Rather, it is the act of returning upon the world of created things after their deaths, assuming them all sacrificially, dying their deaths again for them, and by this doubling saving them, affirming them as alive in the midst of their deaths. So the dead earthlings of "In Country Heaven" praise the vanished earth in the vividness of a memory which turns into description in the present tense: "And, one by one, these heavenly hedgerow-men, who once were of the Earth, call one another, through the long night, Light and His tears falling, what they remember, what they sense in the submerged wilderness and on the exposed hairsbreadth of the mind, what they feel trembling on the nerves of a nerve, what they know in their Edenic hearts, of that self-called place. They remember places, fears, loves, exultation, misery, animal joy, ignorance and mysteries, all *we* know and do not know. The poem is made of these tellings. And the poem becomes, at last, an affirmation of the beautiful and terrible worth of the Earth. It grows into a praise of what is and what could be on this lump in the skies. It is a poem about happiness" (QE, 179, 180).

At the moment when the earth has disappeared, it reappears in all the fullness of its life. To see it as if it were already dead is to know for the first time all we, the living, "know and do not know." Miraculously, the sensible vividness of the world is given back. Only by seeing things from the perspective of their death, only by willing their death, can they be recaptured in their vitality, and, paradoxically, saved from death:

> . . . the closer I move
> To death, one man through his sundered hulks,
>   The louder the sun blooms
> And the tusked, ramshackling sea exults . . . (CP, 193)

But there is no possible distinction in Thomas between image and experience. The watertight compartment of words is still within the stream that is flowing all ways. To make an image of things in terms of the coming death of all things is to experience them in this way. It is for them to *be* in this way. Therefore the poet must "take/The kissproof world" (CP, 23). This is an acceptance which is a defiance, because it is a transcendence. Thomas, the mediator, the Noah, must, like Christ, "unsex the skeleton," make death impotent. He does this not by denying death but by making himself the converging point where everything dies. He must assume in himself the death of all things, and thereby defeat death. Thomas, like Christ, must be able to say:

> I by the tree of thieves, all glory's sawbones,
> Unsex the skeleton this mountain minute,
> And by this blowclock witness of the sun
> Suffer the heaven's children through my heartbeat. (CP, 84)

To "suffer the little children to come unto me" means not to deny or put a stop to the suffering of all created things, all heaven's children. It means sharing their suffering, suffering with them and for them, suffering in one's own heartbeat the necessary suffering of the creation. It is in this sense that "the joy and function of poetry is, and was, the celebration of man, which is also the celebration of God" (PM, 53). To see man from the point of view of death is to see him with God's eyes. To rescue man from death by praise of the beautiful and terrible worth of the earth is to praise the God who has created the earth and is present in all its happenings. God and man are joined together in the watertight compartment of the poem. By a sympathetic identification with the temporal process of the world, an identification which is the act of poetry, the poet can make himself a Noah's ark. He can save things from destruction by participating in their destruction. Such participation is, in the full sense of the words, "an affirmation of the beautiful and terrible worth of the Earth." In this affirmation the poet affirms himself, the ark which contains all things.

To affirm and rescue the earth is to affirm and rescue the self, which at no point in Thomas' experience can separate itself from the totality of the created world. This coincidence of self and world, in all the stages of Thomas' growth as a poet, makes his work another variety of the twentieth-century poetry of reality. Self, world, and deity dwell together in the ark of the poem. "I suffer the earth, therefore I affirm myself and also the God-ordained rightness of whatever happens on earth" — this is Thomas' version of the Cartesian Cogito:

> My ark sings in the sun
> At God speeded summer's end
> And the flood flowers now. (CP, xviii)

VI

Wallace Stevens

We were as Danes in Denmark all day long
And knew each other well, hale-hearted landsmen,
For whom the outlandish was another day

Of the week, queerer than Sunday. We thought alike
And that made brothers of us in a home
In which we fed on being brothers, fed

And fattened as on a decorous honeycomb.

There was once a time when man lived in harmony with his fellows and his surroundings. This harmony was a unified culture, a single view of things. Men thought alike and understood each other perfectly, like the most intimate of brothers. Since they shared an interpretation of the world they did not think of it as one perspective among many possible ones. It was the true picture of reality. Any other interpretation was queer, outlandish, something wild, ignorant, barbarian. Each man felt at home, like a Dane in Denmark, not a Dane in Greece or Patagonia. Just as he possessed his fellows in the brotherhood of a single culture, so he possessed nature through their collective interpretation of it. He was a landsman, an inlander, someone dwelling close to the earth. Since man, society, and environment made one inextricable unity, as of Danes in Denmark, no one was aware of himself as a separate mind. Each was as much at home in the world as the bee in his honeycomb, the dwelling place which he has exuded from his own body and which now forms his food. All self-consciousness was lost in this reflexive feeding and fattening, and man "lay sticky with sleep."

So enduring and beneficent did this order seem that it was impossible to believe that man himself could have made it. Surely, we thought, our happy world must be the gift of some supernatural beings, and these gods must guarantee its rightness and permanence. They seemed outside or beyond our world, "speechless, invisible." They ruled us and sustained us "by/Our merest apprehension of their will." Our culture was revelation of the invisible and speech of the speechless gods.

Suddenly something catastrophic happened, and this happy order was destroyed:

> A tempest cracked on the theatre. Quickly,
> The wind beat in the roof and half the walls.
> The ruin stood still in an external world.
>
>   . . .
>
> It had been real. It was not now. The rip
> Of the wind and the glittering were real now,
> In the spectacle of a new reality.[1]

Once the theater is ruined it can never be rebuilt. The fact that it can be destroyed proves that even when it existed it was not what it seemed. It seemed a divine gift, something as solid as the earth itself. Now man knows that all along it was a painted scene. The true reality has always been the wind and the indifferent glittering of an external world, a world in which no man can ever feel at home.

When the tempest cracks on the theater the whole thing disintegrates: "exit the whole/Shebang" (CP, 37). Men are no longer brothers, but strange to each other. The land withdraws to a distance and comes to be seen as no longer included in man's interpretations of it. Only cold and vacancy remain "When the phantoms are gone and the shaken realist/First sees reality" (CP, 320). As soon as nature becomes outlandish the gods disappear like ghosts dissolving in sunlight. They do not withdraw for a time to an unattainable distance, as they did for De Quincey or Matthew Arnold. They vanish altogether, leaving nothing behind. They reveal themselves to be fictions, aesthetic projections of man's gratuitous values. Having seen the gods of one culture disappear, man can never again believe in any god. "The death of one god is the death of all" (CP, 381; see also OP, 165).

---

[1] The following texts of Stevens' work have been used in this chapter. Each is accompanied by the abbreviation which will hereafter be employed in citations. *The Necessary Angel: Essays on Reality and the Imagination* (New York: Alfred A. Knopf, 1951): NA; *The Collected Poems of Wallace Stevens* (New York: Alfred A. Knopf, 1954): CP; *Opus Posthumous* (New York: Alfred A. Knopf, 1957): OP. Quotations in the initial paragraphs of this chapter come, respectively, from CP, 419, 419, 262, 262, 306.

This vanishing of the gods, leaving a barren man in a barren land, is the basis of all Stevens' thought and poetry. His version of the death of the gods coincides with a radical transformation in the way man sees the world. What had been a warm home takes on a look of hardness and emptiness, like the walls, floors, and banisters of a vacant house. Instead of being intimately possessed by man, things appear to close themselves within themselves. They become mute, static presences:

> To see the gods dispelled in mid-air and dissolve like clouds is one of the great human experiences. It is not as if they had gone over the horizon to disappear for a time; nor as if they had been overcome by other gods of greater power and profounder knowledge. It is simply that they came to nothing. Since we have always shared all things with them and have always had a part of their strength and, certainly, all of their knowledge, we shared likewise this experience of annihilation. . . . It left us feeling dispossessed and alone in a solitude, like children without parents, in a home that seemed deserted, in which the amical rooms and halls had taken on a look of hardness and emptiness. What was most extraordinary is that they left no mementos behind, no thrones, no mystic rings, no texts either of the soil or of the soul. It was as if they had never inhabited the earth. There was no crying out for their return. (OP, 206, 207).

There was no crying out for their return because man knew they would never come back. They would never come back because they had never been there at all. In the impoverishing of the world when the gods disappear man discovers himself, orphaned and dispossessed, a solitary consciousness. Then are men truly "natives of poverty, children of malheur" (CP, 322). The moment of self-awareness coincides with the moment of the death of the gods. God is dead, therefore I am. But I am nothing. I am nothing because I have nothing, nothing but awareness of the barrenness within and without. When the gods dissolve like clouds they "come to nothing," and then man is "nothing himself." Since this is so, he "beholds/Nothing that is not there and the nothing that is" (CP, 10).

This nothing is an annihilating force which rejects everything fictitious. It wipes away each incipient reconstruction of the old harmony before it has had time to crystallize, and sees all "the integrations of the past" as a mere "Museo Olimpico" (CP, 342). The "nothing" is the resolute misery of the man who refuses to accept anything unreal as real and holds to the nothing within as that which destroys the blandishments of appearance. This rejection allows man to retain the nothing that *is* there. For this reason "poetry is a destructive force." As the poem of that title says, the positive nothing is as strong and real as would be a live ox breathing in the breast of a lion:

> That's what misery is,
> Nothing to have at heart.
> It is to have or nothing.
>
> It is a thing to have,
> A lion, an ox in his breast,
> To feel it breathing there. (CP, 192)

The destructive force of the nothing can be seen not only in the bewildering metamorphoses of the rest of the poem (from ox to dog to ox again, then to bear, and finally to man as embodiments of the inner nothing), but also in the dislocation of syntax in the sentence: "It is to have or nothing." The nothing is there in the reader's frustrated attempts to make logical sense of these words, and it is there in the absent object of the verb "to have": It is to have   or nothing. The sentence seems to say that misery is to have either nothing or nothing. If to have nothing is not to have something then man has nothing else.

                      ⌣

What has caused this collapse of man's happy world, leaving him as in a hall of empty mirrors where nothing multiplies nothing? The answer to this question could be historical, an appeal to the world-destroying events which led to the appearance of a relativistic sense of the past in the eighteenth century, to Nietzsche's "Gott ist tot" in the nineteenth, and to the currents of nihilism in our own day. Stevens sometimes writes this way, as in "The Noble Rider and the Sound of Words" (1942). "[I]n speaking of the pressure of reality," he says, "I am thinking of life in a state of violence, not physically violent, as yet, for us in America, but physically violent for millions of our friends and for still more millions of our enemies and spiritually violent, it may be said, for everyone alive" (NA, 26, 27). But the real answer to the question is simpler than this, and in a way more disquieting. It takes no French or Copernican revolution, no catastrophic world wars, no industrializing of the world to overturn everything. A change of place or change of season is enough. Put a Dane in Patagonia and his sense of being at home will be blotted out, never to be unblotted. The first section of "The Comedian as the Letter C" is the story of this dissolution, a dissolution which happens as naturally and irrevocably as the falling of leaves in autumn.

Crispin has been at home in his New England milieu of "berries of villages," "simple salad-beds," and "honest quilts." He has been the "sovereign ghost" of his place, its "intelligence," "principium," and "lex" (CP, 27). A "simple jaunt" from Bordeaux to Yucatan, and then to Carolina by way of Havana is his undoing. The sea is a great heaving monster speaking its own incomprehensible speech, an inscrutable mystery to a mind accustomed to salad-beds, and "mythology of self" is "blotched out beyond unblotching" (CP, 28). At the same time there is an annihilation of the residual sense that there are gods in nature. Triton dissolves to "faint, memorial gesturings,/That were like arms and shoulders in the waves" (CP, 29). The primitive feeling that nature is full of gods is replaced by self-conscious awareness that man has an incorrigible habit of personifying nature. Mythology of self and mythology of the world disappear together. What seemed the work of vast historical changes is accomplished in a moment by the confrontation of a mind equipped with its local mythology and a material reality which that mythology cannot comprehend. The regional fiction reveals itself as hollow, and so dissolves. Now man sees "The World without Imagination" (CP, 27). At the same time the self, deprived of its mythology, shrinks to nothing. The dialogue of the mind with itself commences, and Crispin becomes "an introspective voyager" (CP, 29).

Though this dissolving of the self is in one way the end of everything, in another way it is a happy liberation. There are only two entities left now that the gods are dead: man and nature, subject and object. Nature is the physical world, visible, audible, tangible, present to all the senses, and man is consciousness, the nothing which receives nature and transforms it into something unreal — "description without place" (CP, 339). In conceiving the world in this way Stevens inherits the tradition of dualism coming down from Descartes and the seventeenth century. Like that tradition generally, he is an unfaithful disciple of Descartes. The Cartesian

God disappears from his world, and only mind and matter remain, mind confronting a matter which it makes into a mirror of itself. This bifurcation of reality is the universal human condition, from the creation until now:

Adam
In Eden was the father of Descartes
And Eve made air the mirror of herself,

Of her sons and of her daughters. (CP, 383)

If the natural activity of the mind is to make unreal representations, these are still representations of the material world. "The clouds preceded us/There was a muddy centre before we breathed" (CP, 383); matter is prior to mind and in some sense determines it. So, in "Sunday Morning," the lady's experience of the dissolution of the gods leaves her living in a world of exquisite particulars, the physical realities of the new world: "Deer walk upon our mountains, and the quail/Whistle about us their spontaneous cries;/Sweet berries ripen in the wilderness" (CP, 70). This physical world, an endless round of birth, death, and the seasons, is more lasting than any interpretation of it. Religions, myths, philosophies, and cultures are all fictions and pass away, but "April's green endures" (CP, 68).

"Sunday Morning" is Stevens' most eloquent description of the moment when the gods dissolve. Bereft of the supernatural, man does not lie down paralyzed in despair. He sings the creative hymns of a new culture, the culture of those who are "wholly human" and know themselves (CP, 317). This humanism is based on man's knowledge that "the final belief is to believe in a fiction, which you know to be a fiction, there being nothing else. The exquisite truth is to know that it is a fiction and that you believe in it willingly" (OP, 163). There is "nothing else" — the alternatives are to be nothing or to accept a fiction. To discover that there never has been any celestial world is a joyful liberation, and man says of himself: "This happy creature — It is he that invented the Gods. It is he that put into their mouths the only words they have ever spoken!" (OP, 167).

To discover that man has invented the gods is to find out the dependence of the mind on nature. Mental fictions are derived from material things: "All of our ideas come from the natural world: trees = umbrellas" (OP, 163). Since this is true, the only way to give mental fictions authenticity is to base them on the world of sun and rain and April: "The real is only the base. But it is the base" (OP, 160). When Stevens speaks this way, he is a poet of a happy naturalism. In many eloquent passages he celebrates the joy of "the latest freed man" (CP, 204), the man who has escaped from the gods and is able to step barefoot into reality. This man has shed the old myths as a snake sheds its skin, and can cry in exultation: "the past is dead./Her mind will never speak to me again./I am free" (CP, 117). Liberated from the bad faith which attributed to some never-never land the glory of earth, man does not lose the golden glory of heaven. He transfers to what is close and real, the "in-bar," what he had falsely ascribed to transcendent realms, the "ex-bar" (CP, 317). Culture has always been based on the permanences of sun, air, and earth. Now man knows that this is so. He knows that "The greatest poverty is not to live/In a physical world" (CP, 325), and this brings about a sudden miraculous recovery of the vitality of earth.

‿

But umbrellas are not trees. Even the nakedest man is not part of nature in the same way that stones or trees are. Man possesses imagination, and, though "the imagination is one of the forces of nature" (OP, 170), the peculiar potency of this force is to transform nature, to make trees into umbrellas. In changing nature, the imagination irradiates it with its own idiosyncratic hue. The poet must accept this distortion as in the nature of things. The green of reality is altered by the blue of imagination, and there is no helping this fact. The mind turns to reality and is enriched by it, but it also shapes the real into myths, religions, and other forms of poetry. The worst evil is a victory of one power over the other, a romanticism which kicks itself loose of the earth, or a pressure of reality so great that it overwhelms imagination. "Eventually an imaginary world is entirely without interest" (OP, 175), but, on the other hand, man today is confronting events "beyond [his] power to reduce them and metamorphose them" (NA, 22), and as a result "There are no shadows anywhere./The earth, for us, is flat and bare" (CP, 167). Fresh fictions must now replace the old.

The creation, after the death of the gods, of new fictions, based on fact and not pretending to be more than fictions, is the act of poetry. "After one has abandoned a belief in God, poetry is that essence which takes its place as life's redemption" (OP, 158). In defining poetry as a substitute for religion Stevens is joining himself to a tradition extending from the romantics through Matthew Arnold down to our own day.

The dialogue between subject and object is Stevens' central theme, and it seems that this interchange can become a "mystic marriage," like that of the great captain and the maiden Bawda in "Notes toward a Supreme Fiction" (CP, 401). Imagination and reality can merge to produce a third thing which escapes from the limitations of either, and we can triumphantly "mate [our] life with life" (CP, 222). "If it should be true that reality exists/In the mind . . . it follows that/Real and unreal are two in one" (CP, 485). The red of reality and the blue of imagination join to become the "purple tabulae" on which may be read the poem of life (CP, 424). It is not necessary to choose between Don Quixote and Sancho Panza. Man can have both, and poetry is the search for those fortuitous conjunctions between self and world which show that they are not irreconcilable opposites, but two sides of the same coin, "equal and inseparable" (NA, 24).

The poverty following the death of the gods can apparently be transcended without difficulty. Stevens' real choice is neither for the subjectivism coming down from Descartes nor for the submission to physical nature which he sometimes praises. His tradition is rather perspectivism, historicism, *lebensphilosophie*. He is one of the subtlest expositors of this tradition. His predecessors are Feuerbach, Dilthey, Nietzsche, Ortega y Gasset, Santayana, and Henri Focillon, the Focillon whose *Vie des formes* Stevens calls "one of the really remarkable books of the day" (NA, 46). Like these thinkers, Stevens sees human history as the constant proliferation of forms of art and culture which are valid only for one time and place. These are determined exclusively neither by geography nor by the untrammeled human mind, but everywhere are the offspring of a marriage of man and the place where he lives. The fact that one man's fictions can be accepted by others makes society possible. "An age is a manner collected from a queen./An age is green or red. An age believes/Or it denies," and "Things are as they seemed to Calvin or to Anne/Of England, to Pablo Neruda in Ceylon,/To Nietzsche in Basel, to Lenin by a Lake" (CP, 340, 341, 342).

In human history two things are constantly happening. Men are always being bent to their environment, driven to make their life forms a mirror of the weather of their place, for "the gods grow out of the weather./The people grow out of the weather" (CP, 210), and "the natives of the rain are rainy men" (CP, 37). On the other hand, the mind organizes the land in which it finds itself, as the moon makes concentric circles in the random twigs of a leafless tree, or as the jar in Tennessee orders the wilderness around it and takes dominion everywhere. The jar is a human artifact. Its man-made shape has the power to structure everything radially around it, as the red queen makes a whole age red. The jar is one of the "Imaginary poles whose intelligence/Stream[s] over chaos their civilities" (CP, 479).

Stevens' work can be summed up in two adages: "The soul . . . is composed/Of the external world" (CP, 51); "It is never the thing but the version of the thing" (CP, 332). His poetry is the reconciliation of these two truths, truths which are always simultaneously binding in the endless intercourse of imagination and reality. Words are the best marriage-place of mind and world. In language a people gives speech to its environment, and at the same time it creates itself in that speech. Language is at once the expression of a style of life and the embodiment of a local weather and geography.

～

. . . Of this,
A few words, an and yet, and yet, and yet — (CP, 465)

Apparently this is the whole story about Stevens. From one end of his work to the other he reiterates a single idea, and all his work is an attempt to explore the endlessly variable perspectives from which reality can be viewed by the imagination. He is resolutely carrying out Nietzsche's injunction that man the survivor of God should experiment tirelessly with new truths, new representations, new life forms.

And yet — Stevens' poems are rarely celebrations of the triumphant ease with which man "imposes orders as he thinks of them" (CP, 403). They describe instead a universal fluctuation. This motif is especially evident in *Harmonium*, but it is a constant theme throughout. A great many of Stevens' poems show an object or group of objects in aimless oscillation or circling movement. The space of the poem is filled with things which slip away and evade the observer's grasp. "Life is motion" (CP, 83), and even in an apparently calm scene "invisible currents clearly circulate" (CP, 156). Though Stevens sometimes yields willingly to this mobility and describes with gay felicity "the pleasure of merely circulating" (CP, 149), "the going round/And round and round, the merely going round" (CP, 405), more often there is something disquieting about the reiterated fluttering or undulation. Such poems make the reader feel vaguely uneasy, as if he were a little seasick:

> It comes about that the drifting of these curtains
> Is full of long motions . . . (CP, 62)

> Whether it be in mid-sea
> On the dark, green water-wheel,
> Or on the beaches,
> There must be no cessation
> Of motion, or of the noise of motion,
> The renewal of noise
> And manifold continuation . . . (CP, 60)

Things are curving through space, and even as they move they are vibrating or oscillating, as a wave has its own periodic undulation, but also advances on the dark green water wheel toward the beach. The space of Stevens' poetry is often filled with groups of things moving in this double way, so that the reader is faced with a whole area occupied by a dispersed wavering, like the "casual flocks of pigeons" in "Sunday Morning" which "make/ Ambiguous undulations as they sink,/Downward to darkness, on extended wings" (CP, 70).

The ambiguity of this universal motion goes beyond the fact that things are neither here nor there, but always on the way somewhere else. They are also changing substance. Metamorphosis is the law of life. Like Lady Lowzen, Stevens is someone "for whom what is [is] other things" (CP, 272). His poems are often a series of fluid transformations in which objects modulate into one another by a process which is not metaphorical because all the elements in the series are on the same level of reality. One image melts away and is replaced by another which is a further example of mobility and instability:

> I heard them cry — the peacocks.
> Was it a cry against the twilight
> Or against the leaves themselves
> Turning in the wind,
> Turning as the flames
> Turned in the fire,
> Turning as the tails of the peacocks
> Turned in the loud fire . . . ?

> Out of the window,
> I saw how the planets gathered
> Like the leaves themselves
> Turning in the wind. (CP, 9)

> The going of the glade-boat
> Is like water flowing . . .
> Under the rainbows
> That are like birds,
> Turning, bedizened . . . (CP, 12)

Leaves, flames, peacocks, planets; glade-boat, water, rainbows, birds — the poetic space of such poems is created by the interrelation of a series of images which are equivalents of one another. Each image in "Domination of Black" or "The Load of Sugar-Cane" is another case of the universal turning or flowing. There is no progression from one to another, and each has the same quality of firstness. It is as if the reader were facing the spatial representation of a temporal sequence of metamorphoses, or, one might say, it is like the universe of Heraclitus. There is a constant interchange between the four elements, with air turning into fire at the same time as fire turns into air, and so on, so that the balance remains the same. As in the paintings of abstract expressionism, there is no "beyond" to which the images refer, and they do not appear to exist against a background which exceeds them and goes backward into invisible distances. The black which dominates in "Domination of Black" lies just behind the surface images and expresses more the fear generated by the flux of things than a trancendent power of darkness. The night too is a colored surface and comes striding "like the color of the heavy hemlocks" (CP, 9). The death of the gods exists not only as Stevens' theoretical presupposition, but in the intimate texture of his verse. His images entirely contain their own reality. They are not symbolic. They are what they are. In this they are like physical objects, for these too, in Stevens' world, do not have meaning, nor do they point toward some ideal world which they signify. Natural objects and poetic images simply exist. "A poem need not have a meaning and like most things in nature often does not have" (OP, 177).

This absence of any transcendent reality to which images might refer is related to Stevens' assumption that things are what they appear to be: colored forms in motion. Poetry need concern itself solely with "the surface of things" (CP, 57), for "the aspects of earth of interest to a poet are the casual ones, as light or color, images" (OP, 157), and "art, broadly, is the form of life or the sound or color of life" (OP, 158). This notion leads Stevens to write what might be called expressionist poems,[2] poems which attempt to create, as does much modern painting, a surface of colored forms without depth. These force the spectator to remain close to a primitive level of sensation where the hue, shape, texture, or sound of a thing is more important than the fact that it is an identifiable object. "It was," says Stevens in one text, "the importance of the trees outdoors,/The freshness of the oak-leaves, not so much/That they were oak-leaves, as the way they looked" (CP, 205). This concern with the phenomenology of sensation is apparent in his lavish use of color words, especially in his early poetry. As in Conrad's work, this insistence on colors is a way of bypassing the intellectual perception that the thing has such and such a name, and a way of keeping close to what it may "really be": a colored shape, moving or motionless. Stevens too recognizes that color is anonymous. Even the most delicate nuance of tint can be shared by any number of things. Color is no means of identifying an object and has nothing to do with its individuality. It is an abstract quality which a thing shares with all the other things which are the same color:

> The child's hair is of the color of the hay in the haystack,
>   around which the four black horses stand.
> There is the same color in the bellies of frogs, in clays,
>   withered reeds, skins, wood, sunlight. (OP, 8)

[2] See Michel Benamou, "Wallace Stevens: Some Relations between Poetry and Painting," *Comparative Literature*, 11: 47–60 (1959).

Stevens makes no use of the presentation of a world of qualities as a stage leading to the confrontation of a hidden darkness behind it. For him there is neither darkness nor light behind. There is only the surface of things. Many of his poems present a riot of exotic colors which confronts the beholder with revolving blobs or patches in a shallow space. These shades are often not the colors the things named usually have, but seem to have been put into the poem in order to produce an abstract pattern of colors:

> If awnings were celeste and gay,
> Iris and orange, crimson and green,
> Blue and vermilion, purple and white . . . (OP, 28)

> The yellow glistens.
> It glistens with various yellows,
> Citrons, oranges and greens
> Flowering over the skin. (CP, 196, 197)

> The green roses drifted up from the table
> In smoke. The blue petals became
> The yellowing fomentations of effulgence,
> Among fomentations of black bloom and of white bloom. (CP, 370)

This use of color words is only one example of Stevens' rejection of any beyond. The images in his poems are as primary and self-enclosed, and as superficial, as colors. Their meanings are entirely contained in the nuances which make them what they are. In the absence of any reference in depth, all the referential vibration must be horizontal: a resonance between the images themselves. Nothing exists in isolation. As in Whitehead's philosophy, there is always an interaction of two or more things. The being of each thing depends on these interchanges: "Nothing exists by itself" (CP, 244); "Nothing is itself taken alone. Things are because of interrelations or interactions" (OP, 163). So:

> A man and a woman
> Are one.
> A man and a woman and a blackbird
> Are one. (CP, 93)

If the existence of things depends on relation, then "the inter-relation between things is what makes them fecund" (OP, 293). Like the imagists and the old Chinese poets, Stevens knows that the juxtaposition of images will start vibrations and echoes, perhaps harmonious, perhaps ironic and discordant. The mind naturally creates this musical interaction in its search for coherence. His usual way of exploiting this fact is to set side by side images of different things which share a quality. The meaning of the poem arises from the fecund interrelation of the images. This produces something which is the offspring of the images but different from them. It might be defined as the reader's perception of the one in the many, his recognition that each image is like the others in some way. Poems of this sort are made up of a group of things or actions bound together by being examples of a universal activity which permeates them:

> An old man sits
> In the shadow of a pine tree
> In China.
> He sees larkspur,
> Blue and white,
> At the edge of the shadow,
> Move in the wind.
> His beard moves in the wind.
> The pine tree moves in the wind.
> Thus water flows
> Over weeds. (CP, 73)

In this poem, as in many others, the activity which things share is undulating motion. A wavering vibration pervades the world and binds things together. Each object is another representation of this universal movement, and all things are metamorphoses of one another. The larkspur, the old man's beard, the pine tree, and the weeds are swept through by a piercing force, whether of wind or water, and in this irresistible medium they all waver and sway.

To read Stevens' poetry with attention to its phenomenal characteristics is not at all to find oneself in a realm where reality yields easily to the imposition of imaginary orders. "[N]othing solid is its solid self" (CP, 345). Everything escapes from the mind's grasp and becomes some other thing, or is like some other thing, or is replaced in the center of attention by some other thing. Impermanence is the only permanence in this flat world of circulating colored surfaces. There is no rich echo of nuance and meaning from the poetic tradition, as in Eliot or Yeats. God is dead, and with him died the heaven of consecrated symbols coming down through the Christian or Platonic ages. Stevens' earth is flat and bare, and a bowl of flowers is just a bowl of flowers.

The only possible expansion in these poems is a paradoxical result of this superficiality and narrowness. In each poem the mind confronts a small group of images which interact. Since the meaning of these images is entirely contained in their appearance, they fill up the whole span of the mind. The world is reduced to just these things, as they are, but this reduction is also a widening. The images swell up to become cosmic and universal. In the end nothing remains but a bouquet of flowers or a few elements forming a landscape:

In my room, the world is beyond my understanding;
But when I walk I see that it consists of three or four hills and a cloud. (CP, 57)

This universalizing of particulars is evident in Stevens' constant use of the four primitive elements — bare earth; wind blowing beard and pine tree alike; water, which transforms all things it touches, as Crispin is washed away by magnitude; and fire, absorbing everything in its flaming metamorphosis, leaves, peacocks' tails, and planets. A restricted image like blue and white larkspur becomes an expression of totality by blending with one of these elements. Each cosmic constituent means the same thing. Even bare earth must yield to time and the round of the seasons. Everywhere in Stevens the reader confronts another proof that the sovereign law of reality is change.

⌣

If reality is always moving, so is the other pole of existence. The mind too wavers, now this way, now that, just as does reality. It seeks a happy balance of diverse elements in which things will come right at last, but things do not come right. The mind's inner fluctuations are an exact match for the external wavering of things as they yield to the forces of change:

This is how the wind shifts:
Like the thoughts of an old human,
Who still thinks eagerly
And despairingly. (CP, 83)

The mind shifts like the wind not because it is driven by a universal law of change. Impelled by a rage for order, it wills its own

movement in the search for "what will suffice" (CP, 239). Though
"the mind roam[s] as a moth roams" (CP, 22) in the search for
some way to tranquilize the "torments of confusion" (CP, 27),
it finds that "it can never be satisfied, the mind, never" (CP, 247).
The mind can never be satisfied because "the squirming facts
exceed the squamous mind" (CP, 215). Try as it will, testing first
one way of putting it and then another, the mind cannot impose
peace on the world. Stevens' verse has a tentative, questioning,
experimental quality. He is like a man seeking a magic formula
which will transfigure reality, or like a man improvising on the
guitar, seeking the elusive melody which will no longer be his own
invention but the truth of things playing themselves on the strings:

> Where
> Do I begin and end? And where,
>
> As I strum the thing, do I pick up
> That which momentously declares
>
> Itself not to be I and yet
> Must be. It could be nothing else. (CP, 171)

The imagination wants a complete understanding of the world,
a perfect integration of mind and reality. It seeks a stasis in which
opposites become an indistinguishable unit, "Placed, so, beyond
the compass of change,/Perceived in a final atmosphere;/For a
moment final" (CP, 168). This is the "relentless contact" the mind
desires, that "blissful liaison,/Between himself and his environment" which is Crispin's "chief motive" and "first delight" (CP,
34). The poet searches for images in which "we awake,/Within
the very object that we seek,/Participants of its being" (CP, 463).
Only such a full possession of reality will be escape from undulation.
The central motivation of Stevens' poetry might therefore be defined as a search for immobility.

But fixity is unattainable. Man remains "helplessly at the edge"
(CP, 430), excluded from that center around which everything
would organize itself in neat concentric circles. However hard he
tries to "piece the world together" (CP, 192), it evades his attempts
to order it. In "Metaphors of a Magnifico" (CP, 19) Stevens
experiments with different notions of what happens when twenty.
men cross a bridge into a village. Is it "twenty men crossing twenty
bridges,/into twenty villages" or "one man/Crossing a single

bridge into a village"? The perplexities of the relations between one imagination and another or between several imaginations and reality cannot be untangled. The mind remains baffled, as if it were in the presence of "old song/That will not declare itself," and "the meaning escapes." The meaning of the simplest thing, a bouquet of flowers in the sunlight, always escapes, and the mind remains dissatisfied. "Nothing is final" (CP, 150), and man can never escape the perpetual motion of things.

This motion is the combined oscillation of mind and things, as the mind wanders here and there seeking to capture a reality which is itself eternally changing. Imagination and reality are like two charged poles which repel one another as they approach and can never touch, though the relation between them creates a vibrant field of forces. Existence is neither imagination alone nor reality alone, but always and everywhere the endlessly frustrated attempt of the two to cross the gap which separates them. Attracting and repelling, loving and hating, dependent on each other for their being and yet seeking independence, mind and world perpetuate a dance or round from which all things come. Though imagination yearns for the real, and follows it as a lover follows his beloved, the two can never "walk away as one in the greenest body" (CP, 392). This is the "misery" to which Stevens so often confesses. It derives from the eternal failure of the imagination to step barefoot into reality, and appears in repeated descriptions of a world which is separated from the imagination and seen as cold and dead, so that "The world is ugly,/And the people are sad" (CP, 85). The corpse in "The Emperor of Ice-Cream" appears in a scrupulously sordid scene where "be" has become "finale of seem" (CP, 64). All imaginative coloring has been drained out of reality, and the corpse is merely a corpse. In another poem "The pillars are prostrate, the arches are haggard,/The hotel is boarded and bare" (CP, 135). In such texts the gap between imagination and the world appears in the way the mind impotently confronts a reality altogether flat and unadorned. In other poems the imagination operates in a negative way, as the creator of an interior region of color and splendor which cannot be carried across the emptiness separating it from reality. In one poem the speaker says that there is nothing of "romance" or of "the ideal" in the French flowers she is embroidering on an old black dress.

It would have been different, she says, if she had imagined herself "In an orange gown,/Drifting through space,/Like a figure on the church-wall" (CP, 73). It *would* have been different, and the imagination is present in the Chagall-like figure in the orange gown, but this remains a dream which has been unable to impose itself on reality, just as in another poem Stevens complains that the houses are haunted with ordinary white nightgowns, and not with nightgowns of "green,/Or purple with green rings,/Or green with yellow rings,/Or yellow with blue rings." In such a world no one is going to dream of "baboons and periwinkles" (CP, 66). In "Metropolitan Melancholy" (OP, 32) the poet confesses sadly: "To dab things even nicely pink/Adds very little,/So I think." These dispirited poems lament the death of the imagination, its inability to touch reality and be made fruitful by it. Cut off from imagination reality becomes a matter of white nightgowns. Cut off from reality imagination is a factitious pink paint which cannot cover the ugliness of things.

Each of Stevens' poems incarnates the vibrating flow between images, but also the unreconciled tension between self and world. This produces poems which are a dynamic equilibrium of opposing forces, each pulling the other but also pushing it away. The repelling force is as necessary as the attracting one, for if the images were ever to coincide the poem would disappear. The first poem in *The Collected Poems* contains in miniature all these aspects of Stevens' poetry and is an excellent example of their quality. The opposing energies in the poem, the bucks and the firecat, are interdependent. The bucks go clattering over Oklahoma and then swerve in a "swift, circular line" to the left or to the right when the firecat bristles in the way. The motion of the bucks is determined by the firecat, and the firecat bristles because of the bucks. As long as the two forces confront one another the activity which makes up the poem goes on. The poem is called "Earthy Anecdote." The space of the poem is earthy, objective, but at the same time it is the space of the mind. To speak of the earth is to speak of the mind, and of the relation between mind and earth. The firecat is a fabulous beast which, like the imagination, attracts and repels the realities opposed to it. The poem is as much about that intercourse between self and world which is the source of poetry as it is about the relation between things of the earth. The relation between firecat and bucks is an example of the universal interaction that makes things fecund. The objects in the poem are expanded until they take up all of Oklahoma, and if Oklahoma why not the earth? Earth and mind are reduced to these elements, and motion on one side is possible only so long as there is life on the other. When the firecat closes his bright eyes and sleeps, the bucks stop clattering and the poem ends, just as it would if the firecat and the bucks came together. In the first case the spending of energy disappears as soon as the push and pull between forces comes to an end. In the second case they would annihilate one another if they touched.

Reality resists the mind with a kind of stubborn vitality, and imagination is driven to its extravagant peregrinations not by desire for novelty but by the fact that none of its strategies attain that fusion with life it wants. This "war between the mind/And sky, between thought and day and night" (CP, 407) is the basis of poetry.

⁓

Perhaps the most pervasive form of the search for a truce to this war is willed metamorphosis, perspectivism. This is not the easy reshaping of a passive reality by the sovereign imagination. It is a search for an elusive and uncertain reality. Instead of beginning with reality as a given and then confecting a fictitious picture of it, the imagination must use all its powers to find reality and fix it. "I must impale myself on reality," says Stevens (OP, xxiv). This decision to commit oneself to reality does not lead to an immediate victory. Reality is the poet's "inescapable and ever-present difficulty and inamorata" (OP, 241). Like a shy lady it hides itself away and must be wooed. The poet would see "the very thing and nothing else" (CP, 373), but the very thing refuses to be seen, and elaborate stratagems of self-effacement are necessary to see it. The one thing needful here is humility, for "the humble are they that move about the world with the love of the real in their hearts" (OP, 238).

Reality is hard to reach partly because of its individuality. The thing in itself has an inexhaustible richness, but "the momentum of the mind is all toward abstraction" (OP, 179) and it reduces complex uniqueness to some rationalized version of it. A man says: "That is a pineapple," and fits the pineapple into a schematized conception of it. The particular pineapple in its strangeness eludes the rational mind. Poetry, as Stevens says in a passage he adapts from H. D. Lewis,[3] is an attempt to break the "inexpressible loneliness of thinking" and enrich it with the solid reality of the particular (OP, 236, 237). How can this be done? One way is to see that the pineapple is not a single univocal thing. It is all the possible ways of looking at it. The pineapple changes from moment to moment, as, for example, the light shines on it differently. It also changes as the spectator's feeling changes. A new feeling allows the poet to see new aspects of the pineapple, new connections between the pineapple and other parts of reality. Paradoxically, "our awareness of the irrevocability by which a thing is what it is" (OP, 237)[4] is most quickened not by trying to give one exhaustive view of the pineapple but by multiplying perspectives on it. The first principle of poetry is the assumption that "There are as many points of view/From which to regard [a lady, a pineapple, or any other thing]/As there are sides to a round bottle" (OP, 136).

Poetry must therefore be made up of variations of point of view. These match on a small scale the larger alterations of world view from age to age or from culture to culture. Stevens' perspectivism is not what some of Picasso's sequences of paintings might seem to a naive critic: an initial presentation of the "true" photographic reality, followed by a series of ever more grotesque transformations of this reality. Reality is not possessed initially, and the series of perspectives is an attempt to reach it, as a man might investigate the round bottle by seeing it from all sides. The photographic reality must be broken up in order to approach the alien object which it hides. The strangeness and difficulty of Stevens' verse is an attempt to reveal "a unity rooted in the individuality of objects" (OP, 237).[5] Reality is never visible in its totality at any one time or from any one viewpoint. It "is not what it is. It consists of the many realities which it can be made into" (OP, 178). Poetry must constantly vary its approach, changing it with changes in

---

[3] For the attribution of this text to H. D. Lewis see Joseph N. Riddel, "The Authorship of Wallace Stevens' 'On Poetic Truth,' " *Modern Language Notes*, 76: 126–129 (1961).

[4] The phrase is again borrowed from H. D. Lewis.

[5] H. D. Lewis' words again.

the object and in the spectator's way of seeing the object. "The most provocative of all realities is that reality of which we never lose sight but never see solely as it is. The revelation of that particular reality or of that particular category of realities is like a series of paintings of some natural object affected, as the appearance of any natural object is affected, by the passage of time, and the changes that ensue, not least in the painter" (OP, 213, 214).

Modern painters have used various techniques (cubism, abstractionism, multiple simultaneous perspectives, fauve color, and so on) to destroy stale ways of seeing reality. The poet has similar strategies. A constant one in Stevens' work from the poems and stories in the *Harvard Advocate*[6] to "The Rock" might be called, in echo of the Russian formalists, "making it strange." The poet seeks unusual ways of speaking which will nevertheless strike the reader as fitting. This is achieved by rhythm, rhyme, alliteration, manipulation of syntax, and above all by diction. The most salient quality of *Harmonium* is the elegance, the finicky fastidiousness, even sometimes the ornate foppishness, of the language. Again and again strange words like "spick," "girandoles," "quirky," "clippered," "lacustrine," "princox," "alquazil," or "chirr" turn out, as R. P. Blackmur and others have seen, to be most exact in sound, texture, and meaning. These words, rescued from oblivion in the dictionaries or sometimes coined by the poet, cooperate with the words around them to create an atmosphere as rich and strange as that of a painting by Matisse or Dufy, and as much a new revelation of reality. They bring to light Stevens' special vision of the rich complexity of the individual:

> The lacquered loges huddled there
> Mumbled zay-zay and a-zay, a-zay.
> The moonlight
> Fubbed the girandoles. (CP, 11)
>
> We enjoy the ithy oonts and long-haired
> Plomets, as the Herr Gott
> Enjoys his comets. (CP, 349)
>
> Chieftain Iffucan of Azcan in caftan
> Of tan with henna hackles, halt! (CP, 75)

---

[6] See Robert Buttel, "Wallace Stevens at Harvard: Some Origins of His Theme and Style," in R. H. Pearce and J. H. Miller, eds., *The Act of the Mind: Essays on the Poetry of Wallace Stevens* (Baltimore: The Johns Hopkins Press, 1965), pp. 29–57.

The extravagant witty aptness of such lines, their extreme possession of the "gaiety of language" (CP, 322), is one of the constants of Stevens' style. This is especially apparent in his delightful titles. These sometimes are the best parts of their poems and have only an indirect or ironic relation to its meaning: "Le Monocle de Mon Oncle," "Colloquy with a Polish Aunt," "Two Figures in Dense Violet Light," "The Revolutionists Stop for Orangeade," "The Well Dressed Man with a Beard," "No Possum, No Sop, No Taters," "So-and-So Reclining on Her Couch" — almost any of the titles would do, and Stevens kept lists of hundreds of such phrases, many of them never used (OP, xxxiii, xxxiv).

The notion behind this deliberate fanciness is that each fresh combination of words is a new revelation of reality. Only one collocation of words will invoke just this reality, and the man who is aware of new ranges of reality will necessarily have a gaudy way of speaking. It is impossible to speak directly of the thing in its barrenness, but a new aspect of the thing can be put in words, and therefore reality is never the thing in itself, only some new view of it. "To confront fact in its total bleakness is for any poet a completely baffling experience," and for this reason "only allusion [is] tolerable" (NA, 95). To speak of new things in the old language is to speak still of the old things, for "description is an element, like air or water" (OP, 170), and just as the things of air are determined by their element, so the use of a certain vocabulary will determine the nature of the things which are described in it. "Description is revelation" (CP, 344), and "a change of style is a change of subject" (OP, 171). So Stevens discusses Marianne Moore's way with language in his review of her *Selected Poems* (OP, 247–254) and in his essay "About One of Marianne Moore's Poems" (NA, 93–103). The intimate habits of a poet with syntax, rhythm, and diction are the best indications of that personal tone which is the poet's sensibility, and "language [is] the material of poetry not its mere medium or instrument" (OP, 171). Blessed are they who are extravagantly daring with words, for they shall see the real! Stevens consequently has no patience with those who would limit diction to a stern plainness. "I have never been able to see," he says, "why what is called Anglo-Saxon should have the right to higgle and haggle all over the page, contesting the right of other words. If a poem seems to require a hierophantic phrase, the phrase should pass" (OP, 205).

A single phrase, however hierophantic, will not be enough to uncover reality. Several of Stevens' most elaborate poems are a multiplication of views of the same scene. In the most famous, "Sea Surface Full of Clouds" (CP, 98–102),[7] the "same" poem is presented in five successive versions. Each describes the sea, the sky, the ship, the clouds reflected in the sea. In each case there is another version of the question: "Who, then, evolved the sea-blooms from the clouds?" and of the answer: *C'était mon enfant, mon bijou, mon âme.* The poem makes a subtle variation of the adjectives and images which determine the atmosphere of the scene. Each stanza is a different poem, and each scene is a different scene. The sky and its clouds are reflected in the sea, and there is an elaborate intercourse between them creating every moment a new appearance of the sea surface full of clouds. The clouds and the quality of light in the sky change, and these changes impose themselves on the reflected image in the sea surface. The sea alters too as there is more or less wind, and as the pattern of the surface is wrinkled in one way or another, or is darker or lighter. All the elements of the scene determine one another, and a change in one changes the whole. It is impossible to say that any element is sovereign.

Another power is present: the imagination of the spectator who watches the play of reflections in the sea. The relation between sky and sea is an emblem of the interchange between imagination and reality. Only in the mind of the spectator are the clouds in the sea seen as evolving blooms, and it is the spectator who is reminded by the light of the summer sun on the deck of "rosy chocolate/And gilt umbrellas," or of their variants in the other stanzas. In these variations a change of adjectives changes the scene, but the chocolate and umbrellas, like the sea-blooms, are not present in the real scene at all. The clouds are reflected in the sea, but it is the reflecting soul which makes blooms of the reflections. Words create and recreate the scene, and Stevens thereby demonstrates the mind's dominion over reality. A cunning variation of each of the

[7] See Joseph N. Riddel, " 'Disguised Pronunciamento': Wallace Stevens' *Sea Surface Full of Clouds,*" *Texas Studies in English*, 37: 177–186 (Austin, 1958).

verbal elements makes a new world, and it seems as if he could go on indefinitely remaking it in an infinite number of versions.

Is this really what the poem demonstrates? It could just as easily be taken as an affirmation of the power of reality to transform the mind. The source of the chocolate and the umbrellas is the light on the deck, and how can the reader know that the shift from rosy chocolate to chophouse chocolate and from gilt to sham umbrellas has not been imposed on the passive mind by a delicate change in the quality of the light? The poem may describe not the victory of the imagination but its submission to a reality full of subtle variations which enforce themselves inescapably. The imagination struggles in an unsuccessful attempt to grasp what it beholds in a single version of it. Reality slips away, and the imagination must begin again with different materials in the ever-renewed, never finally successful attempt to fix it down to the last nuance.

Both interpretations of the poem are correct. Just as it is impossible to say whether the sky or the sea is more important in determining the sea surface full of clouds, so it is impossible to say whether imagination or reality is dominant in the making of the poem. The scene changes and the imagination changes and this double change creates each moment a new aspect of the thing. Every novel conjunction may be crystallized in a poem, but in order to keep up with the fluctuations of reality the poet must make poem after poem. That there are five versions is just an accident. There might have been fifteen or twenty-five or five hundred and five. The combinations of imagination and reality can never be exhausted, and the final lines of the poem affirm the power of sea and sky to go on producing "fresh transfigurings" of the scene. This marriage of sea and sky is an analogy for the relation of mind and world which is the true theme of the poem.

～

"Sea Surface Full of Clouds" is like those sequences of paintings which Stevens describes. Each stanza is a new revelation of the underlying reality which all the versions seek and none see solely as it is. The poem depends on metaphor, the most powerful instrument of the perspectivist poet. "A poetic metaphor," says Stevens,

". . . appears to be poetry at its source. It is" (NA, 81). Metaphor differs from other modes of diction in important ways. To make it strange by using an unexpected word will reveal a new aspect of reality, but metaphor does this far better. The unusual word gives only the isolated object, however freshly seen. Metaphor is many-sided. It shows the relation between the object and some other object. Things are what they are because of their interaction with other things. Another way to put this is to say that the resemblance between things is "one of the significant components of the structure of reality" (NA, 71). Metaphor is the means of exploring these resemblances, and poetry is therefore "a satisfying of the desire for resemblance" (NA, 77). Each metaphor brings something secret to the surface. "Reality is a cliché from which we escape by metaphor. It is only *au pays de la métaphore qu'on est poète*" (OP, 179). The nonpoetic reality in which all men live most of the time is a mental husk. Metaphor "creates a new reality from which the original appears to be unreal" (OP, 169). In this sense "the proliferation of resemblances extends an object" (NA, 78). It brings to the surface aspects of the object which no one has seen before, and the ultimate effect of metaphor is to give a heightened and extended sense of reality. Poetry is metamorphosis, but not in the sense that the imagination should use its power to turn things into whatever it likes. Such transmogrifications produce those abortive creations, works "in which neither the imagination nor reality is present" (NA, 11). True poetry sublimates man's apprehension of things. Reality is an essential pole of any metaphor, and a series of metaphors must constantly be coming back to the rock of reality as to the only thing which gives it stability and substance. No such thing as a metaphor of a metaphor exists, for that would be playing with empty mental counters.

Stevens' poetry is full of striking metaphors, as when the speaker in "Le Monocle de Mon Oncle" says that he and his lady are "like warty squashes" (CP, 16), or when he says that the sun is a "strange flower," a "tuft of jungle feathers," an "animal eye," a "savage of fire," a "seed" (CP, 85), or when he invents a cascade of similes and metaphors to describe the wind:

> The wind is like a dog that runs away.
> But it is like a horse. It is like motion

That lives in space. It is a person at night,
A member of the family, a tie,
An ethereal cousin, another milleman. (CP, 352)

Some of the poems are explicitly a study of metaphor. "Poem Written at Morning" (CP, 219), for example, gives an eloquent demonstration of the fact that "the acquisitions of poetry are fortuitous; *trouvailles*" (OP, 169). This means that the images of a poem cannot be voluntarily controlled. They just happen. Metaphor more than any other aspect of poetry comes as it comes, for "true metaphor" is always "fortuitous" (NA, 73). The unforeseen connections of the imagination can never be predicted, its leaps between one part of reality and another. The mind "begets in resemblance" (NA, 76) and gives birth to an unexpected possession of the object.

The poem called "Someone Puts a Pineapple Together" (NA, 83–87) is Stevens' most subtle and elaborate demonstration of the fact that "by metaphor you paint/A thing" (CP, 219). It is both a theory of metaphor and evidence of its power. That Stevens prized the poem is suggested by a reference to it in a poignant poem written at the end of his life and called "As You Leave the Room" (OP, 116, 117). There he lists "that poem about the pineapple" as proof that he has participated in life. The poem is "not what skeletons think about." Skeletons are those who are cut off from reality. "Aristotle is a skeleton" (OP, 168), but Stevens' command of metaphor gives him "an appreciation of a reality" (OP, 117). The poem about the pineapple asserts that "the profusion of metaphor" comes from the planetary interaction of man and the world. Each metaphor touches man at but one point, and rushes away from that conjunction on a curve which is determined by the pull of other planets. Under their multiple pull metaphors proliferate like planetoids: "The ephemeras of the tangent swarm, the chance/Concourse of planetary originals" (NA, 84). The center of this metaphorical activity, the pineapple, is invisible and unspeakable. It is "the irreducible X" (NA, 83), but strangely enough the X "at the bottom of imagined artifice" is also the spectator himself. The unattainable secret at the center of consciousness coincides with the unattainable secret at the center of the pineapple. The "angel at the center of this rind" (NA, 83) is both pure reality and pure imagination.

Since the poet cannot go directly toward the pineapple he must go around and around it and allude to it in different ways, for "the absolute object slightly turned is a metaphor of the object" (OP, 179). His care must be to "defy/The metaphor that murders metaphor" (NA, 84), that is, he must be sure that each metaphor is a true offspring of the conjunction of the planets and not a false tangent in the void. The poem is a series of twelve wildly imaginative metaphors of the pineapple. The fruit is a hut beneath palm trees, a bottle with green genii coming out of it, the sea spouting upward out of rocks, an owl with a hundred eyes, yesterday's volcano, and so on. These are "Apposites, to the slightest edge, of the whole/Undescribed composition of the sugar-cone" (NA, 86). The pineapple is "the sum of its complications, seen/And unseen" (NA, 87), and this "total artifice reveals itself/As the total reality" (NA, 87). The exfoliations of metaphor are a way of putting a pineapple together. Each metaphor is another glimpse of the irreducible X, hiding it and yet revealing it. Another poem about metaphor, "Thinking of a Relation between the Images of Metaphors" (CP, 356, 357), says again that a series of authentic metaphors is a way of moving toward a goal which cannot be attained directly, and the poem about the pineapple ends with a claim that all these "casual exfoliations" (NA, 86) of metaphor gather toward reality, as a swarm of shooting stars point back toward one dark spot in the sky which is their source, or as the intersections of a number of geometrical planes may outline a cone. After the discovery that reality is not something possessed from the start, the multiplication of metaphors seems the best way for the imagination to woo its coy mistress and coax her out in the open.

Is this really so? Stevens wants to know reality, to "call [it] by name" (CP, 407). Metaphor calls the pineapple by the name of something else. This might be acceptable if all the metaphors of an object could be exhausted. It would then be the total of its metaphorical names. But, "in some sense, all things resemble each other" (NA, 71). This simple fact is a catastrophe for the imagination. If the imagination should start out bravely to reach the pineapple by listing all its metaphors, it would never reach its goal. It would become a kind of poetic computer set to explore the permutations of an infinitely variable equation. Day and night, it would still click out its answers. The pineapple is "the coconut and cockerel in one" (NA, 86); the pineapple is "a purple Southern mountain" (NA, 87); the pineapple is a house with "nailed-up lattices" (NA, 86), and so on, endlessly. To possess the pineapple by going away from it toward the things it resembles is as hopeless as to try to reach the center of an infinite circle by going around its circumference. If all things resemble each other the pursuit of reality through metaphor becomes a whirlpool in which the poet can spin forever downward through the proliferation of resemblances.

Perhaps there is an escape from the whirlpool by way of a curious ambiguity in Stevens' discussions of metaphor. Sometimes he talks as if the resemblance between the pineapple and the sea spouting upward out of rocks were objective. At other times he speaks as though the analogy which most interests him is that between imagination and reality. The metamorphoses of poetic imagery are perhaps caused by the imagination itself. It is still true that "every image is the elaboration of a particular of the subject of the image" (NA, 127), but now this elaboration is governed by some feeling in the maker of the image. "Every image," says Stevens, "is a restatement of the subject of the image in the terms of an attitude," and "every image is an intervention on the part of the image-maker" (NA, 128). If the source of the image is the imagination, then the resemblance between things is unreal, a fiction of the mind. Metaphor would then be "the creation of resemblance by the imagination" (NA, 72). This view of metaphor leads to a different picture of its operation. Instead of seeing poetry as a process by which the imagination explores "the resemblance . . . between two or more parts of reality," the essence of poetry must be defined as the resemblance between "something imagined and something real," or even "between two imagined things" (NA, 72). Imagination formerly seemed "a power within [the poet] to have . . . insights into reality" (NA, 115). Now it appears to be "a power within him not so much to destroy reality at will as to put it to his own uses" (NA, 115).

Poetry moves away from reality toward mental fictions, as "the real is constantly being engulfed in the unreal" (OP, 240). The chief analogy is that between the world in itself and transpositions of it into the fictive world of poetry. Things as they are make up one side of the analogy, but the poet's "sense of the world" is the other, and the life of poetry is the metamorphosis by which one is swallowed up by the other. "There is always an analogy between nature and the imagination, and possibly poetry is merely the strange rhetoric of that parallel" (NA, 118). The poet's sense of the world and the corporeal world are paired in an analogy which is like a metaphor. Metaphor is no longer a horizontal relation between the particulars of reality in which the pineapple is seen as yesterday's volcano. Horizontal analogies are the building blocks of a vertical metaphor in which the whole world is transformed into an expression of the poet's mind. The mind has displaced the pineapple as the "tenor" of metaphor. In "Fire-monsters in the Milky Brain" (CP, 331, 332), Stevens says that Adam made all Eden a metaphor by turning it into his mental world. The whole world was his metaphor. What was there before he came was "malformed" until it became the contents of his mind, one version of that fiction man believes in knowing it to be untrue. The poet is a true son of Adam, and his words make "a world that transcends the world and a life livable in that transcendence" (NA, 130).

Transcendent or not, this poetry is unreal. Its transcendence lies in its unreality. Even if the poetry of metaphor is thought of as oriented toward a search for the real it loses itself in the endless multiplication of figures and never touches the thing in itself. "We are ignorant men incapable/Of the least, minor, vital metaphor" (CP, 305), and those analogies which seem to be moving so surely toward reality are governed, not by objective resemblances, but by the poet's sense of the world. Metaphor and perspectivism are instruments of escapism and must be rejected.

Though Stevens does sometimes say that metaphor paints reality, there are many texts in which he repudiates metaphor as evasive and unreal. "Metaphor," he says, is "degeneration" (CP, 444). The "motive for metaphor" is man's unwillingness to face reality directly, his "shrinking from/The weight of primary noon" (CP, 288). The poet must have the courage to reject "The twilight overfull/Of wormy metaphors" (CP, 162), and recognize that "sense exceeds all metaphor" (CP, 431). Knowing this, he must see things "too much as they are to be changed by metaphor" (CP, 430), see them "untouched/By trope or deviation" (CP, 471). He must

"Trace the gold sun about the whitened sky/Without evasion by a single metaphor" (CP, 373), and therefore be justified in saying: "This is the figure and not/An evading metaphor" (CP, 199).

In such texts Stevens categorically rejects metaphor and all its appurtenances. There are also texts where he rejoices in the freedom this rejection grants. It is a freedom to see what is really there and not the opaque film of outmoded fictions. In "Dezembrum" the night sky in winter is purged of its serio-comic mythology:

> Tonight there are only the winter stars.
> The sky is no longer a junk-shop,
> Full of javelins and old fire-balls,
> Triangles and the names of girls. (CP, 218)

"The Man on the Dump" (CP, 201–203) is another eloquent rejection of the old images. They are the bottles, pots, and shoes on the dump, and must be abandoned for the sake of a naked confrontation with reality. Only if the "trash" of metaphor is shed so that the moon and the "freshness of night" are seen without images can we be real men and not images of men. Reality escapes the poet's metaphors and leaves him with an empty fictive shell. Nothing must stand between man and reality, not even the most freshly confected analogy. Only the most unmediated possession of reality will suffice.

⤳

When metaphor fails the imagination must seek to efface itself altogether before reality. Having attempted unsuccessfully to have both Sancho Panza and Don Quixote, the poet finds that he must choose one or the other after all. There is no question which way his choice must fall. "There is nothing in the world greater than reality" (OP, 177), and so the poet chooses for Sancho's commitment to it.

At first it seemed that it would be easy to be a realist. The poet need only disabuse himself of everything fictive and accept the fact that he is a physical man in a physical world. Then he will walk barefoot into reality. This has turned out to be impossible. An essential human experience is the moment when, having rejected everything unreal and committed himself to commonplace reality, a man is amazed to see reality turning into all sorts of other things, flowing like the wind. If he watches a teacup it will change and become ultimately something rich and strange. The source of this change is the imagination itself, for it has an intractable will to metamorphosis and would work its transformations even on a teacup. The only hope seems to lie in annihilating imagination. When the mind has been reduced to a neutral power of seeing, man may be able to see reality without trope or deviation. This destruction of the imagination takes an enormous effort of will, and the act must be constantly repeated or else the deviations of imagination will return. Even when the imagination has been effaced, another heroic effort is necessary to possess even the simplest object with the senses, for "the difficultest rigor is forthwith,/On the image of what we see, to catch from that/Irrational moment its unreasoning" (CP, 398). A multiple energy is necessary, the abnegation of imagination, then the seizing of reality, and finally the expression of this grasp:

> Three times the concentred self takes hold, three times
> The thrice concentred self, having possessed
>
> The object, grips it in savage scrutiny,
> Once to make captive, once to subjugate
> Or yield to subjugation, once to proclaim
> The meaning of the capture, this hard prize,
> Fully made, fully apparent, fully found. (CP, 376)

This text shows what Stevens means when, using a term from Simone Weil's *La Pesanteur et la grâce*, he says that "modern reality is a reality of decreation, in which our revelations are not the revelations of belief, but the precious portents of our own powers" (NA, 175). The human powers which make "man's truth . . . the final resolution of everything" (NA, 175) are not primarily creative. Man's essential power is decreation, "making pass from the created to the uncreated" (NA, 174). Modern man reaches reality by his power to annihilate obsolete mental fictions and reach the uncreated rock of reality behind. A savage rigor is required for this act. Only through the most radical act of rejection can man be sure that "the real will from its crude compoundings come" (CP, 404). Armed with a passion for decreation, and convinced that it is the only way in "these days of disinheritance" (CP, 227), the poet cries: "Let's see the very thing and nothing else./Let's see it with the hottest fire of sight" (CP, 373).

Curiously enough, one of Stevens' terms for this cauterizing is "abstraction," and to see the very thing is, strangely, to "see it clearly in the idea of it" (CP, 380). These unexpected uses of the terms "abstraction" and "idea" hold out a possibility that imagination and reality may be united after all. Apparently Stevens means by "abstraction" the power man has to separate himself from reality, as when he says of the modern poet that, "although he has himself witnessed, during the long period of his life, a general transition to reality, his own measure as a poet, in spite of all the passions of all the lovers of the truth, is the measure of his power to abstract himself, and to withdraw with him into his abstraction the reality on which the lovers of truth insist" (NA, 23). To place reality in the imagination by abstracting it does not mean, however, twisting it into some unreal mental fiction. It means the power to carry the image of the very thing alive and undistorted into the mind. The phrase which gives a name to the first part of "Notes toward a Supreme Fiction" is "It Must Be Abstract" (CP, 380). This means that the poet should abstract himself from the layers of interpretation which have piled up over the years on objects in the external world. He must throw out, for example, what science, mythology, theology, and philosophy tell him about the sun and see the sun as the first man saw it for the first time. He must abstract himself and abstract the sun from all the conceptions man has had of it, and see the sun as a blazing gold disk in the sky. The sun in itself is "inconceivable." It cannot be transcribed into mental conceptions, but it can be perceived, and this is enough. To perceive the sun, the poet must forget all about Phoebus and forget the very name of the sun. Nothing must come between him and the sun when he gives himself to the act of looking at it and seeing it in its being.

To perceive the sun in this way is to see it in the idea of it. At first this seems a strange use of the word "idea." The word is associated with mental concepts and with Plato's heaven of archetypes. But Stevens uses the word "idea" in its original meaning of "direct sense image." To see the sun in the idea of it means just the opposite of seeing it in terms of preconceived ideas of it (the sun as burning hydrogen or the sun as Phoebus Apollo). "If you

take the varnish and dirt of generations off a picture, you see it
in its first idea. If you think about the world without its varnish
and dirt, you are a thinker of the first idea." [8] The beginning of all
progress in knowledge and poetry is a purging of the sight which
"gives a candid kind to everything" (CP, 382), and allows man
to see things in the white radiance of their presence.

If there is any philosophical reference in Stevens' use of the
term "idea," it may be not to Plato but to the *Ideen* of Edmund
Husserl. Husserl also uses the word in its etymological sense, and
his account of the way the world is put in parentheses in order to
reveal its original quality as immediate experience is close to
Stevens' account of the process of decreation. For Stevens as for
Husserl the "idea" of the sun belongs to the mind as well as to
the sun. In Husserl this is the notion of a vast reservoir of a priori
in the mind. These are actualized in individual acts of perception.
This notion is mentioned in the one reference Stevens makes to
Husserl. In "A Collect of Philosophy" he quotes a letter from
Jean Wahl in which Wahl speaks of Husserl's contention that there
is "an enormous (ungeheueres) a priori in our minds, an inexhaustible infinity of a priori" (OP, 194). "This enormous a priori,"
comments Stevens, "is potentially as poetic a concept as the idea
of the infinity of the world." For Stevens too the first idea is an
original possession of the mind, and the chief act of imagination is
to give a glimpse of the world as seen in the first idea of it. "The
first idea is an imagined thing" (CP, 387), and "The poem re-
freshes life so that we share,/For a moment, the first idea" (CP,
382). We reach the perception of the world in the naked idea of it
not through the abnegation of imagination but through its perfect
operation. "[T]he first idea was not to shape the clouds/In imitation" (CP, 383); it was not man's power to make the world over
in his own image. Imagination is ultimately the power of decreation, the power to burn to ash everything not the immediate idea
of the thing. When this is successful imagination and reality become
one, and for a moment the world is seen as it appeared to Adam
before he began naming it.

Imagination is not Eve making "air the mirror of herself"

[8] Letter to Henry Church, October 28, 1942, quoted in Michel Benamou, "Wallace
Stevens and the Symbolist Imagination," in Pearce and Miller, *The Act of the Mind*,
p. 110. This letter is cited again here with the kind permission of Mrs. Holly Stevens
Stephenson.

(CP, 383), but just the opposite, man the mirror of air. In that mirror reality is captured and the invisible at last becomes the mate of the visible. Authentic imagination destroys the false. "It is important to believe," says Stevens, "that the visible is the equivalent of the invisible; and once we believe it, we have destroyed the imagination; that is to say, we have destroyed the false imagination, the false conception of the imagination as some incalculable *vates* within us, unhappy Rodomontade" (NA, 61).

⤴

In accord with this attitude there are throughout Stevens' poetry affirmations that things are exactly what the senses say they are. "To see,/To hear, to touch, to taste, to smell, that's now,/That's this" (CP, 225). Objects seen with true imagination are "too actual" to be changed. They are "things that in being real/Make any imaginings of them lesser things" (CP, 430). Poetry must therefore use the most direct language possible. One penchant of Stevens' mind moves toward this directness and immediacy of sensation:

> The peaches are large and round,
>
> Ah! and red; and they have peach fuzz, ah!
> They are full of juice and the skin is soft. (CP, 224)

Stevens' most radical poem of this sort is "Study of Two Pears" (CP, 196, 197). It is an "opusculum paedagogum," the attempt to make in words a still life of two pears. The poem begins with a categorical dismissal of metaphor: "The pears are not viols,/Nudes or bottles./They resemble nothing else." Things are what they are and nothing more. The poem then proceeds through eighteen lines of meticulous description of the exact shape and color of the pears. They are described as shades of yellow, red, citron, orange, green, and even blue, and the poem concludes with two lines which might be a motto for the poet whose imagination is no incalculable *vates*, but the power of looking with the hottest fire of sight:

> The pears are not seen
> As the observer wills. (CP, 197)

"Study of Two Pears" is perhaps Stevens' most immobile poem. The dizzy fluctuation of reality has been stilled, and the two pears rest in plump fixity on their green cloth, imposing themselves on the spectator's eye. The strength of metaphorical transformation denied to the observer in the first and last lines of the poem is in the middle lines ascribed to the pears themselves. They have an irresistible will to power over their beholder. Their curved forms "bulge" toward the base, their yellow "glistens," and the shades of this color "flower" over the skin as if with an expansive energy. This energy is evident in the way the shadows of the pears are "blobs" on the green cloth. The poem marks one limit of the poet's thought. It expresses a complete renunciation of the idea that "the mind is the terriblest force in the world" (CP, 436, and see OP, 162), an abandonment of the notion that the imagination has sovereign power over reality. Consciousness dissolves into the neutral power of seeing and is at the mercy of the simplest objects.

Poetry can take only one step farther into reality, and that is to make language itself into a substance. Stevens understands the problem posed by the fact that a poem is made of words, not things. If poems are only language then even the most straightforward poem will still be at one remove from reality. As the title of the last poem in *The Collected Poems* suggests, Stevens is never satisfied with the poetry of representation. He wants "Not Ideas about the Thing but the Thing Itself" (CP, 534). Words, however, seem the strongest evidence of man's curse of solitude, his inability to reach "not the symbol but that for which the symbol stands" (CP, 238). Whatever is turned into language is no longer the thing but an idea about it, a mediate sign, not an immediate presence. "The words of things entangle and confuse./The plum survives its poems," "good, fat, guzzly fruit" (CP, 41). Only if words could somehow be brought to participate directly in what they name would they cease to separate man from the real. Otherwise, even if the words are as simple as can be, they will still hold reality at arm's length. "The word must be the thing it represents; otherwise, it is a symbol. It is a question of identity" (OP, 168).

Many modern painters have been obsessed with the fact that even the most distorted representation of a woman or a vase of flowers is still only a picture. They have made paintings lacking in any representational dimension. The paintings are just these thick drops of paint squeezed from the tube, or just this torn piece of old burlap, pasted to the canvas and smeared with black and white paint. Paintings of this sort do not represent the alien sub-stantiality of things by showing a picture of a pair of old shoes, as did Van Gogh, but are themselves manifest examples of matter. Stevens resorts to an analogous technique with words. A poem may start coherently enough, but as it progresses the poet becomes more and more exasperated with the distance between words and things. The language finally dissolves into incoherence and the reader faces words which are nonwords, a thick linguistic paste, like the splotches of paint on an expressionist canvas. By draining all referential meaning out of words Stevens hopes that they will become the thing they represent, or, even more radically, beyond onomatopoeia, that only the sound and appearance of the words will remain. Sometimes this happens in the titles of the poems, as in "Le Monocle de Mon Oncle" or "The Bagatelles the Mad-rigals." Here the witty half-rhymes so fascinate the reader with relationships of sound that he may forget to look for a rational meaning. The same thing often occurs in the body of the poems. It is usually associated with a singsong rhythm, like that of "The Man with the Blue Guitar." The verses become a sort of incanta-tion, as if Stevens hopes that by destroying the ordinary rhythm, syntax, and meaning of poetry in a mad improvisation he might suddenly find himself in tune with something else. Reality, shy as it is, may at last come in to occupy the words:

> And-a-fee and-a-fee and-a-fee
>   And-a-fee-fo-fum —
> Voilà la vie, la vie, la vie,
>   And-a-rummy-tummy-tum
>   And-a-rummy-tummy-tum. (OP, 15)

> Poet, be seated at the piano.
> Play the present, its hoo-hoo-hoo,
> Its shoo-shoo-shoo, its ric-a-nic,
> Its envious cachinnation. (CP, 131)

> Ah, but to play man number one,
> To drive the dagger in his heart . . .

> To strike his living hi and ho,
> To tick it, tock it, turn it true . . . (CP, 166)

This way with words seems to resolve the opposition between imagination and reality by the obliteration of one voice in the dialogue. The mind has effaced itself before reality, and nothing subjective remains but the ignorant eye of the man who sees things as they are, washed clean of human images. Such a man is "responsive/As a mirror with a voice, the man of glass" (CP, 250). He is "the transparence of the place in which/He is and in his poems we find peace" (CP, 251). We find peace because imagination and reality are no longer, like the clattering bucks and the bristling firecat, engaged in an endless push-pull of forces which can neither destroy one another nor leave one another alone. The poems written after this pacification will either be, like "Study of Two Pears," an exact and literal description, item by item, of objective reality, or, in a still further submission to reality, will be made of words which have been drained of meaning and have become inarticulate matter, the "tink and tank and tunk-a-tunk-tunk" (CP, 59) of senseless sound. In either case reality will be unchallenged king.

This peace can never be attained. The poems in which language degenerates toward mere sound are among Stevens' gaudiest, violent acts of the imagination that cut the reader off from reality and invite him to enter an unreal world manufactured out of words. Onomatopoeia as a means of making the word participate in reality becomes delight in sounds for the way they create an ornate inner world in which "everything [is] as unreal as real can be" (CP, 468). Things are no better if the poet tries to become transparent and seeks "the poem of pure reality" (CP, 471). There is no such thing as "the sight/Of simple seeing, without reflection" (CP, 471). "A fictive covering/Weaves always glistening from the heart and mind" (CP, 396). In metaphors as in dreams there is no negation, and to deny that the pears are viols, nudes, or bottles is obliquely to assert that they are these things. The imagination is there just as much when it is invisible as when it is visible. Not to be able to see it means being so much the victim of its enchanting power that it can no longer be distinguished from reality, and there may be an extraordinary moment of insight when a man first becomes aware of "the difference that we make in what we see," the difference that makes what is seen always "a little different from reality" (CP, 344). He has, for example, taken the blue sky for granted as part of the decor of reality. Suddenly he recognizes that there is and always has been a nongeography superimposed on the physical geography. When he looks at the blue sky he is never looking transparently at what is really there, but at "a physical poetry," at "the world of [his] own thoughts and the world of [his] own feelings" (NA, 65, 66). He discovers that he can never live in a "world without imagination" (CP, 27).

The attempt to obliterate one pole of the universal intercourse is bound to fail. The poet lives in "an artificial world" (CP, 252). Even if he returns, "after the leaves have fallen" (CP, 502), to a world apparently without imagination, he is still no closer, in the "blank cold" of winter, to a transparent view of reality. His impoverished vision is as much a fiction as the most grandiose imagination, for "the absence of this imagination had/Itself to be imagined" (CP, 503). On this rock is wrecked the strategy of avoiding fluctuation by a complete commitment to reality.

ᔓ

Reality transformed by imagination dissolves into fiction, and the poet becomes like the people in "Arcades of Philadelphia the Past" who "polish their eyes/In their hands" and never "touch the thing they see" or "feel the wind of it, smell the dust of it" (CP, 225). It has turned out to be just as impossible to reach reality by the abnegation of imagination. There is, however, another strategy. The poet may assume that the real can be reached by rejection of the sensible world. If he abstracts himself from the crudity of individual particulars he may find himself face to face with a pure reality which turns out also to be his own secret self. This way differs from the use of metaphor or perspectivism. It annihilates the objective rather than trying to reach reality through metamorphoses of it.

"Mrs. Alfred Uruguay" (CP, 248–250) sought herself and sought pure being through such rejection. For her "to be . . . could never be more/Than to be," and "her no and no made yes impossible." Her climb up a mountain on a donkey's back was a rejection of tangible things in which "she approached the real." At the same time it was an attempt to reach her buried self. "I have said no/To everything," she cried, "in order to get at myself" (CP, 249). The "anti-master-man, floribund ascetic" of "Landscape with Boat" (CP, 241–243) was the same kind of person. He assumed that the truth lay "like a phantom, in an uncreated night," and that truth was to be reached "by rejecting what he saw/And denying what he heard." He could reach his goal by a succession of negations which would plunge him into a vacuum beyond vacuum. "He had only not to live, to walk in the dark,/To be projected by one void into/Another." Stevens considers in these poems the super-Cartesianism of Mallarmé and Valéry, the idea that reality and selfhood are to be reached by a hyperbolic doubt which puts in question everything tangible and individual for the sake of an imageless purity glimpsed behind. This negation will reach "the neutral centre, the ominous element,/The single-colored, colorless, primitive," "the world beneath the blue,/Without blue, without any turquoise tint or phase,/Any azure under-side or after-color" (CP, 242, 241). Commitment to such a strategy would align Stevens with an important tradition in modern literature, the tradition believing that the ground of things is an anonymous transcendent power which can be attained by the rejection of everything solid, everything formed or colored.

This approach is rarely considered by Stevens, and it is considered only to be denied. One clue to the reasons for his rejection is the fact that he speaks of Mrs. Alfred Uruguay and the floribund ascetic in the past tense. They represent one of "our more vestigial states of mind" (CP, 392), a way which has failed. Mrs. Alfred Uruguay, on her way up the mountain to see the real, is passed by a rider going the other way toward the material existence she has rejected. This rider is "the figure of the youth as virile poet" (NA, 37), to borrow the title of one of Stevens' essays, a "figure of capable imagination" (CP, 249) who makes out of the raw substance of things as they are "the ultimate elegance: the imagined land" (CP, 250). The truth does not lie in a dark void. It is here and now, dispersed everywhere in what man can see and hear. Each man's response to manifold color and sound is also part of the truth. The floribund ascetic had the truth before his senses and did not know it. Stevens remains faithful to this pluralism and to this sense that ultimate truth is close at hand. There is no beyond, and the truth is multiple and diverse. It is everything of which human beings are conscious.

If the idea that conflict can be pacified by negation is dismissed almost as soon as it is considered, another notion is more seriously entertained. This is the assumption that the imagination *is* reality.

Imagination may be "the magnificent cause of being," "the one reality/In this imagined world" (CP, 25). If it is impossible to appease the war between mind and sky by obliterating imagination, just the reverse strategy may work: the destruction of reality. Stevens often feels that there is only one realm after all, the mind. "We live in the mind" (OP, 164). Everything we can know is already in consciousness as soon as we are aware of it. Though there may be extramental things, we can know nothing about them. "There is nothing in life except what one thinks of it" (OP, 162). From the perspective of this idealism there is no quarrel between imagination and something other than itself. There is only a quarrel within the mind between various mental forces. The mind generates its own war, and only the mind can find peace for itself.

If the antagonists make up one family of mental forms, then there seems no reason why they should not live in amicable harmony. The mind is the terriblest force in the world, but not, as it seemed earlier, because it can transform alien reality and make it yield to the will. There is nothing but mind anywhere, and only the mind "can defend/Against itself" (CP, 436, and see OP, 173, 174). If reality is a phenomenon of mental life, the world is my representation. Reality is "a thing seen by the mind,/Not that which is but that which is apprehended" (CP, 468). Since this is so, "imagination is the only genius" (OP, 179), and the "world of poetry [is] indistinguishable from the world in which we live" (NA, 31).

Stevens has completely reversed himself! He once found that it was impossible to efface imagination before reality. Now it seems that reality is a figment of the mind, one of "the creatures that it makes" (CP, 436). Poetry is not the search of the mind for reality. It is a shaping power which "creates the world to which we turn incessantly and without knowing it and . . . gives to life the supreme fictions without which we are unable to conceive of it" (NA, 31). Peace has been reached by the discovery that the world does not exist as a thing in itself. Stevens' poetry is punctuated by accounts of those ecstatic moments when he sees that reality is contained in the mind. At such moments he enjoys a sense of kinglike power and, godlike, disposes things freely, by legislative fiat:

I was myself the compass of that sea:

I was the world in which I walked, and what I saw
Or heard or felt came not but from myself . . . (CP, 65)

The bud of the apple is desire, the down-falling gold,
The catbird's gobble in the morning half-awake —

These are real only if I make them so. (CP, 313)

At such times the poet can say with certainty, "The world is myself" (CP, 361), and, turning to the season as a god might turn to his creation, he can cry: "Thou are not August unless I make thee so" (CP, 251). To say that man should be the transparence of his place means that he should have the courage to recognize that he includes the whole world in his imagination, as an image is possessed by a mirror. When he knows this, the world "will have stopped revolving except in crystal" (CP, 407). Evasive mobility will have become the benign revolutions of a transparent world within a transparent mind. The idea of transparence is of great importance for Stevens. It returns again and again whenever he wants to describe a happy transcendence of the opposition between subject and object. This crystalline clarity does not define the dissolution of imagination into a colorless substance which reality can penetrate. The glass man is the one who has thought long enough and deeply enough to know that the world is already an intimate part of himself, in all its brilliance and solidity.

⁓

This notion that reality is part of the mind is, however, but a momentary hallucination, the outcome of a frantic need to put a stop to endless conflict. The glass man is an illusion, and the idea that reality is a thing seen by the mind is "inescapable choice/Of dreams, disillusion as the last illusion" (CP, 468). It may be last, but it is still illusion, just as much so as the notions that reality is the only genius or that reality is the solid material stuff spread out unequivocally before man, easy to know. In "Saint John and the Back-Ache" (CP, 436, 437), after the Back-Ache has made its proud boast for the power of the mind as the most terrible force in the world, Saint John, here no spokesman for the all-creating word, answers that "the world is presence and not force," and "presence is not mind." The world is not a whirligig revolving toylike within the crystal of the mind. It exceeds consciousness and is able to overturn its systematic reductions in a moment. Some unexpected change is always ready to teach man how little he knows and how overwhelmingly the world is beyond the force of his will. Saint John insists that the presence of the world "fills the being before the mind can think." There is a "dumbfoundering abyss/Between us and the object, external cause," and "The effect of the object is beyond the mind's/Extremest pinch."

After the death of the gods Stevens seemed faced with the relatively easy problem of reconciling imagination and reality, but such a reconciliation is impossible. This way and that vibrates his thought, seeking to absorb imagination by reality, to engulf reality in imagination, or to marry them in metaphor. Nothing will suffice, and the poet is driven to search on tirelessly for some escape from struggle. This seeking is the life of his poetry. It stops only briefly when he is lucky enough to reach one of those times when there is a momentary balance, "not balances/That we achieve but balances that happen" (CP, 386). These balances are only a matter of "perhaps." They may happen or they may not happen. They cannot be brought about by any strategy of the spirit, and they cannot be made to persist. Man's normal state is dispersal, bifurcation. The human self is divided against itself. One part is committed to the brute substance of earth, things as they are, and the other just as tenaciously holds to its need for imaginative grandeur, and searches out such majesty as it can find (CP, 468, 469). Self-division, contradiction, perpetual oscillations of thought — these are the constants in Stevens' work. Is it possible, as some critics have thought, that he is just confused? Is it from mere absence of mind that he affirms on one page of his "Adagia" that reality is the only genius (OP, 177), only to reverse himself two pages later and say just as categorically that imagination is the only genius? Even if such contradictions are intentional, what justification can they have?

It is possible to develop radically different notions of Stevens' aims as a poet, and for each of these it is easy to find apposite passages from the texts. It can be shown that he believes poetry is metaphor, and that he believes all metaphors are factitious. At times he is committed to bare reality; at others he repudiates reality and sings the praises of imagination. Nor is it just a question of contradictions in the logical statements of the prose which are reconciled in the poems. For each position and for its antithesis there are fully elaborated poems or parts of poems. It is impossible to find a single systematic theory of poetry and life in Stevens. If the poet swerves this way and that seeking fixity and escape from contradiction, the critic must find a way to account for this vacillation. Stevens' poetry defines a realm in which everything "is not what it is" (OP, 178). His poetry is not dialectical, if that means a series of stages which build on one another, each transcending the last and moving on to a higher one in some version of the Hegelian sequence of thesis, antithesis, synthesis. It is impossible to organize the stages of Stevens' thought in this way. A new stage merely contradicts the first, and the first remains just as valid in its own way. In fact there is no first stage. They are all equally prior and equally final. There is no progress, only an alternation between contradictory possibilities.

This is related to Stevens' rejection of any transcendent beyond. Dialectical thought usually involves the notion of something hidden or distant, something which can be reached by progressive steps of thought, each a leaping-off place which is dismissed once it is attained. No such series of receding distances exists for Stevens, and therefore he can never move from his initial situation, but turns this way and that in the same place, rearranging elements which he already possesses at the beginning. An example of this is the sequence of the seasons which organizes so much of his thought and gives him so many symbols for poetry. No season is superior to the others. It is not proper to say the bareness of winter, reality untransfigured by imagination, gives way to the "credences of summer" (CP, 372), in which reality is possessed by being imagined well, nor that summer's false unity yields to the "auroras of autumn," and finally to the true rock of winter. The rock is covered with green leaves, and these are a symbol of the blessed validity of the imagination, and of its poems of spring, summer, autumn, and winter. All the seasons are necessary, and all the elements of the universal life are present in each of them. It takes imagination to reach the rock of winter, and reality is still there in "green's green apogee" (CP, 373). There is a "rock of summer" (CP, 375) too, just as the "permanent cold" of winter contains a "vital assumption" which causes the green leaves to come and cover the high rock (CP, 526).

Only by contradiction can Stevens be true to the ambiguous realm in which he finds himself. He can describe this realm only by including both winter and summer, the statement that reality is the only genius alongside the statement that imagination is the only genius. After the death of the gods he finds himself in a place where opposites are simultaneously true. Apparently this situation can be expressed in poetry only by a succession of wild swings to one extreme or the other, giving first one limit of the truth, then its opposite. The poet can escape this oscillation only by finding a way to write poems which will possess both extremes at once

‿

The elaboration of such a mode of poetry is Stevens' chief contribution to literature, and in the meditative poems of his later years he takes possession of a new domain. He writes about the same themes from one end of his poetry to the other, but a change of tone testifies to his increasing awareness of their full implications. The deliberately gaudy language of the early poems gives way to the inward musing tone of the later work. Speaking of the peculiar music of modern poetry, Stevens gives an excellent description of the rhythmical atmosphere of his own later poems: "there has been a change in the nature of what we mean by music. It is like the change from Haydn to a voice intoning" (NA, 125). The music of Stevens' later work is certainly that of a voice intoning. The completely finished unity of the early poems, which makes many of them seem like elaborately wrought pieces of jewelry, is gradually replaced by poems which are open-ended improvisations, created from moment to moment by the poet's breath. They begin in the middle of a thought, and their ending is arbitrary.

"The Man with the Blue Guitar" has a special place in Stevens' work. It marks his turning to the new style. The reader has the feeling that the poem has been going on for some time when he hears the first words, and the last verses are not really an ending. The twanging of the strings continues interminably. The poem could be endless, and in fact three more "Stanzas for 'The Man with the Blue Guitar' " are given in *Opus Posthumous* (OP, 72, 73). The man with the guitar is described in "An Ordinary Evening in New Haven" as a permanent presence, someone always there in the mind's eye watching the poet and reminding him of his obligation to a faithful thinking of life as it is (CP, 483).

Life as it is is a sequence of states of consciousness with neither start nor finish. If a poem is to be true to life it must be a constant flowing of images which come as they come and are not distorted by the logical mind in its eagerness for order. "One's grand flights, one's Sunday baths,/One's tootings at the weddings of the soul/Occur as they occur" (CP, 222). Just as the poem refuses to round itself neatly off with a beginning, middle, and end, so the parts which are given do not organize themselves into a whole, or even into a part of a whole. There is no coherent pattern of symbols and metaphors, each referring to all the others. One metaphor is introduced, developed for a while, then dropped. Another unrelated motif appears, is developed in its turn, disappears, is replaced by another which has little apparent connection with the other two, and so on. "The Man with the Blue Guitar" proceeds in a series of discontinuous short flights, each persisting for only a brief span of time. Each, while it lasts, is like a "half-arc hanging in mid-air/Composed, appropriate to the incomplete" (CP, 309).

The same thing is true of Stevens' other late long poems, "Esthétique du Mal," or "Notes toward a Supreme Fiction," or "An Ordinary Evening in New Haven." These poems do not pretend to be aesthetic wholes, cut off from their creator and set out in the public view like an equestrian statue in the town square. They are meant to catch the broken quality of mental experience as it moves through time in a constant approach toward a goal it never reaches. They keep close to life as it flows and proceed in a series of momentary crystallizations or globulations of thought, followed by dissolution, and then reconglomeration in another form. Each configuration shares with the others only the fact that it is a unique putting together of elements which remain constant. "Thought," says Stevens, "tends to collect in pools" (OP, 170). A man's mental energy tends to organize itself momentarily in a certain form, but life moves on, and a new shape is called for. The mind has a strong resistance to doing the same thing twice, and "originality is an escape from repetition" (OP, 177). "As a man becomes familiar with his own poetry, it becomes as obsolete for himself as for anyone else. From this it follows that one of the motives in writing is renewal" (OP, 220). The man who settles things once and for all becomes like "the man/Of bronze whose mind was made up and who, therefore, died" (CP, 472). Poetry is as evanescent as a snowflake fluttering through the air and dissolving in the sea. It is bound to a time experienced as a sequence of present moments, each real and valid only so long as it is present. "Poetry is a finikin thing of air/That lives uncertainly and not for long" (CP, 155). In the "Adagia" "Poetry is a pheasant disappearing in the brush" (OP, 173). Most succinctly: "A poem is a meteor" (OP, 158).

"The Man with the Blue Guitar" is a sequence of such meteors, and the whole of Stevens' work is an immense poem of this sort. Behind this poem is the flowing of Stevens' life. Throughout this streaming the same elements are constantly present — imagination and reality in unappeasable tension, the hidalgo with his shawl, his guitar, and his demanding stare, the implacable look of life. Each image is a momentary collection of life into a form which focuses its whole energy. While its lasts it has the vitality of what is real and present, but each image is valid only for an instant. It fails to be the reconciliation of tension which would suffice, and therefore poetry remains "an effort of a dissatisfied man to find satisfaction through words" (OP, 165). When the whirlpool dissolves the universal elements are ready to form another shape in the waters. Each poem is another in the endless series of "soliloquies" of "the interior paramour" (CP, 524), another dialogue in the "continual conversation with a silent man" (CP, 359) which generates Stevens' poetry.

The structure of a book of poems by Stevens is on a larger scale like the structure of "The Man with the Blue Guitar." Every poem is a movement toward the perfect poem which never quite gets written. It is a preliminary sketch, a study for a larger work, and the poems follow one another like a sequence of free inventions. In the last year of his life Stevens said: "It is not what I have written but what I should like to have written that constitutes my true poems, the uncollected poems which I have not had the strength to realize" (OP, 246). This tentative, experimental quality is evident in the pattern of his characteristic poems, the way they start casually in the middle of some event or thought, move a little way, and then stop, being careful not to center too fixedly on any metaphor or symbol, surprising the reader with sudden seeming irrelevances, unexpected images or reversals of thought. The poem is a trial flight, something provisional and subject to change without notice. The perfectly finished poems are the ones that remain unwritten and unwritable. If Stevens were to try to write such poems he would only write falsely.

This incompleteness is also evident in his titles, both those for individual poems and those for books. Each poem is a hesitant and uncertain gesture toward a perfection which is never reached. He calls a poem "Prelude to Objects," or "Asides on the Oboe," or "Extracts from Addresses to the Academy of Fine Ideas," or "Debris of Life and Mind," or "Notes toward a Supreme Fiction," or "Prologues to What is Possible," in each case emphasizing the fragmentary, partial quality of the poem, the way it is a piece of a larger whole, something preliminary and unfinished. The titles of his books of poetry suggest the same qualities. The harmonium is a small keyboard organ used at home. The book of poems called *Harmonium* is like a series of improvisations on this amateur's instrument. Stevens wanted to call this first book "The Grand Poem — Preliminary Minutiae." [9] This title would have been a perfect expression of the nature of the poems. *Harmonium* too suggests this notion of tentative fragments. Stevens may have been remembering this, as well as trying to affirm the unity of his work, when he wanted to call his collected poems *The Whole of Harmonium* (OP, xiv). The titles of his other books of poems are just as tentative: *Ideas of Order, Parts of a World, Transport to Summer* (in which one side of the pun gives the idea of motion in the direction of summer), and *The Auroras of Autumn* (an apt phrase to describe poems which are a flickering continuum of light). Only *The Rock* suggests something final and stable, but that title was affixed only after the poet had attained the ultimate immobility of death. Each poem by itself and all the poems taken together demonstrate that "We live in a constellation/Of patches and of pitches,/Not in a single world,"

[9] *Poems by Wallace Stevens*, selected, and with an introduction, by Samuel French Morse (New York: Vintage, 1959), p. viii.

and are therefore "Thinkers without final thoughts/In an always incipient cosmos" (OP, 114, 115).

⌐

Within the "endlessly elaborating poem" (CP, 486) which is life the same sequence of events is constantly recurring. First something happens which decreates, which destroys an earlier imagination of the world. Then man is left facing the bare rock of reality. This happens every year in autumn. When the leaves have all fallen, "we return/To a plain sense of things," and "it is as if/We had come to an end of the imagination" (CP, 502). This clearing away is experienced as a gain. What is removed was a fictive covering of the rock, "something imagined that has been washed away" (CP, 488), and what is exposed is the real in all its clarity:

> It is a coming on and a coming forth.
> The pines that were fans and fragrances emerge,
> Staked solidly in a gusty grappling with rocks. (CP, 487)

The autumnal decreation, as of leaves turning brown and falling, gives the poet a sense of "cold and earliness and bright origin" (CP, 481). It is as if he had returned to the beginning of everything, and were like the first man facing an uncreated world, with everything still to be imagined. This encounter with coldness and earliness is only the beginning. The poet is not satisfied to confront a bare and unimagined world. He wants to possess it, and it can only be possessed by being imagined well. Man is inhabited by a "will to change" (CP, 397) just as fundamental as his will to see the rock of reality exposed in its nudity. Decreation is followed by the reconstruction of a new imagination of the world. Winter leads to spring, the rock is covered with leaves which are the icon of the poem, and what had been the simplicity of beginning becomes the ornate complexity of the end. The poet moves from "naked Alpha," "the infant A standing on infant legs" to "hierophant Omega," "twisting, stooping, polymathic Z" (CP, 469). If the beginning is bare and simple, the end is multiple and encrusted with color, like an illuminated manuscript, or like a splendid robe of state, "adorned with cryptic stones and sliding shines," "With the whole spirit sparkling in its cloth,/Generations of the imagination piled/In the manner of its stitchings, of its thread" (CP, 434).

No sooner has the mind created a new fictive world than this "recent imagining of reality" (CP, 465) becomes obsolete in its turn, and must be rejected. This rejection is the act of decreation and returns man once more to unadorned reality. The cycle then begins again: imagining followed by decreation followed by imagining and so on for as long as life lasts. In this rhythmic alternation lies man's only hope to possess reality. Each imagining becomes outmoded and must be shed as a snake sheds its skin, and with the new season a new imagining of reality comes forth to replace the old. The search for fixity led to perpetual errancy, a distracted wavering this way and that. Nothing, the poet has discovered, is more mistaken than to seek for unchanging stability. Man must yield to time and change, and move fast enough to keep up with them. The "ever-never-changing same" (CP, 353) is the repetition from moment to moment of a situation which is always the same and yet always radically new, and only if man follows this, like a cork bobbing on the waves, can he stay alive.

This new notion of "How to Live. What to Do" (CP, 125) assumes that human existence is radically qualified by time and sees time as a sequence of unconnected moments. "The past is not part of the present" (CP, 291), and as soon as something has receded an instant into the past it becomes unreal. There is no great weight of history determining the present and likely to reappear in it, as there is for Hawthorne or Henry James, and there is no possibility of recovering the past as a viable part of the present through affective memory, as in Wordsworth or Proust. If Stevens is an historicist, he is an odd one who says the "integrations" of the past had validity when they were present, but are of no use now. Stevens never believes, as does Dilthey or Bernard Groethuysen or Robert Browning, that a man can build his life around an attempt to relive the human past and make it come alive again in the present. The poet must consign the past to oblivion in order to live in the only authentic time. In "The Noble Rider and the Sound of Words" he rejects Verrocchio's splendid equestrian statue of Bartolommeo Colleoni. It has come to seem "a little overpowering, a little magnificent" (NA, 9), another case, like Plato's image of the charioteer of the soul, in which "the imagination adheres to what is unreal," and therefore has "lost its power to sustain us" (NA, 7). Any past age or civilization, however grand in its time, becomes artificial and insubstantial, "like a stage-setting that since then has been taken down and trucked away" (OP, 224).

If Stevens, like some other Americans, rejects history, he also rejects his own past. In "The Rock" he denies reality to his own private past as categorically as he elsewhere denies it to the past of mankind. Even the seemingly enduring image of the man with the guitar becomes as obsolete as everything else. It too must be forgotten: "The sounds of the guitar/Were not and are not. Absurd. The words spoken/Were not and are not. It is not to be believed" (CP, 525).

Each moment is born in absolute newness and freedom. It is separated from the others by an infinitesimally narrow nothingness which prevents continuity or interchange. Man must match the ever-renewed freedom of time with an equal freedom on his own part. He must bury the corpses of the past. This is the sense in which "all men are murderers" (OP, 168), for "Freedom is like a man who kills himself/Each night, an incessant butcher, whose knife/Grows sharp in blood" (CP, 292). So Stevens cries: "what good were yesterday's devotions?" (CP, 264). This refusal of the past gives him a possession of the nick of time in all its fleeting vitality: "I affirm and then at midnight the great cat/Leaps quickly from the fireside and is gone" (CP, 264).

The present is the great cat who leaps from the fireside. It can never be seized or held and it lasts only for the blink of an eye. It is so narrow as to be almost nonexistent, and yet in that slender space lies all reality. In "Martial Cadenza" (CP, 237, 238) Stevens celebrates the ecstatic joy of an escape from the usual obfuscations which separate man from the present. He has been living "without time" and therefore has been living in unreality, for "that which is not has no time,/Is not, or is of what there was" (CP, 237). Suddenly he catches a glimpse of the evening star in its perennial constancy. This returns him to the living immediacy of the present, "the ever-breathing and moving, the constant fire" (CP, 238).

⌐

If life is made up of such moments how is it possible to justify the cycle of decreation followed by a new imagining of reality? This progression moves with a slow and stately turning, like the sequence of the seasons which is so often its image. If the poet pauses long enough to write the poem of winter it will already be part of the dead past long before he has finished it, and so for the poems of the other seasons. He must make sterile vibrations among various spiritual climates, always a little behind the perpetual flowing of reality.

There is a way to escape this impasse, and its discovery gives a special character to Stevens' later poetry. The poet can move so rapidly from one season to another that all the postures of the spirit are present in a single moment. If he does this he will never pause long enough at any extreme for it to freeze into fixity, and he will appease his longing to have both imagination and reality at once. An oscillation rapid enough becomes a blur in which opposites are touched simultaneously, as alternating current produces a steady beam of light, and the cycle of decreation and imagining, false if the poet goes through it at leisure, becomes true to things as they are if he moves through it fast enough.

Stevens' poetry contains in its inner development an implicit rejection of technological civilization and its metaphysics. That civilization has been built both theoretically and literally on the idea that it is possible to understand and control reality by doing something to it, whether this takes the form of trying to possess things by turning them into images, perspectives, metaphors, "world views," or whether it is the literal making of machines out of the earth. Stevens, like Gerard Manley Hopkins, sees modern civilization as an obscuring of reality which leaves man in possession of a two-dimensional façade. In "The Common Life" (CP, 221) he describes a modern industrialized town in "these days of disinheritance" (CP, 227). The city is as flat as "a page of Euclid," and the people who live in its "morbid light," a light which has been made at the electric plant, are as depthless as if they had been cut out of paper. To this universal death has man been brought by his irresistible desire to make things over to his own uses. Stevens comes in his later poetry to practice an opposing strategy, no less an act of will. He accepts and names things as they are. This means letting them change as they change. When he does this he finds that each tick of the clock is "the starting point of the human and the end" (CP, 528). In "this present" there is "an air of freshness, clearness, greenness, blueness,/That which is always beginning

because it is part/Of that which is always beginning, over and over"
(CP, 530). The present begins over and over because it has no
sooner begun than it has gone to the end, moved so rapidly that
"this end and this beginning are one" (CP, 506). The elemental
forms of experience are present in every instant of time and in
every season or weather of the soul: mind in its emptiness detached
from reality and seeing it in bare impoverishment, the imagination
covering the rock with leaves, flowers, and fruit, the drying and
falling of the leaves in autumn. Stevens' *Collected Poems* moves in a
slow round through the cycle of the seasons, from the gaudy,
springlike poems of *Harmonium*, like new buds on the rock, through
Transport to Summer and *The Auroras of Autumn*, and then back again
to winter with *The Rock*, but every authentic image, from one end
of his poetry to the other, recapitulates the sequence in a breath.
To see the world in its first idea is to see it in "living changingness"
(CP, 380), to go in an instant from the white candor of the beginning in its original freshness to the white candor of the end in its
multiplicity of imaginative enhancement. The first idea is not only
a certain perception of things in space. It is also an experience of
their participation in time.

"The Owl in the Sarcophagus" (CP, 431–436) is Stevens' fullest
expression of the way time moves from beginning to end in each
moment. The poem is about "the forms of thought," that is, the
universal limits between which human existence moves, for we live
in the mind. If man lives in the mind he dies there too: "It is a child
that sings itself to sleep,/The mind, among the creatures that it
makes,/The people, those by which it lives and dies" (CP, 436).
Man dies in the mind because the mind is bound by time. This
means that it is defined by the fact that it will one day die. Death
does not lie somewhere ahead as an end which will cut short an
existence which has been lived as though it were immortal. Life
dwells within death, and is constantly coming from and returning
to death as its origin, home, and end. The owl, Minerva, the mind,
lives in a sarcophagus, and the poem describes "the mythology of
modern death" (CP, 435). It embodies the forces which determine
the mind's activity, the creatures that it makes. These forces are
always the same within the perpetual present of the mind. They
are "death's own supremest images,/The pure perfections of
parental space,/. . . the beings of the mind/In the light-bound

space of the mind, the floreate flare" (CP, 436). Since the figures of the poem live in mental space, they exist in "a time/That of itself [stands] still, perennial" (CP, 432). This moment is "less time than place" (CP, 433) because it is outside time, though it is the only living part of time. The moment is the dwelling place of space.

The figures of the mythology of modern death are three: sleep, peace, and "she that says/Good-by in the darkness" (CP, 431). Sleep is the beginning, the radiant candor of pure mind without any content, mind as it is when it faces a bare unimagined reality or mind as it is when it has completed the work of decreation and is ready "in an ever-changing, calmest unity" (CP, 433) to begin imagining again. If sleep is the beginning, peace is the end, "the brother of sleep," "the prince of shither-shade and tinsel lights" (CP, 434). "Peace after death" is the end in the sense that he represents the fulfillment of the mind's work. If sleep is prior to life, since "ultimate intellect" is consciousness with no content and therefore not consciousness at all, then peace is the death at the end of life, the death of a consummation of the imagination. Peace is that death man touches in every moment as he goes from the immaculate beginning to its late plural. He is "that figure stationed at our end,/Always, in brilliance, fatal, final, formed/Out of our lives to keep us in our death" (CP, 439).

What of the third figure, she that says good-by? She broods over the brief flash between start and finish which is living reality, surrounded on all sides by death. She dwells in what Stevens calls in another poem "The mobile and the immobile flickering/In the area between is and was" (CP, 474), and presides over the meteor of the moment as it appears out of nowhere, glows, and disappears. Only in the present can man glimpse things as they are. Reality exists in the space between is and was, and the third figure is the embodiment of this presence of the present, a presence which is like a glow in molten iron, such a glow as fades even as we watch it.

This goddess is like the "necessary angel of earth" in "Angel Surrounded by Paysans." She too could describe herself as "A figure half seen, or seen for a moment, a [creature]/Of the mind, an apparition apparelled in/Apparels of such lightest look that a turn/Of my shoulder and quickly, too quickly, I am gone" (CP, 497). Though she disappears as soon as she appears, though she dwells "on the edges of oblivion" (CP, 435), she is the only means

by which man can "see the earth again" (CP, 496). Her speed
allows him to see things as they are, in that quick breath after the
beginning and before the peace of accomplished imagination. If
man can glimpse reality only in the moment, it is also that moment
which endows him with whatever reality he has. The third figure,
she that "in the syllable between life/And death cries quickly, in
a flash of voice,/Keep you, keep you, I am gone," is "the mother
of us all" (CP, 432).

Stevens is here describing the indescribable and embodying the
disembodied. In these poems, as much in their rhythm as in their
meaning, he gives the reader an immediate apprehension of the
ever-breathing and moving present as it goes in an instant through
all seasons and all possible experiences, and then burns out like a
meteor.

⌇

How is it possible to write poetry which will match the mobility
of the moment? Any form of words will apparently be too fixed to
move with a time of such rapidity. Even a short poem is too long
to be a meteor. It transforms the living flow of reality into a clumsy
machine and is already a relic of the past before the last line is
reached.

Stevens gradually learns ways of meeting this situation. He comes
to write a poetry of fleeting movement, a poetry in which each
phrase has beginning and ending at once. Instead of being a solid
piece of machinery interacting with the other parts, every image
is a recapitulation of the coming into being of the moment and its
disappearance. Each is another pheasant disappearing in the brush.
Even if the poem develops a single theme, it must keep beginning
over, for yesterday's devotions are of no use, and the image used in
one line of a poem is out of date by the time the next line is reached.
The poem must be true to the moments as they come, for the moment is everything. Within each image all space is contained. Each
exists "within an instant's motion, within/A space grown wide"
(CP, 440). Acceleration through time, and a speeding to annihilation in the dead past; expansion in space, until the universe is
contained in a few words — the image takes possession of both
space and time, for "a journey in space equals a journey in time"

(OP, 162), and "in the instant of speech,/The breadth of an accelerando moves,/Captives the being, widens — and was there" (CP, 440). These phrases describe exactly the ever-repeated action of Stevens' later poetry, the moment of speech which expands until it contains everything, all space and all the present, and then disappears. The attempt to catch in words this "moving chaos that never ends" (OP, 50) is the central motive of *Transport to Summer*, *The Auroras of Autumn*, and *The Rock*.

A number of linguistic strategies are used in this attempt. Sometimes a single word or phrase catches the motion, as does the image of the aurora borealis, with "its frigid brilliances, its blue-red sweeps/And gusts of great enkindlings, its polar green,/The color of ice and fire and solitude" (CP, 413). With inexhaustible fertility of invention Stevens finds phrases to describe the fluctuation of the moment. Each image is "A new text of the world,/A scribble of fret and fear and fate" (CP, 494). The flowing of water is "a gayety,/Flashing and flashing in the sun" (CP, 533), and the poet speaks of "gawky flitterings" (CP, 294), of the "fidgets of all-related fire" (CP, 352), of "irridescences" (CP, 478), of "coruscations" and "bright-ethered things" (CP, 349), of "these — escent — issant pre-personae" (CP, 522), of "time's bellishings" (CP, 514), of "particles of nether-do" (CP, 509), of reality's "faculty of ellipses and deviations" (CP, 493). The sea changes "from crumpled tinfoil/To chromatic crawler" (CP, 492), and other poems describe "Gold easings and ouncings and fluctuations of thread/And beetling of belts and lights of general stones" (CP, 477), "confused illuminations and sonorities" (CP, 466), "windings round and dodges to and fro,/Writhings in wrong obliques and distances" (CP, 429, 430), and "hats of angular flick and fleck" (CP, 449). Each such phrase is a new way to express the same thing, the mobile flickering in the area between is and was.

Another way to catch the moment is through sequences of images which are metamorphoses of one another. Stevens' last poems return to the motif of constant transformation which appears so often in *Harmonium*, but change is no longer seen as something to be resisted. Now the poet knows that the poem shares in reality only if it keeps up with the dizzy speed of time. A number of passages in Stevens' late work try to do this through a dazzling sequence of metamorphoses. Reality is a theatrical spectacle where things are constantly transformed, as "Scene 10 becomes 11,/In Series X, Act IV, et cetera" (CP, 357). It is as if the spectator were watching a motion picture which had been speeded up so that he could see in a single instant spring blossom into summer and die again in the fall:

> It is a theatre floating through the clouds,
> Itself a cloud, although of misted rock
> And mountains running like water, wave on wave,
>
> Through waves of light. It is of cloud transformed
> To cloud transformed again, idly, the way
> A season changes color to no end,
>
> Except the lavishing of itself in change,
> As light changes yellow into gold and gold
> To its opal elements and fire's delight . . . (CP, 416)

Sometimes the flowing of time is matched by the constant alteration of a series of phrases in apposition. Each phrase is a restatement in different terms of the previous one and confesses its imperfection by the fact that it must be replaced. A phrase is a tangential hinting at something which can never be fully possessed in words. The rapid substitution of one phrase for another keeps up with the motion of time and shares its strength. This change is an effortless acceleration, as if the poet had begun to move with the wind. "We make," says Stevens, ". . ./Variations on the words spread sail" (CP, 490). So he speaks of "a breathing like the wind,/A moving part of a motion, a discovery/Part of a discovery, a change part of a change,/A sharing of color and being part of it" (CP, 518), or describes a bouquet of flowers in a jar as, like lightning, "Crowded with apparitions suddenly gone/And no less suddenly here again, a growth/Of the reality of the eye, an artifice,/Nothing much, a flitter that reflects itself" (CP, 448). Each phrase is good only for the moment and must be replaced by another.

The changefulness of the moment may also be expressed by images of slight variation. Stevens' late poetry is full of things which are neither quite one thing nor quite another, but are poised halfway in an unlikely equilibrium. Colors in these poems are a blend of two or more colors, and each object is "of medium nature" (CP, 448). The poet has to find words which will be true to these intermediate realities, realities which have only a brief existence.

"The enigmatical/Beauty of each beautiful enigma" is constantly becoming "amassed in a total double-thing" (CP, 472), and to parallel this world of nuances there must be a language of nuance. Only if the poet's phrases "Rise liquidly in liquid lingerings,/Like watery words awash; like meanings said/By repetitions of half-meanings" (CP, 497) can the poem express the moment when reality is changed "by an access of color, a new and unobserved, slight dithering" (CP, 517). The reader encounters "half colors of quarter-things" (CP, 288), or "chains of blue-green glitterings" (CP, 449), or "a storm of secondary things" (CP, 351), "belted/And knotted, sashed and seamed, half pales of red,/Half pales of green" (CP, 378), a storm full of "Reflections and offshoots, mimic-motes/And mist-mites, dangling seconds, grown/Beyond relation to the parent trunk" (CP, 365). Primary noon turns to "phantomerei" in the "first gray second" after twelve, and then the poet can no longer see pure green, but "a kind/Of violet gray, a green violet, a thread/To weave a shadow's leg or sleeve, a scrawl/On the pedestal" (CP, 459, 460).

The storm of secondary things is more than a temporal sequence of changes. Each moment is "abulge" (CP, 514) with multiplicity. It is a swarming plenitude of things moving together, "floating like the first hundred flakes of snow/Out of a storm we must endure all night" (CP, 351). Things change from moment to moment and each moment is itself full of an enormous number of activities born of the interchange of imagination and reality. The moment is "a glass aswarm with things going as far as they can" (CP, 519), and in this fullness things are "Blooming and beaming and voluming colors out" (CP, 484), so that the poet can perceive "the infinite of the actual" (CP, 451), the multiplicity which is generated by "The dazzling, bulging, brightest core,/The furiously burning father-fire" (CP, 365). In any moment a man encounters a great crowd of changes all going on at once, "As if the air, the midday air, was swarming/With the metaphysical changes that occur,/Merely in living as and where we live" (CP, 326). If the poet sits on a park bench, he finds himself in a "Theatre of Trope" (CP, 397), face to face with an inexhaustible proliferation of happenings all taking place at the same time:

> The water of
> The lake was full of artificial things,

> Like a page of music, like an upper air,
> Like a momentary color, in which swans
> Were seraphs, were saints, were changing essences. (CP, 397)

The flittering of single words or phrases, a sequence of meta-morphoses or of phrases in apposition, the expression of the nuances of secondary things, the presentation of a world of swarming plenitude — these are Stevens' means of expressing the mobility of the moment. Often they work together, as in "An Ordinary Evening in New Haven" (CP, 465–489), that extraordinary tour de force of Stevens' late manner, one of the triumphs of his art. The poem is a long cadenzalike meditation on the equivalence of poetry and life. It is a supple and sinuous improvisation, constantly generating itself out of its own annihilation. It begins and ends and begins again indefatigably, and gives in "flickings from finikin to fine finikin" what Stevens calls, in words that might stand as an epitome of his later style:

> . . . the edgings and inchings of final form,
> The swarming activities of the formulae
> Of statement, directly and indirectly getting at,
>
> Like an evening evoking the spectrum of violet,
> A philosopher practicing scales on his piano,
> A woman writing a note and tearing it up. (CP, 488)

⏝

After Stevens' experience of the dissolution of the gods it seemed that he was left, like post-Cartesian man in general, in a world riven in two, split irreparably into subject and object, imagination and reality. All his work seems to be based on the assumption of this dualism. Any attempt to escape it by affirming the priority of one or the other power leads to falsehood. But as his work progresses he finds that there is after all only one realm, always and everywhere the realm of some new conjunction of imagination and reality. The later Stevens is beyond metaphysical dualism, and beyond representational thinking. It is no longer a question of some reality which exists already in the world, and of which the poet then makes an image. The image is inextricably part of the thing, and the most extreme imaginative distortion is still based on reality. There is only one mode of existence: consciousness of some reality.

Imagination never exists separately. Reality never exists separately. All that ever exists, anywhere, for man, is imagination-reality, an imaginary reality, or a real imagination.

Imagination is reality, or, as Stevens puts it, "poetry and reality are one" (NA, 81). He makes much use of the form of statement which says "A is B." Among the "Adagia" (OP, 157–180) are many such sentences: "Art . . . is often indistinguishable from life itself." "Poetry is a means of redemption." "Imagination is the only genius." "Reality is the spirit's true center." "The theory of poetry is the life of poetry." "The theory of poetry is the theory of life." "Words are the only melodeon." "God is a postulate of the ego." "The world is myself. Life is myself." These expressions are not tautologies. They affirm the equivalence of the multiple in the one. All entities come together in the realm of things as they are, the realm of the "is" which yokes them together in the unity of being. These equivalences might be run together in a chain: "Imagination is reality is the only genius is life is poetry is the theory of poetry is the theory of life is words is the ego is God is redemption." Stevens in several texts affirms this sort of relation between propositions of the form "A is B" or "A and B are one":

Proposita: 1. God and the imagination are one. 2. The thing imagined is the imaginer.
The second equals the thing imagined and the imaginer are one. Hence, I suppose, the imaginer is God. (OP, 178)

Now, if the style of a poem and poem itself are one; if the style of the gods and the gods themselves are one; and if the style of men and men themselves are one; and if there is any true relation between these propositions, it might well be the case that the parts of these propositions are interchangeable. Thus, it might be true that the style of a poem and the gods themselves are one; or that the style of the gods and the style of men are one; or that the style of a poem and the style of men are one. (OP, 209)

The gods have returned unexpectedly after their seemingly permanent evaporation. They have returned as a postulate of the ego, so that "God and the imagination are one" (CP, 524), or "poetry and apotheosis are one" (CP, 378), or "God is in me or else is not at all (does not exist)" (OP, 172). If God is a postulate of the ego, he is part of reality, for the ego and reality are one. The gods have returned as part of the intertwined series of equations which makes all dimensions of existence equivalent. These dimensions are affirmed simultaneously in every authentic poem. Each image, bare and wintry or gay and summery, contains all the elements, life, the ego, God, imagination, reality. Every image is both original and final. The poet is at the heart of reality and need never move beyond where he is in the first moment. His only obligation is to wait for the next instant and try to equal its novelty with an image which will "catch from that/Irrational moment its unreasoning" (CP, 398).

If all the elements of life are equivalent, imagination and reality are not opposite poles, attracting and repelling one another in irreconcilable tension. They are two names for the same thing. "Real and unreal are two in one" (CP, 485). This discovery makes possible Stevens' late poems, those fluent inventions which affirm themselves neither as imagination nor as reality but as both together. Whatever comes to the spirit is as real as anything can be, and all experiences have the right to be recorded as part of the structure of reality. "The rose, the delphinium, the red, the blue,/Are questions of the looks they get" (CP, 451), and the bouquet is all the things it seems to those who see it. The poet need "seek/Nothing beyond reality" (CP, 471) because everything is contained within it. Since this is true he can, for example, accept effortlessly all the swarming changes which occur as he watches New Haven on an ordinary evening. This recognition of the identity of the elements of life means a radical redefinition of poetry. Words are tangled inextricably in the event they describe. "The poem is the cry of its occasion,/Part of the res itself and not about it" (CP, 473), and therefore "description is revelation" (CP, 344). Words are the vortex of the whirlpool where imagination and reality merge, for "words of the world are the life of the world" (CP, 474). The poet, in this "thesis of the plentifullest John" (CP, 345), has power to make things exist through his creating word.

⤶

"It is a world of words to the end of it" (CP, 345) — this is apparently Stevens' ultimate position: the reconciliation of imagination and reality in a theory of the identity of poetry and life, and the development of a poetry which will sustain this identity. There is one more aspect of his thought, however, and this the most difficult to see or to say.

It begins with a movement toward nothingness in his later poetry. Along with the development of a poetry of the swarming moment there is something different. As its tensions are resolved, Stevens' poetry gets more and more disembodied, more and more a matter of the spirit's alchemicana and less and less a matter of the solid and tangible, the pears on their dish, the round peaches with their fuzz and juice. His verse becomes more and more insubstantial as the oscillations between imagination and reality get more and more rapid, until, at the limit, the poem seems about to evaporate altogether. At the extreme of speed all solidity disappears. The mobility which allows beginning and ending to merge releases something else: a glimpse of the nothingness which underlies existence. When "everything come[s] together as one," with "a kind of cozening and coaxing sound," "disembodiments/Still keep occurring" (CP, 482).

The word or the idea of nothingness comes back more and more often. The motif appears as early as *Harmonium*, but there it is associated with the bareness of winter. Only the snowman, the man who is "nothing himself," is free of mental fictions and can behold "nothing that is not there and the nothing that is." Stevens' later poetry is continuous with this early intuition of nothing, but the theme of nothingness gradually becomes more dominant. In the later poetry nothingness is source and end of everything, and underlies everything as its present reality. Imagination is nothing. Reality is nothing. The mind is nothing. Words are nothing. God is nothing. Perhaps it is the fact that these things are equivalent to nothing which makes them equivalents of one another. All things come together in the nothing. So Stevens speaks of "the priest of nothingness who intones" on the rock of reality (OP, 88). In another poem the wind "Intones its single emptiness/The savagest hollow of winter-sound" (CP, 294). He tells of a room "emptier than nothingness" (CP, 286), or of a moon which is "a lustred nothingness" (CP, 320). He asks for a "god in the house" who will be so insubstantial that he will be "a coolness,/A vermilioned nothingness" (CP, 328), and speaks of metaphysical presences which are like "beasts that one never sees,/Moving so that the foot-falls are slight and almost nothing" (CP, 337). In another poem the first breath of spring "creates a fresh universe out of nothingness" (CP, 517). All things, "seen and unseen," are "created from nothingness" (CP, 486; OP, 100) or "forced up from nothing" (CP, 363), as if, says the poet, "nothingness contained a métier" (CP, 526). The rock of reality is not a substance, material and present before man's eyes. It has come from nothing. If it has come from nothing its source still defines it, and all things dwell in the "stale grandeur of annihilation" (CP, 505). As Stevens says in a striking phrase: "Reality is a vacuum" (OP, 168).

A number of his poems attempt to give a sense of the way reality is a vacuum. In these poems "we breathe/An odor evoking nothing, absolute" (CP, 394, 395). "A Clear Day and No Memories" (OP, 113) describes a weather in which "the air is clear of everything," "has no knowledge except of nothingness," and "flows over us without meanings" in an "invisible activity." "Chocorua to Its Neighbor" (CP, 296–302) is an extraordinarily disembodied poem, the subject of which is a strange shadow, "an eminence,/But of nothing" (CP, 300). "A Primitive like an Orb" (CP, 440–443) is about a "giant of nothingness" (CP, 443), and in "The Auroras of Autumn" a bodiless serpent is present everywhere in the landscape, and yet present as a formless nothingness. These poems accomplish a hollowing out or subtilizing of nature. They attempt to make visible something which is "always too heavy for the sense/To seize, the obscurest as, the distant was" (CP, 441), and give the reader the feeling of what it is like to see reality as less tangible than the finest mist. If it is true that the underlying substance of reality is a vacuum, a "dominant blank, the unapproachable" (CP, 477), then the poet must present it as a nameless, evanescent flowing, hovering always on the edge of oblivion. "It is not in the premise that reality/Is a solid," he says in the last words of "An Ordinary Evening in New Haven." "It may be a shade that traverses/A dust, a force that traverses a shade" (CP, 489). If reality is a vacuum, imagination is no less empty. It is the "nothing" of "Imago" (CP, 439), which lifts all things. Man in a world where reality is nonentity "has his poverty and nothing more" (CP, 427). He is "always in emptiness that would be filled" (CP, 467).

Stevens seemed to be approaching a full possession of plenitude of things, but as the tension between imagination and reality diminishes there is an emptying out of both, until at the moment they touch, in the brevity of a poem which includes beginning and ending in a breath, the poet finds himself face to face with a universal nothing.

~

This apparent defeat is the supreme victory, for the nothing is not nothing. It is. It is being. Being is a pervasive power, visible nowhere in itself and yet present and visible in all things. It is what things share through the fact that they are. Being is not a thing like other things and therefore can only appear to man as nothing, but it is what all things must participate in if they are to exist at all. Stevens' later poetry has as its goal the releasing of that evanescent glimpse of being which is as close as man can come to a possession of the ground of things. The paradoxical appearance of being in the form of nothing causes the ambiguity of his poetry. Man's inability to see being as being causes Stevens to say of it, "It is and it/Is not and, therefore, is" (CP, 440), and yet in the supreme moments of insight he can speak directly of it, in lines which are like a cry of ecstatic discovery:

> It is like a thing of ether that exists
> Almost as predicate. But it exists,
> It exists, it is visible, it is, it is. (CP, 418)

The nothingness is, but it is not to be identified with the hollowness of consciousness. It is "The palm at the end of the mind,/ Beyond the last thought" (OP, 117). Human nature participates in being, but so do all other existences. Wherever the poet thinks to catch it, it disappears, melting into the landscape and leaving just the pines and rock and water which are there, or being absorbed into the mind and taking the mind's own shape. "If in the mind, he vanishe[s], taking there/The mind's own limits, like a tragic thing/Without existence, existing everywhere" (CP, 298). Being is released in the flash of time from is to was, just as it is released in the expansion of perception to occupy space. It is the presentness of things present, the radiance of things as they are, and therefore is "Physical if the eye is quick enough,/So that, where he was, there is an enkindling, where/He is, the air changes and grows fresh to breathe" (CP, 301).

What of the "he" in these passages? Man's sharing in being is the justification for the personification of the landscape which runs through Stevens' poetry from *Harmonium* on. If human nature is part of being, then being appears to man in a human shape if it appears at all: "He was not man yet he was nothing else" (CP, 298). Since being is present everywhere in space, then the perception of things in space takes the shape of some human figure, and this generates the mythological beings who appear in such early poems as "The Paltry Nude Starts on a Spring Voyage" or "Infanta Marina." It is also the origin of the giant appearing again and again in Stevens' later poetry. The giant is the source of everything human, but is also present outside men, "beyond their life, yet of themselves" (CP, 299). So Chocorua describes a "prodigious shadow" at the end of night which hovers over the land like "light embodied, or almost" (CP, 297), and yet at the same time is the base of the human. This strange being in the space of night is, says Chocorua, "a human thing" (CP, 300). He will disappear in the day and "yet remain, yet be." He remains and is as the equal of man and his origin, "not father, but bare brother, megalfrere," yet also "the common self, interior fons" (CP, 300, 301). This generating power is "of human realizings, rugged roy" (CP, 302).

"Chocorua to Its Neighbor" is the first great poem in which Stevens tries to make being perceptible to man, "as far as nothingness permits" (CP, 463), but the attainment of insight into being is the aim of all his later poems. The serpent in the landscape in "The Auroras of Autumn" is the nothingness of occulted being. Being is the true name of the third figure in "The Owl in the Sarcophagus," she who says good-by and in vanishing holds men closely with discovery. The "necessary angel of earth" in "Angel Surrounded by Paysans" is being too, the figure half seen, or seen for a moment, in whose sight we see the earth again. Being causes the "insolid billowing of the solid" (OP, 111) in "Reality Is an Activity of the Most August Imagination," and being is the shade that traverses a dust, the force that traverses a shade at the end of "An Ordinary Evening in New Haven." Being is also, in "A Primitive like an Orb," the "difficult apperception" (CP, 440), the "giant on the horizon" who is "concentrum, grave/And prodigious person, patron of origins" (CP, 443).

In two late poems, "Metaphor As Degeneration" and "The

River of Rivers in Connecticut," Stevens sees being as a river, visible in the shining of the appearances that reveal it, and not to be discovered behind those appearances. It flows everywhere, through all space and time, and through all the contents of space and time. In these two poems he gives his most succinct expression of his apprehension of being:

> The swarthy water
> That flows round the earth and through the skies,
> Twisting among the universal spaces,
>
> Is not Swatara. It is being. (CP, 444)
>
> It is not to be seen beneath the appearances
> That tell of it. The steeple at Farmington
> Stands glistening and Haddam shines and sways.
>
> It is the third commonness with light and air,
> A curriculum, a vigor, a local abstraction . . .
> Call it, once more, a river, an unnamed flowing,
>
> Space-filled, reflecting the seasons, the folk-lore
> Of each of the senses; call it, again and again,
> The river that flows nowhere, like a sea. (CP, 533)

At the heart of Stevens' poetry there is a precise vision of reality. According to this vision, ultimate being is not in some transcendent realm, above and beyond what men can see. It is within things as they are, revealed in the glistening of the steeple at Farmington, in the flowing of time, in the presence of things in the moment, in the interior fons of man. This revelation of being is indeed a difficult apperception, "disposed and re-disposed/By such slight genii in such pale air" (CP, 440). To speak directly of it, to analyze it, is almost inevitably to falsify it, to fix it in some abstraction and therefore to kill it. Though man participates in being he does not confront it directly. It is the center of which each man is an eccentric particle, "helplessly at the edge" (CP, 430). When he tries to reach the center, it disappears. Man can never possess "the bouquet of being" (OP, 109), that fugitive aroma. The best he can do is "to realize/That the sense of being changes as we talk" (OP, 109), and go on talking in the hope that if he is careful to see that "nothing [is] fixed by a single word" (OP, 114), nothing will be, in another sense, fixed momentarily in a word, and he will have another glimpse of being.

The only passage in Stevens' prose which speaks directly of his perception of being is curiously evasive. It is evasive because its subject is evasive. There is something there, Stevens says, but it can only be described negatively, for to define it is to still it and it must not be stilled. The passage is proof that Stevens knows how elusive his central insight is and how difficult it is to speak of it in logical prose:

> I mean that nobility which is our spiritual height and depth; and while I know how difficult it is to express it, nevertheless I am bound to give a sense of it. Nothing could be more evasive and inaccessible. Nothing distorts itself and seeks disguise more quickly. There is a shame of disclosing it and in its definite presentations a horror of it. But there it is. The fact that it is there is what makes it possible to invite to the reading and writing of poetry men of intelligence and desire for life. I am not thinking of the ethical or the sonorous or at all of the manner of it. The manner of it is, in fact, its difficulty, which each man must feel each day differently, for himself. I am not thinking of the solemn, the portentous or de-moded. On the other hand, I am evading a definition. If it is defined, it will be fixed and it must not be fixed. As in the case of an external thing, nobility resolves itself into an enormous number of vibrations, movements, changes. To fix it is to put an end to it. (NA, 33, 34)

To fix it is to put an end to it, but in poetry it can be caught unfixed. The mobile poetry of Stevens' later style is more than an acceptance of the impossibility of avoiding the war of the mind and sky. It is a revelation of being. The poetry of flittering metamorphosis is the only poetry which is simultaneously true to both imagination and reality, and it is the only poetry which will catch being. The ultimate tragedy is that being is transformed instantaneously into nothing, and therefore though the poet has it he has it as an absence. Only a poetry of iridescent frettings will remain in touch with it. In the process of going in a moment through the whole cycle from A to Z, being is released, seen, and annihilated, like those atomic particles which live only a millionth of a second. As soon as it is named, it disappears, but for a moment it is seen. It is and it is not and, therefore, is. After finishing one of Stevens' poems, the reader has the feeling that after all nothing has happened, no change of the world such as science or technology can perform: "And yet nothing has been changed except what is/Unreal, as if nothing had been changed at all" (OP, 117). At the end it *was* there. So Santayana, in "To an Old Philosopher in Rome," lives "on the threshold of heaven," and sees things double, things and the presence of being in things, "The extreme of the known in the presence of the extreme/Of the unknown" (CP, 508). To see things transfigured in this way is still to see them just as they are, in all their barrenness and poverty. This world and the other are "two alike in the make of the mind" (CP, 508), and the old philosopher's ultimate insight, like Stevens' own, is not at all a mystic vision of things beyond this world:

> It is a kind of total grandeur at the end,
> With every visible thing enlarged and yet
> No more than a bed, a chair and moving nuns,
> The immensest theatre, the pillared porch,
> The book and candle in your ambered room . . . (CP, 510)

Merely to see being in things is not enough. It must be spoken. Through words man participates in being, for words of the world are the life of the world. Poetry does not name something which has already been perceived or put in words a pre-existent mental conception. The act of naming calls things together, gathers them into one, and makes present the things which are present. Speaking belongs to being, and in naming things in their presence poetry brings being into the open.

From De Quincey through Arnold and Browning to Hopkins, Yeats, and Stevens there is a movement from the absence of God to the death of God as starting point and basis. Various writers, Browning or Yeats for example, beginning in one or the other of these situations are able to make a recovery of immanence. Perhaps it is Stevens' way, the movement from the dissolution of the gods to the difficult apperception of being, which represents the next step forward in the spiritual history of man. Stevens may be in the vanguard of a movement "toward the end of ontology," as Jean Wahl calls it.[10] Central in this movement is the idea that man's spiritual height and depth are available here and now or nowhere. The last stanza of "A Primitive like an Orb" is one of Stevens' most eloquent statements of his belief that all the words and experiences of man are part of being, eccentric particles of the giant "at the centre on the horizon," the giant who can never be fully possessed

[10] See *Vers la fin de l'ontologie* (Paris: Société d'Édition d'Enseignement Supérieur, 1956).

or spoken in any words, but who is shared by all. If this is the case then the simplest phrase, in all its limitation, is "the human end in the spirit's greatest reach" (CP, 508):

> That's it. The lover writes, the believer hears,
> The poet mumbles and the painter sees,
> Each one, his fated eccentricity,
> As a part, but part, but tenacious particle,
> Of the skeleton of the ether, the total
> Of letters, prophecies, perceptions, clods
> Of color, the giant of nothingness, each one
> And the giant ever changing, living in change. (CP, 443)

VII

William Carlos Williams

As he opened his eyes, he found himself alone, lying in a comfortable place among the trees, quite in the open, with torn branches on all sides of him and leaves, ripped from their hold, plastered in fragments upon the rocks about him. Unfortunately, though, he didn't recognize the place. No one was there to inform him of his whereabouts and when he did begin to encounter passers-by, they didn't even understand, let alone speak his language. He could recall nothing of the past.

In this text alone of his mature work does Williams describe the state of deprivation which was his starting point. It appears only once because it was so soon transcended. The poet does not become himself, nor is his writing possible, until he has gone beyond it. Only in Williams' first published work, the *Poems* of 1909, that pastiche of the romantic motifs he was soon to reject, is there an echo of the experience here described:

But now among low plains or banks which rear
Their flower hung screens o'erhead I wander — where?
These fields I know not; know not whence I come;

Nor aught of all which spreads so touching near.
The very bird-songs I have heard them n'er
And this strange folk they know not e'en my name.

The young man who found himself alone in a strange land was the hero of a long narrative poem, modeled on Keats's "Endymion," which Williams wrote during his medical training, at about the same time that he was writing the poems published in the slender volume of 1909. Though he added more and more scenes to the poem, it remained unfinished.[1] The poem told the story of a young prince taken from his bride at the wedding feast, before the consummation of his marriage, and transported to a strange country.

[1] Williams says in his autobiography that he finally burned the poem, but the manuscript is extant and is now in the possession of John C. Thirlwall. See *The Massachusetts Review*, 3: 307 (Winter 1962) for a facsimile of one page of it.

His wanderings were described as he attempted to recover his past and find his way home again.

The young prince's state of loss was complete. It was the exact antithesis of the condition presupposed in Williams' work after the *Poems* of 1909. Instead of belonging to the place where he found himself, he did not even recognize it. He was detached from his familiar surroundings, like a leaf torn from its tree and cast on the bare rocks of an alien earth. He could not remember the past, when he was married to his locality and invested with all its privileges. He saw the present scene across an empty space, as something strange and unrecognizable, and what he beheld was fragmented, broken branches and torn leaves, the relics of some inexplicable disaster.

The prince was also bereft of language and cut off from other people. These two losses are intertwined. Language is the chief means by which human beings know one another and transform a place into a culture. The prince could not understand the passers-by, nor they him, and so he was forced to endure a terrifying alienation, like that of Yanko Goorall in Conrad's "Amy Foster." A private language is no language, for the essence of language is its use as a means of communication.

Words also join a man to the physical world. The collective naming of flower, tree, rock, and bird brings them into existence for a people, and assimilates them into a culture, giving them a measure, a meaning, and a place. "The only means [man] has to give value to life," says Williams, "is to recognise it with the imagination and name it." Naming and imagining are the same. They are that originating act which creates a culture by "the lifting of an environment to expression." The prince was without a local culture, and therefore he could not recognize the place where he was. His failure to speak the language of the country made him a naked consciousness confronting a world in fragments inhabited by a people speaking words without meaning to him. It is no wonder that he "went on, homeward or seeking a home that was his own." [2]

[2] The following texts of Williams' work have been used in this chapter. Each is accompanied by the abbreviation which will hereafter be employed in citations. *Poems* ([Rutherford, N.J.: privately printed], 1909): P [1909]; *Kora in Hell: Improvisations* (San Francisco: City Lights, 1957): KH; *Spring and All* (Dijon: Contact, 1923): SA; *The Great American Novel* (Paris: Contact, 1923): GAN; *In the American Grain* (New York:

The poet was unable to bring his prince to his native land, and therefore the poem remained unfinished, a potentially endless series of episodes, never accomplishing the leap between homelessness and home. His next long poem, "The Wanderer," comes first in *The Collected Earlier Poems*. It celebrates the homecoming which makes his poetry possible. Here the marriage of the prince is consummated at last. An important letter to Marianne Moore provides the terms in which this homecoming can be understood. The poet praises Miss Moore for recognizing the "inner security" which is the basis of his work. That security, he says, "is something which occurred once when I was about twenty, a sudden resignation to existence, a despair — if you wish to call it that, but a despair which made everything a unit and at the same time a part of myself. I suppose it might be called a sort of nameless religious experience. I resigned, I gave up" (SL, 147). He abandoned his private consciousness, that hollow bubble in the midst of the solidity of the world. The resulting "anonymity" (SL, 147) is assumed in all his work and recurrently affirmed there, as when Paterson, the man-city, asks: "Why even speak of 'I,' . . . which/interests me almost not at all?" (P, 30). To give up the ego means to give up also those dramas of the interchange of subject and object, self and world, which have long been central in Western philosophy and literature. The poet's resignation puts him beyond romanticism. He reaches at the age of twenty the place which Wallace Stevens attains only after decades of struggle to harmonize imagination and reality. After his resignation there is always and everywhere only one realm. Consciousness permeates the world, and the world has entered into the mind. It is "an identity — it can't be/otherwise — an/interpenetration, both ways" (P, 12).

New Directions, 1956): IAG; "An Approach to the Poem," *English Institute Essays: 1947* (New York: Columbia University Press, 1948), pp. 50–75: AP; *The Collected Earlier Poems* (New York: New Directions, 1951): CEP; *The Autobiography of William Carlos Williams* (New York: Random House, 1951): A; *Selected Essays* (New York: Random House, 1954): SE; *Selected Letters*, ed. John C. Thirlwall (New York: McDowell, Obolensky, 1957): SL; *I Wanted to Write a Poem: The Autobiography of the Works of a Poet*, reported and edited by Edith Heal (Boston: Beacon Press, 1958): IWWP; *Yes, Mrs. Williams* (New York: McDowell, Obolensky, 1959): YMW; *Many Loves and Other Plays* (New York: New Directions, 1961): ML; *Pictures from Brueghel and Other Poems* (New York: New Directions, 1962): PB; *The Collected Later Poems* (New York: New Directions, 1963): CLP; *Paterson* (New York: New Directions, 1963): P. Quotations in the initial paragraphs of this chapter come, respectively, from A, 59; P [1909], 17; SA, 41; SL, 286; A, 60.

Williams' work expresses, quietly and without fanfare, a revolution in human sensibility. When he gives himself up to the world he gives up the coordinates and goals which had polarized earlier literature. Romantic poetry, like idealist philosophy, had been based on an opposition between the inner world of the subject and the outer world of things. Since the world is other than the self, that self can ground itself on something external. This tradition remains valid through the nineteenth and early twentieth centuries, down to Yeats and the early Stevens. In Williams it disappears. This is perhaps most apparent, to a reader steeped in romanticism, in a strange lack of tension in his work. Gone are both the profound abysses of subjectivity, so important in earlier poetry, and the limitless dimensions of the external world, through which Shelley's Alastor or Browning's Paracelsus sought a vanishing presence and strained every nerve to reach it. "How foolish to seek new worlds," says Williams, ". . . when we must know that any world warmed by the arts will surpass the very Elysian Fields if the imagination reaches its end there." [3] Only in the *Poems* of 1909 does the image of fathomless space appear, the "soundless infinite blue day" (P [1909], 21), and only there are found examples of the romantic theme of an unattainable presence in the landscape, as in the assertion that poetry will take the reader "to worlds afar whose fruits all anguish mend" (P [1909], 11), or in the last lines of "To Simplicity":

> . . . Hark! Hark! Mine ears are numb
> With dread! Methought a faint hallooing rang!
> Where art thou hid? Cry, cry again! I come!
> I come! I come! (P [1909], 9)

In Williams' mature work, if something exists at all, it dwells in the only realm there is, a space both subjective and objective, a region of copresence in which anywhere is everywhere, and all times are one time. "What is time but an impertinence?" asks the poet (GAN, 65). Since there are no distances there is "no direction" (P, 28), no reason to go one way rather than another because there is no reason to go anywhere at all. To be in one place is already to be in all other places. "I won't follow causes," he says. "I can't. The reason is that it seems so much more important to me that I *am*. Where shall one go? What shall one do?" (SL, 147). Byron

---

[3] "Introduction" to Byron Vazakas, *Transfigured Night* (New York: The Macmillan Company, 1946), p. xi.

Vazakas is an authentic American poet because he "hasn't had 'to go anywhere.' There he is . . . anywhere, therefore *here*, for his effects. And being here, he sees here; and hears here." [4]

This situation means the disappearance of another characteristic of traditional philosophy and poetry: thinking in terms of causality. Western thought has been dominated since Aristotle by the idea of cause, whether this has meant a search for the ground of things in some transcendent being, or whether it has meant conceiving of nature as a chain of cause and effect, each element pushing the next in an endless series. Both kinds of causality vanish in Williams' work. All things exist simultaneously in one realm, and though they may interact they are not related causally. The idea of causal sequence is replaced by the notion of a poetry which "lives with an intrinsic movement of its own to verify its authenticity" (SE, 257). As in other areas of contemporary thought, linear determinism gives way to a system of reciprocal motions, "intrinsic, undulant, a physical more than a literary character" (SE, 256).

It is appropriate that Keats should have been the poet who most influenced Williams in his youth, for Williams might be said to begin where Keats ends. The leap into things which Keats accomplishes by the most extreme reach of the sympathetic imagination is achieved by Williams at the beginning, and attained also is that perpetual present which is expressed in the epigraph adapted from the "Ode on a Grecian Urn" which the poet puts on the title page of his first book: "Happy melodist forever piping songs forever new." "I quit Keats," he says, "just at the moment he himself did — with Hyperion's scream" (A, 61). Williams means of course Apollo's scream. Keats's poetry reaches its climax with Apollo's attainment of immortal knowledge. With that climax it melts into the silence beyond poetry. Williams' work begins with the muteness of what he calls in *Spring and All* an "approximate co-extension with the universe" (SA, 27).

This silence will provide another definition of the place Williams enters when he resigns himself to existence. The romantic or idealist tradition in one way or another presupposes a separation of words from things. Words are instruments which the poet may use to reach and grapple objects in order to close the gap between himself and them. Through words the poet imposes his will on things and

[4] "Introduction" to *Transfigured Night*, p. xii.

so transforms them. The naming of poetry is the creation of a cunning verbal replica which changes things into spiritualized stuff and so assimilates them into the mind. The idea that words "represent" things is deeply a part of the tradition of metaphysical thinking of which romanticism is a version. Williams never uses words in this way. For him things are already possessed before being named. When he gives up he reaches a place which is before language: "Things have no names for me and places have no significance" (SL, 147). This loss of language is radically different from the aphasia of the prince in the early poem. The prince's mutism expressed his separation from other people and the land. Now all things have been assimilated and the need for words has disappeared. If language is the voice of consciousness in its isolation, union with everything can be reached only by leaving it behind. "As a reward for this anonymity," says Williams, "I feel as much a part of things as trees and stones" (SL, 147). His new speechlessness is the silence which follows Apollo's scream. In it he belongs to "a wordless/world/without personality" (CEP, 280).

If trees, flowers, mountains, and meadows are for Wordsworth and Tennyson the dwelling places of a haunting presence, other romantic poets describe the search for a similar ideal incarnated successively in the women they love. To Gérard de Nerval all women are the same woman, and with each is experienced a failure to possess the ideal: "La Treizième revient . . . C'est encore la première;/Et c'est toujours la seule." [5] This theme too no longer has meaning for Williams. If everything is part of himself this includes men and women. The strangers speaking an alien tongue in his early poem are replaced by the men and women of *Paterson*. The latter exist within the man-city and are the poet's mind incarnated: "Inside the bus one sees/his thoughts sitting and standing. His/thoughts alight and scatter" (P, 18). In the same way he says of one of the personae of *The Great American Novel*, a "savior of the movies": "his great heart had expanded so as to include the whole city" (GAN, 49). This expansion is anticipated in the last text in the *Poems* of 1909, where the poet affirms that with the help of "Perfection" he has transcended the "profusion/Of space" and "o'errides all restriction" (P [1909], 22). Perfection is ubiquity in space and possession of its contents, the "fresh variety" of the

[5] Gérard de Nerval, *Oeuvres, éd. de la Pléiade*, 1 : 31 (Paris, 1952).

world which, in another poem from the same volume, leaves the poet "perplexed by detail" (P [1909], 20). The celebrated slogan, "No ideas but in things," is a shorthand expression of the identification of mind and universe presupposed in Williams' work. Other people are no different from inanimate objects and may just as well incarnate the poet's ideas. This obliteration of distances also takes place in the relation between the poet and his readers. "In the imagination," he says, "we are from henceforth (so long as you read) locked in a fraternal embrace, the classic caress of author and reader. We are one. Whenever I say 'I' I mean also 'you' " (SA, 3, 4). To accept the embrace Williams offers means the impossibility of "criticizing" his work, if criticism means viewing with the cold eye of analysis and judgment. The critic must resign himself to the poet's world and accept what he finds there.

If the poetry of the last century and a half has often assumed a distance between man and things or between man and man, an equally important theme has been the distance of God. Here too Williams differs from his predecessors. In his work there is no searching for the traces of a vanished deity, no frantic attempt to find a new mediator between heaven and earth. "Heaven," he says in one of his few references to the idea of another world, "seems frankly impossible" (SL, 147). The disappearance of a distinction between subject and object could be said to mark the end of a tradition which began in its modern form with writers like Montaigne, Pascal, Descartes, and Locke, those explorers of the abyss of subjectivity. The absence of the idea of heaven means the rejection of an even older tradition, Christian and Platonic. Here is everywhere for Williams, and there is no other world to go to.

The resignation to existence which makes Williams' poetry possible is the exact reverse of the Cartesian Cogito. Descartes puts everything in question in order to establish the existence of his separate self, an existence built on the power of detached thinking. Williams gives himself up in despair and establishes a self beyond personality, a self coextensive with the universe. Words, things, people, and God vanish as separate entities and everything becomes a unit. In "The Wanderer" this obliteration of distinctions is poetically enacted. Under the aegis of a muse-lady (whom Williams has identified with his grandmother [A, 60]), the poet is absorbed into the Passaic, swallowed up by "the utter depth of its rottenness"

(CEP, 11), or it can be said that he takes the river into himself, for it is an interpenetration, both ways. After this plunge he possesses all time and space and has complete knowledge of everything: "I knew all — it became me" (CEP, 12).

This phrase is quoted near the end of Book Five of *Paterson*, in a context which shows the poet's awareness of its seminal place in his work. After the absorption of the poet by the river the muse speaks once more to him: "Be mostly silent!" (CEP, 12). Here is attained that silence and anonymity which he describes in the letter to Marianne Moore. This silence is his marriage to all that is.

⌐

"Be mostly silent!" How can this be? In the years after "The Wanderer," Williams was anything but silent. He wrote poems, plays, stories, and essays in a constant stream. How can he have gone from his silence to a justification of literature?

Words as the expression of man's separation from things disappear with the poet's plunge into the Passaic, but this does not mean that language vanishes. It reappears in the new silence as something which already exists, like trees and rocks. Williams' poetry takes language for granted, just as it takes chicory, daisies, plums, and butterfish for granted. His plunge into the substance of things does not reach a shapeless blur in which all distinctions have been lost. The world is within rather than at a distance, but it is still full of things existing in the exactness of their forms. Beside the other things are words. Language has a kind of sanctity for Williams, and most of his vocabulary can be found in any pocket dictionary. There is scarcely a trace in his poetry of that attempt to reconstruct language by deformation which characterizes a writer like Joyce.

Words are first of all things: "But can you not see, can you not taste, can you not smell, can you not hear, can you not touch — words? . . . Words roll, spin, flare up, rumble, trickle, foam — " (GAN, 10, 11). A word is its sound and feel in the mouth when spoken, or the way it looks on the page, black marks against a white background, graphite which could be "scraped up and put in a tube" or ink which could be lifted from the page (GAN, 9). As a painting is made of paint or music of sound, so "A poem is a small (or large) machine made of words" (SE, 256). This does not mean that Williams wants to drain words of meaning and make them dull surds, mute lumps of voiceless matter. "Words are indivisible crystals," and if they are broken up nothing is left but meaningless letters: "Awu tsst grang splith gra pragh og bm" (GAN, 11). To suppose that words in themselves are meaningless would be a return to one form of the dualism Williams has escaped. In the realm where man and things are one there is nothing which is not intrinsically meaningful. To suppose that man ascribes meaning to things is to suppose a separation of subject and object. Every gesture, every flower, every stone has its meaning as part of its substance, and words contain their meaning as an inextricable part of themselves. Like gestures or facial expressions they are ways man affirms his solidarity with the world, proof that meaning is always incarnated, never purely spiritual. "The words," says the poet, "must become real, they must take the place of wife and sweetheart. They must be a church — Wife. It must be your wife. It must be a thing of adamant with the texture of wind. Wife" (GAN, 17). In another sentence the attempt to make words substantial expressed in the repetitions here of "wife" is affirmed as successful: "The words from long practice had come to be leaves, trees, the corners of his house" (GAN, 17).

This acceptance of words as things manifests itself in several ways in Williams' work. Sometimes words are taken as *objets trouvés*. A modern painter makes his collage of bits of newspaper or cigarette packages. Picasso creates a bull's head out of a bicycle seat and handle bars. Marcel Duchamp sets up a urinal as a "ready-made." In the same way Williams makes poetry out of a list of kinds of ice cream, with prices (CEP, 62, 63), or out of street signs (CEP, 353), or out of a fashionable grocery list: "2 partridges/2 mallard ducks/a Dungeness crab/24 hours out/of the Pacific/and 2 live-frozen/trout/from Denmark" (P, 262). Nonverbal things cannot be put into poetry, since poems are after all made of words, but words also are ready-made and may be taken out of their contexts and put into a poem just as they are found. It is not necessary to change something to make it poetic. All things, including words, are already poetic, and what the painter does with bits of burlap and old nails the poet may do with words, put them without arrangement on the page, so they will be present — *there*.

Williams uses in this way quotations from history books, interviews, and letters. The prose parts of *Paterson* are not "antipoetry" set against the poetry of the parts in verse. The prose is poetry too, and the insertion of big chunks of unshaped language as it was spontaneously used is another way of showing that all language is intrinsically poetic. "All the prose," says the poet of *Paterson*, ". . . has primarily the purpose of giving a metrical meaning to or of emphasizing a metrical continuity between all word use. It is *not* an antipoetic device, the repeating of which piece of miscalculation makes me want to puke. It *is* that prose and verse are both *writing*, both a matter of the words and an interrelation between words for the purpose of exposition, or other better defined purpose of the art. . . . The truth is that there's an *identity* between prose and verse, not an antithesis. It all rests on the same time base, the same measure" (SL, 263, 265). The sonnet form or iambic pentameter are preconceived molds, imported from another continent. To force American material into these foreign shapes is to falsify them. Our speech has new rhythms and a new structure: "We've got to *begin* by stating that we speak (here) a distinct, separate language in a present (new era) and that it is NOT English" (SL, 268, 269). The poet's job is to find examples of the American measure, newborn in all their purity, and put them in his poems for all to hear.

The prose of *Paterson* is made of language the poet found already written down. The language in his stories, in his book about his mother, and in some of his poems is living speech, snatches of conversation or soliloquy which he overheard, recorded, and preserved. Many of the stories consist almost entirely of such "auditory scraps from the language (SL, 214). They have no plot, no dramatic climax. Their virtue is to catch the language as it was spoken. A doctor has unique chances to know at first hand the poetic vitality of the common language, and much of Williams' fiction derives from his medical experience. "It is then we see," he says, "by this constant feeling for a meaning, from the unselected nature of the material, just as it comes in over the phone or at the office door, that there is no better way to get an intimation of what is going on in the world. . . . The physician enjoys a wonderful opportunity actually to witness the words being born. Their actual colors and shapes are laid before him carrying their tiny burdens which he is privileged to take into his care with their unspoiled newness" (A, 360, 361).

Speech is an attribute of its speaker, part of what he does or is in the same way that a rose is red or a bit of glass green and shiny. Here again Williams rejects any attempt to make words "spiritual," inhabitants of a detached world of consciousness. A woman's smile, her walk, a child's way of bouncing a ball — these are manifestations of the substance of a person, aspects of the world's body brought to light. Words are gestures too, an uncovering of hidden life. *Yes, Mrs. Williams* is made up largely of the record of things the poet heard his mother say. The disconnected scraps of Mrs. Williams' speech are not an imaginative "portrait." They are the woman herself made visible, each phrase "bringing all together to return the world to simplicity again," showing her as "a valuable thing," "something to look at and to know with satisfaction, something alive" (YMW, 27). In the same way the poems often record with relish the common idiom just as it was spoken:

> Doc, I bin lookin' for you
> I owe you two bucks. (CEP, 427)

> . . . Geeze, Doc, I guess it's all right
> but what the hell does it mean? (P, 138)

To show words as things containing their meaning it is sometimes enough to record the visible words of street signs and menus, the audible words of common speech, but language can get encrusted with old emotions and ideological associations. When this happens its validity is lost. The people of *Paterson* cannot communicate with one another or with the ground which ought to support them: "The language, the language/fails them" (P, 20). Authentic language springs from the present moment. Words pasted over with past associations make up part of that film which hangs between man and reality. "There is a constant barrier between the reader and his consciousness of immediate contact with the world. . . . [N]early all writing, up to the present, if not all art, has been especially designed to keep up the barrier between sense and the vaporous fringe which distracts the attention from its agonized approaches to the moment" (SA, 1, 3). Against this traditional commitment to an art of "the beautiful illusion" Williams sets his art of immediacy. "We have no words. Every word we get must be broken off from the European mass. Every word we get placed over again by some delicate hand. Piece by piece we must loosen what we want" (GAN, 26). There must be a "cracking up of phrases which have stopped the mind." [6] The end of such an appropriation and renewal of language is "to refine, to clarify, to intensify that eternal moment in which we alone live" (SA, 3). This can take place only through a cleansing of words, so that they stand upright on the page, naked and immediate, separate from all previous uses of them, separate even from one another. Marianne Moore uses words in this way, and Williams' praise of her way with words is a covert description of his own aim: "Miss Moore gets great pleasure from wiping soiled words or cutting them clean out, removing the aureoles that have been pasted about them or taking them bodily from greasy contexts. For the compositions which Miss Moore intends, each word should first stand crystal clear with no attachments; not even an aroma" (SE, 128).

How can a word be renewed in this way, "separated out by science, treated with acid to remove the smudges, washed, dried and placed right side up on a clean surface" (SE, 128), with all its primitive strength intact, a thing embodying its meaning? It can be done partly by a chastity in the choice of words. Simple words predominate in Williams' poetry, those words all men must use, so that they always live freshly in the present, reborn of its need. Vocabulary, however, is not enough. A word in itself has no meaning, but is a power of combining with other words. Meaning emerges from the structural relations of a group of words together. Since this is so the naked virtue of a word is often invisible in a sentence. Each word melts into its context and vanishes as a thing in itself, but Williams' aim is precisely to make the word visible as a thing in itself. To allow a word to be absorbed by the language surrounding it is as bad as to let it be swallowed up in its traditional associations. The poet's words must "remain separate, each unwilling to group with the others except as they move in the one direction" (SA, 86). To put down a single word in the middle of a

---

[6] "How to Write," *New Directions in Prose and Poetry*, IV (Norfolk, Conn.: New Directions, 1939), no pagination.

blank sheet of paper achieves nothing but the flatness of a dictionary. Each word must be set against others, for only then does it take
on force and reality, but at the same time it must be used "in such
a way that it will remain scrupulously itself, clean perfect, unnicked
beside other words in parade" (SE, 128, 129).

A manipulation of syntax is one way to reach this difficult goal.
The poet must return to the primitive elements of language if a
new measure is to be created. The sentence must be pulverized and
recreated from the ground up (AP, 57). This does not mean wild,
disordered, or novel grammar. It means isolating the fundamental
ways words combine, concern for the way words grapple with one
another to form meanings. This syntactical energy is concentrated
on in itself. Gertrude Stein is praised by Williams not only for her
"emphasis on the word as object," but for her investigations into the
"grammatical play" of words, her power to reveal "the skeleton,
the 'formal' parts of writing, those that make form" (SE, 115). In
Williams' own poetry such an attention to syntax is everywhere
evident, a focus on what Gerard Manley Hopkins called "the naked
thew and sinew" of the language.[7] Words are grouped in brief
simple phrases which combine with other phrases to form the
grammar of the whole:

> My shoes as I lean
> unlacing them
> stand out upon
> flat worsted flowers.
>
> Nimbly the shadows
> of my fingers play
> unlacing
> over shoes and flowers. (CEP, 224)[8]

---

[7] Claude Colleer Abbott, ed. *The Letters of Gerard Manley Hopkins to Robert Bridges*
(London: Oxford University Press, 1955), pp. 267, 268.

[8] A discussion in *I Wanted to Write a Poem* of the pattern of words on the page and of
the way "the American language must shape the pattern" (IWWP, 65) leads to a
citation of an earlier version of the first stanza of this poem. The revised version is the
result of what the poet calls "the normal process of concentrating the poem, getting rid
of redundancies in the line — and . . . the attempt to make it go faster" (IWWP, 66).
The shorter stanza, says Williams, conforms better to the page; it looks better. Here is
the original version:

> My shoes as I lean
> unlacing them
> stand out upon
> flat worsted flowers
> under my feet. (IWWP, 66)

The simplicity of the sentence structure here, and the emphasis on the tensions between the words makes them stand separate and yet together. Rhythm also works to achieve this end. Williams' metrical effects have an extraordinary power to bring each word out in its "thingness," to make the reader pause over it and savor its tang before going on to the next word. Like the bushes, small trees, and weeds in "By the road to the contagious hospital," each word stands on its own, though sprung from the same ground as the others. The independence of the words in the poem matches the independence of the things they name. The short lines and brief monosyllables of Williams' verse have exactly the opposite effect from the long rapidly rolling blurred periods of Whitman's line, with its tendency to absorb all particulars into one sonorous whole. In the stately slowness of Williams' cadence things and words retain their integrity:

> All along the road the reddish
> purplish, forked, upstanding, twiggy
> stuff of bushes and small trees
> with dead, brown leaves under them
> leafless vines — (CEP, 241)

The poet's characteristic rhythm separates words from one another, or combines several, gently but firmly, into a unit which does not obliterate the outlines of even the most insignificant word. In his verse, as in the growth of things in spring, "One by one objects are defined — /It quickens: clarity, outline of leaf" (CEP, 241). This effect is supported by his way of breaking up his lines. A poem is "a thing made up of words and punctuation, that is, words and the spaces between them" (AP, 52). Just as a modern sculptor shapes space with stone and makes it visible, so Williams' poems bring into the open the white flatness of the page on which the words are printed — not, however, as a "nothingness," the virgin whiteness which the blank spaces in Mallarmé's poems defend. Williams' spaces are full of tension and life, and in them shines that goal toward which the words all singly move. A beautiful early poem, in which rain is the living substance of love, makes this explicit:

> So my life is spent
>   to keep out love

    with which
    she rains upon

                    the world

    of spring

                drips

    so spreads

                the words

    far apart to let in

                    her love (CEP, 75)

A pregnant tension is given to words and the spaces around them by ending a line in the middle of a phrase. Partly this is done to affirm that the sound and weight of a word, in its relation to those around it, is more important than its grammatical connections. Words are treated as things grouped together to form metrical feet, and it is too bad for the grammar if a foot happens to end in the middle of a phrase. The effect of breaking the line in this way is quite different from the isolation of a word in the dictionary. The word at the end of a line may be an adjective without a noun, or a preposition with no phrase to complete it, or a conjunction hanging in the air, as in the following complete lines:

            of red and (CLP, 56)

            be a song — made of (CLP, 33)

            mottled clouds driven from the (CEP, 241)

            It is too old, the (CLP, 45)

            splash of a half purple, half (CLP, 44)

            but (PB, 44)

            flash a (PB, 48)

            of the (PB, 50)

In such lines each word, especially the last, stands alone, with its full vocative or ejaculatory emphasis, but the reader knows that the last word is part of a grammatical construction and will be completed in the next line. The word is not by itself, in slackness, but is endowed with its power of connecting itself to other words in a network of meaning. The word reaches out with all its strength

toward the other words which are for the moment absent. Conjunctions, prepositions, adjectives, when they come at the end of a
line, assume an expressive energy as arrows of force reaching toward
the other words: "of red and →." Going for the moment toward the
void, they go all the more strongly, as a man in isolation reaches
out in longing toward other men and women. Into the white space
surrounding the word go a multitude of lines of force, charging that
space with the almost tangible presence of the various words which
might come to complete the central word and appease its tension.

The poem called "The Yellow Chimney" demonstrates the way
this technique can make words take on substance and presence. A
series of lines end in color-words which are completed with nouns
at the beginning of the next lines: "fleshpale/smoke," "blue/sky,"
"silver/rings," "yellow/brick." This sets up a pattern so that
further lines can achieve the same effect by ending with ordinarily
insignificant words, mere connectives, prepositions, articles, conjunctions, "that," "at," "not," "of," "but," "the." The poem gives
these words too their proper weight and reality. This power to make
the reader see that such words are as much things as are nouns and
verbs is one of the supreme triumphs of Williams' art:

> There is a plume
> of fleshpale
> smoke upon the blue
>
> sky. The silver
> rings that
> strap the yellow
>
> brick stack at
> wide intervals shine
> in this amber
>
> light — not
> of the sun not of
> the pale sun but
>
> his born brother
> the
> declining season (CLP, 50)

Rhythm, syntax, and the placing of the words operate here, as
again and again in Williams' poetry, to achieve, through "the
design of [the] sentences" (SE, 114), that isolation of words from

their logical or abstract meaning for which the poet praises Laurence Sterne and Gertrude Stein: "The feeling is of words themselves, a curious immediate quality quite apart from their meaning, much as in music different notes are dropped, so to speak, into repeated chords one at a time, one after the other — for themselves alone" (SE, 114). Better than the temporal metaphor of music might be a spatial metaphor, like that of "primitive masonry, the units unglued and as in the greatest early constructions unstandardized" (SE, 130), on which Williams models his prose in "The Destruction of Tenochtitlan." The result of his dissociation of words from one another, from their past associations, and from their "dead weight of logical burdens" (SE, 115) is the achievement of that spatiality which Gaston Bachelard and others see as one tendency of modern art. Williams wants his poems to have movement and praises that quality in poetic language. A poet's words should:

> bite
> 　　　their way
> home — being actual
>
> having the form
> 　　　of motion (CEP, 68)

The immediacy necessary for authentic language, however, means that the movement of a poem must be confined to the moment. Even his longest poems, *Paterson*, "The Desert Music," or "Asphodel, That Greeny Flower," produce an effect of simultaneity. In them many actions are going on at once in a perpetual present, the poetic space, and though the images are necessarily sequential they form a chord which exists in a single moment. His shorter poems, though full of movement, are even more obviously spatial. Their motion takes place in one instant, before the reader, on the page, so that a poem like "The Yellow Chimney" is a picture of what it represents, the slender column of words corresponding to the chimney, and the lines of the poem, it may not be too fanciful to say, echoing the silver rings which strap the yellow stack at intervals. Other poems where this form of correspondence cannot be seen are no less spatial. The words are like shapes in a mosaic, all pulling and pushing against one another at once. This spatialization, as well as the tension between words and the page behind them, is expressed in a metaphor from Williams' essay on

Marianne Moore. Her words, like his, are "white circular discs grouped closely edge to edge upon a dark table [which] make black six-pointed stars" (SE, 129).

Words treated in this way become interjections, exclamatory vocables, substances of sound divorced from any abstract meaning and returned to their primitive power as explosions of linguistic energy, each with its own precise radiance. The relations between the words seem less those of grammatical meaning than the attractions caused by the juxtaposition of energies. In this pulverization of language words become atomic particles moving violently like the little wavelets in one of Williams' important motifs — a volume filled with a multiplicity of wriggling forces — waves, worms, stars, yachts contending in the sea.

The poet not unexpectedly endorses Charles Olson's theory of "composition by field" (A, 330). "The poem is made of things — on a field" (A, 333), and therefore is an example of what Marshall McLuhan calls "a mode of broken or syncopated manipulation to permit *inclusive* or simultaneous perception of a total and diversified field." [9] Williams frequently recognizes the way each of his poems is a dynamic motion within a field of forces, as when he says: "You must know by this time that my liking is for an unimpeded thrust right through a poem from the beginning to the end, without regard to formal arrangements" (SL, 50). In the "Prologue to *Kora in Hell*" he defines the poetic space as a moving field which the poet opposes to achieve tension: "The stream of things having composed itself into wiry strands that move in one fixed direction, the poet in desperation turns at right angles and cuts across current with startling results to his hangdog mood" (SE, 15). In another text: "the words must be recognized to be moving in a direction separate from the jostling or lack of it which occurs within the piece" (SA, 86). A sentence "undulates" (CLP, 45), or the space of a poem is defined as "one/jittering direction made of all/directions spelling the inexplicable" (CLP, 44). This space is usually characterized by dissonance rather than by smooth harmony, as Williams affirms when he defends, in an interview with Mike Wallace, the passage in his poetry about two partridges, two mallard ducks, a Dungeness crab: " — if you treat that rhythmically, ignoring the practical sense, it forms a jagged pattern" (P, 262).

[9] *The Gutenberg Galaxy* (Toronto: University of Toronto Press, 1962), p. 267.

Within the field of the poem there must be, as in Stevens' early poetry, a tense equilibrium of opposed energies. Otherwise the words will go toward one pole, gather there, and the poem will disappear along with the field which constituted it. The poem must be "balanced between/eternities" (P, 126). *Kora in Hell* is a sequence of free variations on this theme of polarity. The motif dominant in the prose poems is defended in the commentaries on them: "Between two contending forces there may at all times arrive that moment when the stress is equal on both sides so that with a great pushing a great stability results giving a picture of perfect rest" (KH, 11); "Often when the descent seems well marked there will be a subtle ascent over-ruling it so that in the end when the degradation is fully anticipated the person will be found to have emerged upon a hilltop" (KH, 47). Even in Williams' latest work a whole poem or passage in a poem is often made up of the interaction of a group of ascending or descending energies. Such poems achieve that "rout of the vocables" which the poet praises in Gertrude Stein (P, 258). The words and phrases are like those birds and leaves in Book Five of *Paterson:* "All together, working together — /all the birds together. The birds/and leaves are designed to be woven/in his mind eating and   .   ./all together for his purposes" (P, 270). Language creates an inner space of polarized energies, and this space, with all its contents, moves as a unit toward its goal.

"The Locust Tree in Flower" or *Paterson* or the poems in *Pictures from Brueghel* establish a place of simultaneity. "The mind's a queer sponge/squeeze it and out come bird songs/small leaves highly enameled/and . moments of good reading" (CLP, 195). Within the sponge mind each thing touches the others, interacting with them, quarreling, rebounding, and yet keeping its definite edges and form. Each fills space, permeates it, but remains itself, uncontaminated by the others, and each is at once substantial, mental, and linguistic. To read *Paterson* or "Asphodel, That Greeny Flower" is to enter a region where everything the poet has ever experienced is present together, each item in its particularity ready to be called on when it is needed. This kind of space is expressed by the basic metaphor of *Paterson:* the Passaic River with its falls. The water is the ground of mind, of things, and of language; its roar contains them all. In *Paterson* the plunge into the Passaic which the poet had made in "The Wanderer" is explored in its deepest implications, and flowing water is established as the fundamental metaphor of the new realm Williams' poetry creates:

> Jostled as are the waters approaching
> the brink, his thoughts
> interlace, repel and cut under,
> rise rock-thwarted and turn aside
> but forever strain forward . . . (P, 16)

Words as things incarnating their meanings become a set of fluid energies whose life exists only in the present. Such words, isolated and cleaned, can be put down on the page like splashes of paint on a canvas and allowed to explode into the multitude of meanings which emerge from their juxtaposition. One version of "The Locust Tree in Flower" [10] is an extreme example of this use of words. Here each word has a line to itself, and is surrounded on all sides by the blank page. Logic and grammar almost disappear, but not quite, and prepositions, adjectives, nouns, verbs, and adverbs are put side by side to establish a simultaneous pattern of linguistic forces. This effect is enhanced by the fact that the poem begins with two prepositions, which must be held side by side in the mind as alternatives. Then follow a series of somewhat contradictory adjectives without the article which would be expected before a singular noun. Are these all meant to modify "branch," or will a later noun attract some of them to itself? The words hang freely in the air. Moreover, the verb presupposes a plural subject, so the reader must balance between the possibility that the word "has" may have been left out and the assumption that "come" is to be taken as an imperative. This grammatical uncertainty forces him to hold all the words before his attention at once as he tries various ways to make a sentence of them. He is like a seal juggling thirteen brightly colored balls, and this is exactly what the poet wants. The poem is as much all there at once as the locust tree itself, in its tension of branches, leaves, and flowers. The poem is not a picture of the tree, but is itself something substantial

[10] There is a longer version printed with the shorter one in *The Collected Earlier Poems* (p. 94). Since it was the version printed in *Poetry: A Magazine of Verse*, 43: 3, 4 (Chicago, October 1933), it is presumably earlier. Much insight into Williams' poetic method can be gained by comparing early versions of poems published in periodicals with the final versions in the collected volumes. The changes are almost always in the direction of that terseness which makes each word stand out alone.

echoing in its structure of verbal forces the birth of white blossoms from stiff boughs. In "The Locust Tree in Flower," to borrow Williams' praise for Miss Moore, the "purely stated idea," the idea embodied in words which are things, "has an edge exactly like a fruit or a tree or a serpent" (SE, 130):

> Among
> of
> green
>
> stiff
> old
> bright
>
> broken
> branch
> come
>
> white
> sweet
> May
>
> again (CEP, 93)

Words, nevertheless, are different from splashes of paint or musical sounds. However consubstantial their meaning and their physical presence, they still refer to things other than themselves. The word "parsley" is the name of a small green crinkly plant. Williams cannot escape the referential meaning of words, and curiously enough he has none of that tormenting fear of reference which haunts modern art, no desire to abolish the naming power of words in order to create a poem which will be entirely free of objects, like an abstract painting. In his poetry words are one thing, trees and flowers are another, but both are possessed within the same inner space. As a result he replaces the romantic or symbolist aesthetic of transformation with an art which is calm description, naming one by one the visible and tangible qualities of an object. Texts of this sort abound in his work:

> In brilliant gas light
> I turn the kitchen spigot
> and watch the water plash
> into the clean white sink.

On the grooved drain-board
to one side is
a glass filled with parsley —
crisped green. (CEP, 145)

Such a passage is the exact opposite of a poetry of indirection
or of transposition, Mallarmé's hints at the fan which he never
names or Stevens' tangents of a pineapple. Williams can look
straight at the object because it offers no threat. There is nothing
alien or distant about it. It proposes no invitation to the poet's
violence. The objectivity of his descriptions affirms his security.
The parsley does not need the poem. The poem does not need the
parsley. The parsley and the poem about the parsley are separate
things, each existing within the universal realm made of the poet's
coextension with the world. Poetry of this kind is a way of letting
things be. A good poet, consequently, "doesn't *select* his material.
What is there to select? It *is*." [11]

To let the parsley be in the poem does not mean transposing
the parsley into the poem. It means using the referential meaning
of words to name the parsley in its self-sustaining independence.
The parsley is a stubborn and irreducible fact, nonverbal in nature,
and the poem in the simplicity of its description recognizes it as
such. Just as the parsley is separate from the poem about it, so it
is separate from the things around it. It stands alone in its glass,
side by side with the grooved drainboard, the clean white sink,
the water, the spigot, the gaslight. Each thing has its own intrinsic
particularity, its own precise edges cutting it off from other things,
just as each word in "The Locust Tree in Flower" stands by itself,
surrounded by the white page. There is no blurring, no flowing
of a ubiquitous force which melts distinctions and makes things
alike. In the "Prologue to *Kora in Hell*" the poet affirms that the
value of his poem about the chicory flower (see CEP, 122) is the
way it praises the resolute isolation of the plant. Free of the poem,
it is also free of the things around it: "A poet witnessing the chicory
flower and realizing its virtues of form and color so constructs his
praise of it as to borrow no particle from right or left. He gives
his poem over to the flower and its plant themselves" (SE, 17).
In Williams' world there are no resonances or similarities between
things, no basis for metaphor. There is in fact little figurative

[11] "Introduction" to *Transfigured Night*, p. xi.

language in his poetry. He is deeply suspicious of it. Its place is
sometimes taken by a version of imagist technique, the juxtaposition of dissonant things so that a meaning may emerge from their
contrast:

> Like a cylindrical tank fresh silvered
> upended on the sidewalk to advertise
> some plumber's shop, a profusion
> of pink roses bending ragged in the rain — (CLP, 24)

Most often even this doubling of particulars is not permitted.
Williams has an extraordinary ability to pick a single thing out of
the multitude existing and focus on it with intense concentration,
as if it were the only object in the world, incomparable, unique.
He has the power of "seeing the thing itself without forethought or
afterthought but with great intensity of perception" which he
praises in his mother (SE, 5). His attitude toward things, like
Ezra Pound's, is nominalist. Each object is itself and nothing more
should be said about it: "Although it is a quality of the imagination that it seeks to place together those things which have a common relationship, yet the coining of similes is a pastime of very
low order, depending as it does upon a nearly vegetable coincidence. Much more keen is that power which discovers in things
those inimitable particles of dissimilarity to all other things which
are the peculiar perfections of the thing in question" (SE, 16).

Nor are there vertical resonances. Since there is no "behind"
or "beyond" in Williams' world, no depth or transcendence, there
can be no symbolic meaning in things, no reference to a secret
heaven of ideal values. "No symbolism is acceptable" (SE, 213);
"Those who permit their senses to be despoiled of the things under
their noses by stories of all manner of things removed and unattainable are of frail imagination" (SE, 15). A primrose is just a
primrose, and there are no deep thoughts in flowers, trees, or tables.
The table "describes/nothing: four legs, by which/it becomes a
table" (CLP, 91). The wheelbarrow, in a famous poem, does not
stand for anything or mean anything. It is an object in space dissociated from the objects around it, without reference beyond itself. It is what it is. The aim of the poem is to make it stand there
for the reader in its separateness, as the words of the poem stand
on the page.

If the poem affirms the independence of the object and lets the object be, what good is the poem in itself? The parsley already is, and there seems little use for a poem which merely says that it is. Williams' response to this problem is the basis of his theory of imagination. The poet must make use of the referential meaning of words to relate them to physical objects as a springboard from which they may leap into a realm of imagination carrying with them the things named in a new form. Williams rejects those modern poets who "use unoriented sounds in place of conventional words" (SA, 92). Words should not be wholly independent of things, but they should not be completely attached to things either. That would be the kind of description in which "words adhere to certain objects, and have the effect on the sense of oysters, or barnacles" (SA, 90). Poetry is an effect of the imagination, and "words occur in liberation by virtue of its processes" (SA, 90). How can this freedom be attained? It is not a matter of "a removal from reality" (SA, 90). There must be no return to the idea of the imagination as a power which can take the reader beyond the world. The imagination is one of the conditions or regions of the inner-outer space which is all there is. In poetry words must still have their old meanings, and, therefore, "the writer of imagination would attain closest to the conditions of music not when his words are disassociated from natural objects and specified meanings but when they are liberated from the usual quality of that meaning by transposition into another medium, the imagination" (SA, 92).

This liberation takes place by a paradoxical movement both toward and away from the object, a movement of which the poem about parsley is an example. By illuminating the object exactly, the poem affirms the object's independence and thereby frees the words to execute their dance of imagination above the body of the world. The words carry with them some of the substance of the world and are vitalized by their possession of that substance. The thing "needs no personal support but exists free from human action" (SA, 91), and the poem is real too, but only because it is both related to and free from the thing it names. "The word is not liberated," says Williams, "therefore able to communicate release from the fixities which destroy it until it is accurately tuned to the fact which giving it reality, by its own reality establishes its own freedom from the necessity of a word, thus freeing it and dynamizing it at the same time" (SA, 93). This crucial passage explains what the poet means earlier when he says that "the same things exist, but in a different condition when energized by the imagination" (SA, 75). An image of sublimation is fundamental to his concept of the action of imagination. Poetry lifts things up. Its aim is "to repair, to rescue, to complete" (SL, 147). John of Gaunt's speech in *Richard II*, for example, is not an escape from reality, nor is it a mere description of his state. It is "a dance over the body of his condition accurately accompanying it" (SA, 91). This idea of a free play of words above reality but not separate from it appears again in an image of poetry as like a bird in flight: "As birds' wings beat the solid air without which none could fly so words freed by the imagination affirm reality by their flight" (SA, 91). In another passage, "the poet, challenging the event, re-creates it as of whence it sprang from among men and women, and makes a new world of it."[12]

This tense interaction between words and things is the basis of Williams' repeated affirmation that a poem is "a field of action" (SE, 280). Only if the words are both free of things and related to them can it be said that "poetry does not tamper with the world but moves it" (SA, 91). This avoids both the Scylla of defining art as a mirror of reality and the Charybdis of accepting an art of romantic evasion, a music of pure sounds cut off from life. The poem and the thing are both real, both equally real:

> A rose *is* a rose
> and the poem equals it
> if it be well made. (PB, 141)

Again and again the poet repeats his rejection of any representational theory of art. Poetry is "not a matter of 'representation' " (SA, 45), "nor is it description nor an evocation of objects or situations" (SA, 91). A poem "creates a new object, a play, a dance which is not a mirror up to nature" (SA, 91), "not 'like' anything but transfused with the same forces which transfuse the earth — at least one small part of them" (SA, 50). The prose parts of the original edition of *Spring and All*, never reprinted by the poet, are his fullest expressions of a subtle theory of poetry which rejects both the mirror and the lamp, both the classical theory of art as

[12] "Introduction" to *Transfigured Night*, p. xii.

imitation, and the romantic theory of art as transformation. In their place is proposed a new objectivist art in which a poem is "Not prophecy! NOT prophecy!/but the thing itself!" (P, 242). This new art is becoming increasingly dominant in both America and Europe, and, as this happens, Williams' place as a poet helping to bring about a radical change in literature is more apparent.

If the same energies flow through a poem as flow through the earth, then a poem is "natural" because it is a growth, a process. The poet must try to write "the poem that lifts the dish/of fruit . . . like/a table" (CLP, 91), or compose fiction "so that when [he speaks] of a chair it will stand upon four legs in a room. And of course it will stand upon a four-legged sentence on a page at the same time" (SL, 312). These passages emphasize the activity of the poem. The poem "lifts" the dish of fruit, or "stands up" on the page. Elsewhere the way the essence of poetry is its power to do something is even more explicit. Only if the poem shifts from the adjective which copies a dead nature to the verb which is alive with natural forces can the words be an extension of the processes of the earth, "not 'realism' but reality itself" (SA, 45):

> To copy nature is a spineless activity; it gives us a sense of our mere existence but hardly more than that. But to imitate nature involves the verb: we then ourselves become nature, and so invent an object which is an extension of the process. (SL, 297)

> It is not to place adjectives, it is to learn to employ the verbs in imitation of nature — so that the pieces move naturally — and watch, often breathlessly, what they *do*. (SE, 302)

"Only the made poem, the verb calls it/into being" (PB, 110). The verbal energy of the poem makes it part of nature and asserts the poet's approximate coextension with the universe. Williams ridicules the idea that this means some impossible Roman feast in which man ingurgitates the earth: "the powers of a man are so pitifully small, with the ocean to swallow — that at the end of the feast nothing would be left but suicide" (SA, 28). Through the action of imagination the poet frees himself from this absurd thirst or hunger. When he has rooted himself in objective reality his poems become "as actual, as sappy as the leaf of the tree which never moves from one spot" (SA, 22). His coextension with the universe need be only approximate, for the sap in his poems flows everywhere. This sharing in universal energies produces the sense of "enlargement," of "expansion," which men feel "before great or good work" (SA, 29).

The need to have the poem rooted in the ground of reality is the reason for Williams' insistence that art must start with the local and particular, and raise those to the universal. The poet is "taught by the largeness of his imagination to feel every form which he sees moving within himself" (SA, 27). His problem is "to be both local (all art is local) and at the same time to surmount that restriction by climbing to the universal in all art" (SL, 286). By concentrating on the individual in its uniqueness the poet may reach the universal. The particular *is* the universal. The same forces stream through it as stream through all existence, and therefore the poet "seems to make the world come toward him to brush against the spines of his shrub. So that in looking at some apparently small object one feels the swirl of great events" (SE, 294). It is for this reason that so much depends upon the red wheelbarrow. The wheelbarrow, red and glazed with rain water, occupying silently its small spot in time and space, contains everything. In the same way a single word may concentrate the poet and his world in a breath, as the poet somewhat whimsically proposes in *The Great American Novel:* "I shall make myself into a word. One big word. One big union. . . . I begin small and make myself into a big splurging word: I take life and make it into one big blurb" (GAN, 11). Whatever the specific content of the here and now may be, it can still be said that "all things enter into the singleness of the moment and the moment partakes of the diversity of all things" (SE, 97). The poems about chicory and parsley, like the chicory and parsley themselves, concentrate in themselves the universe, and the basic method of art is that recommended at the beginning of *Paterson:*

> To make a start,
> out of particulars
> and make them general . . . (P, 11)

⤷

A poem written on the basis of this theory of art may be defined as "the mind turned inside out" (KH, 72), or, alternatively, as things turned inside out, taken into a different condition, energized by the imagination. It will also be the reader turned inside out. When a man reads a poem he should enter not so much into the words as into the depths of himself by means of the words, just as a play "should be the/audience itself, come out of itself/and standing in its own eyes, leaning/within the opening of its own ears," "seeing itself/in the action" (ML, 33). Poet, things, and reader are absorbed into the poem and lifted there into a new dimension of intimacy, a place where the unity of mind and world, often obscured or lost, is validated, realized, and possessed. The poem alone "focuses the world" (SE, 242). What is it like inside such a poem?

The major difficulty in reading Williams' poetry is to become accustomed to the ways in which he uses words not as names but as things. This is especially evident in his rejection of visual imagery. Like Charles Olson, he dismisses all "pictorial effects" (ML, 9), all that " 'evocation' of the 'image' which served us for a time" (SA, 20). Eyesight is the most abstract and detached of the senses. It opposes man to a world which he sees from a distance. A poem made of word-pictures compounds these divisions. The reader contemplates language which generates mental pictures of an absent reality. Poem, reader, and world are kept in separate compartments. The aesthetic theory which defines poetry as images for the mind's eye is a natural product of a literate, subjectivistic culture, a culture which would develop photography and the printed book. A poetry of this sort would be a return to the abstraction Williams abhors.

His practice confirms his theoretical choice. His poems are often nonsense if the reader tries to make a coherent mental picture of the sequence of phrases. "To All Gentleness" (CLP, 24–29), for example, moves bewilderingly from the silvered tank to the pink roses bending ragged in the rain, to a girl practicing archery, to a sailor knocked into the sea by the shattering prop of a plane, and so on. *Paterson* is often a sequence of images which seem disconnected if the reader thinks of them visually:

> like a bull
> or a Minotaur
> or Beethoven
> in the scherzo

from the Fifth Symphony
                    stomped
                              his heavy feet
          I saw love
                    mounted naked on a horse
                              on a swan (P, 260)

The sense of bewilderment disappears if the reader understands
that the words are not primarily visual at all. They are meant to
energize the mind in certain ways, and express in their sonority
some quality of matter, thickness and weight, or airy delicacy, or
any one of the other innumerable textures which our senses may
know through words. The poet assumes "that we smell, hear and
see with words and words alone, and that with a new language
we smell, hear and see afresh" (SE, 266). Words marry the reader
to the solidity of things and to their movement. All words are
both verbs and nouns for Williams, both action and matter, and
his poetry is the product of an imagination which puts the mind
within the life of objects. To express this identification in language
the poet must break up the fixities of words and make them flow
together like figures in a dance or ice melted into a stream. "Then
it begins," he says, "that happy time when the image becomes
broken or begins to break up, becomes a little fluid — or is affected, floats brokenly in the fluid. The rigidities yield — like ice
in March, the magic month" (SE, 307). How can this melting
be brought about? It seems plausible enough in theory or as a
metaphor, but words are after all fixed sounds, and even the
volume occupied by the falling Passaic seems bound by the universal laws of space. Any one place in it is excluded from all other
places. The poet must transcend the limitations of logical, visual,
or geometrical space in order to bring into existence the new
poetry of multiple elements in fluid intimacy.

To think of space as always characterized by rigid exclusions
and limitations is to universalize illegitimately one mode of space.
There are other spaces all men and women inhabit, regions less
capable of being deformed by the preconceptions of the logical
mind, and these are dominant in Williams' poetry.

Consciousness is not a separate thing filling a hollow place in a
man's skull. My whole body is conscious, to the tips of my fingers
and toes. The mind is incarnate in "warm self-flesh" (CEP, 182),

and the body is also a means of possessing the world. This is achieved partly through the senses, which are so many different ways of assimilating things. Perhaps even more important is the way the body in action "open[s] up the world" (CEP, 453), and takes it in. The position of my arms and legs, the force of gravity on my flesh, my gestures, gross and subtle movements of my muscles — these make of my body a kinesthetic pantomime internalizing the world. Williams' poems are a dance of words rising from this pantomime. They express that state of bodily knowledge the poet praises in *Kora in Hell:* "A thing known passes out of the mind into the muscles" (KH, 71).

When a thing has passed into the muscles, then language can express the thing by matching the movement of those muscles. Here is another reason for Williams' praise of the verb. His language is often a way of knowing the world through the posture and quality of bodily life which a certain state of the world induces. He thinks with his muscles and bones rather than with ideas: "I have heavy bones, I am afraid — there's little here for me — gravity must drag me down — over the horizon — I'm too slippery — and it doesn't matter — but so it seems" (SL, 64). The reader must accustom himself to words which express the flowering of chicory, the growing of a tree, the flowing of water as if it were happening in the interior of his own body. There is often a soft, muted, thick, blurred quality in Williams' language, something quiet, delicate, almost feminine, and this is the "gentleness that harbors all violence" (CLP, 29), the violence of a power to enter into a natural process and experience it inwardly. In one poem a series of "external" actions expresses the gradual relaxation of a child's body as it falls asleep. The verbs carry the weight of the thickening of consciousness as it is absorbed by the sleeping body:

> Gentlefooted crowds are treading out your lullaby.
> Their arms nudge, they brush shoulders,
> hitch this way then that, mass and surge at the crossings — (CEP, 192)

In the admirable poem about the "contention" of the yachts (CEP, 106, 107), the water through which the boats sail is felt as "an entanglement of watery bodies": "Arms with hands grasping seek to clutch at the prows./Bodies thrown recklessly in the way are cut aside." A wild cherry, in another poem, is "continually pressing back/peach orchards," and this image is equated with "the feel of good legs/and a broad pelvis" (CEP, 140). Another tree is "tense with suppressed excitement" (CEP, 141). Still another is "bent" "from straining/against the bitter horizontals of/a north wind" (CEP, 142). Chicory is bid by the poet to "lift" its flowers, to "strain under them" (CEP, 122), and in spring all plants "grip down and begin to awaken" (CEP, 242). All these images urge the reader to respond to the words with subliminal movements of his muscles mimicking the energy of trees, yachts, plants, or water. "Young Sycamore" is a beautiful poem of this sort. The movement of the poem follows the shape of the tree not as a visual outline but as an "undulant/thrust" from "round and firm trunk" all the way to the "two/eccentric knotted/twigs" at the top (CEP, 332). In the same way a charming poem catches in its rhythm and in the placing of end stops the tension of a cat's feet as it climbs over the top of a jam closet:

> first the right
> forefoot
>
> carefully
> then the hind
> stepped down (CEP, 340)

Sometimes the space of a poem is a multiplicity of things felt together as a tension of muscle against muscle. The transformation of words into vectors of power is accomplished by an emphasis on their weight as expressions of movements within the body. In "Spring Strains" the pun in the title prepares for the energizing of sky, sun, buds, and "rigid jointed" trees in a wrestle of opposing forces which the poem incarnates in its own movement:

> . . . the blinding and red-edged sun-blur —
> creeping energy, concentrated
> counterforce — welds sky, buds, trees,
> rivets them in one puckering hold!
> Sticks through! Pulls the whole
> counter-pulling mass upward, to the right
> locks even the opaque, not yet defined
> ground in a terrific drag that is
> loosening the very tap-roots! (CEP, 159)

In such poems the space the words create is the volume of the body. This body-world has the same kind of intimacy that events inside a man's body have for him. A pain is located in one place, but also permeates the whole body until a man may become one pervasive pain. In the same way Williams' kinesthetic poems transcend the limitations of abstract visual space and bring into existence a realm in which all places are everywhere.

A similar region is created by touch, that most intimate of the senses, the *tactus eruditus* (CEP, 63) every good physician must have. It is not without significance that the title of the little magazine Williams edited in 1932 was *Contact*. Kenneth Burke tells how, "some time after giving up his practice," the poet "said explosively that he missed the opportunity to get his hands on things (and he made gestures to do with the delivering of a child)." [13] A man who brought two thousand babies into the world had certainly much experience of one kind of touching. Many of his poems too are charged with the sense of touch and create in the play of their words a tactile space. The interior of a train station is permeated by "the rubbing feet/of those coming to be carried" and by a "soft light that rocks/to and fro" (CEP, 194). In another poem the poet and his wife, lying on the grass together, dip their hands "in the running water — /cold, too cold," but find it, to their satisfaction, "still wet" (CLP, 198). In a passage in *Paterson* a man describes his experience in a house of prostitution: "you . . . touch the breast, the firmness . . . you touch grasp hold lust feel the curve of a buttock silent-smooth sliding under your palm, the dress, the hand!" (P, 250). In *Kora in Hell* a dance is "hands touching, leaves touching . . . lips touching, cheeks touching" (KH, 44). In one text the poet tells how "whispers of the fishy air touch [his] body" (CEP, 141), and in another "a cold wind winter-long/in the hollows of our flesh" leaves "no part of us untouched" (CEP, 67). "The Shadow" multiplies images of touch to universalize it until the poet is clasped in the embrace of the season, as a stone by the earth, and everything is possessed through touch:

> Soft as the bed in the earth
> where a stone has lain —

[13] "William Carlos Williams, 1883–1963," *The New York Review of Books*, 1 : 45 (1963).

so soft, so smooth and so cool
Spring closes me in
with her arms and her hands. (CEP, 120)

Touch is for Williams more gentleness than violence. The learned touch of the poet-physician makes it possible for him to internalize all things in a single caress. The tactile space is more softly blurred, more passive and yielding, than the kinesthetic one. The world flows together at a touch.

Taste also creates its own kind of space, and it too is far more intimate than eyesight. If a man concentrates on what he tastes, forgetting his other senses, a single flavor will expand to permeate everything. This happens frequently in Williams' work, as in the poem which begins "Waking/I was eating pears!" (PB, 43), or the one about the oyster, "fresh and sweet tasting, to be/swallowed, chewed and swallowed" (CLP, 41), or the one about plums taken from the icebox — "delicious/so sweet/and so cold" (CEP, 354). Justly celebrated is "To a Poor Old Woman," Williams' best poem about taste (CEP, 99). The plums munched by the old woman "taste good to her," but in the end this "solace of ripe plums" is not enjoyed by her alone. It seems "to fill the air" and creates a gustatory space everywhere pervaded by the tang of plums.

Scents have the same penetrating power. Williams has an acute sense of smell, and in a charming poem ("Smell!" [CEP, 153]) ironically reproaches his "strong-ridged and deeply hollowed/nose" for wanting to smell everything, "always indiscriminate, always unashamed," smelling the "souring flowers" of the poplars, the "rank odor of a passing springtime," with as much delight as more lovely aromas. His nose is determined to "taste everything," "know everything," "have a part in everything." In another poem he praises "the smell/of new earth on a stone/that has lain breathing/the damp through its pores" (CEP, 120), and in another "the elm is scattering/its little loaves/of sweet smells/from a white sky!" (CEP, 137). In "A Celebration" there is a "weight of perfume in the air" (CEP, 188), and in "Asphodel, That Greeny Flower" an odor of love has "begun again to penetrate/into all crevices/of my world" (PB, 182). A late poem makes the most pervasive use of smell. Several odors combine to produce an ol-

factory space made up of the interaction of several distinct pun-
gencies:

> . . . odor of excess
> odor of pine needles, odor of
> peeled logs, odor of no odor
> other than trailing woodbine that

> has no odor, odor of a nude woman
> sometimes, odor of a man. (PB, 60)

⤳

Less unusual than Williams' sensitivity to touch, taste, and
smell is his attention to the "complexities of the world about our
ears" (SL, 332), but his auditory space is also characterized by
tactile qualities of closeness and interconnection. Each sound
touches the others without ceasing to be distinctly itself. Aural
space contradicts the laws of geometry. A piece of music seems to
fill the ears of the listener, to be everywhere at once in the world
of hearing. A poetry of the ear shares some of these virtues. So
Byron Vazakas is commended because "he abandoned an eye
habit with all its stale catch, threw all that aside for pure ear."[14]
Special to Williams is his sensitivity to delicate sounds and his
sense of the way one noise has as much power to fill the mind's
ear as does a whole orchestra with its complicated "design" of
sound (PB, 80–82). The "desert music" is an almost inaudible
note which permeates the poet's experiences in Mexico, "as when
Casals struck/and held a deep cello tone" (PB, 119). In the same
way the inarticulate roar of the falls permeates *Paterson*, "inducing
sleep and silence, the roar/of eternal sleep" (P, 28), and in "The
Injury" the sound of a distant "engine/breathing" fills the night
(CLP, 242).

The metaphor of "breathing" is important here. A sound to
Williams is as much inside him as his breath. In another poem a
"cadenced melody" is "full of sweet breath" (CLP, 45), and the
sound of the falls, in *Paterson*, shaking the juniper on its edge,
"is whence/I draw my breath" (P, 33). He praises Vazakas because "he writes as he breathes,"[15] and quotes with approval

---

[14] "Introduction" to *Transfigured Night*, xiv.
[15] "Introduction" to *Transfigured Night*, p. x.

Charles Olson's affirmation that "the line comes (I swear it) from the breath, from the breathing of the man who writes, at the moment that he writes" (A, 331). Poetry is the sound of words more than their abstract meanings, and that sound is the feel of the words in the mouth, the beat of their rhythm as they modulate the breath. The "new measure consonant with our day" (AP, 75) must be based on the sound of our speech, a sound whose rhythms rise from the muscles and the breath as the cadences of a new metric. Authentic language is "the middle brain, the nerves, the glands, the very muscles and bones of the body itself speaking." [16] Sounds for Williams are always close to the tactile, the gustatory, the kinesthetic. His account of the origins of the new measure emphasizes this internalizing of sound: "It began for me as it must always do on the purely physical plane . . . . My ears were keen; I sensed it first through my ears, even as a babe in arms. My uncle, who was a musician, noticed it and spoke of it to my mother: Listen! he said and began to beat a drum. At a certain point in the rhythm he would stop sharply and I, to complete the beat, would come in with my, tum, tum" (SL, 328, 329). Williams has perhaps the most subtle ear of any American poet, and many of his poems are marvels of exquisite auditory harmony, each word fitting perfectly in sound the others. Criticism can only in lumbering awkwardness catch and analyze these evanescent melodies, as, for example, the music of echoing o's, i's, l's, and s's in "Epitaph":

> An old willow with hollow branches
> slowly swayed his few high bright tendrils
> and sang:
>
> Love is a young green willow
> shimmering at the bare wood's edge. (CEP, 212)

The sound patterns of the poems sometimes are explicitly ono-matopoeic, the intertwined birdsong and burbling of a brook (CLP, 73), or the "Wheeeeeee/Clacka tacka tacka/tacka tacka/wha ha ha ha ha" of tree branches in a spring rain (CEP, 66), or the "interminable talking, talking/of no consequence — patter, patter, patter" of a "three-day-long rain from the east" (CEP, 201). Often, both in the poems and in the stories, Williams reproduces

---

[16] "How to Write," no pagination.

the sound patterns of American speech for their own sake, with little attention to meaning:

> "Over Labor Day they'll
> be gone"
> "Jersey City, he's the
> engineer — " "Ya"
> "Being on the Erie R.R.
> is quite convenient" (CEP, 109)

Here snatches of speech become part of the multiplicity of sounds heard on a Sunday morning. The "auditory measure" of "our own spoken tongue" [17] joins the sound of feet, the "scrape of a chair," "a splash of water, the/ting a ring/of small pieces of metal/dropped" (CEP, 109) to form a complex acoustical space. In this poem, as in others, the poet lives in his ears, with an intense concentration on the unique space revealed by hearing.

Eyesight is not exempt from that delicacy which predominates in Williams' way of using his senses and makes soft closeness the primary characteristic of his world. Proper seeing is tactile, not abstract, and "a woman must see with her whole body to be benevolent" (IAG, 182). The gentleness of seeing is, like other gentlenesses, also a violence. Eyesight has a power to grip things in a tight embrace which is as much muscular as visual. The "eye awake" "seizes" parts of the world (CEP, 182), and in another poem "the eye comes down eagerly" to grasp "the contours and the shine" of sea-trout and butterfish on a white plate, to delight in "the fine fins' sharp spines" (CEP, 91). Sight becomes here a kind of touch, and the sharpness of the fins is more important than their shape or color. "To a Solitary Disciple" explicitly opposes two ways of seeing. Williams' follower should not observe passively from a distance the color and shape of a steeple against the sky. Seeing should be used to enter the struggle of lines of force which composes the scene. Eyesight is a tension meeting other tensions and "grasping" them. It pierces the surface and reaches the interior of things:

> See how the converging lines
> of the hexagonal spire
> escape upward —
> receding, dividing!

[17] "Introduction" to *Transfigured Night*, p. xiv.

> — sepals
> that guard and contain
> the flower! (CEP, 167)

In this poem abstract-visual is replaced by dynamic-visual, and eyes join muscles, tongue, and fingers as another way to enter the life of the world and experience it from the inside. Just as a single taste, touch, or sound swells in intensity until it permeates everything, so a visual quality can be universalized until it is everywhere at once. "Yellow, yellow, yellow, yellow" "is not a color." "It is summer" and pervades the details of summer with its yellowness. Even "a piece of blue paper" or "tufts of purple grass" are transformed by the predominant color (CEP, 209). In another poem, an extraordinarily beautiful one, "the stain of love" is a thick yellow light which drips on everything. Light is not weightless or intangible. It is a fluid substance which "eats into the leaves" and "smears" the branches with saffron. In this poem, as in most of Williams' work, there is no emptiness. The space of the poem is everywhere filled with a soft fluid stuff which is both active and substantial:

> There is no light
> only a honey-thick stain
> that drips from leaf to leaf
> and limb to limb
> spoiling the colors
> of the whole world — (CEP, 174)

⤺

This poem is an example of one last way of knowing the world. The honey-thick dripping of yellow light is the ubiquitous stain of love. If there are spaces appropriate to the muscles and to each of the five senses, there also exists a sexual space, perhaps even more important than the others. A man's body is endowed with a sexual sense which has a unique power to polarize the world. Close to the kinesthetic way of knowing, but not identical with it, the sexual sense too takes the world into the body and recreates it there, giving it a special balance and weight according to its erotic values.

This is easiest to see in Williams' relation to other people. Human beings are encountered as bodies endowed with life. Just as the dynamic forces which make up a tree are immediately available through corresponding movements within the poet's body, so the inner life of another person is directly available through his gestures and his facial expressions. The poet's body responds unthinkingly to the body of another person and gives him spontaneous possession of the other's mind. Other people are no more difficult to know and assimilate than flowers or fish. Since their inner lives are incarnated in their bodies and speech they are without hidden consciousness. A passage in *The Great American Novel* shows how the poet and his wife can have no secrets from one another and penetrate easily into the deepest recesses of each other's minds: "He looked at her and she at him. He smiled and she, from long practice, began to read him, progressing rapidly until she said: You can't fool me. He became very angry but understood at once that she had penetrated his mystery" (GAN, 12). Many of Williams' poems demonstrate his power to take possession of another person, usually a woman, in the same way as he takes possession of a plant or a tree. Often a single gesture is enough. The girl "with big breasts/under a blue sweater" is revealed in a moment as she "stops, turns/and looks down" (CLP, 123).[18] Another woman is a physical presence, waking the poet's body in response to her body's life:

> — what a blessing it is
> to see you in the street again,
> powerful woman,
> coming with swinging haunches,
> breasts straight forward,
> supple shoulders, full arms
> and strong, soft hands (I've felt them)
> carrying the heavy basket.[19]

[18] See "The So-Called So-Called," *The Patroon* (Bergen College, N.J., May 1937), pp. 37–40 for another, undoubtedly earlier, version of this poem and Williams' commentary on it: "But there is a dignity in this girl quite comparable to that of the Venus [de Milo]. . . . Why not imagine this girl Venus? Venus lives! . . . [The poem] presents a simple image in the same sort of light that the Athenian placed the Venus — only in not the same context." The poem, he says of the earlier version, "isn't very good because it lacks metrical emphasis." As in the case of the revision of the poem about unlacing his shoes, the poet concentrated the poem, removed redundancies, and organized it into regular blocks so that it looks better on the page. In addition he moved from the impersonality and distance of the past tense to the immediacy of the present, and changed the abstract word "coin" to "dime."

[19] *Al Que Quiere!* (Boston: Four Seas Company, 1917), p. 17. The poem was not reprinted in *The Collected Earlier Poems*.

Williams' fiction is based on this power to put oneself within the life of another person and make him comprehensible by an objective report of his speech, movements, and facial expressions. There is none of the problem of knowing others which has long been a thematic resource in fiction — all that play of perspectives and points of view, product of the assumption that each man is locked in the prison of his consciousness and can know another person only rarely and with difficulty. Williams' characters, like those of Virginia Woolf, penetrate one another completely and are known by a narrator who has transcended point of view so that he stands everywhere in his story at once. His fiction, like that of the French "new novelists," is evidence of a "Copernican" revolution in the art of the novel which puts it beyond the centers of gravity dominant in the novel from Cervantes to Henry James. His stories and novels depend on that power of absorption in another person which he sees as essential in his experience as a doctor: "I lost myself in the very properties of their minds: for the moment at least I actually became *them*, whoever they should be, so that when I detached myself from them at the end of a half-hour of intense concentration over some illness which was affecting them, it was as though I were reawakening from a sleep. For the moment I myself did not exist, nothing of myself affected me" (A, 356).

In Williams' stories and plays he enters into people rather than into flowers or the river, but people too are treated as dynamic forces, energies crisscrossing with one another, loving, hating, always in motion. This means the transcendence of another traditional assumption of fiction. Williams' people are not fixed personalities persisting through time, but are flowing centers of strength, polarizing themselves differently according to each situation. Like the characters in Lawrence's novels, they are capable of undergoing allotropic changes of substance. Williams describes one of his short stories as capable of being seen either as three women in the guise of one, or as one woman in the guise of three. If the human self is a fluid set of forces and not fixed habitual traits, then three people can be one, one person three: "Most of us are not individuals any more but parts of something. We are no one of us 'all' of anything. It is too big for us. So why not write of three people as one? . . . Imagine a woman looking at herself three ways" (SE, 302). *Many Loves* treats simultaneously four intertwined love stories. The play is about the multiple attractions between the characters, heterosexual, homosexual, and the way these forces neutralize one another so that no urge to unity can be satisfied. It is not a drama of stable personalities, but puts in motion a group of interpenetrating energies, each pulled toward several of the others but kept in unresolved tension by contradictory attractions.

The people in *White Mule*, *In the Money*, and *The Build Up* have a similar existence. These novels are products of a methodical objectivism, recording what people said, what happened, and how people felt and acted, without comment or interpretation. *In the Money* shows little Flossie thinking: "This was to be her world, nothing so actual as that which she herself heard and said." [20] The novels are made up of such actualities. There is no "depth," no "symbolism," no "psychology." *White Mule*, says Williams, "had the advantage of the immediate . . . the babies I was seeing every day" (IWWP, 61). It was planned as a novel about infants, and he put in whatever he heard and saw of their behavior at his clinic. All the characters in the novels have the defiant integrity of the newborn. Of the adults too Williams could say what he says of babies: "They don't give a damn what goes on and they let go with everything they have and sometimes it's not too attractive" (IWWP, 61).

Though the novels are flat and objective, nevertheless they have a continuity, for "if there is progress then there is a novel. Without progress there is nothing" (GAN, 9). The progress of the novels is the drive of the life force, which also gives its energy to Williams' prose, a flow like the wind or an irresistible river. The momentum of human existence as it rides time is expressed in the opening pages of *In the Money* and *The Build Up* by motion through space. Gurlie is the central figure of these novels because she most intensely embodies the energy of life. Her vitality creates a specifically human time, a fluid unity made by her effort to fulfill herself, as a tree grows or as a plant comes into flower. Each chapter of these novels, in its concentration on the reality of the moment and its arrow of intention toward the future, is a recapitulation of all the

[20] (Norfolk, Conn.: New Directions, 1940), p. 316.

moments of the past. "Everything exists from the beginning" (GAN, 9), and this means that everything exists in each succeeding moment, each a new example of that "eternal moment" which always remains, "twining in its hair the flowers of yesterday and tomorrow" (GAN, 65). Williams' poems usually give but one moment, one place — the red wheelbarrow by the white chickens, the butterfish on their plate — everything focused in a single event. The novels are no less concentrated. They are a series of instants, each an intense absorption in the present which is the only real and contains in itself all time. This succession demonstrates not only that everything exists from the beginning, but that life is a progress in which every moment contains the whole, "all the past and the future" (GAN, 66). It is therefore proper, paradoxically, that the novels should give an impression of stasis. Though there is movement there is no going beyond the beginning, only a repetition in ever-new forms of what is present in the initial moment: the inexhaustible force of life.

The reaction which gives Williams possession of other people is strongly sexual. Sometimes this response obliterates other sensations and generates a poem which establishes a strongly erotic space made up of the lines of force between the poet and another person. One poem, for example, addresses a young woman curled into the pillows like a kitten, "to make a man clamp his jaws/for tenderness over you" (CLP, 176). Another poem describes the reaction of a group of people to the vitality of a girl with honey-colored hair: "Everyone looked and, passing, revealed/himself/by the light of her hair heavy/upon her shoulders" (CLP, 166). In "The Ogre" the poet brings to light the unmistakably sexual lines of force which his thoughts "put over and under and around" a "little girl with well-shaped legs." Though the girl cannot understand his desire, she feels "the brushings/of the fine needles," as the "tentative lines of [her] whole body" prove (CEP, 154).

More extraordinary is Williams' power to charge a whole scene with sexual meaning. This is a constant mode of his relation to the world, and can be demonstrated in dozens of examples from one end of his work to the other. A tree, a flower, or a landscape is sensed as if it were the body of a desirable woman, and there is a sexualization of everything. A constant alternation between body-words and thing-words makes such poems a covert personification. The poet's desire to possess the world is like his desire to possess a beautiful woman, and the stain of love permeates the world. So, in "Rain," the drops are the woman's pervasive love bathing all things (CEP, 75). Spring is a woman and closes the poet in "with her blossomy hair" (CEP, 120). The elm trees' smell of new bread is the fragrance of the poet's love (CEP, 137), and silver mist and bleached grass are like lovers embraced "limb to limb, mouth to mouth" (CEP, 141). Love arches over the world, like the sky "vast and grey/yearning silently over me" (CEP, 196), or the sky is like "white thighs" and calls forth a response from the "male belly" of the poet (CEP, 203). Autumn is a woman disrobing (CEP, 215), a fine pair of breasts are superimposed on the fountain in Madison Square (CEP, 222), and the love of the poet and his wife manifests itself as the distant city, which in turn is like "a locust cluster/a shad bush/blossoming" (CEP, 385). "Queen-Ann's-Lace" is an admirable poem of this sort. The field full of the white flower is a woman's body, touched everywhere by the man, until the entire landscape expresses an unrelieved sexual tension:

> Each part
> is a blossom under his touch
> to which the fibres of her being
> stem one by one, each to its end,
> until the whole field is a
> white desire . . . (CEP, 210)

This universalizing of sexual desire is dominant in *Kora in Hell*, where the world is often charged with an erotic meaning. *In the American Grain* shows De Soto led to his death by a savage America which is a *belle dame sans merci*, and the basic strategy of *Paterson* is a sexualization of the scene paralleling *Finnegans Wake*. City and surrounding country are a man and a woman in sexual embrace. In *A Dream of Love* the "Doc" says that each man "must create a woman of some sort out of his imagination to prove himself. . . . All right, a poem. I mean a woman, bringing her up to the light, building her up and not merely of stone or colors or silly words — unless he's supremely able — but in the flesh, warm, agreeable, made of pure consents" (ML, 200). The way in which good poetry is like the sexual act is suggested in Williams' praise of *The Pisan Cantos*. Pound has such power over language that "the word — in the present coitus — does lie fertile between the thighs of such sentences." [21] Williams' writing is in fact dominated throughout by the sexual sense. It can be defined as an attempt to bring into existence, with silly words, an erotic space inhabited by a woman of the imagination. His works, taken all together, make a poem which is a woman.

Sometimes a single sense dominates in Williams' poetry and creates a space special to one alone. More often the senses co-operate to bring into existence a realm attainable only by synesthesia, all the body working to internalize things and making it possible for words to incarnate their vitality. With the eye of the mind "directed flexibly *inward*," the reader can then "look *into* the poem" and "*see* the sun rise and hear the winds blow, smell the air, the pure air that is beyond the air — and know the men who are talking." [22] Williams, like Aaron Burr, is a man who needs "to touch, to hear, to see, to smell, to taste" (IAG, 206). If any sense is sovereign for him it is touch, that *tactus eruditus* which he so prizes. The other senses are used no less constantly, but the qualities of touch — softness, gentleness, and immediacy — define their nature too. "A Morning Imagination of Russia" (CEP, 305–308) celebrates the poet's break beyond the urban barriers which have put "a piece of glazed paper" between man and the world. The revolution of the senses which Williams' poetry accomplishes is in this poem described in full, and a comprehensive expression is given to that turning inside out of the mind which makes the new poetry possible. There is "nothing between now," and as a result the earth and the sky are "very close" and when the sun rises it rises "in his heart." Time and space have "wandered into himself," and "the world [is] himself." This triumphant assimilation is attained by the strenuous and yet delicate use of all the senses, but all are modes of touch. Seeing and hearing, and by implication smelling and tasting, are transformed into extensions of the poet's tactile power:

[21] "The Fistula of the Law" [a review of Ezra Pound's *The Pisan Cantos*], *Imagi*, 4: 10 (Allentown, Penn., Spring 1949).
[22] "The Fistula of the Law," p. 11.

. . . We have paid heavily. But we
have gotten — touch. The eyes and the ears
down on it. Close.

~

Apparently there is no farther to go with Williams. Anywhere is everywhere, and there are no directions, nothing to do, nowhere to move after a first moment which contains everything, the senses having taken all objects into a realm where things are ideas, ideas things. The problems which gave rise to action in earlier literature have disappeared: no difficulty in knowing other people; no uncertain approach to external objects by the subjective mind; no pathos of a distant and unattainable God. Poetry in such a world seems to be limited to variations on a first instant which contains everything and appeases every desire.

There is, however, much drama in Williams' work, but it lies in a dimension appropriate to the realm of immanence which he has entered. Three elements are always present in that realm, and these must be brought into the proper relation or life will fall back to some form of inauthenticity. Yet they are mutually incompatible. When one is present the others tend to disappear or to be occulted. Like matter and anti-matter they destroy one another. Only with great difficulty can they be brought into balance. All Williams' work is an attempt to discover ways to do this.

The three elements are the formless ground, origin of all things; the formed thing, defined and limited; a nameless presence, the "beautiful thing" (P, 119), there in every form but hidden by it. The ground is what is always already there, chaotic, senseless, absurd, but fecund, holding within itself the possibility of all forms. The "unfathomable ground/where we walk daily" (CLP, 23) is perpetually new, untouched by time, because it is always in its original state, unshaped, unfixed, a "muddy flux" (P, 156) with an inexhaustible energy of being.

This elemental substance appears throughout Williams' work as the generative source. It is the Passaic, in "The Wanderer," in which the poet is plunged to lose his separate identity. It is the earth, in "Sub Terra" (CEP, 117, 118), the first poem in *Al Que Quiere!* It is "the earth under our feet" in "At Kenneth

Burke's Place" (CLP, 256). It is present in poem after poem as
that which any form has risen from, or stands upon, or is seen
against, the common earth, "the clay of these parts" (CEP, 184)
which exerts its drag toward formlessness on the poet, as the sea
in "The Yachts" tries to pull down the graceful boats. The ground
may be common to all men at all times, but the Europeans coming to America found that "the ground [had] undergone/a subtle
transformation, its identity altered" (P, 29). *In the American Grain*
is Williams' chronicle of the settlers' response to the unfamiliar
texture of an alien ground. It tells of their obliteration of the cultures which had flowered naturally there, the culture of the North
American Indians, the culture of Tenochtitlan, a "whole world
of . . . unique associations" which Cortez destroyed, so that it
"sank back into the ground to be reënkindled, never" (IAG, 32).
The ground is also present in multiple disguises throughout *Paterson*, where the poet has "a mass of detail/to interrelate on a new
ground, difficultly" (P, 30). It is the earth itself, present in one
passage as a tabular account of the forms of rock in layers down
to 2100 feet in a well at Paterson. It is the river and its falls,
shapeless, fluid, an inarticulate roar. It is the fire of Book Three,
"a cataract reversed, shooting/upward" (P, 146). It is the wind
in the same book, and the "alluvial silt" (P, 122) left after a flood,
"a sort of muck, a detritus,/in this case — a pustular scum, a
decay, a choking/lifelessness" (P, 167). Earth, "cyclone, fire/and
flood" (P, 120) — the unfathomable ground is present in all the
elements. Out of these four everything has sprung.

The ground is the source of more than the flowers, trees, and
bushes which grip down their roots and thrust toward the sky in
so many of Williams' poems. Earth, the chatterer, is also father
of speech. Words spring from the ground and each is another
form of the primitive word spoken by the falls in its roaring, like
the "Blouaugh!" of the sea-elephant, which is the speech of the
deep sea (CEP, 71). Each human being, mind incarnate in a
body, has also come from the earth. In "The Cure" the poet tells
his lady of that ground "from which/among the rest you have
sprung/and opened flower-like to my hand" (CLP, 23). Words,
things, people — all three have the same origin, and this guar-
antees their harmonious copresence in the poem. Language, objects, and minds have the same father, and "like father, like son,"

so the words of the poem can be the place where ideas are things. The new measure Williams seeks, with its dance of the vocables, is another mode of the rising of shape from the unfathomable ground.

Though earth is origin of all form the two are radically opposed, as shape is opposed to shapeless, measure to the measureless, the limited to the illimitable. To have one seems to mean the loss of the other. The chthonic vitality of the moist earth is imperceptible in the airy fragility of the flower, and the flower cut off from the earth is dead, like that symbol of separation and inauthenticity in *Paterson:* "a bud forever green,/tight-curled, upon the pavement, perfect/in juice and substance but divorced, divorced/from its fellows, fallen low —" (P, 28). Any form which is disjoined from the living earth is without value. An example of this is the academic mind, dry and abstract, imposing its dead forms on life. T. S. Eliot represents aridity of this sort in poetry, a return to European ideas and poetic forms, an attempt to perpetuate the past, ignoring the novel vitality of the present. "The past is for those who/lived in the past" (P, 219), and those who reverse this law are contributing to that divorce which is "the sign of knowledge in our time" (P, 28).

Williams' animus against the Puritans has the same source. Instead of opening themselves to the new land of America and creating a unique culture resting "upon peculiar and discoverable ground" (IAG, 109), they constructed in a vacuum a false culture modeled abstractly on the old European one: "They must have closed all the world out. It was the enormity of their task that enforced it. Having in themselves nothing of curiosity, no wonder, for the New World — that is nothing official — they knew only to keep their eyes blinded, their tongues in orderly manner between their teeth, their ears stopped by the monotony of their hymns and their flesh covered in straight habits. . . . It is an immorality that IS America. Here it began. You see the cause. There was no ground to build on, with a ground all blossoming about them — under their noses" (IAG, 112, 114). The citizens of Paterson have inherited the immorality on which America was founded. They too are surrounded with the opaque walls of a false culture. Their detachment from reality is especially apparent in the inauthenticity of their language: "They do not know the words/or have not/the courage to use them ." (P, 20). It does not matter whether an abstract form is imported from the outside, or whether an indigenous form is allowed to become divorced from its roots. Whenever a linguistic, physical, or human form is separated from the parent ground it dies. For Williams, as for Stevens, reality lies only in the present moment, and any form must continue to draw its energy from the living earth. Everything must constantly be made anew through reimmersion in the originating soil. Williams' fierce antipathy to all traditionalisms originates in these assumptions. "Root, Branch & Flower" — this was to be the title of his autobiography (SL, 295). The phrase states concisely a basic pattern of his thought.

If the green bud divorced from branch and root dies, it is possible to sink so deeply in the soil that all limitation is lost, and with it the power to flower in a new shape. The city-dwellers of Paterson, divorced from a rooted culture, are like flowers unfertilized by any bee. They return unfulfilled to the formless source:

> They sink back into the loam
> crying out
> — you may call it a cry
> that creeps over them, a shiver
> as they wilt and disappear (P, 20)

In the American Grain celebrates those backwoodsmen, Boone, Houston, and the rest, who "made contact with the intrinsic elements of an as yet unrealized material of which the country was made" (SE, 140). The price for this contact was extreme. They were gradually absorbed by the indistinctions of the wilderness, just as earlier De Soto was lured to his death by the land. The frontiersmen could not return and achieve the triumph of a new form: "Such men had no way of making their realizations vocal. They themselves became part of the antagonistic wilderness against which the coastal settlements were battling. Their sadness alone survives. Many of them could hardly read. Their speech became crude. Their manners sometimes offensive. It was the penalty they had to pay" (SE, 141). In *Paterson* Williams remembers Pound's taunt: "Your interest is in the bloody loam but what/I'm after is the finished product" (P, 50). The finished product, he would answer, can only come from the bloody loam, but, like the hunters who pushed beyond the settlers and were lost in the wilderness, the new American poet may become so imbedded in the earth that he is speechless or speaks indistinctly and so ineffectively: "It is imperative that we *sink*. But from a low position it is impossible to answer those who know all the Latin and some of the Sanskrit names, much French and perhaps one or two other literatures. . . . [W]here foreign values are held to be a desideratum, he who is buried and speaks thickly — is lost. . . . Those who come up from under will have a mark on them that invites scorn, like a farmer's filthy clodhoppers" (IAG, 214, 215). "I am far under them," he says in *The Great American Novel*. "I am less, far less if you will. I am a beginner" (GAN, 26). The achievement of form of whatever sort is subject to a double jeopardy. If the generative urge remains buried in the earth it is not form at all, "no syllable in the confused/uproar" (P, 100), no flower in the shapeless mud, but as soon as it rises altogether free of the ground it becomes a hollow shell.

What vitality disappears? If the earth is just earth, it ought to be possible to give it a permanent form, create a fixed culture which would be valid forever. Why is it that, "unless there is/a new mind there cannot be a new/line, the old will go on/repeating itself with recurring/deadliness" (P, 65)? Why is form false unless, like Antaeus, it keeps touch with the earth?

The answer is that third element, the "hidden flame" (IAG, 204) present in the ground but invisible, and present too in every form but covered up as soon as the form gets fixed in a shape. Only in the moment when the flower rises from the ground is a brief glimpse of the presence released. For this reason validity lies in the process of flowering and not in the flower full blown. Every birth is an uncovering of the secret, but as soon as the child is assimilated into the already existing human community, the flame is shaded, the unique is reduced to common measure: "Thus the birth of every baby, whatever its quality, is a revelation. But the moment it is christened, circumcised or indoctrinated by other means into whatever sect or clan will delimit it from others of its generation, revelation is at an end" (SE, 270). Only when the child and its source are still in living relation is the presence manifest. Authenticity lies in a present moment which moves and changes as form emerges from the shapeless origin. The image of flowering, constantly appearing in Williams' work, is the opening out of the real in the fleeting moment of uncovering before things are dead and fixed. As objects rise from the ground and blossom, the delicate perfume of beauty is released. So, in a good poem "the sentence lives, the movement lives, the object flares up (out of the dark). That is what I mean by reality, it lives again (as always) in our day." [23] In the same way, "each serious American writer in turn," like an object in a poem, "flares up for a moment and fizzles out, burnt out by the air" (GAN, 60).

⸜

What is this hidden flame? "Like all that's universal," Williams says, "it cannot be packed into three common words" (IAG, 204); "one of the characteristics of this rare presence is that it is jealous of exposure and that it is shy and revengeful. It is not a name that is bandied about in the market place, no more than it is something that can be captured and exploited by the academy. Its face is a particular face, it is likely to appear under the most unlikely disguises. You cannot recognize it from past appearances — in fact it is always a new face" (A, 362). In spite of its evasiveness some approach to naming it may be made. Bringing the hidden flame to light is the central motivation of Williams' long career as a writer, but, like Stevens in relation to that "being" which it is *his* goal to release, Williams rarely speaks directly about the presence. It can only be freed by a glancing blow, in a poem or story which is apparently about something else. "Let the words/fall any way at all," he says, "— that they may/hit love aslant" (P, 169). Like Stevens' being, Williams' flame is entirely within things. There is no surreptitious return to Platonism or to any other form of transcendentalism. The presence is as much within the inclusive space, inner and outer at once, as are the ground and the forms which flower on it. Williams continues that "return to earth" which is accomplished in Stevens' poetry, but his flame is less disembodied, less insubstantial than Stevens' being. It is a beautiful *thing*, more noun than verb. Though it too may manifest itself in its hiddenness as "the nul/defeats it all/the N of all/equations," "the blank" (P, 95), it is usually something tangibly actual, "that rock" (P, 95), or the warm light, or the music of a phrase in the common speech.

[23] "The Fistula of the Law," p. 10.

It is incarnated in some objective form which the senses can grasp and is brought to light in the struggles of that form to free itself from the darkness of the unfathomable ground.

Images of substantial light are dominant in the poet's approaches to a name for the rare presence. The placing of words in Marianne Moore's poetry, for example, has the effect of dark objects which cause "the appearance of the luminous background" (SE, 128). Benjamin Franklin did everything he could "to keep the fingers busy — not to realize — the lightning" of the new world (IAG, 155). The aim of *In the American Grain* is by a proper naming of things in American history "to draw from every source one thing, the strange phosphorus of the life, nameless under an old misappelation" (IAG, [vii]). The young poet in *Many Loves* wants "to come through the obscurity/of his surroundings to the flame" (ML, 103), and the "beautiful thing" in *Paterson* is "intertwined with the fire. An identity/surmounting the world, its core" (P, 145). Proper poetry is "multiplex, efflorescent, varied as the day in its forms" (ML, 221), and in literature "it is only in isolate flecks that/something/is given off" (CEP, 272), as though the presence were sparks struck from stone. This image is related to another, perhaps the most expressive of all. The presence of beauty in things is like radium in inert uranium ore. As the radioactive metal turns to lead, a luminous energy is given forth. Beauty is:

> The radiant gist that
> resists the final crystallization
>
> .   in the pitch-blend
> the radiant gist   . (P, 133)

This image expresses Williams' intuition perfectly. The hidden flame is part of the substance of earth, buried secretly there. It only appears in an action whereby something is brought up from hiding to manifest itself as light and form, like the luminous stain at the bottom of the retort in Marie Curie's makeshift laboratory (P, 209).

If the covert radiance of beauty lives in physical objects, it is no less there in human gesture or action. Williams' short stories aim to liberate an obscure phosphorus which is present in the behavior of every man and woman, but thwarted, disguised. Beauty is a thing, an it, but it is as present in human relations as in a flower or in the "colored crystals" which are "the secret of those rocks" (P, 17). Love between human beings, in all its evasions and betrayals, has especially the power to reveal the beauty which is "supremely detached from their acts, from all infidelities. It stands in the full light, APART" (ML, 201). A passage in the *Autobiography* about the poet's experience with his patients gives an explicit description of the shy beauty which is present everywhere. Here again the image of the rare metal hidden in common ore returns:

> We catch a glimpse of something, from time to time, which shows us that a presence has just brushed past us, some rare thing — just when the smiling little Italian woman has left us. For a moment we are dazzled. What was that? We can't name it; we know it never gets into any recognizable avenue of expression; men will be long dead before they can have so much as ever approached it. . . . So for me the practice of medicine has become the pursuit of a rare element which may appear at any time, at any place, at a glance. . . . There's no use trying to multiply cases, it is there, it is magnificent, it fills my thoughts, it reaches to the farthest limits of our lives. . . . It is actually there, in the life before us, every minute that we are listening, a rarest element — not in our imaginations but there, there in fact. It is that essence which is hidden in the very words which are going in at our ears and from which we must recover underlying meaning as realistically as we recover metal out of ore. (A, 360, 362)

These sentences touch the center of Williams' thought and are his most open expression of the third element in the trinity of forces constituting his world. Ground, form, and radiant gist — all three are always there, inextricably intertwined with one another yet hiding one another, so that ground and form are constantly appearing in their nakedness and the flame is constantly withdrawing into secrecy. Nevertheless, momentary balances of the elements occur. Stasis is death, but in flux forms continually rise from the ground and release a fleck of beauty. A woman, a flower, a splendid city, a culture like that of Tenochtitlan, an authentic scrap of speech, a gesture, a cadence, a poem, George Washington's inarticulate actions — all are examples of the same revelation. An admirable passage in *Paterson* embodies in its rhythmic pattern this process of opening, closing, death, and renewal, and shows why Williams is content to be a local poet. Anywhere is everywhere because a universal beauty surrounds each gesture of creation. Paterson is the center of the world, for the center is wherever the poet stands:

> . . . The world spreads
> for me like a flower opening — and
> will close for me as might a rose —
>
> wither and fall to the ground
> and rot and be drawn up
> into a flower again. But you
> never wither — but blossom
> all about me. In that I forget
> myself perpetually — in your
> composition and decomposition
> I find my   .   .
> > despair! (P, 93)[24]

Why "despair"? A time of perpetual renewal seems to guarantee the continuous presence of beauty. Its appearance, however, is followed instantaneously by its disappearance. The radiant gist is always slipping away, fading, falling back into the ground, or being covered up. "It appears, it disappears, a sheen of it comes up, when, as its shattering implications affront us, all the gnomes hurry to cover up its traces" (SE, 287). Even if the flame did not hide itself, no man would be strong enough to face it for more than a moment. "[W]e shrink," says Williams, "squirting little hoses of/objection — and/I along with the rest, squirting/at the fire" (P, 145). No revelation lasts beyond the instant, and so it must be repeated again and again. What forms are taken by this "catastrophic birth" (CLP, 8), and how can the obstetrical poet assist in the delivery of beauty?

The first movement of his imagination is one of descent, of destruction: "However hopeless it may seem, we have no other choice: we must go back to the beginning; it must all be done over; everything that is must be destroyed" (IAG, 215); we must "tear it all apart" until "America is a mass of pulp, a jelly, a sensitive plate ready to take whatever print you want to put on it" (GAN,

---

[24] According to Sister M. Bernetta Quinn the "you" here is identified as God in the title given to the passage in a microfilmed version of the manuscript at the Lockwood Memorial Library of the University of Buffalo (*The Metamorphic Tradition in Modern Poetry* [New Brunswick, N.J.: Rutgers University Press, 1955], p. 109). Here for once the "rare thing" is given a traditional religious name, but the fact that the poet omitted the title from the published version of *Paterson* suggests his reluctance to identify the radiant gist with God.

in its purity? Not at all. The mud is only mud. The "uh" is no
rd. When these are reached all evidence of the beautiful thing
appears. The descent is not an end in itself. When the poet has
nihilated all forms he finds himself plunged in the river, engulfed
roaring noise. "The word" (GAN, 16) is there, but it is in-
dible. Having destroyed everything else Paterson

> discovers, still, no syllable in the confused
> uproar: missing the sense (though he tries)
> untaught but listening, shakes with the intensity
> of his listening   . (P, 100)

Only in a return from the ground can beauty be liberated.
tones invent nothing, only a man invents" (P, 100). Invention
one will liberate the essential word which is the measure of every-
ng. All objects, whatever their configuration, are contained in
at in-between realm where the mind is turned inside-out into the
orld, the world turned inside-out into the mind. To descend to
e elemental ground by a willed destruction of old forms is also a
scent to the poet's own ground, for the two grounds are the same.
elaxation, sinking, and disrobing do not reveal the hidden beauty.
dwells within man, as does the stone, its shelter, but man alone
n free it. He can do this by performing some action which will
cover the crystal in the rock. The poem is a special way of naming
ich brings beauty back into the clear:

> Invent (if you can) discover or
> nothing is clear — will surmount
> the drumming in your head. There will be
> nothing clear, nothing clear   . (P, 103)

After the descent, the return. The opening of the poem accom-
ishes a liberation of the hidden presence. The poet's aim is "from
at base, unabashed, to regain/the sun kissed summits of love!"
, 104). At the end of Book Four of Paterson the protagonist rises
ain from the Passaic, before it runs with him into the bottomless
a. The sea "is not our home" (P, 235), and his descent with the
ver is completed only by an escape from its embracing waves.
his reverses at last the sinking performed in the first three books
Paterson, and, at the beginning of Williams' career, in "The
anderer." The poet's ascent is the flowering of form, but it is not

25). Destruction and descent are interdependent, for only through
demolition can man descend to the root of things. Descent obliterates the last vestiges of abstract consciousness, awareness of the
separate self, and replaces it with an undifferentiated sense of
existence, nebulous, opaque, confused, like the formless earth with
which consciousness has merged. The new poet must be "willing
to smash . . . everything. — To go down into hell" (GAN, 21).
To return to the beginning is to return to the present moment, for
the present is the ever-fresh origin. Only if everything carried over
from the past is destroyed can this moment be reached and within
it the elemental ground which contains all power: "when the form
has been completed, when it has at last flowered, it begins at once
to become sclerotic and has to be broken down once more *to the
elements*" (AP, 57). Ideas, forms of language, poetic forms, metaphors, meters, rhyme schemes, modes of behavior, patterns of
thought — all become detached from the ground as soon as they
exist. They must be demolished at once in order to make possible
new access to the ground. Beauty is hidden — crystals in rock,
radium in pitchblende. The loam is bloody; it hides the principles of
life. An anarchic destruction of all accomplished forms will allow
man to sink into the loam, there to confront the flame of beauty.
We Americans cannot perpetuate the old forms, luckily for us. "We
can't do it. Our feet are too heavy . . . You smile! Yes, we are
not afraid to say now that our feet are too heavy, like our hearts.
They break through. *Nuevo Mundo!*" [25]

The descent which opens a new world is enacted in many
different ways in Williams' work. Whitman is repeatedly praised
for presiding over the destruction of outmoded European forms:
"what he did best was to abandon all the staid usages of writing a
poem and thus bring the sense to unassociated elements of composition" (AP, 68). Like Whitman, the backwoodsmen of *In the
American Grain* had to destroy in themselves what they had inherited
from Europe in order to confront nakedly the new ground. So the
chapter called "Descent" celebrates the disrobing which makes
possible a plunge. Like Whitman or Daniel Boone, Williams does
his share of destroying. His work does not assume that the slate of
history has already been wiped clean, returning things to their

[25] "Introduction" to Sydney Salt, *Christopher Columbus and Other Poems* (Boston:
Bruce Humphries, 1937), p. 10.

primitive elements. The poet must assist in the destructive work, for the radiant gist still remains hidden and only descent will uncover it. He most resembles the surrealists when he is seized by an anarchistic rage to demolish everything, all logical or rational forms, all the continuities of history. The "improvisations" of *Kora in Hell*, for example, are in part parallel to the surrealist enterprise. Like many modern French prose poems they are inspired by Rimbaud's *Illuminations* and try to break down the preconceived forms of the mind to reach the spontaneous ground of thought. The title is Kora *in hell* — Persephone not yet brought back to the sunlight but still submerged in the depths. In one place the poet proposes a reascent: "perhaps we'll bring back Euridice — this time!" (KH, 11). To bring the goddess back to the surface the poet must sink to get her, and this downward penchant dominates in the book. He seems to have been following in anticipation the advice he gives in *Paterson:* "Only one answer: write carelessly so that nothing that is not green will survive" (P, 155). *Kora in Hell* is full of *non sequiturs*, sequences of words which resist logical explication and seem an exact record of what came into the poet's mind when he "scribbl[ed] in the dark . . . often past midnight" (KH, 5): "What can it mean to you that a child wears pretty clothes and speaks three languages or that its mother goes to the best shops? It means: July had good need of his blazing sun" (KH, 14). The notes of explanation which Williams added to the original improvisations sometimes start as if they were going to be rational analysis, but then slip back into obscurity. They are, as the poet admits, "often more dense than the first writing" (KH, 5). "Dense" is a good word here. *Kora in Hell* is a thick murk of words which tries to go back toward the flux of inarticulate sound at the origin of all language. This justifies the description of Williams' work given in a letter from Ezra Pound cited in the "Prologue to *Kora in Hell*": "The thing that saves your work is opacity, and don't forget it" (SE, 8). Williams' implicit denial of the next sentence in Pound's letter ("Opacity is NOT an American quality") is suggested by his later ironic borrowing of the key word here when he wants to distinguish the native Americanism of his work from the foreign quality of Rimbaud and Joyce: "The difference being greater opacity, less erudition, reduced power of perception — " (GAN, 18).

The prose parts of *Spring and All*, written s share the same inspiration. There are Dadai: chapters, lines printed upside down, and a se poet's "secret project: the annihilation of e on the face of the earth" (SA, 5). Only thro act of destruction can the poet reach a mon thing is fresh, perfect, recreated" (SA, 9). T *and All* is the rebirth of things after their an the return to the beginning which leads to s complished. The poem flows steadily dowr Passaic until, in the third section of Book Th of inarticulateness expressed in the pustula flood, a "fertile (?) mud" in which the poet

                — to the teeth, to the very
.   uh,   uh (P, 167)

The attainment of the ultimate descent is the "uh" preceded by a space and the mispl pages earlier, in a sequence of incoherent page. It is appropriate that there should be a in the middle of this sequence, for Williams h to express in the placing of the words that la language before language, which Artaud der of literature.[26]

What is accomplished by this descent to contains all words? Does the poet reach the

[26] See *The Theater and Its Double*, trans. Mary Caroline R 1958), p. 110: "It is a matter of substituting for the s language of nature, whose expressive possibilities will be but whose source will be tapped at a point still deeper, The grammar of this new language is still to be found. G wits." Elsewhere Artaud calls for a use of words themselves Frenchman and the American are even more closely in r the least return to the active, plastic, respiratory source: joined again to the physical motions that gave them bi logical aspect of speech disappear beneath its affective, ph heard in their sonority rather than be exclusively taken for cally, let them be perceived as movements" (p. 119). language, so eloquently expressed here, is strikingly like \ of "cruelty" in Artaud's theater is quite foreign to the Am of language as a magical incantation which will coerce t romanticism have disappeared in Williams.

watched passively, from a distance. It is accomplished within the poem itself:

> The province of the poem is the world.
> When the sun rises, it rises in the poem
> and when it sets darkness comes down
> and the poem is dark   . (P, 122)

The need for the poem to enact the flowering and not merely describe it leads Williams to encounter what might be called the paradox of invention. He remembers that the word "invention" means a finding — "Invent (if you can) discover" — an uncovering of something hidden but already there, and he associates the word with the plunge to the elemental: "But to invent we have actually, as the word radical itself intimates, to return to the root" (AP, 61). Invention does not mean the imposition of shape from the outside on the "alluvial silt." The idea of the poet's mind as the free creator of forms cast outward to organize the formless would be a return to the dichotomy of subject and object, a falling back to romanticism, idealism, and perspectivism. One direction of Stevens' thought is wholly alien to Williams, the direction which leads him to say of Canon Aspirin: "He imposes orders as he thinks of them." Williams would applaud Stevens' rejection of the Canon: "But to impose is not/To discover." [27] Though the ascent to form is necessary, the new pattern must rise spontaneously from the ground, and it must never lose the primitive virtue of the shapeless muck. After the return of everything to pustular scum, Paterson cries: " — of this, make it of *this*, this/this, this, this, this   ." (P, 168).

The frozen forms of language inherited from the past can only be melted to release an authentic language through that free improvisation which Williams advises for all writing. This fluid spontaneity gives his own work, especially his prose, its characteristic drive, the moving energy of a man riding the crest of a wave, vibrating with the life of the water. "Here's a man," he says in *The Great American Novel*, "wants me to revise, to put in order. My God what I am doing means just the opposite from that. There is no revision, there can be no revision — " (GAN, 26). And in an essay: "Write, write anything: it is all in all probability worthless anyhow, it is never hard to destroy written characters. But it is absolutely

[27] The quotations from Stevens are from *The Collected Poems* (New York: Alfred A. Knopf, 1954), p. 403.

essential to the writing of anything worth while that the mind be
fluid and release itself to the task. Forget all rules, forget all
restrictions, as to taste, as to what ought to be said, write for the
pleasure of it — whether slowly or fast — every form of resistance
to a complete release should be abandoned." [28] The new metric
already exists in the sounds of American speech, a "hidden, inner
quality." [29] The poet's first job is to find it there by submitting to
what he hears around him: "The poet's business is to find that
basis, to discover it in the speech around him and to build it into
his compositions." [30]

Still it (the new form) must be *made*, and this is the other side of
the paradox. The poem must rise freely from the mind, and yet
it will not. It comes only through the hard work of the poet: "And
do not believe, I keep repeating, that the form of the age will
spontaneously appear . . . . It is the work, the exhausting work of
the artist who . . . as an inheritor of all the skills of the past will
MAKE the world today" (AP, 61). The poet must do something,
and yet that doing must not be the application of artificial form.
Invention is both a creating and a discovering. "This combination
of order *with* discovery, with exploration and revelation, the vigor
of sensual stimulation, is of the essence of art." [31] The "relativistic
or variable foot" (SL, 335) which Williams long sought, is both a
novel ratio, invented by the poet as a new measure or basis for our
culture, and at the same time it is something found by the poet in
the cadences of the speech around him: "When a man makes a
poem, makes it, mind you, he takes words as he finds them inter-
related about him and composes them — without distortion which
would mar their exact significances — into an intense expression of
his perceptions and ardors that they may constitute a revelation
in the speech that he uses" (SE, 257). Here is a perfect expression
of the paradox of invention! The poem is made, composed, and yet
it must use words as they are already interrelated in common
speech, without distortion.

This can be done only by a process of composition which grows
from within rather than being imposed from the outside. Beginning

[28] "How to Write," no pagination.
[29] "To Write American Poetry," *Fantasy — A Poetry Quarterly* (Pittsburgh, Summer
1935), p. 13.
[30] "To Write American Poetry," p. 13.
[31] "Introduction" to *Transfigured Night*, p. xii.

up to his eyes in the mud, the poet must rise with the world to new form, for the rising takes place within the poem, within the poet. The paradox of invention can be resolved by seeing that the new measure is not something external to the poet. It is uncovered inside, through the hard work of raising the mud to shape. Unless the poet lets himself be the place where the new measure appears, in difficult birth, it cannot come to light. This is a justification for Williams' association of the new measure with modern physics, as when he says "relativity gives us the cue" (SE, 340) or connects "such an apparently minor activity as a movement in verse construction" with "Einstein's discoveries in the relativity of our measurements of physical matter" (SL, 332). Gone are absolute space and absolute time, measured by a God standing outside the universe and endowed with a divine clock and yardstick. Relativity replaces the absolute. There are only innumerable local centers, each as valid as any of the others, each inextricably involved in time, space, and matter, each radiating its own unique power to measure them. The rejection of absolute time and space means the rejection of absolute measure, but not the rejection of all measure. Measure must now be relative, rooted in a particular place. Poetry is still essentially rhythm, as it has always been, but just as "nothing in our lives, at bottom, is ordered according to that [old] measure," so "poems cannot any longer be made following a Euclidian measure, 'beautiful' as this may make them" (SE, 337). The ultimate source of measure is no longer a transcendent God. It is an immanent presence, the radiant gist hidden everywhere in the soil, manifesting itself differently every time a new form emerges from the dark. The new poetic foot must therefore be "variable." It must measure speech freely, as it lifts into form, not mold it according to some fixed pattern. It must renew itself each moment, for Williams' universe, like that of the American primitive painters, is "a beginning world, a re-beginning world" (SE, 336). Each new line must be allowed to ascend from the obscurity into the light, there to take its intrinsic shape according to a measure revealed anew each moment.[32] The flower grows from the pattern seed

---

[32] In the last years of his life Williams was writing a book on metrics and the new measure. The incomplete manuscript is in the Beinecke Library at Yale. It is a fuller working out of the ideas about meter already expressed in his published work and includes, somewhat unexpectedly, discussion of the history of metrical practice in English as well as American verse.

buried in the fathomless ground, and yet it unfolds only through the slow growth of stem and leaves lifting the blossom into the air. Every flower is different from the others, though all manifest the same measure. The flower both makes itself and is made. In its tense life the paradox of invention is transcended. The poem, as it rises within the poet, must be like the flower. In this way it can avoid false form in one direction, and, in the other, permanent immersion in the speechless roar. This balance can be attained, if at all, only with great difficulty:

> How to begin to find a shape — to begin to begin again,
> turning the inside out : to find one phrase that will
> lie married beside another for delight   .   ?
> — seems beyond attainment   . (P, 167)

One way to this equilibrium is through the poem of stasis. In many of Williams' poems a single object, a flower, a person, a tree, rests motionless, poised in its presentness. It may have existed before, already sprung from the ground, complete, but it has just now entered into the poet's awareness. In the embrace which is the poetic naming it flowers anew, and thereby releases a fleck of beauty. So, in one poem, "the leafless beachtree/shines like a cloud" (CEP, 301). This is a motionless flowering, the fixed presence of beauty in things. Such poems reveal the ultimate meaning of a definition of poetry as letting things be. Often the object chosen is insignificant, "ugly," "antipoetic," plants like mullen, Queen Anne's lace, chicory, "the small, yellow grass-onion" (CLP, 153), trees like the locust, items of our civilization like "Picture of a Nude in a Machine Shop" (CLP, 107) or "a fat boy in/an old overcoat, a/butt between/his thick lips" (CLP, 90). These poems have especially that quality of joyful amazement so characteristic of Williams' poetry. Everything that exists, by the very fact that it exists, delights the wide-awake poet, however sordid, broken, or ugly it may be. This joy is his response to the sheer presence of things, each object preserving defiantly its individuality:

> It's the anarchy of poverty
> delights me, the old

yellow wooden house indented
among the new brick tenements

Or a cast-iron balcony
with panels showing oak branches
in full leaf. (CEP, 415)

When the mind concentrates on such insignificant objects they seem to grow larger until they fill the inner space of the mind. The richness of the universe can be concentrated in the poise of "a girl with one leg/over the rail of a balcony" (CEP, 259), or in a glimpse of "little frogs/with puffed-out throats,/singing in the slime" (CEP, 161). One of the most beautiful of such poems is:

Between Walls

the back wings
of the

hospital where
nothing

will grow lie
cinders

in which shine
the broken

pieces of a green
bottle (CEP, 343)

There is a scrupulous bareness here. Everything is cut down to a minimum, presented with complete objectivity. No reference to subjective feelings, no mention of a human presence. The objects exist within an anonymous human space, the poem. It is in the present tense, and what is there in the now — hospital walls, cinders, broken pieces of a green bottle, light — is cut off from past and future, fixed in a perpetual present. The world is reduced to these poor fragmentary elements surrounded by nothing, just as the words, brief and few, which make up the poem are placed on blank white paper. This is the poetry of humility — no capitals, no marks of punctuation, no figures of speech, no "poetic" diction. So sparse is the poem that two little words, "of" and "the," scarcely worth looking at, must make up a whole line as best they can. The poet, in his poverty, seems not to have enough words for the job and must make do with the handful left in his truncated dictionary,

like a starving artist making a painting with two daubs of paint left
in a tube almost squeezed dry. Everything with a halo of tradition
or a literary resonance is omitted. Just as the pieces of the bottle
are broken and lie against a waste surface, so the words in the
poem are separated from one another by their location on the page.
Each line is a fragmentary bit of incomplete grammar, a preposition and an article with no noun ("of the"), three verbs in a row
with no subject or object ("will grow lie"), an article and an adjective with no noun ("the broken"), a single word starkly alone
("nothing," "bottle"). If the poem were reduced any further it
would disappear.

When almost everything is removed, the plenitude of what remains shines forth a thousand times brighter. To multiply, subtract,
this is Williams' strange arithmetic or chemistry of art: " — to
dissect away/the block and leave/a separate metal:/hydrogen/the
flame, helium the/pregnant ash   ." (P, 207). Like radium,
the broken pieces of green glass in "Between Walls" shine with
the light of universal beauty. When nothing remains but the bits of
glass and the poet fixes these with his full attention, the presentness
of things present becomes a revelation of that fugitive radiance
which all things hide. The poem means, he says, "that in a waste
of cinders loveliness, in the form of color, stands up alive" (SL, 265).
In the same way words, cut off from past and future, and from all
preformed literary tradition, are freed to reveal their innate linguistic energy as nodes of power in a verbal field. Reaching out to
combine with other words, their yearning is satisfied only in the
next line, after the reader has crossed over the blank on the page
and the blank in the meter, the pause. The meter works to transform words into things containing their meaning, as the broken bits
of glass contain beauty and do not refer beyond themselves. The
measure is a delicate breath pattern accommodating the words as
they are and bringing them out in their unique shapes of sound
rather than distorting them by some preconceived pattern. There
is a progressive effacement in the rhythm, the first line in each
two-l線 unit having as many as five syllables, the second, in all
cases but one, only two. The sound pattern, like the meaning, is a
shape so delicate and evanescent, so unsupported by anything
around it, that it seems at every moment about to vanish: "the
back wings/of the" followed by a blank, the apparent evaporation

of the poem, leaving a bare page, which fills more than half the sheet. As the words are effaced, something else appears, "nothing," the nothing of the fourth line, but nothing as the momentary manifestation of beauty, that "rare thing."

In such poems the personality of the poet is obliterated in a total adhesion of the mind to the object in its actuality. The thing fills the mind, the mind enters into the thing, and the words of the poem are born of this identification, flying off from it to make the presence manifest. The poem depends on an enormous power of concentration. Nothing else exists, neither before nor after, no depth or breadth in space, no separable thought of the poet, only the thing-thought-word in inextricable combination. Within this unitary realm the pieces of green bottle appear on the cinders, are allowed by the poet to reveal their own measure, in the words, and in so doing to bring to light the radiance else hidden. Williams' whole art is here, the three universal elements of his poetry brought momentarily into perfect balance in vibrating tension.

⤶

This equilibrium is only momentary. The presence brushes past the reader and is gone, leaving him staring at mute bits of green bottle or dead words on the page — there before him, but meaningless. Other modes of Williams' poetry attempt to hold the presence longer before it disappears. One way to do this is to write poems about moving objects rather than static ones. A great many of the poems catch a special form of motion. Some thing or person is stilled in the moment of change, often while making a stylized movement like a ballet dancer. In that fleeting gesture the thing reveals its form, and while it lasts the presence is visible. The tempo of these poems is slow and stately, and then stops. The poet apparently feels that he can catch the secret hidden by a movement if he slows it down in his verse. A Negro woman, "carrying a bunch of marigolds/wrapped/in an old newspaper," waddling down the street, "looking into/the store window which she passes," is "an ambassador/from another world" (PB, 123). Another poem is like a slow-motion picture which is suddenly stopped altogether, leaving two people in the midst of a gesture:

> The sun was on her
> as she came
> to the step's edge,
> the fat man,
>
> caught in his stride,
> collarless,
> turned sweating
> toward her. (CLP, 86)

The girl with big breasts under a blue sweater:

> stops, turns
>
> and looks down
> as though
>
> she had seen a dime
> on the pavement (CLP, 123)

Another (famous) poem catches the figure 5 in gold on a red fire-truck as it speeds by, frozen for a moment in the flick of an eyelid (CEP, 230). In another the blue jay "crouched/just before the take-off" is "caught/in the cinematograph" (PB, 48). Another shows two starlings reversing in the air just before landing on wires — "to/face into the wind's teeth" (CLP, 88). In another a girl is:

> . . . balanced
>
> idly
> tilting her weight
> from one foot
>
> to the other
> shifting (PB, 50)

These poems, and dozens more, seize something in motion and fix it in words as a perpetual gesture. Motion and stillness are reconciled to preserve the virtues of both. As long as the gesture lasts the three elements are in balance and beauty is kept in the open.

In reality, though, the gesture passes. Only in the poet's words is it perpetuated, "peacefully continuing in his verse/forever" (PB, 53). In many poems the motion is completed by the end of the poem, there is a return to stillness, and, with that, a return to confrontation of the static object, hiding its secret once more. Another kind of poem achieves more successfully a mode of perpetual motion. If a multiplicity of diverse elements exist together they generate in their tension an oscillation which seems to go on indefinitely in the confines of the poetic space. The play of one thing against another causes both to move and in moving to release a fleck of the light they hide. "Dissonance/(if you are interested)/leads to discovery" (P, 207) — this is the technique not only of *Paterson* but of many of Williams' shorter poems. Some of these, like "Overture to a Dance of Locomotives" (CEP, 194, 195), "Romance Moderne" (CEP, 181–184), or "Morning" (CEP, 393–396), represent the diverse details of a single scene — all the poet sees in a railroad station, or walking through the Italian section of his city, or what he sees and thinks as he is driven through the countryside on a rainy day. Other poems, like "To All Gentleness" (CLP, 24–29), "Della Primavera Trasportata Al Morale" (CEP, 57–64), "A Good Night" (CEP, 192, 193), or "Struggle of Wings" (CEP, 291–293), mix heterogeneous details from various times and places of the poet's experience. They all exist together in the single space of the mind and can be called on at will to form the continuity of the poem, a jagged pattern of dissociated pieces juxtaposed. The strategy of these poems is to go from fragment to fragment in a rapid sequence of metamorphoses. Each new phrase clashes with the one before and strikes from it a spark of the hidden light. This is also the method of *The Great American Novel*, which moves without transition from stream of consciousness reveries in the present to the inner life of a little Ford, the heroine — "she was very passionate — a hot little baby" (IWWP, 39) — to discourse on the nature of literature, to scenes from American history, to bits of the conversation of Williams' mother, to quotations from advertisements, to scenes of contemporary life, and so on. All times and places of America are unified in the poet's mind, balanced there in a realm which is identified with the ubiquitous air, the same wind which blew over Ponce de Leon's soldiers now shaking a girl's heavy skirt about her knees and modulating the poet's breath as he speaks the "one word" the girl must hear (GAN, 29–31). The aesthetic theory of such works is stated in "Struggle of Wings":

> Out of such drab trash as this
> by a metamorphosis
> bright as wallpaper or crayon
> or where the sun casts ray on ray on

flowers in a dish, you shall weave
for Poesy a gaudy sleeve (CEP, 293)

The images chosen for such metamorphoric sequences are usually "drab trash" indeed, bits and pieces of America, bric-a-brac of an ugly culture, shop signs, menus, the backyards of the poor, field weeds, "cabbages and spuds" (CEP, 292). Sometimes the apparently poetic is followed suddenly by the antipoetic, as in "The Cod Head," a poem catching beautifully the life and motion at the edge of the sea. It ends with " — a severed cod — /head between two/green stones — lifting/falling" (CEP, 334). The interaction of miscellaneous and incongruent images produces a bright flash of revelation which is the farthest reach of poetry. It is "a meaning plainly antipoetical" and yet, by such metamorphoses, "all there is is won" (CEP, 292).

Another version of the liberation of beauty through the interplay of diverse elements is given in the poems and stories about the tension between person and person. Such works have a special importance. A human being is in one sense just another inhabitant of the poetic space and can be possessed in the same way as a bit of broken bottle or a tree. Like a flower, a woman hides the universal beauty and can be brought to reveal it. People, however, are especially its guardians, for only through their encompassing presence can it be brought out of its secrecy in flower or rock. If there are no people, beauty remains invisible. People have a special proximity to the rare element which "reaches to the farthest limits of our lives." Through his possession of a human being, by way of a gesture, a phrase, or an embrace, the poet can capture not the local glimpse of beauty he gets from a flower but a pervasive perfume transfiguring all things. The rock or tree must be worded in poetry to free the hidden flame. Other people are already poetry. Their simplest words reveal beauty in a way no stone can. Only a man invents, and any living man or woman is always performing the miracle of resurrection which lifts the flame of beauty into the light. The interaction of one person with another has therefore a virtue superior to the clash of thing with thing within the poetic space. The reciprocity of love is best of all. An admirable passage in a late poem tells how something secret is brought to the surface in the stress of relationship between two lovers. The rhythm of the lines echoes the give and take which releases beauty:

> There is, in the hard
> >   give and take
> >   >   of a man's life with
> >   >   a woman
> a thing which is not the stress itself
> >   but beyond
> >   >   and above
> that,
> >   something that wants to rise
> >   >   and shake itself
> free. (PB, 77)

‿

The poem of the motionless thing, poems of the single gesture, poems of multiple elements in tension, poems of intersubjectivity — all incarnate beauty and reveal it. All, however, have a flaw: they seem to forget the earth. These poems address themselves to things which have already risen from the ground. It may be for this reason that beauty is so often occulted in them or breathed only evanescently. As soon as form has risen free of the ground it becomes an opaque screen hiding the presence. The poems of multiple objects in metamorphoric sequence, for example, can be seen as mere poetic "mobiles" — each a dance of motionless images circulating in a fixed poetic space, both ground and beauty forgotten. One such poem is in fact called "Perpetuum Mobile: The City," and is a series of urban images "milling about," expressive of endless unsatisfied desire:

> Let us break
> >   through
> and go there —
>
> in
> >   vain! (CEP, 386)

This poem, like other similar ones, is a "testament of perpetual change" (CLP, 103), but nothing is attained through the changes, nothing but a rearrangement of the original elements. One of Williams' most important poetic modes seems to avoid this tendency: the poem which follows in its development the rise of form from the ground and the concurrent release of beauty. All Williams' poems in a sense describe flowering, since things appear before the reader in their words and rise there to a new manifestation. This may not be evident, however, in poems about fixed things or about moving things which are wholly there from the beginning of the poem. Better, from this point of view, are poems which show the actual birth of form from the formless earth. It is proper that the poet should cry: "Saxifrage is my flower that splits/the rocks" (CLP, 7), for the poems which go from rock to flower contain all the elements of existence in momentary copresence. In them "the rocks/the bare rocks/speak!" (P, 242).

Many of Williams' best poems enact from within a flowering. Here again the poet recalls Rimbaud. Central in both are images of birth, of dawning, and of spring, and central in both is the need to associate primitive elements in a new organization which will preserve their freedom. Williams' aim in the renewal of the poetic line is exactly parallel to his aim in other dimensions of life: "Return to the simpler constructive elements of the line — to shake free from the constrictions that have grown into the line and its stanzaic combinations — and to permit a freer (thought-governed) association of the elements" (AP, 61). Williams differs from Rimbaud in more often limiting his images of birth to a single object. In *The Great American Novel*, for example, "the bosom of the earth sprays up a girl balancing, balancing on a bicycle" (GAN, 10). Sometimes, however, he presents a plurality of births, as in another text from the same book: "Up out of the trees with a whirr started the sparrows. With a loud clatter the grouse got up at his feet. The ground was full of mushrooms" (GAN, 22). It is characteristic of Williams that his images of multiple birth should be such commonplace things as sparrows and mushrooms, and more often he shows, not a swarm of birds rising from a tree at dawn or a whole field of mushrooms, but a single tree lifting trunk, branches, and leaves to the sky, or two birds rising against foliage:

> The black, long-tailed,
> one then, unexpectedly, another
> glide easily on a curtain
> of yellow leaves, upward —
>
> The season wakens! (CEP, 454)

Rimbaud, moreover, wants complete freedom from the ground, while Williams' things must remain rooted, even at some cost to their freedom, for only rooted things are alive. The birds and squirrels in "The Yellow Season" hold fast to their tree:

> . . . loveliness
> chirping and barking stands
> among the branches, its
> narrow-clawed toes and furry
> hands moving in the leaves — (CEP, 454)

Many poems follow a sequence from earth to final flower, a process given succinctly in a brief poem called (paradoxically) "Descent": "From disorder (a chaos)/order grows/ — grows fruitful" (CEP, 460). This flowering is not easy. The poems emphasize the tremendous effort necessary to get the plant up through the hard ground and into the light where it can blossom. This stress is recreated in the words of the poem. It is a happening within the poet himself. The chicory must strain to lift its bitter stems out of the scorched ground (CEP, 122), and in "By the road to the contagious hospital" the bushes, weeds, and small trees grip down with their roots and begin to awaken (CEP, 242). The latter poem in its original printing in *Spring and All*, follows the announcement that "at last SPRING is approaching. . . . THE WORLD IS NEW" (SA, 11). It fulfills the rebirth after universal annihilation announced in the prose. Often the poems of flowering catch a plant or tree in the moment of reawakening, when "unopened jonquils/hang their folded heads" (CEP, 362), or "the grass by the back door/is stiff with sap" (CEP, 187), or the "blue-grey buds [are]/crowded erect with desire against the sky" (CEP, 159), or "the birches are opening their leaves one/by one," and "black is split at once into flowers" (CEP, 228). In these poems the enormous pressure working toward form is wonderfully expressed, an energy "from under, as if a slow hand lifted a tide" (CEP, 188), so that there is a "pushing" against the sun "of sumac buds, pink/in the head/with the clear gum upon them," or of "swollen/limp poplar tassels on the/bare branches" (CEP, 190).

Sometimes this dynamic tension between form and ground manifests itself in a trembling of the thing. The pull in both directions is so great that the tree or flower shakes in its place. This oscillation is evidence of its contact with the hidden vitality of the ground. In *Paterson* a juniper bush, rooted by the falls, "trembles frantically/in the indifferent gale," and the branch of a sycamore sways "slightly/on a long axis, so slightly/as hardly to be noticed" (P, 30, 32). Though the swaying of the branch can scarcely be seen, it contains the power of all the elements and is "in itself the tempest" (P, 32). The juniper bush and sycamore branch are good examples of the way each thing in Williams' world is clearly and precisely itself, yet has a softness of outline, an obscure shaking. This blurring of edges shows that it is rooted in the unfathomable ground and, in its push toward revelation, is in resonance with all other things. Vibrating with them, it becomes a concentration of universal life.

In another place in *Paterson* the energetic thrusting of the earth toward the sun is expressed in the "grasshopper of red basalt, boot-long," "carved to be/endless flight," which "falls from an under-mined bank/and — begins chirring!/AND DOES, the stone after the life!" (P, 62, 63, 64). The stone grasshopper is a perfect reconciliation of earth's primeval vitality with the accomplished form of a creature that can fly. In other poems the explosion into flower is not stilled in a perpetual present of reconciled tension, but is followed with delicate slowness from beginning to end, so that the effect is of a containing of growth within the limits of the poem. The poem is a process which goes on moving, a motion from seed to flower, and the opening of beauty is not stopped but pos-sessed. A magnificent example of this sort of poem is "The Crimson Cyclamen" (CEP, 397–404). It follows with masterful linguistic accuracy that almost indescribable thing, the development of a plant from "roots/dark, complex from/subterranean revolutions" to the blossoms in which "color has been construed/from empti-ness/to waken there," "each petal/by excess of tensions/in its own flesh/all rose." Other poems of flowering universalize a single appearance of form and make it expand to be a blossoming of the whole world. In "Catastrophic Birth" (CLP, 8, 9), for example, the "big she-Wop" gives birth to another child, but her parturition is like the eruption of a volcano "by violence lost, recaptured by violence," and hence of the universal bringing forth of beauty in the "compact" revelation of poetry. Once more the poet emphasizes the counterviolence resisting the violence pushing toward birth: "Unless the shell hold/the kernel is not sweet./Under violence the meat lies regained" (CLP, 8).

It is easy to see why this is so. All Williams' poems about the birth of form try to maintain for as long as possible the moment when new life appears from the ground. Only then are the three elements present in pregnant tension. An instant later the baby is born, named, and assimilated into the human world; the volcanic eruption is over, and "the broken cone breathes softly on/the edge of the sky, violence revives and regathers"; the blossom has come to full flower and stands in the air, already beginning to die, no longer a showing forth either of the ground or of the evasive presence. The moment of flowering is revelation. When the flowering is fulfilled "the revelation is complete" (CLP, 9), and the poet is returned to his despair. Only if he could find some way to sustain a continual flowering could he possess indefinitely ground, form, beauty, and so conquer his despair.

⤙

Just such a poetry is developed at the end of the poet's life. This poetry is a triumphant reconciliation of the three elements in a perpetual balance. Instead of moving from ground toward form to release a spark of beauty but then falling back, or holding all three separately in precarious tension, each line or phrase of these poems gathers the elements into inextricable union. Rising and sinking are not sequential but simultaneous. Each line flows from the unfathomable ground into its unique measure and so brings beauty to light. The next line does the same, and the next, and so on. Like a fountain sustained by underground pressure and shining in the sun, these poems hover effortlessly at just the right distance from the source, each line following the last before the poem has had time to sink. The poem is held in constant renewal away from the ground, yet still touches the ground, and in that balance the radiant presence remains visible.

The masterpieces of this form are Book Five of *Paterson*, "The Desert Music," and "Asphodel, That Greeny Flower." In these Williams reaches the summit of his art. The fourth book of *Paterson* ends with the rising of the poet from the river. The fifth book is a taking possession of the new space where he finds himself after his plunge with the river and final emergence. It is not, as might seem, a return to separate form, the poet bound by the surface of his body, caught in his private thought. He rises with the world contained in his body and its thoughts. The space of *Paterson Five* is a triumphant fulfillment of the aesthetic of *The Great American Novel*. Time has been transcended and all the elements of the poem are there together, touching one another, interacting with one another. The unicorn hunt in a tapestry, Audubon following "a trail through the woods/. . . northward of Kentucky" (P, 245), a letter from Allen Ginsberg, Brueghel's "Nativity," a passage from Mezz Mezzrow's *Really The Blues*, a woman the poet has seen in the streets of Paterson — all are assembled in one place, and the poem can move in a moment from one to another, for all are possessed at once. The symbol for this unification is the dance. The elements of the poet's world circle around one another in harmonious measure, and *Paterson Five* ends with an image of poetry as a dance:

> We know nothing and can know nothing   .
>   but
> the dance, to dance to a measure
> contrapuntally,
>   Satyrically, the tragic foot. (P, 278)

In "The Desert Music" the satyrs' dance, origin and end of poetry, returns, and with it the music which permeates every detail of the poet's visit to Juárez, rising above the dance of the vocables as a new auditory form of beauty:

> Now the music volleys through as in
> a lonely moment I hear it. Now it is all
> about me. The dance! The verb detaches itself
> seeking to become articulate   . (PB, 120)

Finally there is "Asphodel, That Greeny Flower," the extraordinary love poem of Williams' old age. This poem has the quiet mastery of supreme attainment. Like *Paterson Five* and "The Desert Music," "Asphodel" gathers the world together and the lines rise continuously from a center which is everywhere. Since the lines ascend one by one from the same unfathomable ground, each is the equivalent of the others, the same and yet different. Flowers are facts, poems flowers, and "all works of the imagination,/interchangeable" (PB, 178). Each object could be substituted for any of the others, for all say the same thing, do that one thing which all poetic speech does — perpetuate the dance. In the extreme reach of his imagination the poet enters a space where:

                              no distinction
          any more suffices to differentiate
                         the particulars
                                of place and condition (PB, 162)

Interchangeability enters in yet another way, for in "Asphodel"
beauty is expressed not in a single image, of dance or music, but
in a group of images all standing side by side in the poem to say
the same thing, each saying it perfectly but in a unique way. The
space of the poem is the poet's memory. Everything which has ever
happened to him is brought back in its substantiality, "a whole
flood/of sister memories" (PB, 154). It is also, and pre-eminently,
the space of love, for "Asphodel" is a poem "of love, abiding love"
(PB, 153), the poet's final affirmation of his love for his wife and of
the way the relation between them creates and sustains the world.
The poem is also the space of language, of a murmuring speech
which the poet prolongs defiantly and yet precariously, with infinite
gentleness, against time and death:

          And so
                         with fear in my heart
                                I drag it out
          and keep on talking
                         for I dare not stop.
                                Listen while I talk on
          against time. (PB, 154)

The space of the poet's sustaining speech is the realm of the
imagination, "the place made/in our lives/for the poem" (PB,
159). This place is also the sea, or rather the waves on the surface
of the sea. The sea is the profound depth from which all things
have come to dance like waves as the lines dance in the poem. The
"sea/which no one tends/is also a garden" (PB, 156), earth giving
birth to flowers as the sea to waves. Sea, garden, poem, love, and
memory are equivalents, and "the glint of waves," "the free
interchange/of light over their surface" (PB, 165), is the play of
words in the poem, the blossoming of flowers in a garden.

These images lead to others. The poem is speech in defiance of
death. Here, at the very end of Williams' career, death appears in
his world for almost the first time. It is another name for the unfathomable ground. The poem flowers from it and yet contains it.

As Asphodel is the flower of hell but still triumphs over the darkness, so the space of the poem is not hell but is the flower which rises above death, for "love and the imagination/are of a piece,/swift as the light/to avoid destruction" (PB, 179). This leads to a final group of images, once more interchangeable with the others. Asphodel, the flower of hell, is the atomic bomb, since "the bomb/also/is a flower" (PB, 165). The exploding bomb is equated with a distant thunderstorm over the sea which the poet watches with his wife. The poem prolongs indefinitely the moment just before death. It is speech in the shadow of death and dwells in the light of a perpetual present, between the lightning and the thunderclap, between the sight of the exploding bomb and the coming of annihilating heat. In "Asphodel, That Greeny Flower" light, the sea, memory, speech, the garden, and love are the same, and the poem maintains forever in living poise the moment between birth and death. As long as that moment lasts the flame of beauty is held in the open:

> The light
> for all time shall outspeed
> the thunder crack. (PB, 181)

This radiant promise is the climax of Williams' writing, and the climax too of the development so far of twentieth-century poetry. Beginning with a heritage of romanticism and the dualism which usually accompanies it, twentieth-century literature has sometimes, as with Conrad, gone to the limits of nihilism, or sometimes, as with Eliot, recovered a new version of Christian immanence. Yeats, Thomas, Stevens, and Williams have gradually developed a poetry beyond subjectivism and beyond dualism. This poetry presupposes a new understanding of reality. Only a reality which includes the human life that is lived in it makes possible a poetry which is "the cry of its occasion,/Part of the res itself and not about it." [33] In the work of Yeats, Thomas, and Stevens can be witnessed the difficult struggle to go beyond the old traditions. Williams goes farthest. He begins within the space of immanence and his work is a magnificent uncovering of its riches. The section in Book Two of *Paterson* beginning "The descent beckons/as the ascent beckoned" (P, 96) is more than the poet's first use of the novel measure of his

[33] Wallace Stevens, *The Collected Poems* (New York: Alfred A. Knopf, 1954), p. 473.

last poems. It also affirms his right to dwell in a new space and a new time. The poem describes the "accomplishment," "renewal," and "initiation" of memory, but memory here is identical with the endless present of "Asphodel, That Greeny Flower." In "The descent beckons," as in Williams' other late poetry, space and the mind are identical. This space, a domain of plenitude and enlargement, coincides with a time which continually reaches out toward a goal of perennial freshness. Time is a dimension of space, a function of its life as it moves onward in the ever-new moment between origin and end. "The descent beckons," in its expansive openness to the future, may be taken as a comprehensive description of the realm entered by the poetry of reality:

>   . . . the spaces it opens are new
> places
>   inhabited by hordes
>   heretofore unrealized,
> of new kinds —
>   since their movements
>   are towards new objectives (P, 96)

Index